The Eagle and the Dragon

Westward strays the eye
Richard Wagner, *Tristan and Isolde*, I, 1.

For Agnès Fontaine

The Eagle and the Dragon

Globalization and European Dreams of Conquest in China and America in the Sixteenth Century

Serge Gruzinski

Translated by Jean Birrell

polity

First published in French as *L'Aigle et le Dragon* © Librairie Arthème Fayard, 2012

This English edition © Polity Press, 2014

This work, published as part of a program providing publication assistance, received financial support from the French Ministry of Foreign Affairs, the Cultural Services of the French Embassy in the United States and FACE (French American Cultural Exchange).

Polity Press
65 Bridge Street
Cambridge CB2 1UR, UK

Polity Press
350 Main Street
Malden, MA 02148, USA

ISBN-13: 978-0-7456-6711-9
ISBN-13: 978-0-7456-6712-6 (pb)

A catalogue record for this book is available from the British Library.

Library of Congress Cataloging-in-Publication Data

Gruzinski, Serge.
  [Aigle et le dragon. English]
  The eagle and the dragon : European expansion and globalization in the 16th century / Serge Gruzinski.
    pages cm
  Includes bibliographical references.
  ISBN 978-0-7456-6711-9 (hardcover) – ISBN 978-0-7456-6712-6 (papercover)
  1. History, Modern–16th century.   2. Civilization–History–16th century.
  3. Discoveries in geography–History–16th century.   I. Title.
  D228.G7813 2012
  909′.5–dc23
                              2014016825

Typeset in 10.5 on 12 pt Sabon
by Toppan Best-set Premedia Limited

For further information on Polity, visit our website: politybooks.com

Contents

Acknowledgements

The members of my history seminar at the Ecole des hautes études en sciences sociales know how much I owe to their questions, comments and criticisms. No historical research can be done in isolation, and global history, even more than other forms of history, demands an interchange of ideas, a bringing together of skills and encounters between researchers from the four quarters of the globe. Carmen Bernand, Louise Bénat Tachot, Alessandra Russo, Alfonso Alfaro, Décio Guzman, Boris Jeanne, Pedro Gomes, Maria Matilde Benzoni, Oreste Ventrone and Giuseppe Marcocci, all budding researchers, whatever their age, have supplied the energy, the horizons and the confrontations that are essential to global history. Nevertheless, though never a solitary enterprise, a work of history remains above all an individual adventure. The Ecole des hautes études en sciences sociales continues to be a special place, where one can depart from well-trodden paths, run risks and imagine the future of a discipline which might resume its place at the head of the social sciences by showing that it has learnt to break through the barrier of times and civilizations.

Foreword

Serge Gruzinski is one of the leading French historians of his generation (he was born in 1949). He began as a historian of early modern Mexico, but has gradually widened his scope to encompass the history of Latin America (including Brazil), and more recently the history of early modern globalization (globalization, whether economic or cultural, may have accelerated in the last few decades but the trend goes back much further). In his latest book, Gruzinski focuses on two parts of the early modern world, Mexico and China.

Most of us, even historians, do not think of sixteenth-century China and Latin America as having much to do with each other (apart from the goods sent from China to Manila and then taken to Acapulco by the so-called 'Manila galleons'). It is the achievement of Serge Gruzinski to show us that we were wrong. *The Eagle and the Dragon* is a fine example of what the French call *histoire croisée*, sometimes translated as 'connected history' or 'transnational history', an approach to the past that focuses on economic, political or cultural links between different parts of the world.

Histoire croisée is sometimes presented as the successor to an older 'comparative history' that examines both the similarities and the differences between societies but has little to say about possible connections. In my view, however, these two approaches are complementary rather than contradictory. Serge Gruzinski obviously agrees. He is interested in connections between the two empires of Spain and China, the eagle and the dragon, but builds this study around comparisons and contrasts, notably between Spain's conquest of Mexico and Portugal's failure to conquer China. Offering a fascinating example of 'virtual' or 'counter-factual' history, Gruzinski imagines what might have happened if it had been Portugal that succeeded and Spain that failed. After all, the conquest of Mexico by Hernán Cortés with a force of only a few hundred Spaniards was far from inevitable.

In short, the great merit of this relatively short book, besides bringing little-known details of the relations between the two empires to our notice, is to stimulate reflection about what makes empires vulnerable and, more generally still, about such questions as how different paths might have been taken at certain points in history and why things actually happened in the way that they did.

Peter Burke

Introduction

Andromache: 'The Trojan War will not take place, Cassandra!'
Jean Giraudoux, *The Trojan War Will Not Take Place*, I, 1

Some writers of the first half of the twentieth century came across the paths that led me from Mexico to China. It was from Jean Giraudoux that I got the idea for a title, long ago – *The Chinese War will not take place* – but I had to abandon it. Paul Claudel vividly depicted worlds we are now perhaps better placed to understand. In the 'Days' of his play of 1929, *The Satin Slipper*, people from all four quarters of the globe converse one with the other. 'The Scene of this play is the world, and more especially Spain at the close of the Sixteenth Century', Claudel explained. In what he described as 'compendiating countries and periods',[1] he made no claim to be a historian, but he plunged his readers into all the turmoil of a globalization. It was not the first globalization, nor would it be the last; Claudel's was the globalization that came rapidly in the sixteenth century, in the aftermath of the Portuguese and Spanish expeditions. Both the Aztec Eagle and the Chinese Dragon then experienced the first consequences of a European immoderation.

This globalization was not the same as European expansion. The latter mobilized huge quantities of technical, financial, spiritual and human resources. It was a consequence of political choices, economic calculation and religious aspirations which combined, for better or worse, to despatch soldiers, sailors, priests and merchants thousands of kilometres away from the Iberian Peninsula, into every part of the globe. This Iberian expansion sparked chain reactions, even caused shocks so seismic they destabilized whole societies. This was the case in America. In Asia Iberian expansion came up against forces stronger than itself, when it had not got bogged down in the marshes and forests of Africa. The image of an inexorable European advance – whether its heroic and civilizing virtues are celebrated or it is held up to contempt – is an illusion that has proved difficult to dispel. It derives from a linear and teleological vision of history which continues to mislead both historians and their readers.

What is incorrect in the case of Iberian expansion is even more so in that of globalization, which may be defined as the proliferation of links of every type between parts of the world previously unaware of each other or in only the most distant contact. The globalization of the sixteenth century affected Europe, Africa, Asia and the New World, as interactions of unprecedented intensity began to take place between them. A web was being spun around the planet, still fragile, full of huge holes, always liable to tear at the least pressure, but indifferent to political and cultural frontiers. The protagonists in this globalization included the African, Asian and Amerindian populations, who all played a part, willy-nilly. However, it was the Portuguese, the Spanish and the Italians who supplied most of the religious, commercial and imperialist energy, at least at this period and for more than 150 years. As the Chinese servant in *The Satin Slipper* says to Don Rodrigo, Viceroy of the Indies: 'We have captured each other, and there is no way of getting unstuck'.[2]

How much of this was perceived by contemporaries? Their gaze was often more penetrating than that of the historians who have studied them since. Many people in the sixteenth century, and not only Europeans, grasped the magnitude of the developments taking place around them. For the most part they conceived them in religious terms, on the basis of the perspectives opened up by mission. But globalization also impacted on the minds of many who were conscious of the speeding up of communications between the different parts of the world, the discovery of the infinite diversity of landscapes and peoples, the extraordinary opportunities for profit opened up by investments on the other side of the world and the limitless expansion of known spaces – and the attendant risks. Nothing seemed to be beyond the curiosity of the travellers, though they were frequently unable to go anywhere without the assistance of their indigenous guides.

The discovery of America and the conquest of Mexico can be attributed to historical figures like Hernán Cortés and Columbus. This is questionable, but convenient. The distance of centuries and our increasingly galling ignorance encourages us to accept such shortcuts. But globalization had no author. It was a response, on a global scale, to the shocks set off by the Iberian initiatives. It caused many histories suddenly to become intertwined, with unexpected and previously unimaginable consequences. It was in no way an inexorable and irreversible process, mechanically accomplishing a preconceived plan leading to the standardization of the world.

It is thus mistaken to believe that our own globalization was born with the fall of the Berlin Wall. It is equally illusory to see it as a gigantic tree sprouted from a seed sown by Iberian hands in the sixteenth century. Yet our own age is indebted to this distant period, and in a variety of ways, if we accept that the absence of direct links or linearity does not turn the course of history into a series of chance events and happenings lacking in significance. It was in the sixteenth century that human history began to be played out on a world stage. It was then that connections between the different parts of the world began to accelerate: between Europe and the Caribbean from 1492, between Lisbon and Canton from 1513, between Seville and Mexico from 1517, and so on. There is another reason, which is central to my book: it was with Iberian globalization that Europe, the New World and China became world partners. China and America play a major role in the globalization of today. But why and how did they come to stand face to face on the world chessboard? And why does America today show signs of exhaustion, while China seems poised to deprive it of its first place?

In an earlier book, *What Time is it There?*, I discussed the nature of the links formed in the sixteenth century between the New World and the Muslim world. These regions were then confronted with the first consequences of European expansion throughout the globe. Columbus believed that his discovery would provide the gold which would enable Christians to recapture Jerusalem and vanquish Islam. The Ottoman Empire, for its part, was made uneasy by the sight of a continent unknown to the Koran and Islamic scholars and succumbing both to the faith and to the greed of Christians. It is impossible to discuss the globalization that has gradually given the world a common history without considering what has happened since the sixteenth century between the Islamic lands, Europe and America. But is this enough? If the addition of a fourth part of the world was the founding act of Iberian globalization, the irruption of China onto European and American horizons was another major upheaval. The fact that it was roughly contemporary with the discovery of Mexico ought to have attracted attention before now, but, long focused on Mesoamerica, we had forgotten that it was not the end of the world, but rather, as the ancient Mexicans claimed, the centre.

The Iberians hoped to conquer China on two occasions in the sixteenth century, but their aims were never achieved. 'The Chinese war will not take place', to paraphrase the title of Giraudoux's famous play. Some, belatedly, will regret this. Others, like me, will reflect on what we can learn from these dreams of conquest, contemporary with the colonization of the Americas and the exploration of the Pacific Ocean. China, the Pacific, the New World and Iberian Europe were the major players in a history that was created by their encounters and their confrontations. It can be summed up in a few words: in the same century the Iberians failed in China and succeeded in America. This is what is revealed by a global history of the sixteenth century, conceived as another way of reading the Renaissance, less stubbornly Eurocentric but probably more in tune with our age.

1

Two Tranquil Worlds

What frightens me in Asia is the vision of our own future which it is already experiencing. In the America of the Indians, I cherish the reflection...of an era when the human species was in proportion to the world it occupied.

Claude Lévi-Strauss, *Tristes tropiques*
(trans. J. and D. Weightman, p. 150)

In 1520 Charles V, Francis I and Henry VIII were the three rising stars of Latin Christendom: regent of Castile since 1517, crowned king of Germany in 1520, Charles the Great had been born with the new century; Francis I had been king of France since 1515, Henry VIII king of England since 1509.[1] Meanwhile, in Portugal the ageing Manuel the Fortunate was still vigorous enough to marry the sister of the Tudor king. Faced with their French and English rivals, Charles the Great and Manuel of Portugal nurtured oceanic ambitions which would project their kingdoms towards other worlds. In November 1519 a Spanish adventurer called Hernán Cortés, at the head of a small troop of foot soldiers and cavalrymen, made his entry into Mexico. In May 1520 a Portuguese ambassador, with even fewer men, entered Nanking. It was here that the ambassador Tomé Pires was received by the emperor of China, Zhengde. Korean sources reveal the presence of some Portuguese in the imperial entourage, where they would have enjoyed the services of a guide and interpreter, the Muslim merchant Khôjja Asan.[2] In Mexico, and at this same period, Cortés met Moctezuma, leader of the Triple Alliance, or, if preferred, the 'Emperor of the Aztecs'.

The Two Emperors

Let us look first at Zhengde. It was in Peking, in June 1505, that Zhu Houzhao succeeded his father, the Emperor Hongzhi, under the imperial name of Zhengde. The tenth Ming emperor had acceded to the throne at the age of fourteen and he died in 1521.[3] His reign was much criticized by the chroniclers. According to them, Zhengde neglected affairs of state in favour of a life of pleasure. He liked to travel outside the Forbidden City, leaving his predatory eunuchs to amass fortunes.

In reality Zhengde was also a warrior who tried to escape the tutelage of the senior civil servants in order to revive the tradition of openness, even cosmopolitanism, of the preceding Mongol dynasty, the Yuan. He spent most of his time away from the imperial palace and he liked to surround himself with Tibetan monks, Muslim clerics, artists from central Asia, and Jurchen and Mongol bodyguards; when, that is, he was not meeting foreign ambassadors who had travelled to Peking. He even prohibited the slaughter of pigs so as to improve relations with the Muslim powers of central Asia. In 1518 and 1519 he personally led military campaigns in the north against the Mongols and in the south in Jiangxi. In 1521 he decided to crush a rebellious prince and had him executed in Tongzhou. This did nothing to improve his image; or that at least is the impression left by the official chronicles and gazetteers that appeared after his death, all of which present his reign as a time of disorder and decay (*moshi*). An exodus of peasants to the mines and the towns, the rise of parvenus, the abandonment of traditions, 'local customs' made to undergo 'a sea change',[4] harsh exactions by officials, unease and unrest among the people, the growth of illegal trade with the Japanese – the verdict of the official histories is hardly complimentary. Added to which were natural catastrophes, a flood and a famine in 1511, which they were quick to blame on the crisis then afflicting society. But not the whole of society; it was also an age when new fortunes were too many to count, when production everywhere increased and when international trade was more prosperous than ever before.[5]

In 1520 the ruler of China, in a drunken stupor, fell from the imperial boat into the waters of the Grand Canal, the principal artery connecting the north and south of the country. The fever or pneumonia he caught as a result of this enforced immersion killed him the following year, on 20 April, aged only thirty. It was icy water that had led to his death, and as this was the element of the dragon, some chroniclers believed that dragons had been responsible for his untimely end.[6] Only a few months earlier, mysterious creatures had disturbed the calm of the streets of Peking, attacking passers-by and wounding them with their claws. They were called 'Dark Afflictions'.[7] The Minister of War restored order and the rumours died down. Zhengde, who had always been curious about strange phenomena, had met the Portuguese embassy not long before his death. To his contemporaries and their successors, however, this episode counted for little. It did not earn him the posthumous and tragic fame that would be attached to the person of the *tlatoani* of Mexico-Tenochtitlan, Moctezuma Xoyocotzin. A film of 1959, *The Kingdom and the Beauty*, made at the height of the Communist era, was not enough to immortalize the adventures of a sovereign who had disguised himself as a man of the people the better to indulge his pleasures.

We know a great deal, but at the same time very little, about Moctezuma Xoyocotzin. The Aztec world is even less familiar to us than the Chinese world and it has acquired an enduring tragic aura. Indians, Spanish and mestizos have all left biased and contradictory pictures of Moctezuma Xoyocotzin: either reasons had to be found for the collapse of the indigenous kingdoms, or the prowess of the Spanish conquest had to be glorified.[8] Grandson and successor of Ahuitzotl (1486–1502), Moctezuma was born around 1467. He was a mature and experienced ruler in his fifties at the time of the arrival of Hernán Cortés. The ninth *tlatoani*, he reigned from 1502 to 1520 over the Mexicas of Mexico-Tenochtitlan; he also dominated Texcoco and Tlacopan, his partners in the Triple Alliance – the 'three heads'. Western tradition has made him emperor of the Aztecs.

The chroniclers invest him with warlike virtues he had apparently demonstrated at the beginning of his reign, but he seems to have made little use of them against the conquistadors. He strengthened his control over the noble elites and reorganized the upper echelons of the administration, dismissing some of those who had served under his predecessor; he altered the calendar – the full significance of this will emerge later; and he led numerous campaigns against the enemies of the Triple Alliance, but with only modest success. The defeat he suffered at the hands of Tlaxcala (1515) shows that it was not necessary to be Spanish or to have horses and firearms to get the better of him. Like his Chinese fellow ruler the Emperor Zhengde, he kept a menagerie full of exotic animals. He resembled him, too, in his liking for women; the chronicler Díaz del Castillo confirms that he was 'free of sodomy', a matter on which the Spanish needed constant reassurance. Moctezuma met his death at the hands either of the Indians or of the Spanish. According to the histories written after his death, his reign was punctuated by evil omens, which the 'priests of the idols' were unable to decipher and which were later associated with the Spanish conquest. His wretched death has inspired films and operas.[9] Unlike the Emperor Zhengde, he has an imperishable place in Western history and in the European *imaginaire*.

These two emperors had nothing in common except the fact of being caught up in the same history. In November 1519 Moctezuma encountered the Spanish in Mexico; a few months later Zhengde met the Portuguese in Nanking. I will return to this coincidence, but after a brief introduction to what China and Mexico represented at the dawn of the sixteenth century.

The China of Zhengde and the Mexico of Moctezuma

In 1511 the Portuguese took Malacca and the Spanish seized Cuba. The Iberian fleets were then only a short distance from, as it were, two huge icebergs, whose visible tips they were preparing to explore. For a few years yet, Mexico and China would escape the expansionist fever then consuming the Iberian Crowns and their subjects.

The two countries had little in common, other than being next on the list of Hispano-Portuguese discoveries ... or conquests; and other than the strange – to European eyes – fact of having experienced millennia of history which had unfolded quite apart from the Euro-Mediterranean world. China and Mexico had followed trajectories alien both to Judeo-Christian monotheism and to the political, juridical and philosophical heritage of Greece and Rome, though without ever having been exclusively inward-looking. It is true that, while the Amerindian societies had developed without any sort of relationship with the outside world, contacts had long existed between the Chinese world and the Mediterranean (by way of the famous Silk Road). We should not forget that China had always been in communication with a part of Eurasia, if only by welcoming Indian Buddhism, allowing centuries of Islamic penetration or sharing immune resistances; these last, when the crisis struck, were cruelly absent in the case of the Amerindian populations.

What were China and Mexico like in the second decade of the sixteenth century? China was an empire (although some prefer to talk of 'the Chinese world'),[10] whereas ancient Mexico was far from a politically unified whole. Archaeologists prefer the much broader concept of Mesoamerica, given that 'Mexico' evokes a national reality that emerged in the nineteenth century and is wholly anachronistic for the period under discussion here. In any case, it is not my intention here to compare China and Mexico. I aim rather to provide a brief sketch of each on the eve of the Iberian arrivals, with the emphasis on the crucial features which help to explain the way they each reacted to European intervention, particularly in the areas that are pivotal whenever there is a clash of civilizations: the ability to move rapidly on land and sea, the art of collecting and circulating information, familiarity with operating at a continental and intercontinental level, the capability to mobilize material, human and military resources at short notice and unexpectedly, a propensity to think on a world scale. These strengths – part technical, part psychological and intellectual – would all play a part in Iberian expansion: without capital, ships, horses, firearms and writing, no far-flung expansion was conceivable, with all it involved in the spheres of the movement of men and material, logistical support, fact-finding and spying campaigns, methods of extracting and transporting wealth and, what is too often forgotten, the creation of a world consciousness.

A brief appraisal is inevitably unsatisfactory, and even more so in the case of Mesoamerica because, in our communal memory, China and ancient Mexico do not loom equally large. The sudden influx of Spaniards into their new conquest inspired a plethora of accounts and descriptions, but the pre-Columbian period remains largely obscure, remarkable advances in archaeology notwithstanding. The ancient Mexicans had no writing, the Chinese had been writing for at least 3,000 years. Chinese sources are consequently abundant, whereas the historian of America has to make do with European testimonies and a handful of indigenous and mestizo accounts which are inevitably distorted by the trauma of conquest and the constraints of colonization. The indigenous worlds of the fifteenth century will probably always be obscure to us. The Chinese world speaks to us still, and will probably speak to us more and more.

Zhongguo

Zhongguo, the 'Middle Kingdom'... Compared with the New World and the rest of the globe, Imperial China beat all records for antiquity. The Chinese Empire dated back to the third millennium before the Christian era, with the dynasty of the Xia. By contrast, the Mexica and Inca empires, the giants of the American continent, had accumulated between them barely a century of existence by the time of the Spanish conquest. The continuity and antiquity of China, its sheer size, its human resources – more than 100,000,000, perhaps even 130,000,000 inhabitants[11] – and its incalculable wealth would all be discovered by the Iberians with amazement; they would take pleasure in describing them to each other, before repeating them to the rest of Europe.

Above all, the Chinese empire was a huge administrative and judicial machine, perfected over the centuries, which controlled the country through a host of mandarins, eunuchs, magistrates, inspectors, auditors, judges and military leaders; except on the northern frontiers and the coasts, the army played only a subsidiary role. This machine was replenished by way of competitive entrance examinations, which assured continuity of rule between the court of Peking, the provincial capitals and the lowest levels of the empire. There was no nobility, nor any great lords, but a generally educated gentry. Many of them, thanks to examination success and familial or regional support, were able to embark on an upward path which took a handful of the most talented and best supported to the imperial capital. The 20,000 employees of the Confucian bureaucracy and the 100,000 eunuchs can give the impression, seen from Europe or from Mexico, of a vastly overstaffed administration.

In reality sixteenth-century China was a notoriously under-administered monster.[12] As in every administration, corruption oiled the wheels where imperial control, too distant, too slow or too sporadic, proved ineffective. Corruption was at its worst on the southern coasts, where prosperity was largely based on overseas trade. The Portuguese were to be lucky beneficiaries of this. Nothing is perfect; mismanagement, revolts and banditry mean we cannot idealize the Celestial bureaucracy, but we should recognize that it was unique in the world in having the capacity to administer such large populations and spaces. It was with this bureaucracy that the emperor clashed: the liberties he took with court rituals and practices, his military ventures, his curiosity about external worlds and his universal ambitions were all repugnant to the educated members of the administration, whose values were different.

But China was also a world of great merchants. They traded in corn, silks, salt, tea and porcelains. The increasing congestion of the Grand Canal, crucial axis of north–south traffic, testifies to the scale of this trade.[13] In the early sixteenth century the merchants gained in power vis-à-vis the gentry, who looked down on them as parvenus. Their dynamism was contrary to the principles of Confucian morality, as they preferred the uncertainties and expedients of the market to the stable, ordered and sane world of the countryside. However, the old model was still so powerful that it imposed itself on the new classes. The merchants of Huizhou, great exporters of corn and tea and fortunate beneficiaries of a salt monopoly, tried to improve their image by attaching themselves to the world of the educated and the high civil service.[14] The gentry, meanwhile, found it difficult to resist the luxury goods – ancient porcelains, exotic fruits and plants – these prosperous merchants imported, often from distant locations. The temptation was all the stronger in that the collection or consumption of rare and precious goods has always been a 'must' among members of the gentry. It is hardly surprising that the curiosity aroused by the strange objects introduced by the Iberians encouraged the opening of links with the Europeans, and hence contact between the two worlds.

Trade, postal services and the army all had the benefit of a road network, a relay system and a series of canals and bridges of a density and efficiency remarkable for the period, when they are compared with anything contemporary Europe had to offer. Horses, sedan chairs and flat-bottomed boats crisscrossed the country. The state of the roads and the number of bridges – of dressed stone or pontoons – fascinated European visitors, who could hardly believe their eyes.[15] The development of agriculture was equally astonishing: fields as far as the eye could see, not a square centimetre of land left uncultivated, armies of peasants toiling in the rice fields.

The growth of agriculture and technology benefited from the diffusion of the printed book, particularly visible in the late fifteenth century. Publishing had become a highly profitable enterprise and ventures such as the Shendu publishing house, in Fujian, projected the image of a dynamic country, in many spheres more 'advanced' than Christian Europe. It was the boom in publishing which made possible the printing and reprinting of standard works, the Confucian canon, normative texts like the Ming code and the ordinances of the same name and imperial histories. This success was also due to the spread of reading. One is inevitably reminded of the irruption of printing into fifteenth-century Europe; with the difference that in China printed texts, 'which make it possible to embrace the world from the room one is in',[16] were neither a new nor a recent development, and had for centuries existed alongside an orality that was still predominant. This revolution was long in the past for the Chinese of the sixteenth century. Writing was the spearhead of an administration that was impressive for its time; it encouraged deep philosophical reflection, but it was also useful to the – often rebellious – free spirits who, from deep in the provinces, expressed opinions and reactions to the things of this world. Gazetteers flourished everywhere, spreading news, divulging techniques and knowledge, forging contacts between the different parts of the empire and keeping count of the flights of dragons that portended catastrophes.

To speak of 'Chinese thought' leads inevitably to generalities that fail to convey the diversity of its ideas or the originality of its innovations. From the beginning of the fifteenth century examination candidates had access to compilations of neo-Confucian texts with which they were expected to be thoroughly familiar. These writings, like the *Great Collection of the Four Books*, nurtured an orthodox thought inherited from the Song and found throughout the empire, which would influence the thinking of the bureaucracy until the beginning of the twentieth century. It would be a mistake, however, to imagine an intellectual sphere exclusively devoted to the world of the classics. Confucian orthodoxy was also open to Buddhist influences, it assimilated quietist tendencies which prioritized the internal experience of the mind above the external life, and it tolerated deviations encouraged by the social transformations of the age. Scholarly culture and popular culture intermingled, here as elsewhere, while syncretist strands combined Confucianism, Taoism and Buddhism in the idea that these three teachings were all one.[17] It was the primacy accorded to the spiritual experience over the doctrinal corpus which explains these phenomena of convergence and this fluidity of the religious traditions.

Some fascinating figures stand out on this intellectual horizon. Wang Yangming (1472–1529) was one of the most remarkable and his thought dominated the Chinese sixteenth century. Wang emphasized individual intuition and insisted on the predominance of the mind, because the mind was first in what was a unity:[18] 'the mind of the saint conceives Heaven-and-Earth and the myriad beings as one body. In its eyes, all the men in the world – whether they are strangers or family, distant or close, as long as they have blood and breath – are his brothers, his children'. Thus one must 'make one body with the myriad beings'. Convinced that 'knowledge and action are one and the same', Wang Yangming also preached the necessity of engaged thinking. Other thinkers reacted against Confucian orthodoxy by seeking unity on the side of the *qi* and by maintaining that there was nothing else in this world than energy (Wang Tinxiang, who died in 1547). Even more radical tendencies appeared around a man such as Wang Gen (1483–1541), founder of the school of Taizhou, famous for its free interpretation of the Confucian texts. China had little reason to envy the Europe of Erasmus and Luther.

Anahuac

In Chinese, 'China' can be said as *Hai nei*, 'within the [four] seas'. In Nahuatl, the language of the Aztecs and of central Mexico, the Indian land is called *Anahuac*, that is, 'by the waters'. The idea of a continent surrounded by water is also picked up in the expressions *cemanahua/cemanahuatl*, 'the whole world, the world which goes right to its end', as if China and Mexico had got together on the word. *Uey atl*, the 'Great Water', which meant the ocean, but also the revenants,[19] surrounded the emerged world of the ancient Mexicans. Behind its dead and its impassable wall of water, Anahuac was another tranquil world.

Not for long: in 1517 the Spaniards who had set off for Cuba first skirted the coasts of the Gulf of Mexico. It was from their boats that they saw the continental land we call Mesoamerica, then home to a medley of distinct peoples, languages, histories and cultures. The region had no cause to be jealous of China as regards antiquity, but its links with the past had largely been broken. For the populations who were about to welcome the Spaniards, the great city of Teotihuacan, contemporaneous with the apogee of the Roman Empire, was lost in the mists of time, and memory interpreted a common patrimony in very different ways, according to place: Maya in the Yucatán, Zapotec and Mixtec in the region of Oaxaca, Nahua in the Valley of Mexico. Not only did the absence of writing of an alphabetic or ideographic type make any attempt at historical reconstruction difficult, but the Nahua peoples who had settled on the *altiplano* from the twelfth century had brought other memories with them, which had to some extent erased those which had preceded them. Thus the Mexicas had done everything to present the foundation of Mexico-Tenochtitlan as something quite new, although other groups had already lived on this site.

To which should be added a relationship to time that was totally different from ours, as it mobilized memories which reproduced the past by emphasizing cycles and repetitions, though also including some doses of linearity. Two Moctezumas had reigned over Mexico-Tenochtitlan, one in the middle of the fifteenth century, the other at the time of the Spanish invasion. The history of the second is remarkably reminiscent of that of the first, as if care had been taken to highlight the analogies rather than bring out the particularities. In constantly mirroring and duplicating, this cyclical memory was an obstacle to the reconstitution of facts to which Western history has accustomed us. The image of the past as we understand it emerges hopelessly confused. This was a way of thinking ill-equipped to confront the unexpected or the unthinkable in their absolute singularity – as happened with the irruption of the Iberians. On the contrary, it tended to reduce them to familiar norms, without having the benefit of the centuries of relations with foreigners which had been the experience of the Chinese. The Ming Dynasty never forgot that it had its roots in the expulsion of the Mongols who had invaded and subjected the China of the Song.

The diversity that characterized Mesoamerica was mirrored in its political fragmentation. At the beginning of the sixteenth century a coalition based in the centre of the country, the Triple Alliance, brought together under the aegis of Mexico-Tenochtitlan and the Mexicas (our Aztecs) city states of Nahua culture which dominated a large part of the *altiplano*. But the Nahuas of the Triple Alliance were not alone in their occupation of Mesoamerican space: Purepechas in the northwest, Mixtecs and Zapotecs in the south, Totonacs in the east, Otomis and others all resisted the Triple Alliance, while on the Yucatán Peninsula the heirs of the great Mayan societies were the first to make contact with the Spaniards. With between 200,000 and 300,000 inhabitants, the Aztec capital, Mexico-Tenochtitlan, was one of the largest cities in the world. Nor was it the only city on the *altiplano*: Texcoco, Cholula, Tlaxcala and several others were all religious, political and economic centres of a vitality that would surprise the invaders.

Whereas China had a colossal administrative machine operating in a relatively unified territory, the Aztec Empire existed in name only. It was largely, as we will see, a creation of Hernán Cortés and of the historiography he inspired. There was an inflation on all sides, designed to give added lustre to the Spanish victory, or added poignancy to the Indian tragedy. In fact, Mexico-Tenochtitlan and its allies imposed their authority by means of raids and predatory expeditions which were not always successful. In the absence of roads and draught animals, the constant expansion of the sphere of influence of the Triple Alliance came at the cost of a diminution of the political and economic control it was able to exercise.[20] Ruling did not mean systematically dispossessing the enemy of his resources and his gods; rather, it meant extracting tribute and securing guarantees of loyalty, that is, hostages. These victors did not seek to change those they vanquished, whereas the Chinese had long sinicized the non-Han groups and the Iberians were preparing to Westernize the Amerindians. It is not that the Mexicas had deliberately chosen this weak form of empire, without intensive settlement or political integration. Rather, they had developed it so as to extract maximum profit, catching most of the peoples of the region, allies or enemies, unprepared. The Spanish victors would play by different rules.

The 'imperial' administration was essentially based on representatives of the Triple Alliance recruited from the ranks of the nobility, the *calpixqueh*, who were responsible in each region and in some forty provincial capitals for collecting the tribute.[21] At the local level this task was deputed to tax collectors or *tequitlahtoh*, who were dependent on the *calpixqueh* higher up the scale. Some of the tribute ended up in Mexico, the rest was used to maintain the garrisons stationed in the provinces. There was nothing remotely comparable to the countless mandarins, judges, soldiers and customs officials the Portuguese came up against everywhere they went.

The warriors played an important role in Mexico and their strong-arm tactics regularly compelled the other lordships to pay tribute and deliver captives to the Mexican capital and its allies. It seems likely that the Spanish invaders, who were above all men of war, felt less ill at ease than if they had had to face squads of educated administrators. Though the Indian soldier was very different from the Spanish soldier. The Nahua ethic prioritized single combat and the taking of prisoners. It promoted an intense individualism which fostered a spirit of fierce rivalry even in situations of extreme danger on the battlefield. It was for the individual warrior to triumph over the enemy and to remember that flight was punishable by death.[22] The obsession with maintaining rank and with winning and retaining privileges – sometimes even to the point of sharp practice – was hardly conducive to collective operations in which the coherence of the group mattered more than the courage of the individual. The pitiless gaze of the other, ready to denounce the most trivial infraction,[23] if it has not been exaggerated by the colonial sources, suggests a rigidity at the heart of the military elites that was ill-adapted to face sudden and unforeseen situations.

Admittedly, these fine principles were hardly applied to the letter. The confrontations with the Spanish quickly revealed Indians who were much more flexible in their movements and choice of tactics. This was in the first place because there was no real permanent army; Mexico and its allies assembled contingents of men who fought in a more or less coordinated manner against local rebels or traditional enemies. It is surprising to find the latter constituting pockets of insubordination at the very heart of the sphere of influence of the Triple Alliance, as in the case of the Tlaxcaltecs. This is to be explained by the limits of any intervention, which quickly became apparent. Any movement of troops, even on a small scale, posed logistical

problems: no locomotion except on foot and, everywhere, the rug-
gedness of the landscape. The necessity of carrying everything on
men's backs made heavy demands: at least one porter was needed for
every soldier if the equipment and foodstuffs were to keep up with
the expeditionary corps. To heavy weights was added a lack of suitable roads; *tamemes*, or human bearers, would survive the Spanish
conquest, until they were replaced by beasts of burden.

In countries where – unlike China – roads, canals and rivers were
practically nonexistent, the strike force mobilized in time of war
remained limited and the means for exerting pressure on the defeated
likewise. Here, there was no slow process of integrating conquered
peoples, but rather periodic recalls to order, accompanied by the
beheading of the enemy elites, systematically sacrificed on the altars
of Mexico-Tenochtitlan. At any moment, the intrusion of a new
player was likely to challenge the balance of power favourable to the
Triple Alliance and threaten Mexica hegemony. As a result, it was
always at the mercy of the exacerbation of the particularisms that
were rife throughout the *altiplano*. The Tenochcas had humiliated
their immediate neighbours of Tlatelolco, who paid them back in
kind; the allies of Texcoco resented the arrogance of Mexico-
Tenochtitlan; the Nahuas of Tlaxcala had for generations fought
against those of the Valley of Mexico; the Purepechas of the Michoacan
did everything in their power to prevent the northwest expansion of
the Triple Alliance.[24] Recently settled in the Valley of Mexico, the
Mexicas had to struggle to impose their legitimacy, overcome the
resentment of their allies and frustrate their traditional or potential
enemies.

So, 'Mexica empire' – or house of cards? We must be careful not
to project the unhappy fate of the Mexicas back onto their last years
of splendour. In other circumstances they might have consolidated
their position and there might one day have been an empire worthy
of the name.

Paradoxically, the most serious threats, whether effective or perceived as such, came from deep within the empire, not from its distant
frontiers or even its coasts. It was the city of Tlaxcala, some 200
kilometres from Mexico City, which resisted the coalition, whereas
no power strong enough to rival the Triple Alliance developed to the
north or south of its sphere of influence; even less an enemy fleet, a
possibility that remained unthinkable for the ancient Mexicans. Their
conception of the world made this impossible: they believed that the
Earth was a disc or a rectangle divided into four parts, surrounded
by a gigantic sea whose furthest points rose up to support the vault
of heaven. For the Mexicas, defence and attack were conceived of as

a confrontation of enemies close at hand, not for repulsing an alien suddenly emerged from the ocean.

As with China, our category of religion, the distinction between sacred and profane and the very idea of divinity serve to obscure the beliefs, myths and rites of the ancient Mexicans. Academic habits encourage us to apply these terms to types of behaviour and forms of consciousness which are extremely difficult for us to comprehend. They generally prevent us from questioning them and they explain a sort of mental block with regard to them which few authors are able to escape.[25] It was fundamentally through their relationship to time that the Mesoamerican societies tried to master their fate and that they constructed the meaning they gave to the world – a time, as I have already observed, irreducible to ours.

It was necessary to gain time in order to push back the end of the world, and it was this constantly maintained tension which lay behind the omnipresent practice of human sacrifice, in the course of a scrupulous performance of the rites fixed by the *tonapohualli* calendar. There was no dogma, as was the case in China, too, even less orthodoxy. The nonexistence of canonical texts, whether in the Chinese, Judeo-Christian or Muslim sense, may explain the apparent absence of religious deviation and the silence of the sources. Or it may be that the discretion of the indigenous informants conceals debates which emerged within the *calmecac* colleges, perhaps concerned less with essentials than with the appropriateness of the rites, the pre-eminence of such and such a god, the interpretation of the divinatory calendar or the accuracy of the calculations intended to assure its absolute correctness. It is possible that the contradictory narratives and interpretations surrounding the figure of the god Quetzalcoatl retain the traces of serious dissent that had resulted in rupture, exile or suicide. The variants that can be detected in the traditions which have been preserved reveal, at all events, the diversity of the points of view; they also tell us that particularisms were generally expressed through the cult of a founding god who was opposed to the local divinities.

There is the same opacity with regard to the rules of everyday life. A ruthless ethic seems to have regulated relations within the family and the group, but the often admiring descriptions of the Spanish monks raise many questions. Fascinated by the austerity, not to say Puritan rigour, of what was still there for them to see, and anxious to preserve the vestiges of the heritage of the vanquished, they may have reinterpreted indigenous norms and behaviour in ways that made them comprehensible, acceptable, even compatible with the new Christian faith.[26]

Less than a century later, the Jesuits who settled in China similarly idealized local customs and engaged in an enterprise of the same mould, aimed at separating the wheat – the Confucian ethic – from the chaff – the beliefs and 'superstitions' of the ordinary people and the 'idolatries' of the bonzes. But the Chinese were able to resist this cleansing campaign, whereas the Indians of Mexico had no choice: they had to form, not always unwillingly, the first Christendom of the Americas. In any case, the evidence of the educated of both empires presents us with images and ideas that are too coherent; it is not easy to see what they conceal.

Two Worlds of Thought

Can we speak of 'educated' if Anahuac was populated by societies without writing – or, to be more precise, without alphabetic or ideographic writing, because pictographic systems, together with the use of a medium of *amate* bark or animal skins, served to record a vast range of information, and in particular to draw up calendars; consultation of the latter played a major role in the organization of society and the way in which this society faced life on earth (*tlalticpac*).

Here, they did not represent; they took fragments from the visible and the invisible which they organized and fixed in colours in what we today incorrectly call codices and which the Spanish called 'paintings'. In the absence of written texts to be copied, pondered and glossed, there was a far greater investment in the image, as compared with Latin Christendom or China. However, this image did not function in the mode of representation, because it was of the order of the *ixiptla*: at every level, it rendered the invisible palpable and present, in the polychrome form of the great codices, the monumental perspective of the buildings and the mass impact of the ritual parades which regularly took over the great cities.

From the Great Temple to the roads and canals, the periodic processions of the gods, priests and captives, and the routine practice of human sacrifice – conceived both as food for and offering to the gods and as repayment of a debt – mobilized lives and accumulated wealth before squandering them for ever. The ritual dramatized the moment, speeded time up or slowed it down. In short, it manifested and animated in the eyes of all the numinous foundations of the world and its implacable operation. Human organs, precious objects, animals and plants were telescoped or superposed in the constant interplay of correspondences between creatures, words and things, all bearing the imprint of the divine and the sacred. The human heart cut out of the breast of the sacrificial victim evoked the prickly pear and its purplish colour, but fruit and heart in their turn suggested the red, rising sun. This was not symbolism or metaphor,[27] nor was it a language that would remain hidden in the pages of a book, Chinese or European. Everything converged in sumptuous and costly productions that would be repeated as long as the gods lived. 'Production' is too light a concept, 'myth' too literary a term. The 'myths' encompassed physical, collective and olfactory experiences, such as the stink of decomposing flesh and blood, the sight of humans being butchered in societies where the butchering of animals was unknown, or the scenes of collective drunkenness produced under the influence of *pulque* (the fermented juice of the agave) and hallucinogens. The myths were experienced as communal plunges into the beyond of death and the sacred, both structuring and traumatic. These were much more than texts to be recited by heart, or subjected to exegesis, from a seat by the fireside, pen or brush in hand.

It is difficult to go deeper. Chinese thought, however remote from us it seems, is not indecipherable, at least if one makes the effort. Yet the thinking of the ancient Mexicans remains forever inaccessible, and that of those who survived the Conquest was indelibly marked by colonization. It is true that so many things separate our intellectual world from China and from Mexico that the two worlds can become strangely confused; perhaps because they each represent an alternative and a challenge to our own ways of thinking?

Are there any real similarities? *Anahuac* and *Zhongguo* seem to share principles that are not ours: the idea that there is no absolute and eternal truth, that contradictions are not irreconcilable, but rather alternatives, and that, instead of emphasizing words that excluded, both worlds preferred complementary oppositions – the yin and the yang of the Chinese, or the water-and-fire of the Nahuas, *atl-tlachinolli*. Did the omnipresent breath, the *qi*, flow or vital energy, which animates the universe, both spirit and matter in constant circulation, equate to the Mexican *tona*? Was the world conceived on either side of the Pacific as 'a continuous web of relations between the whole and the parts', rather than as a sum of independent units each endowed with an essence?[28] Should we explain some of these proximities by systems of expression which bear no relation to alphabetic or phonetic writing? Can we say of each Chinese ideogram, as of each Indian pictograph, that they are 'one thing among things'? In the linguistic field, the absence of the verb 'to be' in the classic forms of the two languages surely had some impact on the conception and configuration of the relationship to the world.

It has to be admitted that these similarities are not without their appeal. It may be that, given the impossibility of accessing the thinking of the ancient Mexicans other than through the European filter, the model of Chinese thought might open up other approaches. It might help us, if not to understand, at least to get closer to the irreducible singularity of the *ixiptla* of the Indians. Nevertheless, in our desire to draw on this reserve of non-Western thinking, we must be careful not to fall prey to optical illusions that result from flaws in our own vision.

2

Openness to the World

The history of European expansion has long divided the world into the invaders and the invaded. The activity and inexhaustible curiosity of the Europeans have been contrasted with the inertia of local societies, turned in on themselves and closed to the outside world. China, imagined as asleep ('When China wakes...'), sealed off from the external world or hunkered down behind its Great Wall, has suffered from this image. And in the case of Indian America, isolation from the world has been seen as one of its defining features.

What is incorrect for China is incorrect for America, too. The Mesoamerican societies had never been societies cut off from, even less ignorant of, each other. Not only does the history of this region consist of a succession of migrations which constantly confronted and mixed populations, but religious, political and artistic exchanges in the age of Teotihuacan, and probably long before, impacted on the whole of Mesoamerica, while the endless 'flower wars' and far-flung raids produced regular clashes between peoples.

The World According to the *Pochtecas*

To these contacts we should add the long-distance trade conducted by the *pochtecas* of the Triple Alliance, a group whose autonomy was disliked both by the warriors and the princes. Accustomed to travelling abroad, visiting distant lordships and speaking other languages, always informed about events elsewhere, able when necessary to merge into a hostile background by adopting the clothes, language and customs of others, it is hardly surprising that the *pochtecas* were a source of unease to the warriors of Mexico-Tenochtitlan. They were seen as possessing a flexibility and a mobility – not to say cosmopolitanism, though the word is anachronistic – which they themselves lacked. Their ties with their native city were never exclusive. Long-distance trade linked the centres of the *altiplano* to the northern provinces, to the coasts of the east and west and to the regions of the Gulf (Vera Cruz and Tabasco); and – further afield – to Central America (Chiapas, Soconusco and Guatemala). From here, other routes led by other networks and other relays to Colombia, and even Ecuador.

Thus there were plenty of people prepared to travel long distances. They took the customary precautions, of course, because the movements of merchants, like every other aspect of life, were subject to signs in the same way as those of connoisseurs of the occult and pilgrims. Travellers were careful to respect the days of the divinatory calendars they always carried with them. In these calendars Nahua, Mixtec and Mayan signs mingled in syncretic combinations which reveal the fluidity of the religious traditions and testify to the intermixing of ideas about which we are still poorly informed.[1] Like long-distance trade, forms and ideas had been crisscrossing Mesoamerica for centuries, even millennia.

But mobility was impeded in numerous ways: there were no draught animals and there was no use of the wheel, even if archaeology tells us it was known. Together with the mountainous landscape and the poverty of the hydrographic networks, these handicaps complicated and slowed down the circulation of men and things, if we take China or Europe as reference points. Porterage on the backs of men limited the weight and volume of the loads that could circulate, effective though it was in the absence of true roads. The Spanish colonizers grasped this and had no shame in swiftly taking advantage of this purely human solution. The absence of the wheel was a serious drawback compared with China or Europe: the Amerindians were unfamiliar with either glass or steel and had no machines for transport, for defence (no cannon, harquebus, crossbow or catapult), for production (no looms, no mills) or for communication (no printing).

At the beginning of the sixteenth century the machine did not yet give Europeans an overwhelming advantage, but it had already set them on the path towards a conception of the world in which men would increasingly depend on machines for their existence, their survival and their success. The ability to create machines and know how to use them was both a strength and a sign of modernity, whether Chinese or European. The Amerindians would learn this at their cost.

The Emperor's Fleets

'Medieval' China was very far from the closed and unchanging country that we, in our ignorance, like to imagine it as. It had embarked in the fifteenth century on a maritime expansion which extended as far as the shores of East Africa. Earlier, it had been the cornerstone of a Mongol rule that stretched as far as the plains of Poland and Hungary. The official withdrawal to within the frontiers of the empire, after the abandonment of the great expeditions led by the Chinese Muslim Zheng He, was only relative. On the one hand, there was an active Chinese diaspora settled in South-East Asia;[2] on the other, the China of the Ming Dynasty, in power since 1368, was very far from renouncing its supremacy over this part of the world. Relations with Tibet and the oases of Central Asia, the Mongols and the Jurchen of the north, the Koreans and the Japanese of the east, and with South-East Asia testify to the extent of its spheres of influence and to the complexity of the policies it needed to pursue in each case. The existence of a government department responsible for contacts with the external world, the curiosity about and knowledge of foreigners and the circulation of men and books mean we cannot see China as a world shut away behind its lines of fortification.

Admittedly, contacts with the outside world, hence with a barbarous and inferior world, were disliked by Confucian scholars and a source of unease to high civil servants. In 1436 the government forbade the construction of seagoing vessels.[3] Some forty years later, the archives of the great maritime expeditions were destroyed. It was not until 1567 that the ban proclaiming the 'closing of the seas' (*haijin*) was lifted.[4] Foreign trade was permitted only if it was strictly controlled, and the imperial fleet was made responsible for tracking down clandestine activities, on the Fujian coast and elsewhere. Draconian measures were employed to discourage any dealings with foreigners. Those Chinese who engaged in long-distance trade, fitted out large vessels, showed a readiness to take risks, corrupted customs officers and brazenly enriched themselves were looked at askance. Nevertheless, nothing held back either the race for profit or smuggling in the first decades of the sixteenth century. The import of cloves, pepper and sappan wood was so profitable that the Chinese merchants, always the more numerous and more enterprising, were in fierce competition with each other.[5]

The Portuguese landed in an empire which may jealously have guarded its frontiers, but which was not impermeable to the outside world. We are beginning to gain a better appreciation of its prodigious human diversity and to see beyond the classical bland image which the men of letters tried to present of it, and to pay proper attention to the eunuchs, the women and the ethnic and religious minorities, Buddhist and Muslim, who had other visions of the world.[6]

The Frontiers of Civilization

China had both land and maritime borders.[7] The Triple Alliance had only the former, as the sea did not separate it from any other human society. But both governments had a special relationship with their northern steppes, inhabited by nomadic peoples. In both cases, the contrasting lifestyles fostered among the sedentary population the notion that they and they alone were in possession of that particular quality we call 'civilization'. In China this belief had been associated since the distant times of the Xia, the Shang and the Zhou with one region, *Zhongguo*, 'the kingdoms of the centre', situated in the 'nurturing embrace of the Yellow River'.[8] It was from *Zhongguo*, it was believed, that *wen*, a term often translated as 'culture' or 'civilization', had emerged. Which meant that the peoples who lay outside *Zhongguo* could not be *wen*, that is, civilized. To begin with, *wen* was a value system which spread of its own accord due to its irresistible attraction for those who were without it. In the imperial era it became a way of life to be imposed by force in the lands absorbed by 'the kingdoms of the centre', *Zhongguo*.

The history of pre-imperial and imperial China was punctuated by frequent invasions from the north, of which the first was probably that of the Zhou in the second millennium BCE.[9] As a general rule the invaders settled, became sedentary and adopted the customs of the 'civilized'. This was the case with the Mongol invaders who ruled China until 1368 and also, centuries later, with the Manchus who would destroy the Ming Dynasty.

The history of Mesoamerica also exhibits a dynamic by which the peoples of the north were drawn to move south in search of civilization. The frontier between the arid zone and the cultivable zone shifted with climatic changes, leading to population movements that were impossible to control.[10] The Mexicas, like the other Nahuas, were the first to recognize that they were not autochthonous, but people from elsewhere, who had left the mythical Aztlan in a heroic migration that had brought them to the new Aztlan, Mexico-Tenochtitlan.[11] By settling, they changed, and they acquired the characteristics of the sedentary populations and the agrarian and urban communities of which they were anxious at all costs to become part. They were the very opposite, in a sense, of those people on the move, heading for the other side of the world, the Spanish and the Portuguese. The Mexicas went to great lengths to acquire the local roots they lacked, whether seeking to 'rewrite' the past or to cling on to the island of Mexico and the lakes and lands of the Valley. The construction of the Great Temple, *ombilicus mundi*, is striking testimony to this quest for historical depth and this physical and metaphysical attachment to the centre of the world. The Mexicas and their allies were new arrivals both on the *altiplano* and in history. In fact this was also true of the Ming, who acceded to power some fifty years after the foundation of Mexico-Tenochtitlan. One understands why, in both cases, these new masters tried to appropriate the heritage of those who had preceded them, Song, Yuan or Toltec.

The Nahua priests and rulers knew how deliberately to magnify the feature which distinguished them from those they no longer wished to be. Civilization as they conceived it was expressly linked to the heritage of the legendary Tula and to the creativity of its inhabitants, the Toltecs, 'painters, authors of books, sculptors', carvers in wood and stone, builders of towns and palaces, master craftsmen in the art of the feather and ceramics.[12] Miguel León-Portilla has argued that the word *toltecayotl* has a meaning equivalent to what we call 'civilization', a concept which included the skills and the knowledge derived from ancient times and from the *altiplano*. However, the rulers of the Triple Alliance also knew that they came from the north and that they had a past of privations, migrations and wandering, when they had been simply Chichimecs.[13] In the sixteenth century the word 'chichimec' became, under European influence, synonymous with pillager, nomad and barbarian, with the primitive Indian clothed in animal skins and reduced, for his survival, to hunting among the cactus.

There was a clear contrast, therefore, between the 'barbarian' and the 'civilized', but it was expressed in very different terms in Mexico than in China or Europe, because in Mexico the 'civilized' proclaimed themselves former 'barbarians'. Was it not the first Chichimec emigrants who had merged with the Nonoalcas to found Tula, the city – or, if preferred, civilization – par excellence?

The Sea

For the Chinese the sea had long been the domain of the Isles of the Immortals. The coast is still dotted with islands devoted to divinities, such as the island of Putuoshan, off the Zhejiang coast south of Hangzho, where there lives, it is said, the bodhisattva Guanyin; or Meizhou Island, off the coast of Fujian, where Mazu, Empress of Heaven, is venerated.[14] But for centuries, even millennia, the 'South Seas' had ceased to be unknown and impassable and had become, instead, a zone of dense traffic with South-East Asia.

The coasts had long been areas of intense activity. Since at least the Han (–206/–220), large ships had been built there, and tributary and commercial embassies from the other countries in the region received. Since the fourth century foreign merchants had arrived in increasing numbers, soon to be joined by Buddhist monks from India and South-East Asia, who spread their ideas and beliefs throughout southern China. Under the Tang Dynasty, with the establishment of direct relations with the Persian Gulf and the Red Sea, merchants from western Asia arrived, settled and introduced Islam. Driven by the monsoon winds, the vessels of the new arrivals landed at Guangzhou (Canton), which experienced a period of rapid growth. In 684 and 758 these unprecedented contacts led to incidents with the local authorities, involving 'Persians and Arabs', who were accused of disturbing the peace. Communities of foreign merchants settled in Yangzhou and Guangzhou, where there were many Muslims by the end of the ninth century. Islam was not the only religion to come knocking at the door. The Chinese coast also received Manicheans, Nestorian Christians, followers of Brahmanism and, by the thirteenth century, the first Roman Catholics. In the thirteenth and fourteenth centuries, visited by people of different languages, ethnicities and beliefs, the coast took on a cosmopolitan air. So prosperous was southern Fujian that the port of Quanzhou (Zaytun in Arabic) in the fourteenth century was to maritime China, it has been said, what Shanghai would be in the 1920s and Hong Kong in the 1970s.[15] And it is to a Jewish merchant from Italy, Jacob of Ancona, that we owe a fascinating description of this port, which traded with the whole of South-East Asia.

It would be surprising, therefore, if the Chinese themselves had not taken advantage of this activity to set sail, trade with Korea and South-East Asia and feed a diaspora that kept on growing. This was the context for the famous expeditions of the early fifteenth century, which took sea routes frequented for centuries and visited the coasts of Arabia and East Africa. In the fourteenth and fifteenth centuries the scale of this commercial traffic drove the Ming Empire to reassert its control over trade by awarding certain ports a monopoly of maritime activities. Officially, everything had to be done through tributary embassies, whose frequency, composition and maritime and land itineraries were fixed. Offices were opened, closed or moved over time, though total control of relations with the outside world was never achieved.[16] The Portuguese who went to China found interlocutors with centuries of experience in dealing with foreigners and an administration determined systematically to filter everything arriving from the South Seas.

At the same time, the many coastal islands attracted smugglers, outlaws and pirates who flouted imperial power. The more the empire proclaimed its desire to stop private traffic, the more these clandestine and predatory activities flourished. This lawless zone was famous for its barbarity and its cruelty.[17] This, too, was a world the Portuguese would come to know, and to which they would quickly adapt.

In Mesoamerica, trade was essentially overland. The coast had no fleet, even less ships capable of sea voyages, although the Mayas had rowing boats suited to tropical coastal navigation. Compared with the China of maritime networks, ports, imperial fleets, coastguards and customs officials, not to speak of the China of smugglers, this Mesoamerica surrounded by almost empty seas gives the impression of being on another planet. Also, unlike the Chinese, who had turned their backs on long voyages, though without having forgotten their advantages, and the Iberians, who were now discovering their attractions, benefits and risks, the Mesoamericans expected nothing of the waters surrounding them. Though certain objects washed up on the shore at the beginning of the sixteenth century aroused the Indians' curiosity: 'they brought Moctezuma a Spanish trunk, which must have come from a ship wrecked in the North Sea [Atlantic], in which they found a sword, rings, jewels and clothes; Moctezuma gave these gems to the lords of Tezcoco and Tacuba, and, so as not to worry them, he told them that his ancestors had hidden them and carefully put them aside, and he asked that they treat them with proper respect'.[18]

The master of Mexico may have preferred to conceal the truth for fear of fuelling speculation about the predicted end of his reign. But this text was drawn up well after the conquest, when the die had already been cast. The ancient Mexicans could hardly have imagined what an unpredictable fate the emerald waves of the divine water had in store for them.

A History Played Out in Advance?

In the face of European expansion, it may seem obvious to us today that Mexico did not stand a chance, whereas China was well equipped to repel invaders arriving by sea. But these are opinions reached with the benefit of hindsight and under the influence of later interpretations, which clog up our minds. Was this Mexico of more than 20,000,000 inhabitants, without iron, machines and writing, really doomed to destruction at the hands of a few thousand Spaniards? Had the Mexicas reached their apogee, so were feverishly scanning the Eastern Sea for the signs that would foretell their rapid decline? It is equally absurd to believe that the Spanish were consciously planning the conquest of Mexico, a land of whose existence they were totally ignorant.

What stands out from this brief survey must surely be the diversity of peoples, things and situations that the Portuguese and the Spanish discovered, round about the same time. What did these discoveries boil down to? At the moment of contact, the Iberians had no way of penetrating the societies they found – always assuming we can do this better today. Yet it was they, and for a long time only they among Europeans, who were left to observe, describe and understand the worlds they suddenly found within their grasp – not one world, but many worlds at the same time. This should convince us, once and for all, that to think in terms of the European facing the Other, or the Other facing the European, is no more than an academic exercise which inevitably obscures what happened between the Iberians and the rest of the world in the sixteenth century. It is because they were forced to operate in many different registers – with Americans, with Asiatics, with Africans and with Muslims – and so face a plethora of othernesses (though not necessarily always experienced as such), that they helped to lay the foundations of the globalization which was then beginning to emerge. They had at the same time embarked on the path to modernity, a modernity that was de-centred, constructed outside Europe, in dialogue with other civilizations. What is important is not so much to discover whether they understood – or not – those they encountered (as if, once again, there is somewhere a truth to be discovered, and as if we are better placed to discover it today), as to take account of the means they mobilized in order to engage with humanities that were unknown to them; even if they then, whenever they could, forced them into submission.

In the second decade of the sixteenth century, at the heart of the Valley of Mexico, an avalanche of signs and disturbing prodigies created a sense of unease, constrained the power of Moctezuma and heralded sinister arrivals. The skies of Western Europe were equally disturbed at this same period. Fantastic night battles terrorized the countryside around Bergamo in 1517, causing much ink to flow.[19]

The skies of China were hardly calmer. For the first six years of the reign of the Emperor Zhengde, dragons spared the Celestial Empire. However, from the summer of 1512 their visits began to multiply. First came a fiery red dragon; then, on 7 July 1517, nine black dragons flew over the River Huai, 'at the point where it crosses the Grand Canal'. A year later the sky of the Yangzi Delta was traversed by three dragons breathing fire. They hoovered up a score of ships, spreading panic and causing countless deaths. Eleven months later, above Lake Poyang, there erupted a battle between dragons such as had never been seen since 1368, when the Mongol dynasty had fallen. In China visits by dragons boded ill; they denounced an unworthy emperor or a disastrous policy, or they presaged catastrophes. Apparitions proliferated when the dynasty vacillated, no longer capable of correctly carrying out the mandates of Heaven.

Neither Europe nor America had a monopoly of heavenly prodigies. Every society in the world, large or small, was too imbued with the habit of associating them with times of crisis for us to regard what was seen by the Chinese, the ancient Mexicans and the Europeans as anything other than coincidence. Nevertheless, they all belonged to worlds that were ignorant of each other. At the dawn of the sixteenth century, the skies, like the civilizations, were still strictly compartmentalized.[20]

3

Because the World is Round

By about 1515 the Spanish settlers in Cuba were turning their attention to the vast lands which lay to the west and south of their island. The first expedition to the coast of Mexico left in 1517. The third, that of Hernán Cortés, set out in 1519. After an exhausting but ultimately victorious war, the conquest was confirmed on 13 August 1521 by the seizure of Mexico City and the collapse of Mexica rule. Mexico came under European control, and the rest of the continent followed. Whether Latin, French, Dutch or Anglo-Saxon, the New World would for a long time to come be prey to the European countries that had conquered, colonized and westernized it.

The first sustained contacts between the Portuguese and the Chinese began around 1511 in Malacca, where there was a large colony of immigrants from the Celestial Empire. The first appearances of the Portuguese on the coasts of China date back to at least the year 1513, and were repeated in the following two years. In June 1517 a Portuguese embassy, which had set sail in eight vessels, left Malacca for Canton, where it remained until January 1520, before setting out for Peking. It was the first diplomatic mission sent by a European power to the Middle Empire. In May it reached Nanking, then, in summer of that year, it arrived at the imperial court in Peking. But the mission was suddenly cut short and its members thrown into prison. The Chinese authorities were not content simply to put these intruders behind bars; they physically eliminated them, as a bunch of spies and robbers with hostile intentions. From this point China managed to keep the Europeans at bay until the middle of the nineteenth century. It may not entirely have escaped foreign invasions,

Manchu, Japanese or Western, but unlike India and the rest of Asia, it never let itself be colonized.

Parallel Histories

Why not compare these parallel histories, which tell of the divergent fates of large portions of the globe, Indian America and China?[1] It is more than a matter of a simple parallelism. The Iberian expeditions to the coasts of Mexico and China may not have been part of a concerted operation, but neither was their temporal coincidence pure chance. The two events derived from a common dynamic. The sixteenth century saw many parts of the world come into contact with Europeans. This set in motion processes which can only be understood at a global level. With the benefit of hindsight they appear irreversible and they emerge as the first signs of a unification of the world that is generally dated, quite anachronistically, to the end of the twentieth century. Distant in space but synchronic, both symmetrical and complementary, these movements have escaped the attention of generations of historians in thrall to historiographical and geographical divisions inherited from the nineteenth century, and still surprisingly current today.

Yet we need only put these histories side by side to see aspects of the intercontinental landscape created in the sixteenth century by the entry onto the scene of two new European powers, Castile and Portugal, whose amazing sea voyages across the globe put them in contact with worlds of which they were wholly, or almost wholly, ignorant. The shocks and collisions which rapidly ensued were often deadly. They can be explained by a conscious desire to dominate the planet, or by an imperialist and Western 'logic' which irresistibly took the Iberians – those for whom 'the world had neither limit nor end' – round the globe.[2] But such a unilateral vision ignores the fact that it takes at least two to make a meeting. The modalities of the contact, the intensity of the shocks and their repercussions differed according to place and to partner. The trauma was not the same in Mexico as it was in China, even if in both cases it affected people and forces totally unprepared for the confrontation.

Connected Histories, or the Race for the Moluccas

There is an even more direct link between these parallel histories: the 'Spice Islands', located on the fringes of South-East Asia and consisting of the Banda Islands and the Archipelago of the Moluccas (Maluka in Indonesian). The Banda Islands produced nutmeg and mace, Ternate and Tidore produced cloves. These spices, much sought after by both Chinese and Europeans, were commodities in a world-wide trade which was hugely profitable and which involved commercial chains stretching from South-East Asia to the Mediterranean of Alexandria and Venice. Confident they had the maritime means to seize the Spice Islands, hence short-circuit the innumerable intermediaries in this legendary trade, the Portuguese and the Castilians embarked on a race against each other, executing a pincer movement, the former by the east, the latter by the west.

In 1493 the Treaty of Tordesillas divided the world into two equal halves between Castile and Portugal. The pole-to-pole demarcation line bisecting the Atlantic was easy enough to follow, but the other dividing line, the Anti-Meridian, was as unclear as it was virtual. Did the Archipelago belong by right to the Portuguese or was it in the half awarded to Castile? The two camps clashed with each other, therefore, first diplomatically, then through their pilots, sailors and soldiers, over a boundary whose location was uncertain, situated on the other side of the Earth. At stake was control of the spices which the Banda Islands and the Moluccas produced in abundance.[3]

Masters of the sea route via the Cape of Good Hope, it was the Portuguese who were the first to approach and then reach their goal. In 1505 Manuel encouraged the search for *descobrimentos* (discoveries) in the direction of Malacca. The year after, anxious to ward off a Castilian threat – so close did the New World seem – he ordered a fortress to be built, either on the spot or nearby. It was impossible to operate in this region, however, without some anxiety regarding the highly enterprising merchants known as the *Chins*, not mentioned by Marco Polo. In 1508 the king became impatient and asked Diogo Lopez de Sequeira for information about these *Chins*. The Portuguese had encountered them in northern Sumatra, where they had been offered Chinese porcelain.[4] In July 1509, in Malacca, the Portuguese fleet came face to face with some Chinese junks. All passed off peacefully, however. They invited each other to dinner and questioned each other about their respective countries. It is to this encounter that we owe what is probably the first physical description of the Chinese. Contact was made and the atmosphere became more relaxed. The Chinese were clearly not Muslims, but were they really Christians, as the Portuguese at one point believed?

In 1511 the soldiers and sailors of Lisbon seized Malacca from the Sultan Mahmud Shah. The port became a crucial base for the Portuguese advance in western Asia. Malacca was then home to numerous communities of merchants. Its new masters aligned themselves with the Tamils and the Keligs, but sent the members of the Gujarati community packing.[5] Although they had rejected Chinese offers of collaboration, contacts developed with the merchant community which had settled in the great port. In 1512 one of its representatives set sail for Lisbon. A projected voyage to China the same year was abandoned, although the Portuguese had already reached the Moluccas and the Banda Islands. They had achieved their goal.

The Castilians had not lost all hope of getting their own access to the spices. In 1512 Ferdinand the Catholic decided to send the Portuguese João Diaz de Solis in the footsteps of his compatriots. He was to sail to the Moluccas, take possession and then fix, once and for all, the position of the line of Tordesillas, 'which would in future and forever be known and clearly established'. He was also to take Ceylon, Sumatra, Pegu and, while he was about it, the 'country of the Chinese and junks'.[6] A map then circulating in Castile located Malacca, the Spice Islands and the Chinese coast on the right, that is, the Spanish, side of the line.[7] So, before anyone had any notion of the existence of Mexico, the Castilians were signalling their designs on China. This project exasperated Lisbon. Manuel of Portugal was furious and the expedition of Solis did not, in the end, take place. But had Castile really abandoned its plans? In 1515 Ferdinand asked Solis to set out in search of a passage between the Atlantic and the sea which Balboa had discovered in September 1513, that southern sea which would be called the Pacific Ocean. No such luck! Not only was the Rio de la Plata not the hoped-for opening to Asia, but João Diaz de Solis ended up in the stomachs of the Indians.

Nevertheless, the world being round, the Portuguese knew that the Spanish efforts to advance in a westerly direction would one day bring them to the Far East. So they set out to consolidate their presence in the China Sea and the Moluccas by every means and as speedily as possible. This explains the embassy which Manuel decided to send to Peking in 1515. The Portuguese of Malacca lost no time. A letter of 1512 describes the preparations for a voyage to China, though it was aborted due to the opposition of the Muslim intermediaries, who proposed to block the route to Canton.[8] In May 1513 Jorge Alvarez erected a stela or *padrão* on the Chinese coast. Two years later, a Portuguese cousin of Christopher Columbus, Rafael Perestrello, left Malacca 'to discover China' and landed at Canton. He returned to Lisbon three years later, having completed the first round trip between Portugal and China.

Castile had not given up. In 1518 another Portuguese navigator who had gone over to the enemy, Magellan, revived the project of

Solis to reach the Moluccas by the western route.[9] Magellan was familiar with the region. He had lived for some years in Portuguese Asia and taken part in the conquest of Malacca and the exploration of the Sonde Archipelago. In 1519 Magellan's stopover in Brazil aggravated Lisbon's fears. This time, the Pacific would be reached, then crossed from east to west.

The Portuguese had other grounds for their fears, which seem absurd to us today. The discovery of new lands between the Antilles and Asia might give rise to another threat, one that was already visible on the globes, whether those conceived by Johannes Schöner in 1515 and 1520, which showed a ridiculously small Pacific, or others, made in the 1520s, which linked Central America to Asia.[10] This erroneous idea of a supposed proximity would survive even the failure of Gómez de Espinoza, the navigator who tried unsuccessfully to re-cross the Pacific and reach the Antilles in one of the ships of Magellan's fleet.[11]

It is difficult, as a result, to dissociate either Portuguese designs on South-East Asia or Castilian activities in the New World from the conquest of the Spice Islands. It was the conquest of the Moluccas which mobilized the Crowns of Castile and Portugal, with its global perspectives, its prospect of inexhaustible riches and its share of infernal rivalries. Mexico as such was still in limbo, but China was already emerging on the horizon. One of the chroniclers of Magellan's expedition, Maximilian Transylvanus, laid it on the line: 'Our ship has traversed the whole West, gone round the bottom of our hemisphere, then penetrated the Orient, to return at last to the West.'[12]

This feat, beyond that of the Argonauts, had the result of obscuring the first aim of the voyage, which had been to take possession of the Spice Islands and settle in the most distant part of Asia; which meant coming close to China. This was suggested, in Spain, by the chronicler Peter Martyr of Anghiera: 'You the Spanish will follow the setting sun, as the Portuguese have followed the rising sun, and will arrive to the east of the Moluccan Islands, which are not very distant from the country where Ptolemy placed Cattigara and the Great Gulf, gateway to China.'[13]

The Columbian Precedent

It is not enough to relocate the Portuguese and Castilian enterprises within the perspective of the search for spices. The initiative of Lisbon to make contact with China inevitably evokes one of the clichés of the epic of Christopher Columbus, his desperate desire to reach Asia.

It has too quickly been forgotten that the oceanic continuation of the Spanish *reconquista* had never been the conquest of America, but the quest for a passage to Asia. As the *Memorial de la Mejorada* recalls, Columbus had been charged by the Catholic Kings with 'searching for and discovering the Indies, the islands and the lands of the Far East, by sailing westward from Spain.'[14]

This was what disturbed and outraged the king of Portugal, all the more so as, in the mind of Columbus, the space beyond the Cape of Good Hope, stretching from the Indian Ocean to the islands he had discovered, rightfully belonged to the Crown of Castile.[15] In a sense, for Castile, the West was Asia – a distant world, but one that had haunted the Mediterranean *imaginaire* since Antiquity, and was known to be real. This notion was so deep-rooted that Spanish America would retain its name of the 'West Indies' until the nineteenth century. And the indigenous peoples of the continent, from Patagonia to Canada, even today, are for us Indians. America began by being an accident and an obstacle in Spain's race for the East, and it is the task of the historian to show that its 'invention', that is, the way in which we have progressively imagined it, is as inseparable from our relationship with Asia as it is from our relationship with Islam.[16]

4

A Leap into the Unknown?

What did people in Europe know about the China of Zhengde and the Mexico of Moctezuma at the beginning of the sixteenth century? In reality, nothing, even though the Portuguese had been visiting the coasts of India for some time and the Spanish circulating in the Caribbean. Neither China nor Mexico had as yet established themselves on European horizons. Were the Iberians thus first launching into the unknown or into a void? And was this an early indication of the European propensity to take an interest, whatever the cost, in *terrae incognitae*?

The metaphor of a leap into the unknown is seductive but misleading, as it fails to take account of the frame of mind and practice of the sailors. They were not sailing into the unknown. Since the beginning of the fifteenth century the Portuguese had been engaged in the gradual, and for a long time tentative, construction of a thalassocracy, drawing on their maritime experience and the knowledge they had gathered from a variety of sources. They had made a giant leap forward in connecting Africa and then the Indian Ocean to Lisbon and Europe. After this, the Portuguese sailors lapped up the miles at an unprecedented rate: having landed on the coast of India in 1498, they reached Malacca in 1511, the Moluccas in 1512 and China in 1513. All this would have been impossible, even inconceivable, had they not been able to make use of the mercantile routes and information networks that had existed in the Far East for centuries. Past masters in the art of accumulating knowledge and even more of putting it to good use, the Portuguese were never steering into unknown waters. The Castilians, too, though they had far less experience than their neighbours, also believed they knew where they were going. Seen from the ports of Andalusia, Marco Polo's China, Cathay, loomed in the West.

The Cathay of Marco Polo

The Portuguese were familiar with the work of the Venetian Marco Polo, a copy of which, in Latin, was in the library of King Duarte (1433–8). However, it was in the second half of the fifteenth century that its influence was most directly felt. About 1457–9 the map made by the Venetian Camaldolese monk, Fra Mauro, for King Afonso V of Portugal drew heavily on his work, in particular for the names of the Chinese towns and provinces: Cambaluc, Quinsay, Zaiton (Zaitun), Mangi, Cathay and Zimpagu (Cipangu, that is, Japan). Years later, a letter from the physician Paolo del Pozzo Toscanelli, astronomer to the city of Florence, addressed to the Lisbon canon Fernão Martins, would cause much ink to flow.[1] It was in June 1474 that Toscanelli explained to his correspondent that it was possible to reach the Indies by crossing the Atlantic. He sent him a map, and drew his attention to a port of unimaginable wealth where huge cargoes of spices were landed. The country had a large population, the prince who ruled it was called the Great Khan and his palaces were located in the province of Cathay. Toscanelli had this from the mouth of an ambassador to Pope Eugene IV. Quinsay was situated in the province of Mangi, near to Cathay, and its name meant the City of Heaven. This Florentine scholar also provided figures, for example, for the distance between Lisbon and the 'very great city of Quinsay', which was twenty-six spaces marked on the map, each representing 250 miles. 'From the island of Antillia [supposed to lie in the middle of the Atlantic], which you know, to the very noble island of Cipangu, is ten spaces'. This information, passed on to the canon of Lisbon, and through his intermediary to King Afonso V of Portugal, was all taken from Marco Polo's text.

The expectations aroused by Marco Polo probably circulated more quickly than his book, which remained for a long time largely inaccessible to readers in the Iberian Peninsula. It was in Castile that it had the most spectacular effects. In 1492, for the first voyage of Columbus, sailors were recruited by the lure of the prospect of discovering a land where the houses had roofs of gold – a publicity coup inspired by Marco Polo's *Travels*.[2] But what was the link between the Genoese and the Venetian?

It is not now believed that Columbus had read Marco Polo before he set out for the New World. His knowledge was probably limited to what he had gleaned from the famous letter of Toscanelli. It was only in the spring of 1498 that he started to read the *Travels*, a copy of which had been sent to him by the Bristol merchant John Day.[3] Nevertheless, the figure of the Great Khan was constantly in Columbus' mind, as it was in that of Queen Isabella, who sent the Genoese letters of credence which he was to present to the King of Kings and other lords of India.

Everything Columbus saw and discovered was interpreted – and he was not alone in this – in the light of the information on Toscanelli's map. Or, to be more precise, Columbus did not discover anything: he recognized and he rediscovered, and even his last expedition was still presented as a further stage in an ordered progression. On the first voyage, still not spying land on the horizon, Columbus believed he must have bypassed Cipangu. He thought his best plan would then be to sail directly for the *terra firma* of the 'city of Quinsay to deliver the letters of Her Highness to the Great Khan, seek a reply and return with it'.[4] That is, he would make for the continent of Asia.

At first he thought the island of Cuba must be Cipangu, then that it was 'the land and kingdoms of the Great Khan or their borders'.[5] So he must be before Zaytun and Quinsay, 'a hundred leagues more or less from both of them'. Columbus selected an ambassador, Rodrigo de Xeres, and a New Christian, Luis de Torres, who knew Hebrew and Chaldean, to go ashore and find the Great Khan. This mission, which also included two Indians, was to approach the ruler of the country 'on behalf of the king and queen of Castile', offer him gifts and friendship and, of course, collect information about 'certain provinces, ports and rivers the Admiral knew of'. Columbus had not lost his senses. The people of Caniba, who had been described to him by the Indians of Hispaniola, had to be 'the people of the Great Khan, who must be somewhere near',[6] and he never budged. It was after his second voyage that Columbus located the Chinese port of Zaytun (Quanzhou), made famous by Marco Polo, at the height of Cape Alpha and Omega (Punta de Maisi, at the eastern end of Cuba); for him, this was where the West ended and the East began.[7] The New World of Columbus lay always in the shadow of China.

The maps of the period confirmed this vision of the world by stubbornly persisting in representing the same far-off lands. On the mappa mundi of Henricus Martellus Germanicus, now in the British Library (1489 or 1490), we see Ciamba (Champa), Mangi, Quinsay and Cathay, here taken to be a town. The map known as the Yale (1489) shows Cipangu at 90° west of the Canaries; Lisbon is situated at 105°

from Cipangu and 135° from Quinsay. This was how the world was seen in a Florentine workshop on the eve of the first voyage of Christopher Columbus. In 1492 Martin Behaim (Nuremberg) built a globe that was probably based on different versions of the work of Marco Polo; he calculated that not more than 130° separated Europe from Asia and placed Cipangu at 25° from the land of Mangi, that is, from China.[8]

Although it had long been under attack, Marco Polo's book continued to be influential in Europe. It is hardly surprising that it should first become accessible to those who felt most directly concerned by what it contained. In 1502 a German from Moravia who had spent seven years in Lisbon (1495), after an earlier brief stay in Seville (1493), translated Polo's *Travels* for Portuguese readers unfamiliar with Venetian, Tuscan, French or Latin. This was the printer and polygraph Valentim Fernandes, a correspondent of Albrecht Dürer, Conrad Peutinger[9] and Hieronymus Münzer. It was he who made the Portuguese discoveries known to the people of northern Europe, in rather the same way as the Milanese Peter Martyr of Anghiera would extol the exploits of Columbus and the Castilians from the Court of Castile.[10]

The Preparation of the Voyages

In reality, the Portuguese expedition to China was based on much more solid information than a letter from a Florentine frequenter of papal audiences or the writings of Marco Polo. It had been conceived and meticulously prepared in Lisbon. Goods from Asia had been regular arrivals in the great port on the River Tagus since the last years of the fifteenth century. Among them had been brocades and porcelain from China, well before Portuguese ships had reached that country.

The objective had a name, the 'land of the Chins', and it gradually acquired a physical, human and material existence. The conquest of Malacca had brought the Portuguese into contact with a significant Chinese community which had been settled there for some time. By 1512 a Chinese had been sent to Cochin, and from there to the Court of Lisbon. A map of Javanese origin dispatched from Malacca enabled the king of Portugal to locate the land of the Chins. Some Chinese books reached Lisbon that same year and, two years later, Manuel offered one of them to Pope Leo X. In Rome this book, as we will see, attracted the attention of the great humanist Paolo Giovio, who could hardly contain his surprise and admiration.[11] China had arrived in Europe by way of its precious objects even before the Portuguese set foot on its soil. And if it is true that it is to China that we owe the invention of printing, it had already impacted on the world of educated Europeans some decades earlier, handing them, indirectly, one of the chief tools of the European Renaissance, the printed book.

The Portuguese in Asia had access to more direct and much more abundant information. Since the first voyage of Vasco da Gama (1498) they had moved in seas that teemed with informants of every sort. In Malacca not only did the factor of King Manuel, Tomé Pires, know his Asia, but it was probably in 1515 that he completed a remarkable treatise of economic and political geography, the *Suma oriental*, which described all the resources of the Asia the Portuguese had discovered.

Several pages in this book were devoted to the land of the Chins, two years before its author set foot on its shores. It is as if Hernán Cortés had compiled a description of Mexico and North America without waiting to land in Yucatán. The 'things of China', Pires said, 'are made out to be great, riches, pomp and state in both the land and the people...it would be easier to believe as true of our Portugal than of China'.[12] He noted how white the inhabitants were, described their clothes and came up with innumerable similarities and comparisons ('as we are', 'like we have in Portugal', 'as we do'). The faults of the Chinese of Malacca – 'they are not very truthful, and steal' – were well known, but this applied mainly to 'the common people'. It was the first time that a European noted the use of chopsticks among these people, who also ate pork and praised Portuguese wine. The Chinese women, like many women in Asia, also attracted Pires' attention: they were as white as Europeans, looked like Spanish women and were as heavily made up as the ladies of Seville.[13] In fact these could only have been women he had glimpsed in Malacca.

The country he had described to him was covered with cities and fortresses. The king, who lived in Cambara (Khanbalikh), was never seen by the people or the grandees. It was in Cambara that this ruler periodically received the homage of the neighbouring kingdoms, Champa, 'Cochin China', 'Liu Kiu' (Ryû Kyû), Japan, Siam, Pase (Pazem, on the island of Sumatra) and Malacca, in accordance with a ceremonial that was punctiliously and jealously observed. The vassal states regularly sent ambassadors laden with the best their country could provide, and the Son of Heaven showered them with presents in return. According to what Pires had been told, the sovereign received them concealed behind a curtain. The envoys saw only the 'vague shape of his body' and communicated with him only through intermediaries. Pires was as yet unaware that he would one day lead a mission to China, hence would himself one day come up against the rigidity of the imperial protocol. Not only was the king inaccessible, but the kingdom was hermetically sealed. No Chinese left for Siam, Java, Malacca or Pazem without the consent of the governors of Canton. No foreigner left the kingdom without the express authorization of the sovereign. Any junk which broke these laws had its merchandise confiscated and its crew was put to death. A word to the wise...[14]

Canton was the Chinese town about which most was known in Malacca. Once again, without realizing it, Pires was becoming familiar with a place in which he would later spend many years, probably the last years of his life. Some of his information came from the merchants of Luçon (the Philippines), 'who have been there'. Situated at the mouth of the great river, Canton was the country's principal trading port. His informants described a city built in stone on a flat terrain, surrounded by walls '7 fathoms thick and as many high', with monumental gates at regular intervals. Canton had several 'ports', which sheltered many large junks. The ambassadors who went there were accustomed to engage in their commercial activities in the town or outside, some thirty leagues from Canton. Here were the islands where the missions berthed while they waited for the official of Nanto, a port on the coast, to announce their arrival to the authorities of Canton and arrange for merchants to come to value their cargoes and calculate the dues to be paid. The experts pocketed the taxes and asked what sort of merchandise to bring from Canton to satisfy the visitors. It was explained to Pires that everything was done outside Canton for fiscal reasons and so as to ensure the security of the town, too often exposed to the threats of corsairs. The Chinese feared the Javanese and Malaysian junks, which were far superior to those of the empire – or, to be more precise, kingdom, Pires never using the word empire. He concluded that one of these large ships would be enough to decimate Canton, which would be a 'great loss' to China. This was a conviction that never faltered among the visitors from Lisbon.

How many days did it take to reach China from Malacca? Twenty, or not more than 15 taking advantage of the monsoon winds. What was the best time to leave? The end of June. How long did it take to travel from China to Borneo? A fortnight.[15] But the journey there and back took seven or eight months. What could be sold to the Chinese? Pepper most of all, small quantities of cloves and nutmegs, and a host of other items ranging from elephant tusks to Borneo camphor. Where should you berth when you arrived from Malacca? On the island of Tunmen. What could be bought in China? Mainly silks, pearls, musk, large quantities of porcelains and even sugar, not to mention the cheap trinkets like those that arrived in Portugal from Flanders.[16] Where did these goods come from? White silk from Chancheo (Ch'uan-chou), coloured silks from Cochinchine and damasks and brocades from Nanking. Where else could you stay other than in Canton? On the coast of Fujian, much further northeast, especially if you were planning to go as far as 'Lequios' (Ryû Kyû). But it was Canton that was the 'key to the kingdom of China'. And as you can never be too careful, you should beware of the ordinary people, who were 'not very near to the truth', while the great merchants and the purchasers of pepper seemed to trade 'honestly'.

So, Pires knew everything, or nearly everything, that was necessary in order to visit the Celestial Empire. He was remarkably well informed when we remember that nothing had been known about China ten years before, which is humbling, considering our claim to know everything in record time today.

Malacca, Crossroads of Asia

Pires owed his knowledge to his stay in Malacca, a port which had become, by the beginning of the fifteenth century, a vital hub in this part of the world. Malacca, which sought Chinese protection at an early stage, had been a frequent port of call for the fleets of Admiral Zheng He (1371–1433).

The town was home to a cosmopolitan population of merchants who had arrived from all the great ports of Asia, and it was a subject on which Pires could hold forth at length. It was probably one of the best possible places in which to acquire information about the maritime routes in this part of the world and about the communities of merchants who frequented them. Pires was not alone in seeking information about China. His compatriots Francisco Rodríguez in 1513 and Duarte Barbosa in 1516 also collected all sorts of facts: about the manufacture of porcelain and silks and the protocol of the embassies received at the Chinese court, and a description of the maritime route – the 'Road to China' – which led from Malacca to Canton.[17]

In 1514 and 1515 a Florentine merchant, Giovanni da Empoli, summarized in two letters what he had learned about the Chinese, both those in Malacca and those on the continent. China, he said, was notable for 'the greatest wealth and greatest objects in the world'.[18] He also spoke about the town of Zerum (Zaytun), which was where the king of China lived, whom he identified as the Great

Khan of Cathay.[19] Was he perhaps the first to grasp that the China of Marco Polo and the China of the Ming were not the same? In 1516 another Florentine, Andrea Corsali, produced in his turn a summary of existing knowledge, taking advantage, like others, of the new information provided by the pioneering expedition of Jorge Alvares.

Pires' voyage was thus by no means the first. By 1513 Jorge Alvares had reached the Chinese coast. A year later another expedition was entrusted to Rafael Perestrello, a Portuguese second cousin of the son of Christopher Columbus, then viceroy of the Indies, Diego Colón. In the spring of 1515, at the head of three junks, Perestrello sailed for China. He was not alone. The Portuguese and the Italians had already taken the same route. It was from Canton, in November 1515, during his first stay in Asia, that Giovanni da Empoli wrote a letter describing China in a few powerful images: the towns, the population, the wealth, the buildings – they all seemed to him extraordinary. Da Empoli died off the Chinese coast in a fire on his ship, in 1517.

On the Portuguese side, people were already beginning to move into a post-Marco Polo age, in which Ming China began to eclipse the Cathay of the Mongols. The scholars of Europe were much slower to update their knowledge. Their maps continued to repeat what Ptolemy and Marco Polo had written about this part of the world, while those used by the Portuguese sailors, which they jealously guarded, had taken note of the discovery: they kept the latest information about the Chinese coast and the Pearl River Delta secret.

Were the New Indies in Asia?

If the Spanish colonists in the Caribbean could believe they were within reach of prosperous trading societies, it was thanks to the expectations and delusions disseminated by Christopher Columbus, who was convinced he had come close to Japan and the Empire of the Great Khan. For the reasons outlined above, Marco Polo's *Travels*, which few had read but many had heard talked about, interposed itself between Castile and the New World. Now, in the first years of the sixteenth century, the Venetian traveller found a new public in Lisbon and Seville. Polo's book was published in Portuguese in 1502, quickly followed by a first Castilian edition, which came out within a year in Seville. Does this mean that the port of the Guadalquivir was planning to press hot on the heels of the port of the Tagus? Why translate Marco Polo side by side with the text of 'Micer Poggio, a

Florentine who discusses the same lands and the same islands', that is, the account of the voyages of Nicolò de' Conti? Paradoxically, the aim was not to provide grist for the Columbus mill but, on the contrary, to supply arguments for those who refused to confuse his Indies with Marco Polo's Asia.

In the prologue to his translation the Dominican Roderigo de Santaella explains his book and reveals that he was very much more than a simple translator. Laden with titles, apostolic proto-notary, archdeacon, canon of Seville, Santaella was an intellectual of high standing in the kingdom of Castile. A humanist educated in Bologna and Rome, author of numerous works of Christian morality, a proponent of clerical reform and a great connoisseur of art, he pondered the identity of the Castilian discoveries in the Western Ocean. His translation of Marco Polo was explicitly aimed at Columbus. In the first years of the sixteenth century, when the latter was on his fourth voyage, Santaella rejected the idea that the western isles were part of the Indies described by Marco Polo.[20]

The prologue responded to the atmosphere of uncertainty prevailing among the Seville elites, which was in sharp contrast to the assurance with which the Portuguese were forging ahead. The discovery of the Antilles had caught the imagination of 'many of the common people and of men of higher status'. Were these the islands of King Solomon, and hence an outlier of Asia? Santaella stated categorically that the islands discovered by his compatriots belonged to a fourth part of the world: 'It seems that Asia, Tharsis, Ophir and Lethin are in the East whereas the Spanish Antilles are in the West; their position and their nature are very different'. Those who defend the contrary position 'deceive many simple people with their baseless inventions'. By popularizing the Venetian's text, the translation of Marco Polo was to expose the stupidity of Columbus's claims. The only possible conclusion was that the Indians were not Indians and it was time to stop confusing the West with the East. The notion of the West began to take shape, a West which was a distinct entity and no longer the paltry appendage of a sumptuous East.

Santaella was not hostile to the great discoveries. What could be more agreeable or more exciting for those with a thirst for knowledge than to take an interest in 'the parts of the world', in particular those that were inaccessible to them and known only to a very small number of people? Santaella addressed himself to the count of Cifuentes, to whom he dedicated his translation, and to the nobility, that is, to the Court, but also to the large number of clergy and merchants who lived in the great Andalusian city. He knew how to please the sort of people who were always on the lookout for new things, never before seen or described, avid to discover 'the grandeurs of the lordships, the provinces, the towns, the riches and the diversity of the nations and of the peoples with their laws, their sects and their customs'.

Santaella was aware of the upheavals caused by the Iberian expeditions. Indeed, it was this that had prompted him to reread Marco Polo in a new light. The veracity of Polo's accounts had often been questioned, and they could seem highly improbable if seen only from the vantage point of 'our Europe', a Europe before the discoveries. But they were not quite so startling if they were put in the context of the Castilian and Portuguese discoveries, which had come thick and fast. The voyages of the Iberians had opened up such a range of possibilities and so enlarged horizons that they made the unbelievable and the improbable seem quite ordinary. The marvels described by Marco Polo became more credible as a result; Polo was indeed an 'authentic author', and his book incontestably a first-hand account of the eastern part of the world. And it was precisely because he had told the truth that it had to be accepted that the new islands were not in any way connected with Asia. It was reading Polo in Castilian that brought home the unprecedented nature of the discoveries.

Santaella also advanced another, subtler and more profound argument. Polo's work was not only of 'geographical' interest. It should also be read 'so that our people will not fail to benefit from it in many ways'. It provided Christians with much food for thought. First, it was remarkable evidence for the admirable diversity of divine creation. The true believer need only stand back a little from the world with which he was familiar to see more clearly how lucky he was to have received the faith, 'by creating between the barbarous people and the Catholic people a difference analogous to that which separates dark from light'. Better still, this realization would awaken the desire to spread knowledge of God to these pagan peoples, 'to these innumerable souls', by 'sending as elsewhere workers, as the harvest is abundant. And at the end of the day, seeing the way in which the idolaters and pagans, about whom there is much in this book, serve and honour their false gods and their insensate idols, the people will awaken and emerge from their heavy sleep and their grave negligence to hasten to serve and follow our true God'.

Here, in a few lines, we have the outline of a vast programme of Christianization directed at the rest of the world, the 'other parts', a programme announced and formulated even before the Castilians were aware of the existence of the populations of Mexico or Las Casas had taken up the defence of the Indians.

The Asiatic Dream

Was Santaella's offensive powerful enough to overcome the hunger
for Asia which tormented the Castilians in their rivalry with the
Portuguese? Spanish interest in this part of the world did not go away.
Nor was it confined to Polo. The voyage to India of Nicolò de' Conti
as recorded by Poggio came out in Granada in 1510; two years later
one of the very first works to deal with the Portuguese explorations,
Martín Fernández de Figueroa's *The Conquest of the Indies of Persia*,
was published in Salamanca. Meanwhile, in 1521, it was the turn of
John Mandeville, who had so stirred the imagination of Latin
Christendom in the fourteenth and fifteenth centuries, and who was
republished in Valencia.[21]

Even in Central America, the Spanish still dreamed of Asia. Take
this letter from a Milanese who had settled in Castile, Peter Martyr
of Anghiera, who recounts rumours that had reached him. This
reporter missed nothing: 'On 14th October of this year 1516 I was
visited by Rodrigo Colmenares, about whom I have already spoken,
and a certain Francisco de la Puente...Both of them, one who had
heard talk of it, the other who had witnessed it, said that there were
many islands in the southern sea, to the west of the Bay of St Miguel
and the island of Rica, where trees grow and flourish that bear fruit
similar to those of Colocut, which, with Cochin and Camemori, is
the spice market for the Portuguese; they deduced that not far away
there began the land which produces every sort of aromatic sub-
stance'.[22] There was no shortage of people eager to explore this new
promised land. The places mentioned – Colocut (Calicut), Cochin
and Camemori (Cannanore) – are certainly taken from the book of
Fernández de Figueroa, *The Conquest of the Indies of Persia*, where
the three ports of the Indies appear in exactly the same order.
Everything indicated that Asia was very near.

The Leap into the Void

Why did the idea that Asia was within arm's length survive so long?
Because if Santaella was right, and if Marco Polo's Indies were not
Santaella's Indies, the belief that they had arrived in 'known' territory
collapsed – and with it the enthusiasm of the sailors and the confidence of the investors who counted on recuperating their losses from
the wealth of Asia. Suddenly, the leap into the unknown became a
leap into the void, and further exploration was going it blind. A

comparison of furthest Asia and North America on the planisphere of Waldseemüller (1507) is startling: whereas the almost familiar shapes of Cathay and Cipangu appear at the far right-hand side of the map, at the other side, and at the same height, we find an immaculate, enigmatic white; here, ten years later, would be Mexico, which as yet no one knew existed. Our North America is given the name *Terra ulterius incognita*. Six years later, in 1513, another map of Waldseemüller still showed an empty space. And every navigator and every investor has a horror of the void.

From Cathay to the void, and from the void to discovery. Before 1517 nothing had filtered through about the societies of ancient Mexico. And it was not the exploration of Golden Castile that would point the way. A witness as prolix and an observer as indefatigable as Bartolomé de Las Casas, settled in Santo Domingo in 1503 and then in Cuba from 1512, seems to have heard nothing to make him suspect that strong societies had developed on the continent. But who could have imagined for a moment that there existed a New World on the other side of the Atlantic, one that was covered with rich cities and that, to cap it all, these kingdoms were thousands of leagues from Asia?

The Spanish were about to confront societies which had never had any contact with the rest of the world. Here there were no Muslim intermediaries, no local maps to be interpreted, no more or less nebulous memories to be unravelled, no Mesoamerican diaspora settled in the islands to facilitate the encounter. For the Spanish who set blindly out, the situation they discovered was doubly surprising, as was recalled, some time later, by a veteran of these expeditions, Bernal Díaz del Castillo. Not only had 'this land [the peninsula of Yucatán, reached in 1517] never been discovered before and till then not been known about', but the Castilians found themselves face to face with an urban civilization in America: 'from our ships we saw a great town ... and as the population was large, and as we had never seen anything like it on the island of Cuba or on Hispaniola, we called it Great Cairo'.[23]

5

Books and Letters from the Other End of the World

The amazement caused by all this novelty was just as strong on the Peninsula. As early as 1492 the Milanese Peter Martyr of Anghiera was an attentive and lucid chronicler of the projects of Columbus and his successors. He was indefatigable on the subject of the unprecedented nature of the discoveries; he said it and repeated it to two successive popes, Adrian VI and Leo X: from these 'unknown' lands and men flowed 'new, unimaginable and truly astonishing things'.[1] His enthusiastic description of the gifts Cortés sent to Valladolid in March 1522 set the pattern for the way in which educated Europe would perceive the great civilizations of Mexico. The discs of gold and silver, the necklaces of semiprecious stones and other 'little gold bells', the 'tiaras', the 'mitres', the plumes, the feather-work fans beguiled by their beauty and by the extraordinary skill demonstrated by their creators.[2] The reaction was unanimous, whether it came from the Spanish Dominican Bartolomé de Las Casas or the German painter Albrecht Dürer.

'Their Books are Like Ours'

Some curious books were also included in this collection. For Peter Martyr, there was no doubt that the Indians wrote. For paper or parchment – 'the material on which the Indians write' – they used a fine skin which resembled that of the 'fruits of the edible palm tree'.

Peter Martyr got everything explained to him: you began by stretching the leaf to give it its final form. When it had hardened, you covered it with 'something that resembles plaster or another material of the same type'. The leaves were not joined together, but arranged in a large number of accordion pleats. Once it had been folded, the object formed a block of square parts bound together by a 'resistant and flexible bitumen'. 'Covered with plaques of wood, [the books of the Indians] look as if they have emerged from the hands of a skilled binder'.

Indigenous paper, book manufacture, handling, nothing escaped this Milanese humanist, who also pondered the nature of the writing he had before his eyes. The Amerindian glyphs were 'formed of squares, brackets, bows, crests and other objects aligned as with us'. They seemed to him 'almost like Egyptian writing', which he had seen at close quarters during his travels in Egypt.[3] A friend of his, the apostolic nuncio Giovanni Ruffo da Forli, made the same comparison: 'In the little squares are figures and signs in the form of Arabian and Egyptian characters which have been interpreted here as being the letters they use, but the Indians have been unable to explain in a satisfactory manner what they are'.[4] The alternation of pictographs and drawings even suggested a comparison with the innovations then fashionable in European workshops, recalling 'the way printers are often accustomed these days, in order to attract clients, to insert in general histories and even in books for entertainment plates which represent the protagonists in the story'.

'Once they are closed, their books are like ours'. One feels that Peter Martyr was determined to play down anything that might differentiate Europe from the New World, though his assertion seems today somewhat hasty, if not reductive. It is true that he also enthused about the riches of their contents: 'Their books...contain, as far as one can see, their laws, the order of their sacrifices and their ceremonies, their accounts, astronomical observations and the ways and times for sowing'.[5] This statement was probably based on explanations provided by the envoys of Cortés, Francisco de Montejo and Alonso Hernandez Portocarrero.[6] It was crucial because, if the Mexican books were the repositories of juridical, religious, astronomical and agricultural knowledge, it suggested that the inhabitants of these countries had access to the tools necessary to the functioning of a policed society and to its projection into the future.

It is hard to imagine, in fact, a more appealing presentation of the Mexican societies. But nothing is perfect. There was a down side, and it was a serious one. These newly discovered societies practised human sacrifice, in particular of children. Our humanist did his best to understand this, recapitulating the explanations provided by the Indians.[7] Nevertheless, he was still enchanted by the spectacle of the gifts brought back from Mexico, and in the end it was this fascination that won out: 'I do not think I have ever seen anything whose sheer beauty is so eye-catching'.[8]

'In China There Are Printers'

By 1512, as noted above, one Chinese man had been dispatched to Cochin, and from there to the court of Lisbon. It is highly probable that he either took samples of ideographic writing with him or produced them on the spot. If not, it would have been enough to open the first Chinese book that had arrived on the banks of the River Tagus, at about the same time, or to have leafed through the *Notebook of Chinese Paintings* mentioned in the inventory of the royal wardrobe,[9] to get some idea of the skill of the artists of the Celestial Empire. In 1514, as we have seen, King Manuel had offered a book to Pope Leo X. In Rome it attracted the attention of the humanist Paolo Giovio;[10] it may well be that the enthusiasm demonstrated some years later by Peter Martyr was inspired by that of his illustrious colleague.

The emblematic scene of this scholar casting an informed eye over the things of another world had a precedent in Rome. Posterity has forgotten Paolo Giovio, a Lombard and one of the most prominent intellectuals of his age, one of those agile minds that are so much of their time that they end up disappearing along with it. Faced with Chinese books, Paolo Giovio could not conceal his admiration, but in his case it was the printing process itself that impressed him most: 'There are [in China] printers who print according to our own methods books containing sacred stories and rites on a sheet of which the largest side is folded towards the inside in square pages. Pope Leo has been kind enough to show me a book of this type which was given him as a gift, together with an elephant, by the King of Lusitania, so it is easy to believe that examples of this kind had reached us, before the Lusitanians had penetrated India, through the Scythians and through the Muscovites as an invaluable aid for our literature'.[11] Paolo Giovio would later disseminate the idea that printing had been brought from China by a merchant rather than invented from scratch in the Germany of Gutenberg.[12] This was intended as a blow to the pride of a country guilty of having sheltered Luther and his followers.

The question of the Chinese origin of printing would continue to be a subject of much debate. In the sixteenth century the Goan physician Garcia da Orto, the Portuguese historian Jerónimo Osorio and the Italian Jesuit Giampetro Maffei all repeated Paolo Giovio's version. It was not a trivial debate. Not only was China a country which produced books and which had mastered printing, but Europe would be in its debt. Unlike Mexico, whose productions remained distant curiosities or recalled a bygone past like that of ancient Egypt, China had gifted Christendom with a technique which could hardly leave a humanist indifferent: the invention of the printed book. However great the general ignorance with regard to China, it had already, through printing and trade in its precious objects, infiltrated the courts of Europe.

Americanism and Orientalism

Lisbon would have an opportunity to compare the books of China and of Mexico. In 1521 Manuel of Portugal received from Charles V one of the codices sent by Cortés, the *Codex Vindobonensis Mexicanus*, which then passed into the hands of Clement VIII.[13] It was not a Mexica book the Lisbon court had before its eyes, but a Mixtec painting, probably brought to the Vera Cruz coast among the gifts presented to the conquistador. The references to the story of the feathered serpent god Quetzalcoatl in the codex must have escaped Cortés, just as they escaped the Iberian sovereigns who later examined it. At least, shortly before his death, Manuel had the opportunity to observe that the civilization discovered by his Castilian neighbours for his posthumous son-in-law Charles was as impressive as the China he himself had had in his sights.

Mexican or Chinese, the books came from living and contemporary worlds, of which they presented a remarkably positive image, even in the eyes of an educated Italian. In a Europe where writing was valued and ancient manuscripts collected, Chinese books and Mexican codices were unequivocal indicators of civilization, indispensable in 'placing' societies about which nothing had previously been known. Writing and its adjuncts were seen as indispensable repositories for memory, hence any historical continuity. Paolo Giovio made a point of the stories found in these Chinese books, while Peter Martyr suggested that the Mexican books reported 'the deeds of the ancestors of each king'.[14] So both China and Mexico passed the test with flying colours at a time when, for many people, the Ottoman Empire conjured up the image of a barbarous nation, destroyer of Greek and ancient culture.[15]

These objects had very different life expectancies. The writing and arts of China had time on their side and a future ahead of them. By contrast, no one then realized that the Mexican codices were the last manifestations of an art and a technology doomed to annihilation or irrevocable decline. As it happened, the die was not yet cast on the other side of the Atlantic when Peter Martyr saw the codices. But the admiration of the humanist from Milan would not prevent the ravages of the conquest and it is disturbing today to compare these paeons of praise with what the future held in store. Peter Martyr wrote at what proved a brief moment in the relationship between Europe and Mexico, that of discovery, before conquest and destruction. Portuguese, Italians and Castilians appear here in the same guise, that of collector. Mexican curiosities were valued for their refinement, their strangeness and their singularity. Chinese books fell into the same category, in which intellectual value and technical skill ranked high. For Castile, war, booty and destruction very quickly replaced collecting. In Lisbon, it had been from the beginning an element in a trading relationship: goods arriving from China were first and foremost precious commodities with high added value. With hindsight the Mexican books seen by Peter Martyr, like the treasures sent to Charles V, fixed both the instantaneity of a civilization destined to imminent ruin and also, for a long time to come, an image of a Mexico fossilized in its feathers and its pyramids. Trade with China, on the other hand, continued to supply the West with luxury goods that were expensive to procure.

For the moment, both Peter Martyr and Paolo Giovio – who would become one of the great experts on the Ottoman world – helped to launch disciplines that would occupy a crucial place in the history of European thought: Americanism and Orientalism. These two humanists were among the first in Europe 'scientifically' to observe, describe and interpret objects originating in China and America,[16] exploiting global information networks which, via Seville or Lisbon, converged on Rome. Other Italians before them had produced and disseminated information about other parts of the world: to cite only the most recent, Ludovico di Varthema, whose voyage to India and South-East Asia was published in Rome in 1510,[17] and Amerigo Vespucci, whose authentic or apocryphal writings came out from 1503.

Peter Martyr and Paolo Giovio were not content simply to accumulate new information. They set out, as humanists, to interpret it. Their thinking on the subject of distant worlds drew on their classical training, which assured their authority while at the same time providing them with the tools with which to conceive the relationship of Christendom to Mamluk Egypt and the New World (Peter Martyr) or to China and the Ottoman Empire (Paolo Giovio), even to compare America to Asia (Paolo Giovio). Both the voyages and the collections of Giovio and the letters of Peter Martyr revealed the contours of a republic of letters which now set itself the task of making known the new realities of the oecumene. One of the consequences of Peter Martyr's correspondence with the Italy of princes, prelates and the Roman Curia was the initiation of the first scholarly contacts between the New and the Old Worlds. In addition to the Casa de la Contratación in Seville and the Court of Lisbon, which polarized information about the new lands, the Italian networks assured its diffusion throughout Europe by exploiting diplomatic and ecclesiastical channels and printing.[18]

These networks were not all active at the same time. Knowledge of China spread in Europe only from the middle of the sixteenth century, not so much because the Portuguese were deliberately more discreet, but because China was a much more difficult nut to crack than Indian Mexico. The latter was magnificently served by the letters and the *Decades* of Peter Martyr (1530), the *Letters of Relation* (*Cartas de Relacíon*) of Cortés (published from 1522) and the *Chronicles* of Fernández de Oviedo (1535) and Lopez de Gómara (1552), to quote only the texts that achieved a wide circulation.

Chinese resistance is not the whole explanation. The material about China collected by the Florentines and the Portuguese long remained primarily in manuscript. To my knowledge, only the letter of the Florentine Andrea Corsali was published, in record time for the age: dispatched from Cochin in January 1516, it arrived in Florence in October and emerged from the presses of Stephano Carlo da Pavia in December of the same year.[19] Admittedly, the lack of printed versions did not prevent the *Livro das cousas* of Duarte Barbosa from being translated into Castilian in 1524 through the efforts of the Genoese ambassador and the Portuguese cartographer Diogo Ribeiro, then into German in 1530, and cropping up in 1539 in San Salvador do Congo.[20] Magellan owned a copy in Portuguese. Information about China continued to have a low profile; it was aimed almost exclusively at specialists who read Portuguese and was presented in a form ill-suited to arouse the enthusiasm of the educated public of the Renaissance.

Everything changed in the second half of the century. China emerged into the spotlight, whereas Mexico had already exhausted its quota of admirers and the curious. Pioneering writings like the first letter of Giovanni da Empoli, the *Suma oriental* of Tomé Pires and, in an abbreviated version, the *Livro das cousas* of Duarte Barbosa had to wait until 1550 to be published by Giovanni Battista Ramusio in the first instalment of his *Navigations and Travels*.[21] After this, new Italian editions came thick and fast: 1554, 1563, 1587–8,

1606 and 1613 for the *Suma oriental*; 1554, 1563, 1587–8, 1603 and 1613 for the *Livro das cousas*.[22] In Portugal, meanwhile, the third *Decade* of João de Barros came out only in 1563, conveying a host of information about events on the coast of China in the second decade of the sixteenth century. Already, however, other works, this time exclusively devoted to China, had caught the attention of educated circles in Europe.

Letters from China and Mexico

The first contacts between Europe, China and Mexico, though contemporaneous, have not received the same degree of 'media hype'. The extraordinary epic of the conquistadors and the miserable fate of the Aztec empire continue to fascinate, whereas the discovery of Ming China and the failure of Tomé Pires have never caught the imagination. Yet both sets of events continue to influence our contemporary world. Marco Polo had no need to conquer China or benefit from the invention of printing to bequeath us a masterpiece, *The Travels*, destined to be read for centuries. Success or failure are not enough, it would appear, to explain these different treatments. Nor is the remarkable skill as a writer displayed by the future master of Mexico; in Hernán Cortés the conquest of Mexico found its Julius Caesar, who fixed for ever its triumphant image. The Portuguese ought to have been able to rely on the writing skills of Tomé Pires, whose *Suma oriental* shows him to have been equally capable of recreating the singularity of the lands he visited. The eye of Pires was as keen as that of Cortés, which makes his silence all the more regrettable. Pires did not return from China alive, and if he ever managed to smuggle a manuscript out of his Cantonese prison it has not survived. His companions in misfortune, however, wrote letters.

It is letters, therefore, which enable us to follow the progress of the first contacts. Those of Hernán Cortés, copied, discussed, published and translated, have become so famous as to rank among the first manifestations of a Western literature born on the American continent. Those sent from Canton, by contrast, written by obscure Portuguese, are scarcely known, even today, beyond the Lusophone world.

Cortés sent a total of five 'letters of relation' to Charles V, in July 1519, October 1520, May 1522, October 1524 and September 1526.[23] They not only circulated within the court but quickly had the good fortune to attract the attention of European printers to events in Mexico. Jacobo Cromberger published the first letter in November

1522, only three years after it was written. The following year a German from Zaragoza, Jorge Coci, published a second letter, illustrated with engravings taken from an edition of the *Decades* of Tite-Live, to which he gave a title as interminable as it was sensational, exalting the size of the cities, the wealth of the trade, the splendour of Tenochtitlan and the power of Moctezuma.[24] In March 1523 Jacobo Cromberger published the third letter in Seville. In 1524 a Latin translation of the second and third letters came out in Nuremberg, thanks to Pietro Savorgniani, who compared Cortés to Alexander and Hannibal. It included a document of major importance: a plan of Mexico-Tenochtitlan, probably based on a sketch sent by Cortés in the early 1520s. This image was so successful that it was reprinted in Venice the same year, this time with captions in Italian. By this stage Germany could follow events in Mexico through three printed letters and the diary of Albrecht Dürer, who visited an exhibition in Brussels of the treasures sent by Cortés. In 1525 Cromberger published the fourth letter in Seville, a year after it had been written in Mexico. Further editions and translations followed over the centuries.

The first printed book to deal with Mexico was written by the humanist Peter Martyr of Anghiera; this was the *De nuper sub D. Carolo repertis insulis*, published in Basel in 1521. The reception in Spain of the objects from Mexico and the arrival of a handful of Indians had been the occasion for meticulously orchestrated presentations which inevitably attracted the attention of the diplomats. One of these was the humanist Gaspar Contarini, who, in his letters, kept the Venetian Senate informed about the conquest of Mexico. And it was in Venice that, in 1528, Tenochtitlan became one of the most famous islands in the world, alongside Japan (Cipangu), thanks to Benedetto Bordone and his *Isolario*.[25] Inspired by the Nuremberg engraving, the image of the town was amended in ways that accentuated its resemblance to Venice.[26] It became so deeply embedded in the imagination of the Venetians that Mexico, with its lake and its canals, became a model for the management of the waters of the lagoon for the humanists of the city of St Mark.[27] In the following decades, information spread like wildfire, reaching the heart of Europe and providing material for the *Kosmografie Česká* (1554), which referred for the first time in Czech to the powerful city of Temixtitan (Tenochtitlan).

So it is on the testimony of Cortés that our European vision of the conquest of America has been constructed and reconstructed, because it reveals him as an exceptional storyteller and peerless stage manager as well as the conqueror of a prestigious empire. Not only was his testimony direct, it was hot from the press. In a situation he did not understand, Cortés constantly came up with interpretations whose effects were always carefully calculated. He never forgot that he was writing to the Emperor Charles V. True, there was always a time lag between the lived moment and its later interpretation in a letter, but it was a good deal shorter than in the case of other direct accounts of the conquest such as the *Relación breve de la conquista de Nueva España* of Fray Francisco de Aguilar (about 1560) and the *Historia verdadera de la conquista de Nueva España* of Bernal Díaz del Castillo (1568). These histories, written decades after the events they describe, re-read the incidents of the conquest in the light of information gathered much later in a New Spain which had to justify both Castilian domination and the annihilation of the society of the defeated. Aguilar and Díaz del Castillo told a story whose outcome and whose various episodes they already knew, whereas in his first letters Cortés was still groping in the dark. For the historian this difference is crucial, because it gives us access to the original intentions of the enterprise before it was presented as the ineluctable consequence of the first colonization of modern times. It then emerges that the ventures of Pires and Cortés had many points in common.

On the Portuguese side we lack, as already noted, the testimony of the man who led the enterprise, and who may be seen, all else being equal, as the alter ego of Hernán Cortés. Not only has Tomé Pires left no major written work on China, but the letters he sent from Nanking to Jorge Botelho and Diogo Calvo are lost, depriving us of what must have been an exceptional first-hand account of his meeting with Zhengde, ruler of the Celestial Empire.[28]

The few Portuguese letters to have escaped the disaster seem to have been written around 1524.[29] Their authors were Cristovão Vieira, one of the members of the Portuguese embassy, and Vasco Calvo, probably a merchant, who arrived on the Chinese coast only in 1521. These two observers had eyes as sharp as those of the conquistador of Mexico and, as we will see, were equal to him in ambition. These letters have not enjoyed the same historiographical posterity and survive only in copies discovered in the Bibliothèque nationale of Paris at the beginning of the last century.[30] The history of relations between China and the West has usually passed over this Portuguese pre-history and ignored these direct sources.[31] These two Portuguese may not have had the same literary talents as Cortés, but they nevertheless reveal gifts of penetration as exceptional as the situation they faced, alternating between global opinions and a sharp sense of detail, a panoramic view and personal experience. As with Cortés, their immediate reactions throw light on the clash between worlds ignorant of each other, a crucial moment if we are to understand the take-off of globalization at the dawn of the sixteenth century.

In the case of Portugal and Castile we have later accounts transmitted by the great chronicles of Portuguese expansion. João de Barros in his *Década da Asia*, Fernão Lopez de Castanheda in his *História dos descobrimentos e conquista da India pelos Portugueses*, Gaspar da Cruz in his *Tractado em que se contem por extenso as cousas da China* and Fernão Mendes Pinto in his *Peregrinação*, all, like their Castilian counterpart, provide later accounts, precious but written from a different standpoint than that of Calvo and Vieira, when all plans for the conquest and colonization of Chinese territory had been abandoned.[32]

The Gaze of the Others

The letters of Cortés and the Portuguese give us only the European version of these events. Where they also report the reactions of their adversaries, that is, of the Indians and the Chinese, they tell us only what they saw and what concerned or confirmed the Iberian vision – a bias that should come as no surprise.

Did the others remain silent, paralysed by shock or surprise? This was true neither of the Chinese nor the Mexicans, but it was the Castilian expedition which left the deepest imprint, in line with the cataclysm it provoked. It was only in the nineteenth century that indigenous texts took their place alongside the Spanish sources, eventually creating what Miguel León-Portilla called, in a phrase which has become famous, the 'vision of the vanquished'.[33] These often poignant texts helped, notably in the second half of the twentieth century, to rekindle interest in the conquest of Mexico and to inspire research which seeks to reconstruct the point of view of the indigenous peoples.

For Mexico we have a group of texts produced by Indians or mestizos, the most important being an illustrated history of the conquest written in Nahuatl in the mid sixteenth century, thus more than a generation after the events it describes.[34] It owes its existence to the work of reconstruction carried out by the Franciscan Bernardino de Sahagún as part of his general history of New Spain.[35]

The Chinese material I have used here comes from dynastic histories, provincial chronicles and the biographies of important persons.[36] These texts are difficult to decipher, even for an eminent sinologist like Paul Pelliot. What can we learn from his meticulous research, which teems with observations whose import is often disconcerting? The Chinese sources that stick closest to events present the version favoured by the administrations of Peking and Canton. This is why they are sometimes at odds with statements made by the Portuguese. A decade or so later, however, new sources, which are often contradictory, leave us perplexed. It seems that, with the passage of time and fading memories, the Chinese sources confused the Portuguese ambassador, Tomé Pires, with a Muslim ambassador who went by the name of Khôjja Asan. Both these men had connections with Malacca, but the former came from the city conquered by the Portuguese, whereas the latter, according to Paul Pelliot, was the envoy of the former authorities of this place.

To add to the confusion, the *Mingshi* (or *Ming-che*) refers to a mysterious Houo-tchö Ya-San, who may be Tomé Pires, or a Chinese interpreter of the Portuguese embassy, or even one of the Muslims who accompanied the Portuguese mission. At all events, the man who was executed in Peking in 1521 cannot be Tomé Pires, the *kia-pi-tan-mo* of the Chinese sources, who died some years later. It may have been a Muslim of Malay origin,[37] who, according to the *Ming-chan tsang*, knew Chinese and the language of the barbarians. Other sources claim that a certain Khôjja Asan was executed in 1529 in Canton and associate this Asan with the Portuguese Pires. It may be that, under torture, this man confessed that he was only a false envoy, or even that he was a Chinese in the service of the Portuguese.[38] A few decades later, to muddy the waters even further, Khôjja Asan is presented as the Portuguese ambassador and complicit in the abuses perpetrated by a Muslim from central Asia who enjoyed favour at court, Sayyid Husain.[39]

How is this confusion of identities to be explained? In part it is due to the fact that the Chinese had no idea who the Portuguese really were. If they took this Khôjja Asan to be the Portuguese ambassador, or a Chinese in service of the Portuguese, it is probably because the new masters of Malacca were believed to come from an Asiatic or Muslim country situated to the southwest of the ocean, somewhere south of Java or northwest of Sumatra.[40] The Chinese never grasped the absolute singularity of their visitors. The same was true of the ancient Mexicans, who took their hosts to be the inhabitants of a mysterious *altepetl*, an unknown lordship, *Castillan*, but still an *altepetl* like their own.

The Retrospective Illusion

So the sources are, as is usually the case, incomplete and biased. However, there is a further obstacle to be overcome, that of a teleological history. There is always a tendency to distort what happened between the Iberians, China and Mexico after 1517, to tailor events to their known consequences and project onto this particular moment the interpretations or silences which the Chinese, Portuguese, Spanish and Mexicans were quick to provide after the event in order to make both comprehensible and acceptable a past that was problematic in all it contained that was unforeseen, unexpected and, for some, intolerable. There is no such thing as a raw historical fact, any more than there is a pure culture or an original story. Nevertheless, we can try to retrieve from under the blanket of the accumulated certainties, clichés and things left un-said of history what the arrival of these aliens in China and Mexico represented, at least on the European side.

There is a further risk, that of substituting for different histories which confront each other a unitary story, and of imposing its truth on whatever material – always laconic – it proves possible to discover. In which case a global history is no more than a new manifestation of Western history. We may also believe, as I do, that it is not only a matter of adopting another perspective, of shedding a new light which does no more than produce a past which can be interrogated today. Historians are tireless restorers, but they never forget that what they restore, whether it be the Middle Ages, the Renaissance, the discovery of the New World or something else, never has an original, but is primarily and invariably the product of earlier constructions and rewritings done after the event, and is constantly in need of being done once again.

To compare the Mexican coast and the China Sea is also to mitigate our ineradicable Eurocentrism and make new questions emerge. It is to reconnect the links which national historiographies have broken and to subject the newly reconnected elements to a global reading in which they interact with each other, and no longer only with Europe. It is by shifting the focus, and no longer only by inverting the points of view, as in the already distant age of the 'vision of the vanquished',[41] that we can hope to achieve a history that makes sense in our own age. With all these precautions taken, let us see what a global reading of the Iberian visits reveals.

6

Embassy or Conquest?

It was not Hernán Cortés who discovered Mexico. His expedition had been preceded, hence involuntarily prepared for, by two separate 'contacts' initiated from Cuba. This island, conquered in 1511, the year Malacca fell to the Portuguese, became the Antilles base for a series of raids and expeditions of reconnaissance. It is only with hindsight that they appear as stages on the road to Mexico. By contrast, Malacca, major hub for South-East Asian trade, did not have to wait for the arrival of the Portuguese to become the gateway to China. In this city of more than 100,000 inhabitants, the Portuguese found Asiatic traders of every description,[1] an active Chinese diaspora and a wealth of commercial and political information regarding this part of the world. They knew they were on the threshold of the Moluccas and of China, and their military presence – the seizure of Malacca had been notably violent – changed the name of the game throughout the region.

It was all very different in Cuba. Here, the Spanish were on their own and soon ran into trouble. After the execution of the indigenous chief Huatey, burned alive in 1512, Indian resistance ceased to present a threat to the Spanish presence and the settlers soon found themselves too numerous for an over-exploited island. They thought only of finding a practicable way out for as many people as possible.[2] The longing to escape which soon pervaded the island encouraged hopes that were projected onto the mainland; they were well aware that other Spanish, further south, were in the process of exploiting 'Golden Castile'.

Makeshifts and Muddles

The first Spanish expedition left Cuba in February 1517, on the initiative of a band of some hundred settlers who were seeking an alternative to yet more razzias in the surrounding islands. Their idea was 'to go in search of new lands'.[3] The expedition was placed under the leadership of Francisco Fernández de Córdoba. It consisted of three ships, three pilots, one of whom was Antón de Alaminos, a priest and – who knew what the future held? – an inspector or *veedor*, officially responsible for collecting the king's fifth on the wealth, 'gold, silver or pearls', they might find. What had been no more than a hunch soon became a reality. They were not well equipped; 'our fleet consisted of poor men', there were not enough cables for the rigging and not enough barrels that did not leak to hold their supplies of fresh water.

This little band set off, at the mercy of the winds, 'heading west, without knowing the shallows or the prevailing winds or currents at this latitude'. Unlike the Portuguese, the Spanish navigators sailed into unknown seas, without the assistance of the local pilots who abounded both in the Indian Ocean and the China Sea; the risks were immeasurably greater. Among the successes of this first voyage were the discovery of Yucatán, the first contacts with Indians living in agglomerations and properly clothed (those of the islands had been naked) and the capture of two natives destined to serve as interpreters – 'they both squinted'. On the downside were some scuffles which turned out badly for the Spanish (they lost fifty men, that is, half the party, at Pontonchan),[4] fear and a hasty retreat back to their ships: 'God willed that we escaped alive with great difficulty from the hands of these people'.

A makeshift expedition, inadequately equipped raids, failure all along the line; for a trial run, this was a veritable disaster. It was nearly a nightmare, and it contradicts the long-held image of the Indians of Mexico as paralysed by the strangeness and the weapons of their visitors. In fact, their stubborn resistance was equalled only by their ability to spread the news and sound the alarm all along the coast. It was not by chance that the Spanish were greeted at Campeche, their second stop, by cries of 'Castilan! Castilan!',[5] as if they were already only too well known. In any case, the affair was the very opposite of a carefully orchestrated discovery and conquest. It was more like a bad Western – in which the Palefaces got beaten – than Europe swallowing up America.

Conscious of all that was at stake, the governor of Cuba took things into his own hands and in 1518 dispatched a new and stronger fleet of four ships. Juan de Grijalva and his band of 240 men were given a mandate to 'get all the gold and silver they could', but also to 'settle' if the occasion arose. And, on the spot where Vera Cruz would later be founded, Grijalva loudly proclaimed that he did indeed intend to 'settle',[6] that is, colonize, the region. Had the Crown authorized this? It is far from clear. In any case, Grijalva returned to Cuba without pressing ahead. The expedition was half successful. Either the Indians avoided contact or they were brutally repulsed with swords, falconets and swingletrees. When contacts were attempted, barter proved disappointing: the people of the Rio Tabasco gave a categorical no to Spanish demands. 'They have a lord; then we arrive and, knowing nothing of them, at once try to force one on them; it would be better for us to think twice before we make war on them' – this was the message which the Castilians thought they detected behind the Indian hostility.

Communication had improved during the previous year, but no one knew what the Indians were talking about when they kept saying, each time louder than the last, 'Colúa, Colúa' and 'Mexico', and pointing in the direction of the setting sun. There could be no plan, obviously, to conquer a huge country of which our budding conquistadors had no knowledge. In particular, they had no idea that Moctezuma had been watching their every step since the first expedition, or that he had given instructions to his governors on the coast to negotiate with the new arrivals in order to find out who they were and what were their intentions.[7]

This second expedition has left several powerful images, such as the dozens of large white flags waved by the Indians on the banks of the Rio de Banderas to attract the attention of the visitors, hailed with loud cries, or the shields covered with tortoiseshell which gleamed in the sunlight on the beach, and which the soldiers thought was gold. Another disappointment was their later discovery that the 600 hatchets they took back to Cuba, which they also believed to be of gold, were actually made of cheap brass. The expedition was beginning to verge on the farcical.

Lacking enough equipment and men, the conquistadors were obliged to set off back to Cuba. At Champotón, in the modern state of Campeche, encouraged by their victory the previous year, 'proud and arrogant...and well armed in their own fashion', the Indians fell on the Spaniards. The attackers eventually had to retreat, but they refused to parlay with the invaders. The chronicler Díaz del Castillo attributes this ill will to the two Indian interpreters: 'they must not have said what they were told to say, but quite the opposite'.[8] The Portuguese of China would later encounter the same problem, a reminder of the extent to which the Iberians were at the mercy of their intermediaries.

Grand Designs in Lisbon, Intrigue in the Caribbean

From the beginning, everything marked the Portuguese enterprise as different from that of the Castilians. Not least its origins: the Portuguese penetration of China was an operation conceived in the highest reaches of the state in Lisbon. When the new governor of India, Lopo Soares de Albergaria, landed in Cochin in September 1515, he was accompanied by Fernão Peres de Andrade, the man King Manuel had decided to send as captain-major (*capitão mor*) of a fleet with a mission 'to discover China'.[9] Peres de Andrade was expected to choose from among his entourage an ambassador who would make official contact with the Chinese authorities.

But did Manuel the Fortunate have more than a diplomatic operation in mind? There were strong economic and strategic reasons for the king to take an interest in this part of the world. The Crown intended to establish a commercial presence and assume control of the pepper trade between the Moluccas, Sumatra and the Celestial Empire.[10] It also needed to arm itself against the threat of Castilian interference. To which should be added Manuel's dream of seizing Jerusalem and exercising an imperial responsibility over the whole world.[11] '[The king] was counting on...being declared suzerain of the largest possible number of sovereigns in Asia'.[12] It was for all of these reasons that Manuel extended his diplomacy to Christian Ethiopia, which might provide a precious ally against the Moors of Egypt and join the great offensive against the Muslim worlds that he hoped to launch. In countries as distant as Ternate, east of Indonesia, Kilwa, on the African coast, and Chaul, in India, the native populations found themselves forced to pay tribute to the king of Portugal.

The extension of Portuguese suzerainty as far as China was thus part of Manuel's conception of Portuguese kingship, and his ambitions went hand in hand with the idea that the profits of trade with this part of the world would help to consolidate the young Estado da India and finance the route of the Cape of Good Hope. This dream of universal sovereignty – recorded by Valentim Fernandes in his translation of Marco Polo – may not have involved the military conquest of Asia, but it did not exclude laying the foundations of a maritime empire, and this is what the governor Afonso de Albuquerque set out to do by taking the Archipelago of Socotra (1506), Ormuz (1507), Goa (1510) and Malacca (1511). This was in spite of the fact that, even in Portugal, the policy of imperial expansion was opposed by elements among the nobility and by commercial circles hostile to these interventions on the part of the Crown.

On the ground, in Goa and Malacca, the expedition to China was well organized. When the leader of the expedition, the captain-major, Fernão Peres de Andrade, aged twenty-six, had to choose an ambassador, it was to Tomé Pires that he turned. It would have been difficult to find a greater specialist in the Far East. Born around 1468, Pires was the son of a *boticario* (apothecary) of King Jean II and himself *boticario* of a prince of the royal family. He had left Portugal for India in April 1511 to take up the post of 'factor of the drugs',[13] responsible for procuring spices for the Crown. He had disembarked in September and, eight or nine months later, he was sent to introduce order into the royal accounts in Malacca, which he reached in July 1512. It was here, almost straightaway, that his abilities and the opportune death of the royal factor enabled him to land the jobs of 'scrivener and accountant of the factor and controller of the drugs'.[14] During the course of his stay, in 1513, he made the long journey to Java, from which he returned with a cargo of 1,200 quintals of cloves. His many occupations, interrupted for several months by serious fevers, nevertheless left him with the time to collect exceptional information about the whole of Portuguese Asia. At the end of January 1515 he left Malacca having almost completed his great life's work, the *Suma oriental*, which would remain for at least a century an indispensable summary of the economic geography of the region.

Yet we should not forget the commercial dimension of this book, which is full of geopolitical and ethnographic observations revealing the acuity of Pires' eye. He was always attentive to local practices. His stays in Cochin, Cannanore and Malacca had brought him into contact with all sorts of Asiatic merchants and familiarized him with an amazing range of languages, customs, beliefs and cultures. He was one of the best experts on Asiatic questions and the local officials did not mistake their man. His curiosity, his shrewdness, his knowledge of the region and of spices together with his grasp of economics made him an ideal candidate to lead an embassy from Manuel to China, where he would encounter all the obstacles that would be put in the way of Europeans by a society that felt itself under attack.

In fact Pires had gone back to India with the intention of returning to Lisbon with the considerable fortune he had amassed. However, his reputation and his good relations with Peres de Andrade persuaded the new governor Lopo Soares de Albergaria to send him back to Malacca with the captain-major. It would be hard to imagine a better-prepared enterprise, given all Portugal had put into it in means and in knowledge. It was a voyage conceived in Lisbon but entrusted to men who knew how to make the best use of the human resources they found locally. Nevertheless, nothing is perfect. The operation encountered various imponderables. First came a false start: in February 1516, in Sumatra, the fleet of Peres de Andrade and Pires joined the ship of an Italian, Giovanni de Empoli, loaded with pepper for China, but the precious cargo burned along with the boat. The expedition returned to Malacca, which it left a second time in August 1516. This was despite the arrival of the monsoon and against the advice of Peres de Andrade, and, as the captain had predicted, bad weather forced its return to port. These setbacks notwithstanding, in June 1517 the great Portuguese expedition set off yet again for China, which it reached on 15 August.

Pires was of humble origins. His family was connected with the court, but of no particular importance. We may be reminded of that hidalgo of Medellín, who owned Indians in Cuba in *encomienda*, called Hernán Cortés. Both men left the Iberian Peninsula in the hope of making their fortunes. Neither of them were isolated individuals. Cortés was part of the entourage of the governor of Cuba, Diego Velázquez, patron of his marriage to Cátalina Suárez; Pires prided himself on being a 'friend' of the captain-major Peres de Andrade. The similarities end here. Pires, aged 52, was a commercial agent, an expert in all things Asian and the advance guard of royal power; Cortés, aged 32, and a former student of law, had his legal knowledge and a few rich friends, but no prior experience, little or no money to invest, and the best that can be said of his relations with the government that had sent him to discover 'these rich countries'[15] is that they were erratic. They were alike, however, in that neither of them showed any signs of a long-considered personal project. Cortés seems not to have been interested in the two first expeditions to Mexico (1517/1518); Pires had been on the point of returning to Europe when he was sent to China.[16]

European expansion, and with it Iberian globalization, was as much an affair of individual destinies as of grand political projects; more policy making on the hoof than well-oiled machine with clear objectives.

The Asia of Spices, but not the New World

Just as Manuel had his dreams of crusading and Asia (he seems to have been obsessed with the capture of Mecca and recovery of Jerusalem),[17] the Crown of Castile, too, in 1517, had other preoccupations. Ferdinand the Catholic had died in 1516. The young Charles who succeeded him, the future Charles V, became regent for his mother Joanna the Mad. He was only seventeen years of age when, in September 1517, he landed in Asturias to take possession of his kingdom. By May 1520 he had left a Spain on the edge of explosion to deal with affairs in Germany and become King of the Romans at Aachen. It was not until July 1522 that he returned to Castile.[18] The overseas territories were thus not at the forefront of his concerns. Indeed, the conquest of Mexico by Cortés – in 1521 – took place while the emperor was preoccupied in northern Europe by the upsurge of Lutheranism. If Charles thought of Tordesillas, it would be less because of the treaty dividing up the world that bore its name than because it was the castle in which his mother, Joanna the Mad, was confined; as long as she lived, she shared his throne. If he thought of Portugal, it would be because he had decided to make his elder sister Leonora of Austria, then aged twenty, marry his uncle, King Manuel.

Did the future emperor have no interest at all in the overseas territories? This was not quite the case. Charles V was not a man to increase his possessions by conquest, an idea that was quite alien to him. The heir of the dukes of Burgundy, the young king of Castile and Aragon and future emperor of the Germanic Holy Roman Empire took possession of those inheritances which accrued to him and loudly proclaimed his right to those he was refused – in the event, the duchy of Burgundy. Charles's imperialist logic was essentially one of patrimonial recuperation: his empire 'was not imperial in any sense of conquest. It was based on the most peaceful of all foundations, on the rights of family'.[19] To which we should add both 'internal' difficulties – the antipathy of Castile to the Flemings in the young prince's entourage and the revolt in Germany of the monk Martin Luther – and some major European problems, among them the war with France and the question of Milan. The imperial dream of universal domination did not take off until some years later.

The division of Tordesillas was not, however, entirely absent from Charles's thoughts. We should not forget that he received Magellan in late February or early March 1518 – it was in April that Grijalva, at the head of the second expedition, set sail for Mexico – or that he agreed to his project to discover 'islands, mainlands and precious spices', either by finding the Western passage or by taking the Portuguese route via the Cape of Good Hope. Ignoring the recriminations of the ambassador of Lisbon, Charles gave every assistance to preparations for the expedition which set out in September 1519.[20] Any idea of conquest was excluded in advance. Orders were given to establish friendly relations with the natives and, above all, not to make war on them.

For Charles, Magellan was first and foremost an expert on all things Asian, both an experienced navigator and an authority in the mould of Tomé Pires. He had been in Malacca between 1511 and 1512. He had taken part in the seizure of the town, which he left only on 11 January 1513.[21] He probably met Pires, who had lived there since July of the previous year. In any case, he benefited from information collected by one of his friends, perhaps even a cousin, Francisco Serrão. The latter had been the first Portuguese to reach the Moluccas, where he decided to stay, becoming a counsellor to the Sultan of Ternate. He had corresponded with Magellan and knew everything that was to be known about the Moluccas; he was also, inevitably, a source of information for Pires and his *Suma oriental*. The fact that Serrão had written to Magellan, and hence sent messengers from one end of the world (the island of Ternate) to the other (Castile), makes one wonder whether his old friend might also have succumbed to the Castilian sirens, as the Portuguese claimed. Two friends separated by thousands of kilometres were in charge of the projects of two European monarchies both pursuing the same path on the other side of the globe. Magellan, Serrão, Pires: this first network reveals how Iberian globalization already heeded neither time nor space.

Through the Portuguese defector, the emperor kept an eye on the distant Moluccas and the gold mine of spices. Asia instead of the New World: in Spain, Charles and all those who had invested in the project waited impatiently for news of the expedition while, at the same time, and nearer to hand, the conquest of Mexico was about to begin. When Magellan died off Cebu, in April 1521, Cortés was preparing for the siege of Mexico City. The Mexica capital fell in August, three months before the survivors of Magellan's expedition reached the Spice Islands and Tidore.

So, unlike the enterprise of Pires, which could hardly have been more official, the expedition of Cortés was not a concern, even less a priority, of the young prince or his councillors. It is impossible to see it as an expression of an imperial project involving the New World. When, in 1519, the third expedition departed, the future mastermind of the conquest, Hernán Cortés, was no more than a henchman of the governor of Cuba, himself the devoted servant of Juan Rodríguez de Fonseca, bishop of Burgos, aged seventy, who, from Castile, pulled all the strings on the Antilles stage. Nevertheless, while one would not have thought that this Mexican episode was in any way connected with the events in China, it was, paradoxically, the Asia of spices and China, and not Mexico, which was the deliberate, proclaimed and longed-for goal of the Iberian enterprises. The discovery and conquest of the New World has since so monopolized our attention that it has been forgotten that the Iberian governments were directing all their energies towards a quite different part of the world.

With few exceptions, history books on both sides of the Atlantic, and the historiographies of Europe, Mexico and Latin America, continue to present the venture of Hernán Cortés as a planned conquest of the Aztec Empire inscribed in the genes of the conquistadors – and of modern Europe. This is a retrospective illusion like so many others that the historian encounters or spreads along the way. It was only by stages, and even more because it succeeded beyond all expectations, that the rash adventure eventually assumed the significance which Cortés took it upon himself to give it, with the assistance first of his companions and then of his chroniclers. Meanwhile, in the case of the venture of Tomé Pires, it was the disaster in which it ended that has reduced it to the proportions of a diplomatic blunder or a non-event.

In both cases the Iberians were adding to their knowledge of Asia and the Antilles, agents of an aggressive expansion which proved itself for over twenty years in both Asia and the Caribbean; however, the Amerindians turned out not to be such tough adversaries as the Muslim Asians, who had to be confronted both on land and at sea. Not all the conquistadors were Castilians. The Portuguese Peres de Andrade, who was to lead the embassy to Canton, took part in the attack on Kilwa (1505),[22] the victory of Calicut (1506), the assault on Patane (1507) and the battle of Diu (1509).[23] These episodes remind us that Portuguese expansion in this part of the world and at this period had a strong aggressive and military dimension, which culminated in the seizure of Malacca in 1511. It was with eighteen ships and 1,200 men that the viceroy of the Indies, Afonso de Albuquerque, seized the Malayan city.

If we compare this progress in Asia with the exploration and occupation of the Caribbean, the flag of conquest was undeniably in the hands of the Portuguese. The Spanish knew this, and had to settle for hearing about their exploits or reading about them in the book published by Martín Fernández de Figueroa in Salamanca in 1512. When you spoke about conquering the Indies, you had to look East, as the title of his book proclaimed: *Conquista de las Indias de Persia e Arabia*. Here, the Castilian reader learned all about the 'four thousand places discovered and conquered' by Manuel's men and about 'the battles his fleet has made famous and immortal by dint of fierce combat'.[24]

The Portuguese Landing on the Coast of China

It was in June 1517 that Manuel's embassy left Malacca headed for China. According to the Chinese sources, in 'the twelfth year [1517]' or 'the thirteenth year [1518], [the Portuguese] sent an embassy'.[25] It was several weeks later, on 15 August 1517, that Fernão Peres de Andrade landed on the island *da Veniaga*, identified as Tamão in Portuguese and Tunmen in Chinese, and situated between the mouth of the Pearl River and the River Xi.[26] This island was regularly used as a staging post by foreign merchants arriving on the Chinese coast. It appears that a first Portuguese, Jorge Alvarez, had already in 1513 berthed at Tunmen to trade and to erect a stele or *padrão*, sign of Portuguese settlement.

It was here that the new arrivals began to construct huts and a stockade with a view to settling in. Impatient to reach Canton, one group decided to force the hand of the Chinese coastal authorities, who had instructed them to await their permission before proceeding up the Pearl River. Disregarding this directive, they sailed on to Canton. Once arrived at the town, they had the bright idea of signalling their arrival by launching a few salvos of cannon fire, which terrorized the inhabitants, not accustomed to such noisy and excessive displays. Never, according to the Chinese, had boats sailed like this right in the heart of the city. The boats cast anchor and the group was received at the 'postal relay', a sort of hotel for the reception and lodging of foreign missions.[27] It was situated on the quay of Mussels, south west of the town, hence outside the walls, on the river bank. Here the Portuguese were confined, though not exactly locked up, as they took advantage of the confusion created by the feast of the Lanterns, on 24 February 1518, to treat themselves to a tour of the city walls.[28] This enabled them to stretch their legs, satisfy their intense curiosity and collect information of a military order, in other words, engage in a little espionage.

Called to order and told to behave, the Portuguese were instructed in the correct conduct to be adopted in the presence of the viceroy

of the province, Tch'en Kin. According to one Chinese source, he
had given orders that they should be initiated into the rituals of protocol in the sanctuary of Guangxiao, while also sending a report to
the emperor seeking to know what policy to adopt with regard to
these strangers. Guangxiao was the mosque of Canton, an ancient
sanctuary founded in the seventh century, suggesting that the Chinese
authorities had taken the visitors to be Muslims: 'These people who
had pointed noses and eyes with rings under were very similar to
Muslims'.[29] According to other sources the Portuguese were received
in the great Buddhist temple of Canton; in which case, the Europeans
must have been seen not as monotheists, but as members of a Buddhist
sect and worshippers of images. We are also told that the Portuguese
liked to 'read Buddhist books'. While waiting here the envoys learned
to genuflect and then bang their heads on the ground. Meanwhile,
the authorities drew up an inventory of the products they introduced:
branches of coral, camphor of Borneo, gilded breastplates, coarse
silks of red, glass prisms, a sword with three edges and a cutlass of
flexible and extremely sharp iron.

The mission consisted of twenty-four persons: in addition to Tomé
Pires, six Portuguese, three of them domestic servants, a dozen servants originally from the Indian Ocean and five interpreters, *jurabaças* – a word of Malayan origin – or *lingoas*. The reply from Peking
was slow in coming. The Portuguese waited. At last, the response of
the court arrived. It took the form, it seems, of an imperial edict
stipulating that the visitors should be sent packing after being paid
for their merchandise.[30] However, the members of the embassy were
not deterred by this flat refusal.

All this while, the Portuguese who had remained in Tunmen, living
in huts on land or on their ships at anchor, caused much talk by their
habits and their practice of trading in slaves. All sorts of rumours
circulated among the peasants and fishermen in the surrounding area.
The foreigners were accused of capturing children and eating them:
'On various occasions, they seized little children of less than ten years
old and roasted and ate them. For each one, they paid a hundred
pieces of gold and the young thugs took advantage of this to trade
[with them]'.[31] I will return to this claim.

There were other reasons why the European settlement was a
source of concern to the Celestial authorities. King Manuel wanted
to eliminate Asiatic competition in the Chinese market. To this end,
Lisbon planned to open a maritime route first between Cochin and
Canton, and then between Pazem and the Chinese port. In each case,
it would be necessary to build a fortress on the Chinese coast. Only
a strong settlement on the threshold of the empire could assure the

Portuguese presence in the region. All this, of course, must be done without consulting the Chinese authorities and on the assumption they could replicate on Chinese soil their experiences in Asia and Africa. The plan to create a military base, staffed with veterans of Portuguese victories and battlefields (Azamor or Morocco, Ormuz, Goa, Malacca), from which to make expeditions of discovery using ships built locally, is not without echoes of the way, at about the same time, the Castilians were advancing in the Antilles and the Gulf of Mexico.

The Spanish Landing on the Coast of Mexico

Cortés, too, needed a base on the Mexican coast. He chose the Bay of San Juan de Ulúa, not far from the site of the future port of Vera Cruz; and the word he used to describe his foundation was *fortaleza* (fortress).[32] The bay had an unsavoury reputation. The Spanish of the second expedition had found an island there, which they named 'Isle of Sacrifices', because they had come upon some bloodsoaked victims: 'Two boys with their chests cut open, and their hearts and their blood given as an offering to this accursed idol'. It was a distressing sight: 'It moved us to great pity to find these two lads dead and to see such cruelty'. By contrast, the island in the estuary of the Pearl River where the Portuguese landed, and where they made themselves at home, had long been a commercial port of call, hence its name, *Veniaga*, which means 'trade' in Malay. The Chinese and the Mexicans had a very different relationship to the high seas. However, if the Spanish had understood what lay behind the sacrifices, it might have given them an indication of the power of the Mexicas: according to priests they met on the island, it had been the people of Culua – for which read Mexico-Tenochtitlan, deep in the interior – who had ordered these offerings to a god who, Bernal Díaz del Castillo would much later learn, was the all-powerful Tezcatlipoca. The Spanish understood Ulua, and not Culua, and gave this name to the sinister island which became San Juan de Ulúa.

It was opposite this island that the Spanish pitched their camp. But let us at this point recall how Cortés had come to be here. In 1518, seduced and 'filled with joy' by the information reported by Juan de Grijalva, the governor of Cuba, Diego Velázquez de Cuellar, had appointed a settler with no military experience, Hernán Cortés, to lead a third expedition. The governor was becoming increasingly impatient. He had not yet obtained from the Emperor Charles V authorization to colonize, that is, in the language of the day, 'to engage in barter, conquer and settle'. Cortés was therefore instructed only 'to engage in barter', and not 'to settle', although in Cuba the governor was already trumpeting the contrary, so sure was he of obtaining from the court the grandiloquent title of governor (*adelantado*) of Yucatán.[33] Concretely, and in hopes of more, the Spanish had a mandate to explore the surrounding region and pick up anything they could, but not to establish a permanent settlement. On 18 November Cortés and his friends, who had other ideas, left Santiago de Cuba in a hurry, to the rage of Diego Velázquez. They headed for Yucatán and landed on the coast of Tabasco, acquiring on the way two precious interpreters, Jerónimo de Aguilar and La Malinche.

It was only some months later, on their return to the Bay of San Juan, opposite the infamous Isle of Sacrifices, that, on 22 April 1519, the enterprise took a quite different direction from that desired by the governor of Cuba – though not in line with some grand scheme, its results known in advance. Meanwhile, Tomé Pires and his men were still languishing in Canton, waiting for a signal from Peking.

When the ships of Cortés arrived, the Indians enquired as to the origin of the caravels. Cortés had made contact with the local caciques, to whom he made gifts of European clothes, including two shirts, two doublets and some caps and breeches.[34] Presents were exchanged. According to Cortés the local chief was delighted: 'He was very happy and contented'. The tropical region may have been unhealthily muggy, with its labyrinth of lagoons and swamps sweltering under the heat, but it seemed to please the new arrivals. The country was occupied by people originally from the *altiplano*, sent there by the master of Tenochtitlan. The Nahua language predominated, therefore, as did Mexica influence. There was even a tax collector, or *calpixqui*, appointed by Mexico-Tenochtitlan, residing near the mouth of the River Papaloapan, at Tlacotalplan.[35] The Spanish were still unaware of all this, of course, but they were delighted to find gold and pleased by the warm welcome of the Indians.

It was at this point that the expedition openly changed course. Manipulated by Cortés, the captains took the decision to settle and 'found a town (*pueblo*)', where there would be 'a court of justice' so that 'in this land also You [Charles V] might have sovereignty'. They then asked Cortés – in an act of political ventriloquism – to appoint alcaldes and magistrates (*regidores*) to administer the town 'forthwith', even making a pretence of threatening him should he refuse. Cortés gave in and founded a town which was called the Villa Rica de la Vera Cruz. The new municipality met the very next day; it declared that the powers of Cortés as representative of Diego Velázquez had expired, then hastily appointed the newly discharged captain as 'chief judge, captain and leader, whom we might all respect'.

The Castilians began to behave as if on their home ground, like the Portuguese in Tunmen. They chose a site that was sufficiently flat and marked out spaces for the future square, church and arsenals. Everybody, even Cortés, lent a hand in the construction of the fortress, digging the foundations, making tiles and bricks, carrying water and victuals. They built battlements and barbicans. Soon they erected a pillory in the square and a gallows outside the town, in short, provided themselves with everything they needed to make them feel at home, safe and equipped to administer justice in good and true form. The passages devoted to this episode by Díaz del Castillo help us to imagine the activities of the Portuguese on the island of Tunmen, too, and the crucial quality of versatility shown by the Iberians in situations of this type. It was not long before houses, a church and a fortress rose from the ground.

Another episode links the two histories, revealing how both these nations had an immediate tendency to behave as if they were in conquered territory. On the Chinese and Mexican coasts alike the new arrivals demonstrated their contempt for the established authorities. While the Portuguese of Tunmen were accused of having roughed up the tax collectors sent by the authorities of Canton, the men of Cortés manhandled and arrested the men sent by Moctezuma to collect tribute. Cortés justified his behaviour by explaining that he wanted to rein in the barbarous demands of the Mexicas; it was primarily an effective way of impressing the local populations. These actions, here as in China, vividly demonstrate the predatory instincts of the invaders, who had every intention of getting their hands on the local wealth, accountable to no one. They foreshadowed the time when the Spanish conquerors of Mexico would appropriate the indigenous tribute, which the Portuguese of Canton similarly proposed to do and would gladly have done, if only China had been Mexico. At all events, whether it was at the court of Peking or the court of Mexico, the offensive initiatives of the intruders caused anger and a demand for reprisals.[36]

Cortés had thus broken with the governor of Cuba. Even if he had behaved with more tact, his actions would have been decisive. The page of Diego Velázquez was well and truly turned. The sleight of hand was also a mini coup d'état. The former henchman of the protégé of the bishop of Burgos was no more than a usurper and traitor who had put his life at risk; all the more so when, on 1 July, our potential conquistador learned that Diego Velázquez had at last received the expected authorizations from Castile.[37] If there was, or was to be, a conquest, it was officially for the governor of Cuba, and him alone, to organize. It is hard to believe that Cortés the mutineer, in these circumstances, was in a position to plan the conquest of a powerful empire. At the very most he demonstrated his intention of establishing himself on this part of the coast. He spent long nights writing and seeking possible answers. He had to pass two major tests: he must convince the emperor of his good intentions and he must make his settlement permanent and viable in the eyes of his companions.

Cortés Careers off Course, the Portuguese Have Designs

So Cortés sent emissaries to plead his cause at court. Through their intermediary, he offered – what else could he do? – to head up the conquest of this 'vast and heavily populated' land, and do it much better than his former protector could have done – and he accompanied his proposition with magnificent gifts for the regent Charles; as the saying goes, '*dadivas quebrantan peñas*' (gifts break rocks).[38]

These gifts were political tools: they had to provide tangible proof of the existence, on the other side of the ocean, of an extraordinary civilization, beyond all comparison with those of the island tribes or Golden Castile. Cortés's representatives had to demonstrate to the court that the captain's apparent disobedience deserved the indulgence of the sovereign. The game was certainly worth the candle. Cortés claimed to have explained himself in a first letter addressed to the emperor, in which he had justified the unjustifiable. No trace of this letter survives. Was it lost or did it never exist?[39] If the former, no one could criticize Cortés for having refused to render his accounts; but there was no possibility of anyone using this mysterious missive – because it had gone astray – and the statements he had committed to writing to demonstrate his perfidy and cunning.

Emissaries and gifts thus took to the ocean, headed for Spain – escaping the clutches of Diego Velázquez – in the hope of defusing the situation and saving the necks of Cortés and his companions (26 July 1519). Charles received them in Tordesillas, in March of the following year, and then in Valladolid in April. The battle was far from won, and Cortés's fears were well founded. His envoys had to face the friends of Diego Velázquez and the all-powerful Fonseca, bishop of Burgos, who had for years ruled the roost in all things Indian. The humanist Peter Martyr of Anghiera describes the atmosphere prevailing at court. He himself might enthuse about the gifts brought to the emperor, but he recalls that the king's Council criticized the attitude of the conquistador. If he is to be believed, the emissaries of Diego Velázquez and the lobby which supported him did not mince words: 'They are robbers on the run, guilty of lese-majesty'; for these rebels, they demanded the death penalty. The imminent conquest of Mexico was always within a hair's breadth of losing its hero. More specifically, it was Cortés's initiative in founding Villa Rica, a 'colony' in the Roman sense of the term,[40] that was the focus of the dispute; no one raised the issue of the conquest of a land larger than Spain, even though the gifts and the gold were enough to excite widespread envy. This, at least, is how it looked to Peter Martyr in 1520, and how he described the situation to Pope Leo X and the Roman Curia.

At this point the conquest of Mexico was still only a *pronunciamento* launched by an unknown man in an unknown land, which was probably rich but which was certainly hostile. Meanwhile, was the Portuguese embassy in Canton really intended as no more than a diplomatic exercise? What were the intentions, or rather what was the mindset, of the Portuguese who comprised it and who found themselves immured there, thousands of kilometres from Lisbon? The sources leave little doubt: not only was the possibility of conquest not ruled out, it is explicitly referred to in the correspondence of Vieira and of Calvo, his companion in misfortune, our most direct witnesses. The envoys from Lisbon might not be born conquistadors to quite the same degree as their Castilian rivals, but they never ruled out the idea of an armed expedition when arriving in a newly discovered land. The strolls along the walls of Canton were not only a way of passing the time for tourists caught up in what seemed an interminable wait. The members of the embassy were tasked with collecting as much information as possible on the means of defence and forces of the Chinese, in particular in the region of Canton, and they seized every opportunity. This is revealed in their letters, which are full of sensitive information which they conscientiously transmitted to their superiors and all of which was aimed at preparing for an intervention and then a military occupation.

What does Cristovão Vieira say about Canton and its strategic importance? 'The port of call for the whole country of China is Canton'. It was *the* port of China, as Hong Kong would be later: 'It is more favourable than others to trade with foreigners'. However, it was also 'the place and the land the most susceptible in the world to

being subjected'. Once he was fully informed, he concludes, King
Manuel would not hesitate to undertake this conquest: 'It offers
greater honour than the government of the Indies'. Many factors
would militate in favour of an armed intervention. Fed up with their
ill-treatment, the Chinese people wanted nothing more than to rise
up against the detested mandarins. They were waiting only for a
Portuguese landing: 'Everyone wishes to rebel and hopes for the
arrival of the Portuguese of Canton... everybody is waiting for the
Portuguese'.[41] The revolt of the countryside against the mandarins,
precipitated by the arrival of the Europeans, would quickly spell
starvation for the city of Canton, which would then fall like a ripe
fruit. The lack of fighting junks left the great city with only its ramparts for protection. Once taken, it would only need two fortresses
to be built to hold the town: one on the north flank, because 'from
there you can seize the city', the other on the side of the mandarins'
landing stage. The tone is peremptory – there was not a moment to
be lost. It would need even less time to put this plan into action than
to write about it.

The haste was based on an analysis of the supposed weaknesses
of the Middle Empire. Chinese domination was recent and fragile:
'Until now, they have not had lordships of their own, but they have
gradually taken over the land of their neighbours, which is why the
kingdom is huge, because these Chinese are full of duplicity and it is
from this that their presumption, arrogance and cruelty derives; and
this because up to the present, they, who are a cowardly, weak people,
lacking arms and without any experience of war, they have always
won land from their neighbours less through force of arms than
through guile and hypocrisy, and they arrange matters so that no one
can do them any harm.'[42]

The Castilians of Cortés were conquistadors-in-waiting who played
for a while the role of ambassadors. The Portuguese of Pires were
ambassadors who expected to be treated as such, but who harboured
all sorts of bellicose ulterior motives. Looked at more closely, or
rather when we systematically compare the sources at our disposal,
the two projects begin to appear less diametrically opposed than at
first appears. Precious light is shed on the often confused circumstances in which worlds connected and contacts were made at the
dawn of modern times: the initiative might be local (Cuba) or metropolitan (Lisbon); it might be planned from the outset (Pires) or
totally unpredictable and impossible to control (Cortés). It was
always complicated by dark calculations and it produced in the
Europeans, as, for that matter, in their hosts, too, ambivalent behaviour which was accentuated by the total novelty of the situation in

which they all of them found themselves. When closely observed, the expected clash of civilizations (in its Europe/China or its Europe/ Mexico variants) resembled for the moment a game of cat and mouse, without anyone yet being in a position to tell which was the cat and which the mouse.

The March on Peking (January to Summer 1520)

In August 1519 a second Portuguese fleet, led by Simão de Andrade, landed in Canton. It made contact with the embassy, but left China in the summer of 1520. It was by now six months since Pires had left for Peking. In Canton the Chinese authorities had begun by flatly rejecting the Portuguese request. Detained in the city, the embassy had been obliged to wait almost a year before it received permission to travel to the capital. Things were beginning to move at last. The Portuguese, according to the *Mingshi*, had managed to corrupt one of the eunuchs of the commission for the maritime affairs of Guangdong and for the security of the frontier posts.[43] The embassy set off on 23 January 1520 and stopped in Nanking, where it seems to have met the emperor.[44] Zhengde had returned from tours in the north and northwest of China in 1518 and 1519, at the instigation of his favourite, the eunuch Jiang Bin. Another ambassador, Tuan Muhammed, was close on the heels of Tomé Pires. Sent by the king of Bintan (formerly of Malacca) to complain about the Portuguese, he had left Canton in the first half of 1520 and he too was now in Nanking.

Pires was in Peking during the summer of 1520, perhaps in the Imperial Suite. Yet he had to wait until January 1521 before he got even a glimmer of the possibility of an official audience. In the hope of facilitating his plans, the Portuguese ambassador had acquired the support of a eunuch who wielded great influence at court, Ning Cheng, and the emperor's favourite, Jiang Bin.[45] It was probably the latter who made it possible for Pires to meet the emperor in person in Nanking. Things moved so slowly because the emperor, who was near Peking, at T'ong-tcheou, between 5 December 1519 and 18 January 1521, had been warned against the mission of Tomé Pires and delayed his response as a consequence of accusations made in Canton, Nanking and Peking. Nevertheless, in the capital, the authorities received the Portuguese envoys respectfully. They had plenty of time to familiarize themselves with the ceremonial with which Manuel's ambassador was ready to comply.[46] But was Pires ever going to be officially received?

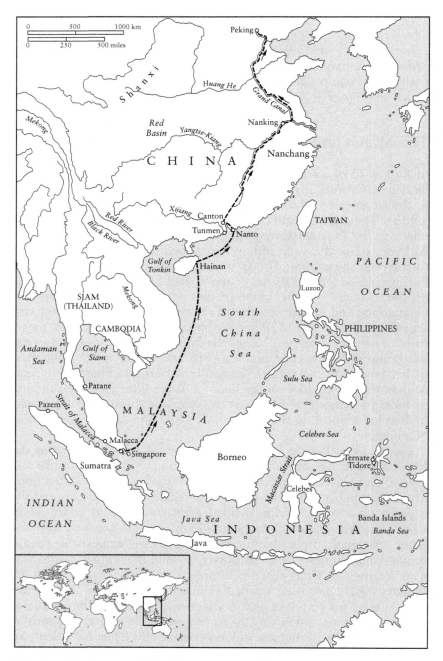

Map 1. The Route of Tomé Pires: Malacca-Peking, June 1517–summer 1520

The March on Mexico (August to November 1519)

While Pires was kicking his heels in Canton, the conquistador in Mexico was feeling his way. He pondered the balance of power and collected information about what seems to have become his goal from Easter 1519: Mexico-Tenochtitlan. Most of all, he tried to negotiate alliances and get his presence accepted locally. Treaties were made with more than thirty *pueblos* of the Sierra, essentially Totonacs, who had little love for the Mexicas.[47] It was in this context that Villa Rica de la Vera Cruz was founded.

Cortés wanted to see the Aztec capital with his own eyes and to meet Moctezuma. The destruction of his ships ruled out any retreat in the manner of Grijalva and led up to the departure, on 16 August 1519, of an expedition consisting of 300 foot soldiers or *peones*, fifteen mounted soldiers, 400 Totonacs and 200 *tameme* porters to carry the artillery.[48] Everything seemed to go smoothly. The Indian chiefs were apparently delighted to pass under Spanish rule: 'They were very well pleased to be Your Highness's vassals and my friends'. They were warmly welcomed at Cempoala, Sienchimalem (Xicochimalco) and Iztaquimaxtitlán, where the Spanish stayed for a

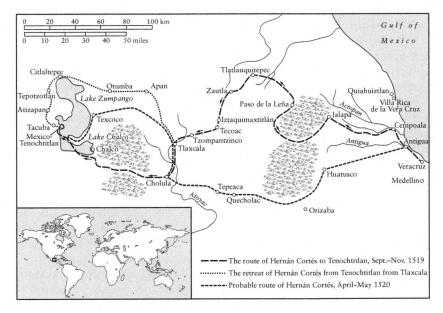

Map 2. The Routes of Hernán Cortés in Mexico

week. Cortés reassured his hosts by claiming he was only passing through, wishing to see Moctezuma, and 'going for no other purpose'. It would have been like a walk in the park but for the chilliness of the mountains, which decimated the Indians of Fernandina (Cuba), who 'had not enough to wear'.[49]

It is difficult, in these circumstances, to speak of a conquest proceeding according to a well-laid plan, with the blessing of the colonial and imperial authorities and the support of all the Spanish forces established in the islands. Diego Velázquez was still a long way from admitting defeat. The governor of Cuba hastily raised a troop and a fleet to put down the rebellion. This force, twice as large as that of Cortés, set out in March 1520. It ought, in principle, to have eliminated the rebel without difficulty; it would then have been necessary to start all over again. Seen from the metropolis, the future of Cortés looked bleak. In fact the news of his rebellion reached Castile shortly before the uprising of the *Comuneros* of Castile. The countryside erupted in June 1520 and the unrest was only ended by the victory of Villalar, in the province of Valladolid, nearly a year later (23 April 1521). It is hardly surprising, in the circumstances, that the initiatives of Cortés were looked at askance. The party of the governor of Cuba, which was very active and influential at court, was confident of obtaining from King Charles the head of a rebel who was unknown either to the sovereign or his councillors.[50] But their manoeuvres failed, as did the fleet launched in pursuit of Cortés.

Unable to intervene in person either in Cuba or at court, Cortés attempted to score points locally by an inexorable advance in the direction of Mexico. The conquest, strictly speaking, had not yet begun, but Cortés had resolved that nothing, and certainly not the hostility of the Indians or the fears of his own troops, was going to stand in his way. Before the gates of Tlaxcala, things became complicated. Forced to engage in their first battle, the Spanish lost over fifty men. To those who bemoaned this, Cortés replied: 'Better to die as brave men, as the old songs say, than to live dishonourably'.[51] An indigenous ally attempted, with no more success, to make the captain see reason by using an argument which the Chinese would use against the Portuguese, much later, when they seemed likely to invade: 'Beyond this province, there are so many people that a hundred thousand men will fight against you now and, when they are all dead or defeated, an equal number will arrive, and they will go on, for a very long time, replacing each other and dying, a hundred thousand after a hundred thousand, and you and your men, since you claim to be invincible, will die from exhaustion with the effort of fighting them'.[52] The vagaries of fate and the precariousness of the situation did not escape Peter Martyr of Anghiera, whose comment on the news from distant Castile was: 'Our men, however, have not always been victorious; often luck turned against them and sometimes the barbarians who refused to accept guests destroyed whole armies of ours'.

The sources provide contradictory images of the expedition. From a distance, and after the event, Peter Martyr gave it the ultimate accolade by comparing it to the war waged by Julius Caesar against the Helvetians and the Germans, or the war between Themistocles and the hordes of Xerxes. The conquest of the Gauls! Was it possible to imagine a more illustrious, more classical and more rational model of conquest? The size of the advance force, as described by Cortés, added to the grandeur of the enterprise: no fewer than 100,000 Tlaxcaltecs had proposed to accompany the Spanish on their march on Cholula and Mexico![53] On the ground, it was a very different story. The members of the expedition, panicking, had a far less glorious example in mind: they compared Cortés to the 'valorous Pedro Carbonero of Cordoba', leader of a medieval band, as popular as legendary,[54] who had led his men into an impossible battle against the Moors.[55] It had been a disaster: the Moors had left not a single Christian alive. So Cortés 'had led them into this place from which they could never escape'.[56]

Cortés chooses immoderation

So this was still no cold imperialist conquest, directed from on high, but rather the reckless folly of one man and his entourage, of a captain of dubious legitimacy who could count only on God and himself, and whose venture might at any moment end in disaster. Cortés did not hesitate to report the words of his companions, who called him a fool. But he was a fool who knew what he was doing. To brush aside accusations of rebellion and emerge triumphant from his duel with the governor of Cuba, Cortés had no alternative but to seize the lands of Moctezuma and give his initiative a legal, blameless, imperial and Christian facade.[57] In these circumstances, the conquest of Mexico appears neither as a carefully considered choice nor as the fulfilment of a political project: it was a matter of life or death for one man. On the ground, faced with an anxious and exhausted band of men who wanted only to get back to the coast, Cortés was reduced to brandishing the lure of wealth and glory in battles yet to be fought.

The situation seemed hopeless, which encouraged immoderation. Cortés was ready to promise anything: 'We were in a position to

win…the greatest dominions and kingdoms in the world'. The
Spanish, by fighting, would win 'greater honor and renown than any
generation before our time'.[58] Cortés positioned himself on the world
stage by presenting himself as a planetary predator, and stood alone
against fate, in a conquering frenzy which took on the task of attacking the greatest powers on earth and laying them low. If modernity
is indeed the leap into the monstrous described by Peter Sloterdijk,[59]
and the ability to assume full responsibility for the crimes committed
or to be committed, Cortés was a vehicle of modernity. His project
was crazy; but was it any crazier than the projects of the Portuguese
of Canton or the propositions of Tomé Pires, who, before he knew
he would lead an embassy to China, grandly prophesied: 'With ten
ships, the governor of the Indies who has seized Malacca will subju-
gate the whole of coastal China'?[60]

The immoderation of Cortés's plans might well have been a source
of anxiety to the first recipient of these letters, the Emperor Charles,
the very opposite of an insatiable conqueror. But it would end up
being coincidental with the ideals of universal monarchy and *domi-
nium mundi* which the Chancellor Mercurio Gattinara had begun to
inculcate into the young prince.[61] Nevertheless, it was still too early
for the project to 're-found [a] universal empire with a Christian
mission and the goal of fighting against Islam' to be applicable to the
conquest of the New World.

Cortés had to employ great ingenuity so as to avoid displeasing
the emperor while at the same time finding the words that would
force his hand and extract a pardon. Here, his pen worked wonders.
The version he provided in his second letter (October 1520), written
when the objective (Mexico-Tenochtitlan) had been achieved and he
had a clearer idea of what Mexico represented, was a travesty of
everything that had happened. The vision was both heroic and 'politically correct', and it was visually spectacular, not to say Hollywood-
ian before its time. It was this vision which a posterity greedy for
sensationalism would remember. The enterprise was elevated to the
status of 'conquest and pacification'. The country was 'marvellous'
– the word keeps recurring. It was:

> a very large and very rich province called Culúa, in which there are
> large cities and marvellous buildings, much commerce and great
> wealth. Among these cities there is one more marvellous and more
> wealthy than all the others, called [Tenustitlan], which has, with
> extraordinary skill, been built upon a great lake, of which city and
> province a powerful lord called Mutezuma is king; here things terrible
> to relate befell the captain and the Spaniards.[62]

The emphasis was all on the Indian towns of the *altiplano*, described in a crescendo which reaches an apotheosis with the presentation of the metropolis of the Triple Alliance, Mexico-Tenochtitlan.[63]

The bombast of Cortés made an immediate impression which far exceeded his hopes; it mesmerized Latin Christendom, infiltrating into the European *imaginaire*, as far afield as Bohemia and Poland, clichés and scenes whose fame contrasts with the silence surrounding China. Europeans would 'see' Mexico long before they 'saw' Peking. The famous engraving of the Aztec capital, taken from a letter sent by Cortés, was endlessly reproduced and discussed. Yet the description of China given by Vieira after his account of the embassy of Pires was equally astounding.[64] It was the first to be provided by an eyewitness who had travelled in the interior of this country. But it went almost unnoticed.[65]

Cortés continued to present himself in the best possible light. It was as a visitor,[66] as a helping hand acclaimed everywhere he went, or as an envoy of the Emperor Charles V, ready to return home once his mission was accomplished, that he is portrayed in his letter. And it was in this light that he presented himself to the Indian princes: 'Your Majesty had received news [of the existence of Moctezuma] and...had sent me to see him...and that I was going for no other purpose'. What did it matter that the indigenous peoples did not use alphabetic writing! Everything was allegedly settled with them by the written word ('the proceedings and agreements I had made with the natives of this lands') and by papers which, of course, had got lost in the turmoil of the conquest. Everything was designed to show the reluctant conquistador in a favourable light: from the supposedly scrupulous use of the *requerimiento* 'in good and due form with the interpreters I took with me',[67] to the legitimate defence forced on him by monstrously unequal assaults – 100,000 Tlaxcaltecs against forty crossbowmen, thirteen horsemen, five or six harquebuses and half a dozen guns.[68] Was he supposed to have let himself be massacred?

Blockages

What had the Indians of Mexico committed themselves to with regard to the distant and unknown master whose emissary Cortés claimed to be? Were the Spanish, in their eyes, any more than a bunch of brutally effective mercenaries, whose favour or whose services it was prudent to gain?

Cortés's journey was punctuated by exchanges of gifts and gestures of welcome, to which he said in reply whatever he chose. Crucially,

however, the expedition met with a courteous but firm refusal from
Moctezuma. The first 'official' embassy from the master of Mexico
was received during skirmishes between the visitors and the Tlaxcalan
troops. 'Six chieftains of rank, vassals of Mutezuma, came to see me
with as many as two hundred men in attendance. They told me that
they had come on behalf of Mutezuma to inform me how he wished
to be Your Highness's vassal', and pay an annual tribute, 'provided
that I did not go to his land, the reason being that it was very barren
and lacking in all provisions and it would grieve him if I and those
with me should be in want'.[69]

The Portuguese embassy, stuck in Canton, came up against a
similar barrier and for similar reasons: there could be no question of
allowing Europeans to approach the capital. Neither Peking nor
Mexico-Tenochtitlan wanted foreigners setting foot deep in their territory; the Mexicas were as adamant as the Celestial authorities. The
Chinese barrier would remain in place for months; it was lifted only
by dint of the persistence of the Portuguese mission and its ability to
negotiate, first locally and then at court, alliances which opened up
the route to Peking. It is the same persistence that we see in Cortés,
who struggled to convince the Mexicas of his good intentions while
at the same time consolidating his position at the heart of the *altiplano*: he speaks in his letter of his 'determination'. Conquest or
embassy, the first stage of Iberian penetration unquestionably aroused
the hostility of the local powers. Nevertheless, against all expectations, the invaders managed in both cases to overcome the opposition
they encountered, in fact to force the hand of their adversary.

The first stage was taken up with talking and negotiation. In
Tlaxcala, 'noble messengers from Moctezuma' repeatedly visited
Cortés; they told him that other envoys awaited him in Cholula. The
envoys circulated between the Tlaxcaltec city and Mexico-Tenochtitlan.
Cortés, who found himself under conflicting pressures from the
Tlaxcaltecs and the Mexicas, decided to exploit the ill feeling between
the two enemy camps: 'When I saw the discord and animosity between
these two peoples I was not a little pleased…I manoeuvred one
against the other'.[70] Having arrived at Cholula, 'city of temples', he
continued to ponder the intentions of the Mexicas: were they laying
a trap for him? He made threats: 'Since [Moctezuma] did not keep
his word or speak the truth, I had changed my plans: whereas, before,
I had been going to his land with the intention of seeing him and
speaking with him in order to have him as a friend and to converse
with him in harmony, now I intended to enter his land at war, doing
all the harm I could as an enemy'.[71] Moctezuma managed to placate
him by offering him a sumptuous gift, 'ten gold plates and fifteen

hundred articles of clothing'. The *tlatoani* claimed he was not party to the intrigues of the Cholultecs and assumed the role of deceived master unable to control events. Cortés took advantage of this to concoct the image of a deceitful prince who amply deserved to be removed from the scene.

At the end of what was still not a conquest, but rather a series of diplomatic offensives, Moctezuma eventually accepted that Cortés was going to come to Mexico: 'Once he understood my determination to go and see him...he would accommodate me in that great city where he lived'. Nevertheless, once arrived in the province of Chalco, Cortés faced new pressures: Moctezuma 'begged me...to turn back and not persist in going to his city'. Cortés quoted the pressing nature of his mission while remaining extremely courteous: 'I replied that were it in my power to return I would do so to please Moctezuma'. At all events, 'once I had seen him, should he still not wish me to remain his company, I would then return'. At Amecameca, that is, closer to Mexico, he received a new embassy. Once again, he escaped a surprise attack thanks to the precautions he had taken. There arrived an umpteenth ambassador, brandishing threats, who exhorted Cortés one last time to stop his advance, 'for I would suffer many hardships', a point on which these lords 'urgently and earnestly persisted'.[72] Cortés did nothing. Tired of resisting, Moctezuma decided to allow Spanish troops to come to him; at Iztapalapa they received gifts of welcome, slaves, clothes and gold. Mexico-Tenochtitlan was ready to receive Cortés.

How are we to understand Moctezuma's volte-face when we think of what the fates had in store? A comparison with events in China suggests several possibilities. A handful of Portuguese managed to get themselves received at the heart of the empire, surmounting all the obstacles placed in their path. Why might the court of Peking and the Triple Alliance decide to allow the visit of these foreigners? A first response might be to consider the obstacles put in their way as trials inflicted to test the visitors' intentions and their ability to adapt to unknown territory. In both cases, the identity of the intruders presented as much of a problem as their motives. It created a margin of uncertainty, which demanded from their hosts an effort of the imagination and a degree of flexibility. Neither Pires nor Cortés gave the appearance of classic invaders; they were neither Mongols nor Tlaxcaltecs. The Chinese and the Mexicas had to work out for themselves what their arrival meant. As different interpretations were put forward, local reactions evolved. The importance attached to this new presence, whether it was commercial or military, quickly suggests comparisons: one thinks of the Cantonese merchants attracted by the overtures of the Portuguese, or of the Tlaxcaltec lords by no means displeased to add the military power of the new arrivals to their own troops. In both China and Mexico the rivalry both between periphery and centre – between Canton and Peking or between the Vera Cruz Coast or Tlaxcala and Mexico-Tenochtitlan – and within the central government itself created fertile territory for the reception of a foreign body which would introduce a new element into the political scene. The Chinese sources, too, do not conceal the bad relations between Zhengde and the central administration.

Little is known about the reactions of Moctezuma's entourage or about the friction within the Triple Alliance that encouraged the *tlatoani* to receive and offer hospitality to his future conqueror. For Cortés, it was essential above all to save face in Spain, which is probably why his version of events paints a picture that is too good to be true. It was in Cortés's interests to present the warm welcome and offers of alliances coming from a majority of the indigenous groups as signs of voluntary submission to an undisputed authority. In Tlaxcala the envoys of Moctezuma had 'spontaneously' proposed to pay tribute to the emperor.[73] When Cortés invoked 'Moctezuma's friendliness' towards him, it was as much to explain the reasons for his success to this hostile audience as to give a pacific and legitimate character to his march.

Meeting the Emperor

In both China and Mexico the expeditions included an episode that was to be the highlight of the voyage: the meeting with the emperor. In the Chinese case, this took place in Nanking in the spring of 1520. According to Cristovão Vieira: 'In the year 1520, on 23 January, we set out to meet the king of China; in May we were with the king in Nanking; he instructed us to proceed to Peking to conduct our business there; on 2 August, we wrote to Canton about what had passed with the king'.[74]

The description of the meeting with Zhengde is frustratingly circumspect, although it refers to detailed letters sent to Canton, now lost. Other Portuguese sources do little more to satisfy our curiosity.[75] They tell us that the Portuguese had experienced something quite exceptional: 'In Nanking, we saw the king in person, enjoying ourselves contrary to the custom of the country, because normally the king never leaves his apartments and, since the land of China has been the land of China, the king permits few to contravene this custom and few strangers see the king as I tell you we saw him'. A few details convey just how close the envoys got: 'He did us much honour and he enjoyed seeing us; he played draughts with Tomé Pires, sometimes in our presence; he instructed us to dine with all the grandees, and so far this has happened three times. He visited the ships we travelled in. He made us bring out all the chests; he took such clothes as pleased him and gave permission to Tomé Pires for us to go to Peking, where he would look into our affairs'. The remarkable familiarity of the contacts was not a fabrication. The reception in Nanking, in its simplicity, was in marked contrast to the pomp and grandiloquence of Cortés's reception in Mexico. It may be that the intervention of the emperor's favourite, Jiang Bin, possibly bribed by the Portuguese, facilitated matters and that Zhengde was not displeased to wrongfoot his ministers.[76]

We will probably never know whether the emperor played Chinese chess – *xiangqi* – with Pires, or whether Pires taught him one of the board games then in fashion on the Iberian Peninsula, ancestors of our draughts and other backgammons.[77] The use of a Portuguese word for the game, and Zhengde's apparent curiosity on this occasion, suggest that it was a game played on a board marked out in a given number of squares with pieces in the form of discs, called 'tables', made of wood, bone or ivory (our future draughts pieces), and six-sided dice.[78] In these circumstances, it seems more likely that Zhengde wanted to learn a new, foreign game than that he wanted to compete with an opponent who was a complete novice on a Chinese chess board. It would hardly be surprising if Pires carried equipment for games with him on his travels; games were an excellent way of passing the time and provided some distraction on pretty risky expeditions. It is also known that games circulated from one end of Eurasia to the other, and that European chess and Chinese chess probably had a common origin in northwest India around 500 BCE. What changed with the arrival of the Portuguese was that the age-old itineraries travelled by caravans and by games, at the cost of innumerable adaptations and transformations, were suddenly short-circuited. Worlds which had previously had only distant, indirect and sporadic relations with each other came into direct contact, and this contact might come about through games.

This was equally true of Mexico. The daily contacts between the entourage of Cortés and Moctezuma were based on exchanges of gifts and clothes and on a passion for gambling, which seems universal. Díaz del Castillo, on one occasion when he was mounting guard, remembered seeing Cortés playing at *totoloque* with the *tlatoani*: 'The game they called by this name was played with small, highly polished balls, made of gold specially for this game; they threw from a little distance with the balls and with discs which were also of gold, and they won or lost, in five tries, certain jewels and precious pieces they staked'.[79] Everybody laughed, Moctezuma most of all, to see one of the future conquistadors, Pedro de Alvarado, contriving to cheat: 'He went in for plenty of *ixoxol* when he was counting the points'.[80]

As described here, Moctezuma appears a great and liberal lord. But was the Mexican *tlatoani* really no more than a king from out of a chivalric romance? Under the cliché, beneath the prodigious courtesy, other concerns emerge which derive from the way in which the indigenous societies conceived games of chance. For Moctezuma, whatever the secret dealings, whatever the opposing parties, it was fate and fate alone that would determine the outcome. The *tlatoani* acted as an attentive follower of portents and auguries, eager to know which way the pendulum would swing in the absence of a helping human hand. Let a game prefigure and reveal the outcome, an outcome which would see the loser doomed to absolute disaster, the victor to unalloyed triumph.[81] There were no half measures with the Mexicas: the losers in a ball game were sacrificed down to the last man. Moctezuma belonged to a world where the warrior of yesterday could die tomorrow under the obsidian knife of a priest performing the sacrifice. Should we say that the Mexicas 'played' with destiny and time, whereas their more prosaically minded visitors enjoyed themselves and lined their pockets? This would be to forget that the Castilian expedition included an astrologer, Botello, who had no hesitation in consulting the fates. This suggests that for Cortés, too, the results of the game might prefigure the fate which awaited him and his companions...[82] In Nanking, people were more likely to believe that the game would be determined by the accumulation of points, hence by experience and shrewdness, and that chance played a much smaller part. But we must be careful not to make Tomé Pires or Zhengde too much like us.

In this year of 1520, in Nanking and Mexico, obscure Europeans who had never come remotely close to their own sovereign found themselves face to face with the 'masters of the world', in principle inaccessible to ordinary mortals. In one case they played draughts, in the other skittles. Both were ways of being entertained, but also of relaxing in a particularly stressful situation, for the Europeans as well as for Moctezuma, who was then, or so Cortés claimed, his visitors' hostage. These worlds did not connect at a stroke, and gambling games helped to deal with the unexpected or simply to kill time, which was not always exclusively devoted to spying on or laying traps for each other. In both cases curiosity was as strong a factor as the desire to conquer or possess. And the curiosity was not all on the side of the new arrivals. Moctezuma and Zhengde were men of power, repositories of age-old traditions and esoteric knowledge. It is easy to forget that, for them, time spent in the company of these bizarre creatures who had come from elsewhere, who were totally ignorant of the most elementary customs and codes of China and Mexico, but who possessed other forms of knowledge, might be intriguing, even fascinating. In any case, the monotony of the daily round, which extends across societies and cultures, was interrupted for a brief moment. Though the crass ignorance of local custom – as on the part of the huge Spaniard who could find nothing better to do all night when keeping watch than masturbate – shocked the master of Mexico-Tenochtitlan, who complained about it then and there.[83]

In Mexico, unlike Nanking, the episodes of this type did not precede the official encounter. They happened weeks after an event to which both parties had attached exceptional importance, as shown by the mobilization of so many resources and men in the case of the Mexicas, and by the splendour ascribed to it in Spanish accounts. The meeting between Cortés and Moctezuma was also a moment of high importance because it became, as described by Cortés, central to the theme of his second letter. To reveal to his readers the splendours of the American Venice, and to describe for the emperor the surrender of Moctezuma, seemed the only way he could hope to achieve a pardon for his rebellion. This means that it is difficult, if not impossible, to distinguish what Cortés saw and understood at the time from what he transmitted to Europe a few months later.

The discovery and the description of the 'great city' marked, by any standard, a turning point in the history of Spanish expansion in America. A threshold was crossed, which provided Cortés with the best possible justification. After the conquest of the 'savage' of the islands (had this been anything more, in a sense, than a tropical rerun of the conquest of the Canaries?), and after the Columbian false hopes of reaching the Empire of the Great Khan, the Spanish had at last reached a world worthy of the effort, a world we would call 'civilized', and everyone, Cortés in the forefront, soon realized this: 'These people live almost like those in Spain, and in as much harmony and order as there, and considering that they are barbarous and so far from the knowledge of God and cut off from all civilized nations, it is truly remarkable to see what they have achieved in all things'. For the *señorío* of Moctezuma was not only 'almost as big as Spain',[84] but it incarnated the emergence between Europe and East Asia of a continent which had many societies and which had remained without contact with the rest of the world or with the revealed God. They had done much more than discover new lands, they had come face to face with another humanity which had appeared from nowhere. Cortés knew how to inflate the global and historical significance of his expedition by proclaiming the conquest of the 'greatest kingdoms in the world' and the most glorious enterprise there had ever been.[85] This way he might be able to exchange his reputation as trouble-maker of the islands for the immortal plumes of the conqueror.

To justify his actions in the eyes of the Crown, the jurists and the theologians, Cortés needed Moctezuma to have made a spontaneous submission. This alone could ward off questions about the legitimacy of the conquest. It provided the conquistador with a fault-free, unquestionable progress, with no false note, and it endowed his ini-tiative with huge worth by adding a new empire to the one his master, Charles, already possessed: one 'might call oneself the emperor of this kingdom with no less glory than of Germany'.

How did Cortés manage this? By bluffing; by putting into the mouth of Moctezuma an argument which explained the *tlatoani*'s submission as a voluntary act of restitution. Were the Mexicas not just as much strangers in this country as the Spanish? We are not 'natives of [this land], but foreigners who came from very distant parts'.[86] They had not come alone. A chieftain, now long gone home ('he returned to his native land'), had brought them to Mexico. It was in the nature of things, therefore, that his descendants – the Castilians – should one day arrive to claim what was their due. So Moctezuma abdicated his power and, like the Japanese Emperor Hirohito in January 1946, renounced at the same time his divine nature: 'See that I am of flesh and blood like you and all other men, and I am mortal and substantial'. By a prodigious acceleration of history, Moctezuma embraced a secularized vision of the world even more rapidly than his people would pass from copper to steel.

What happened next was deemed to confirm the prince's friendly feelings towards the invaders. It was as if Moctezuma had jumped at the chance to submit to Caesar: they felt 'such good will and delight on the part of Moctezuma and all the natives of the aforementioned lands that it seemed as if *ab initio* they had known Your Sacred Majesty to be their king and rightful lord'.[87] A thousand miles from the ad hoc-ery, compromises, false steps and many blunders which had marked the Spanish progress on Mexican soil and their installa-tion in Mexico City,[88] Cortés presented a scenario in which everything had gone according to plan. The pen of the future conquistador produced one of the founding myths of Western expansion by pre-senting his emperor with the fait accompli.

Reading Cortés, this infiltration stood so much to reason, this intrusion was so 'expected', so clothed with good intentions, so imbued with the conviction of being in the right and in tune with history, that one ends up believing that things could not have happened any other way. It had been written for the Indians as for the Spanish: 'For a long time [the Indians] have known'. As for the Emperor Charles: 'He had known for a long time...' of the existence of these distant vassals, as if the emperor had always known of the existence of the Aztecs! It only remained for the Indians, without need for either war or defeat, to deliver themselves bound hand and foot to their visitors, who did not even need to be their conquerors: 'Anything that I might have shall be given to you whenever you ask', said Moctezuma.[89]

This is also a textbook illustration of a practice introduced into the Caribbean, that of the *requerimiento*, or appeal for the voluntary submission of the populations encountered; except that this time it was applied at the level not of an island tribe but of a continental power, not to say whole civilization. This did not happen without some manipulation, which Cortés openly admitted. It seemed to him, he said, that it was prudent to make them believe that 'Your Majesty' was the one they were waiting for. Too bad if the emperor was not, in reality, the 'Messiah' awaited by the Indians! Mexico City, unforgettable backdrop to an episode Cortés brilliantly reconfigured for his master, was worth a little white lie! How could one not succumb to 'the magnificence, the strange and marvellous things of this great city of Temextitan [Tenochtitlan]'?[90]

7

The Clash of Civilizations

We must not receive their ambassador, and must let them know plainly whether they are obedient or recalcitrant in our eyes. We must order them to restore the [occupied] territory to Malacca; only after this is done shall we consent to their bringing tribute. Should they remain obstinately fixed in the illusion, we must issue manifestos to all foreign peoples to make known their crimes, and punitive expeditions must be sent against them.
Report of the imperial censor K'ieou Tao-long (second semester 1520).[1]

In both Mexico and Nanking, it all began peacefully. For the moment, there was no clash of civilizations. The unexpected arrival of the Iberians was marked by a number of blunders: illegal settlements, by the Portuguese at Tunmen and by the Spanish at Vera Cruz; the refusal to comply with the orders of the local authorities, who wanted to keep them at a distance; and even a few violent incidents, of which the merchants of Siam and the *Calpixquis*, or mandarins of the fisc, were the chief victims. Both the Spanish and the Portuguese found themselves in situations in which they were totally at sea; they were not without experience to draw on, in the Caribbean, on the coast of India or in Malacca – but the reactions of their adversaries, be it Indian societies or the Chinese Empire, remained unpredictable.

Awkward Situations

Tomé Pires entered Peking around 1 August 1520. He was lodged, says Vieira, in the enclosed buildings reserved for foreigners. He then needed to be officially received. So as to conform to Chinese protocol, he communicated the letter from King Manuel to the Minister of Rites. In fact several letters were handed to the Chinese authorities. One of them, which was sealed, was only to be opened in Peking. The other, written in Chinese, was a message from Peres de Andrade, in a translation provided by interpreters recruited in Malacca.[2] These interpreters had not contented themselves with translating the Portuguese into Chinese, they had also put the letter into a form that would be acceptable to the court of Peking. As a result, the Portuguese found that they had professed their allegiance to the Son of Heaven. When Tomé Pires learned what the translators had done, he protested, which quickly put him in an awkward situation. For, if Manuel's envoys had not come to perform an act of submission, the translated letter was in Chinese eyes a sham, the envoys liars and the embassy a farce. So the letter of introduction was not accepted. Pires had to wait for the emperor to return to Peking before a decision as to his future could be taken.

If the Portuguese found themselves in a difficult situation, it was also because the senior officials regarded them with hostility. Everything suggests that they had put obstacles in the way of the European delegation during the interminable 2,000-kilometre trek from Canton to Peking. The senior secretaries Yang T'ing-houo and Mao Ki had put pressure on the emperor when he was still in T'ong-tcheou, before his return to Peking.[3] The imperial censors wanted to wait for the arrival of the ambassador Tuan Muhammad, sent by the ousted sovereign of Malacca, who did not reach the Court until some time after January 1521. The Malayan envoys had warned Peking that the Portuguese had come to China to act as spies; they were robbers, whose practice was to lay a brick and build a house on the lands they intended to appropriate. This was what they had done in Malacca. Nevertheless, the Emperor Zhengde seemed ready to tolerate these strangers, who were obviously – but was this their fault? – unfamiliar with local customs.

So Pires had to be patient. It was from other foreign envoys that he picked up the details of the ceremonial in which he was preparing to participate in Peking, since in Nanking he had seen the emperor only in private audience. Neither Barros nor Vieira shows any sign of unease at the prospect of doing homage to the emperor. In the event, however, Pires was never to receive permission to go to the Imperial Palace and prostrate himself three times before a wall behind which the emperor was supposed to be.[4] The death of Zhengde on 20 April 1521 meant that the contacts made in Nanking were worthless. All the ambassadors who were in Peking were sent packing. Pires had to set off back to Canton.

The situation in Mexico was scarcely more encouraging. Cortés realized the seriousness of the trap presented by the lakeside capital. The visitors, who numbered at most 500, probably fewer, would be at the mercy of between 200,000 and 300,000 Mexicas who lived in the town, if only for lodgings and food. If supplies were not forthcoming, they and their horses would die of hunger and thirst. There could be no question of seizing Moctezuma, for fear of provoking a chaotic situation of which they would be the first victims. Cortés would nevertheless claim the contrary in his second letter. If the Mexicas were to be seen as a people in revolt against Charles, hence the target of a riposte presented as an act of self-defence, he had to invent a story of submission, and, to make this submission more complete, Moctezuma had to be the hostage of his visitors.[5] Strangely, from November to May, Cortés did not think fit to inform the emperor of the capture he was supposed to have carried out. The contradictions in the sources, in which Moctezuma is in turn a prisoner kept closely confined and a sovereign kept under only lax constraints, destroy much of the credibility of Cortés's version.[6]

For his part, the *tlatoani* had long avoided clashes with the intruders; battles in Mexico, even if they went badly for the Europeans, risked loosening the grip of the Mexicas over their allies of the Triple Alliance. To expose himself to a pitched battle would be to provide the Spanish with an opportunity to demonstrate their formidable effectiveness. It was necessary at all costs to avoid losing face before the other cities of the Valley. And incidents inside the town, due to the combined fury of the Spanish and their Tlaxcaltec allies, might lead to unrest and destabilize his power. The *tlatoani* had other reasons for temporizing, preferring to wait for the reception of the tribute and the end of the rainy season. Everything militated against openly opposing his inopportune visitors.

In this situation the rulers of Mexico did not remain passive spectators. Always on the alert, Moctezuma dispatched spies to keep watch on the intruders' route. He had pictures of the Castilians painted, as much to know what they looked like and what sort of weapons they carried as to act from a distance on their representations. One has the impression of him in permanent session of a veritable 'crisis cabinet', kept informed on a daily basis by a series of reports of the progress of the new arrivals.[7] If we are to believe the chronicler Diego Durán, who gives a very European cast to things, the *tlatoani* ordered that the archives be consulted to search for precedents and to identify the new arrivals. This was not necessarily all loss, since the hypothesis of a 'return to the country', whether or not in the form of a return of Quetzalcoatl, would eventually pervade the minds of the Indians. In Mexico, the observations and tests continued once the army of Cortés was installed in the town. Everything suggests that Moctezuma was never unaware of anything that was going on; he was well informed about the arguments and the intentions of the Spanish even before their arrival and their encounter in Mexico.

The Spanish needed time: time to improve relations with their indigenous allies, time to rethink their use of the horse, which was effective but very exposed to the shots of the Indians, time to devise the relief and arming of a naval force on the Lake of Mexico, time to establish a link which would ensure a permanent supply of reinforcements by sea and time to make the paralysing efficacy of their brutal interventions felt.[8] All these advantages, taken together, were likely eventually to cause some of the Indian peoples to come over to their side. For the moment, the invaders were content to familiarize themselves with their surroundings; and also to ponder the possibility of a conquest.

The Deaths of the Two Emperors

When he learned, early in May 1520, that a Spanish fleet had left Cuba with the intention of arresting him, Cortés left Mexico, leaving most of his men behind. The risk was twofold: falling into the hands of the envoys of Diego Velázquez, on the one hand, abandoning his men to the mercy of the Mexicas on the other.

The threat from Cuba was soon dealt with. However, in Cortés's absence, Mexico rebelled. He had no sooner returned than the trap closed around him. He was dismayed: 'the greatest and most noble city of all the newly discovered part of the world would be lost, and with it all we had gained'.[9] It seems that it was in these circumstances that Moctezuma became the hostage and the prisoner of the Castilians. The Spanish then took refuge in their palace, which had been turned into a fortress, with 3,000 Tlaxcaltec allies. The Mexicas tried to starve them into submission. Projectiles rained down on the Europeans. Eighty men were wounded on the first day of the attack, including the captain. So hostilities had broken out in the middle of the town even before the conquest had begun. Cortés tried hard to make use of Moctezuma by getting him to persuade the Indians to lay down their arms, but he soon lost this, his best, weapon: according to the European sources, the *tlatoani* was seriously wounded by a stone and died three days later; according to the other camp, it was the Spaniards who executed him.

The leaders of the Mexican offensive then urged Cortés to leave the country immediately. The numerical superiority of the Mexicas was overwhelming and the situation appeared hopeless. A daytime retreat would be a catastrophe, a counter-attack suicidal: 'they had calculated that if 25,000 of them died for every one of us, they would finish with us first, for they were many and we were but few'.[10] All the intruders could do was flee during the course of a stormy and tempestuous night, sustaining huge losses: hundreds of Spaniards, 45 horses and 2,000 Indian 'friends' lost their lives. This was the disastrous episode to which posterity would give the name the *Noche Triste*.

Spurred on by the death of the *tlatoani*, the revolt of Mexico-Tenochtitlan marked a decisive turning point. The pro-war party had triumphed, and was determined this time to get rid of the foreigners whatever the cost. It was only now that the visitors were forced into a war without mercy.[11] It was not yet a war of conquest; rather it was a headlong flight, testimony to the state of unpreparedness and the military inferiority of the Spanish. Those who survived, and who had barely escaped annihilation, were far from having donned the mantle of conquerors. The battle had begun by turning in favour of the Indians.

In China, too, the death of the sovereign transformed the situation of the visitors, but for very different reasons. Zhengde died on 20 April 1521, of the after-effects of pneumonia. The Chinese administration lost no time. The deceased emperor's favourite, Jiang Bin, was disgraced, arrested and quickly executed along with his four sons. All the foreign envoys were expelled. We read in the *Shilu*: 'On that day...the barbarians who had paid tribute from Kumul, Turfan, Fo-lang-ki [the Portuguese] and other places were all recompensed, and instructed to return to their country'.[12] When the new emperor Jiajing entered the capital, on 27 May, Pires was no longer in Peking, which he had been forced to leave between 2 April and 21 May. The change of ruler had led to a change of policy, and the accumulated hostility against the dead emperor was given full rein. The cliques which congregated around the young heir – he was aged thirteen – set about purging the imperial entourage and erasing all trace of the preceding reign. The 'House of the Leopards', where Zhengde had liked to stay, was closed when the ambassadors regarded as having enjoyed too much favour were sent away. However, unlike the other envoys, Tomé Pires alone left without either gift or honorific title.

The Portuguese ambassador had no idea what awaited him in Canton. In the spring of 1521, just when Pires had taken the road south, a flotilla of Portuguese ships loaded with pepper and sappan wood, under the command of Diogo Calvo, had entered the harbour of Tunmen (Tamão), where it appears to have unloaded its cargo without incident. The retaliatory measures taken in February by the Minister of Rites, which included a ban on any foreign ship approaching the Chinese coast, had not yet extended to Canton. Portuguese ships continued to frequent Tunmen in the early summer. The Chinese fleet mounted a blockade. Some Portuguese who were in Canton, including Vasco Calvo, were arrested. In June, Duarte Coelho forced the blockade of Tunmen with a strongly armed junk and another vessel chartered by the merchants of Malacca. The *haido* (admiral) of the province, Wang Hung, decided to launch an attack, but the Portuguese artillery repelled his forces.

The battle had already dragged on for forty days when two other Portuguese ships appeared, which managed to escape the Chinese and return to Tunmen. It was here that, on 7 September 1521, the decision was made to leave. Taking advantage of darkness, the Portuguese fleet left its mooring. In the small hours, the Chinese caught up with it and battle commenced. The Portuguese escaped disaster only thanks to a terrible storm. This was their first *Noche Triste*. They managed eventually to reach open sea and fled from China, as the Castilians had fled from Mexico the previous year. They reached Malacca at the end of October. It was soon after this that the embassy of Tomé Pires reached Canton. It was immediately placed under surveillance.

Since August 1521 the Chinese of Canton had been afraid that the new arrivals might come to the aid of Pires and his company.

> At this moment, [the authorities of Guangdong] drew up another report stating that, among the seagoing ships, there was some whose [occupants] said they were [people] of the kingdom of the Fo-lang-ki who had come to assist the ambassador [Tomé Pires] with clothes and provisions, and [the authorities] demanded that they pay taxes in accord with the regulations applicable to the foreign merchandise which these people were carrying.

The matter was submitted to the Minister of Rites, who replied:

> The Fo-lang-ki are not a kingdom which [is allowed] to come to the court and offer tribute. What is more, they have invaded a neighbouring [country] whose king had received the investiture from China; they had behaved violently and broken the law; they brought merchandise for the purpose of trade, and gave the false pretext of coming to the aid [of their ambassador]. Further, the feelings of the barbarians are unfathomable; if they stay for a long time, they might well engage in

espionage. It would be prudent to instruct the Mandarins responsible for surveillance to expel them all, without allowing them to go any deeper into the country. In future, if barbarians from overseas arrive on agreed dates to offer tribute, they should pay taxes as laid down in the regulations. As for those who do not submit to the verifications or who come with merchandise other than on agreed dates, all relations with them should be broken off.[13]

Peking recommended responding to the appeal for help from the Malay ambassador, but without sending the Chinese fleet. Malacca should be restored to its ruler with the assistance of Siam and the neighbouring countries.

So when he reached Canton at the end of September, or even late August 1521, Tomé Pires found an extremely tense situation. There are suggestions in the sources that some women helped to enliven another period of enforced inactivity. Pires was effectively a hostage in Cantonese hands. The Chinese had decided to subject him to some diplomatic blackmail: they demanded that he negotiate the return of Malacca to its legitimate sovereign. For the Malays, who had sent an embassy to Peking, had also been sent back to Canton. They arrived with an official letter to be handed to Pires, intended for the king of Portugal, with a copy for the governor of Malacca. The letter was presented to Pires in October 1522. It demanded the restoration of Malacca to its legitimate ruler. The threats, the tone and the reflections of the Minister for Rites reveal the mistrust now felt for the intruders: 'The land of the Franges [Portuguese] must be a pretty small place close to the sea and, since the world had been the world, an ambassador from that country had never arrived in the land of China'.[14] The Chinese authorities were not content with closing the door. They called for the destruction of the fort of the *Ilha de Mercadoria* (Tunmen) and the departure of the Portuguese from Malacca. They demanded to know exactly how many Portuguese there were in Malacca, Cochin and Ceylon. And in order to get a better idea of the capacity of the enemy and deprive them of any technical or military superiority, they even instructed the Portuguese to build 'galleys' and manufacture gunpowder and bombards.[15] Pires refused to enter into a negotiation for which he had no mandate.

The Second Portuguese Disaster

In the meantime, a new Portuguese fleet, consisting of five ships and one junk from Malacca, under the leadership of Afonso de Melo

Coutinho, had arrived in Tunmen in August 1522. He had been forbidden, however, to trade or to communicate with Tomé Pires. During August, Melo Coutinho tried to take by force the headquarters of the Chinese forces in Nanto (Nan-t'eou). An indecisive battle began. The Portuguese managed to resist the dozens of fighting junks for a while, but were eventually overwhelmed by sheer force of numbers. They finally withdrew after fourteen days of combat, having suffered heavy losses in men and ships.[16]

> [The first year of Jiajing] they finally ravaged the Bay of Si-ts'ao. The 'Commander of defensive measures against the Japanese' and the po-hou [centurion] Wang Ying-ngen led the offensive. A man of Hiang-houa [a garrison], P'an Ting-keou, was the first aboard; the rest followed; forty-two men were taken alive, including Pie-tou-lou and Chou-che-li, thirty-five heads were cut off [as well] and two ships [of the Fo-lang-ki] were seized. Those who remained of the bandits [the Portuguese] brought three more ships which resumed the battle. [Wang] Ying-ngen died fighting. These bandits were defeated and fled. The imperial troops obtained their cannon, which were named *fo-lang-ki*. The *fou-che* [commander of the fleet of Guangdong] Wang Hong had them brought to the court.[17]

According to another Chinese source:[18]

> the *haidao* Wang Hong [wanted] to drive [the Portuguese] out with troops; but they refused to leave and, on the contrary, using their cannon, they attacked and defied our troops. From that moment, our men watched them from a distance, fearing them, and dared not approach. Someone suggested a means, that is, to send good swimmers who, entering the water, would pierce and sink the [Portuguese] ships, and capture all on board. Wang Hong, as a result, was recommended for [more senior] posts.[19]

The Chinese fleet had clearly suffered one or more setbacks before resorting to this stratagem.[20]

On the Portuguese side, Vieira appraised this second disaster: one ship had exploded, another had been scuttled, two others, those of Diogo de Melo and Pedro Homem, had been captured and some forty Portuguese had fallen into enemy hands.[21] The wounded were summarily executed as soon as they arrived on the Chinese ships: 'Because their wounds and their fetters made them cry out, they cut off their heads on the junks'.[22] The Chinese sources also emphasize the capture of a foreign '*fo-lang-ki* named *Pie-toulou*', that is, Pedro Homem, who in reality had escaped since he died in the naval battle. It seems that the victors resorted to the ruse of presenting one of the Portuguese as the ambassador so as to magnify their victory.[23]

For Vieira and his companions in misfortune, 14 August 1522, with the arrival of Melo, was the day the expedition turned into a nightmare. The members of the Portuguese embassy who were held in Canton were thrown into prison. Exposed to the vengeance of the Chinese administration, mandarins, soldiers and eunuchs, they endured all sorts of mental and physical ordeals: 'our arms are swollen and our legs skinned by the tight chains'. Vieira recorded their calvary and kept count of the dead. Many of the prisoners died of hunger and cold.[24] The women who had accompanied the expedition were sold into slavery.

In December 1522 the judges of Canton issued a final sentence: 'The petty sea robbers sent by the great robber have come treacherously to spy out our country'. The intruders were nothing but robbers and their merchandise stolen goods, 'the booty of bandits'. In the following spring an edict set a date for the execution of the prisoners. On 23 September the sentences were carried out. The Portuguese were led through the principal streets of the town and suburbs of Canton before being executed by crossbow bolts. 'These twenty-three men were cut into pieces, for each one the head, the arms, the legs, the genitals placed in their mouths and the trunk cut in two at the level of the belly'. In his letter Vieira lists one by one the Portuguese, African and Indian victims of the Chinese; he describes the nature of the punishment administered and records the number of deaths and the cruelties inflicted with an indignation that is almost comical when one remembers the brutality with which the Iberians customarily behaved in territory they conquered or visited. The Asian and Chinese collaborators suffered a similar fate, including the crews of the junks which had brought the Portuguese to Canton: 'Many died from drowning or blows or hunger suffered in prison'. Some Siamese were beheaded and their bodies impaled for having brought Portuguese prisoners into China.[25]

The Chinese authorities banked on the spectacular nature of the executions making an impression on the crowds and discouraging any collaboration with the foreigners:

> So that everybody would see them, those in Canton and those in the country, to make them understand they should not deal with the Portuguese and so that people would not speak of the Portuguese ... Their heads and their genitals were taken, carried by the Portuguese in front of the mandarins of Canton, exhibited in the middle of dances and rejoicings, hung up in the streets and then thrown into the rubbish,

and it has since been agreed that no more Portuguese would be accepted in this country nor any other foreigner.

How better to instil in the minds of the people of Canton and its environs the idea that the Portuguese were a filthy crew, from an insignificant country? Or provoke the xenophobia of the crowds since, in the eyes of the educated Chinese, every foreigner was a savage and a 'barbarian' *(fan-ren)*.[26] As a result, dozens of Portuguese who ventured onto the Chinese coast were beaten up and executed. In 1523, or perhaps May 1524, Pires, too, was probably executed. The Chinese sources refer to the killing of the 'arch criminal' Huo-chê Ya-san.[27] Even today, the fate of Tomé Pires remains shrouded in mystery, as there is a tradition that he escaped execution, was exiled and died in a town in the interior of the Empire.

In their misery, the Portuguese of Canton were still careful to distinguish between those responsible for their crushing defeat, the mandarins of Canton, and the imperial authorities:

> Thanks to these goods and to those of the five junks, the mandarins were greatly enriched; these robbers have no longer been in Canton for a long time now, they have been sent into other provinces as is the custom, now they have been elevated into dignitaries of the kingdom.[28]

The victims insisted on the local nature of the plot, and denounced a scandalous denial of justice: 'This is not justice, this is the justice of three thieving mandarins'.[29] It was a diplomatic way of minimizing the affront to the Crown of Portugal, of exercising tact with regard to Peking and, finally, of not recognizing the scale and the radical nature of the Chinese reaction.

In any case, the Portugal of John III, who had succeeded to the throne in 1521, lost interest. The new king abandoned the universal ambitions of his father and made no attempt to retaliate. He preferred to concentrate his efforts east of Malacca and strengthen the Portuguese presence in the Moluccas. In 1524 he ordered the construction of a fortress in Sonde to respond to a new danger, 'that the Castilians might seize this territory, knowing that there were large quantities of pepper there'.[30]

The Revenge of the Castilians

Cortés's expedition did not end with his *Noche Triste*. Unlike the Chinese, the Mexicas had not had the satisfaction of ridding themselves of all their enemies. But, though Cortés escaped a disaster like that suffered in Canton, it was by the skin of his teeth and at the cost of heavy human losses and the humiliation of a *Noche Triste* when the conquistadors had been forced into a headlong flight, drenched to the skin, coated in mud and soaked in blood. The contrast between events in China and Mexico was not as great as all that. It is mistaken to oppose Chinese lucidity and resourcefulness to Mexican unawareness and naiveté, or the unflagging determination of the mandarins to the prevarication of the Mexica leaders. The Chinese and Mexican reactions were less different than might be supposed. They were equally complex and equally violent in both cases. The violence of the Indians – bodies slaughtered, sacrificed and devoured before the eyes of their peers – had its counterpart in the quartered bodies of the prisoners of Canton. The Spanish had been within a hair's breadth of disappearing from the historical scene, like Pires and his men and the soldiers of the two Portuguese fleets, massacred by the Mexicas. Nevertheless, the Mexican and Chinese responses were not equally effective, and it is the brutalities of the Spanish which have been remembered by posterity.

Once he had left Mexico, the wounded Cortés retreated with his men and his horses on the point of exhaustion. The Indians harried this band of wounded warriors who 'believed that it was [their] last day'.[31] It was a miracle that the Tlaxcaltec allies did not turn against what remained of the Spanish troops to 'regain their former liberty'. On the contrary, these indigenous peoples remained faithful to their new ally. It was at this moment that Cortés chose to embark on the conquest of Mexico – what he called 'the pacification of the country' – rather than dig in on the coast in the hope that help would arrive, and present his project as the recovery of 'the great city of Temixtitan, and...the other provinces which are subject thereto'.

If he was not to appear a traitor who had fled the field, Cortés had to be punishing an Indian revolt which had broken out 'for no good reason'. The war, therefore, was triply justified in his eyes: legitimate self-defence – 'to protect our lives'; recovery of what had been lost; and the battle against barbarity and idolatry. The introduction of the notions of propagating the faith and battling against barbarity completed an argument which managed to combine every aspect of colonial imperialism. And as if that were not enough, Cortés added the notion of just vengeance and the settling of accounts: the enemy were not an innocent people who had been invaded, but rebellious vassals who had broken their word. The raison d'être and the Machiavellian nature of the way the arrival in Mexico had been presented now emerge more clearly: Moctezuma had to have handed his country over to the foreigners for the breaking of the ties to be presented as a 'great treachery'.[32]

Cortés was immoderate as always: facing the tens of thousands of Indians on the battlefield at Tlaxcala by a mere 'forty horse men and 550 foot soldiers, eighty of whom were crossbowmen and harquebusiers' with 'eight or nine field guns but very little powder'.[33] More than his weapons, men and horses, it was the support of several Indian lordships that gave Cortés the advantage over his adversaries. The 'pacification' of the settlements of the *altiplano* accustomed his army to Indian warfare and won over new groups, even from the enemy camp. It was negotiation as much as the success of his army that enabled Cortés to return and lay siege to Mexico.

The operation was carefully planned and prepared. It had the benefit of an unexpected ally: the epidemic of smallpox which erupted after the expulsion of the Spanish from Mexico-Tenochtitlan (June 1520). It was probably not decisive in their victory, because the sickness affected the conquistador's indigenous 'friends' equally badly, but it made a huge impact on the Mexicas.[34] The construction of a fleet of brigantines proved a masterstroke. It gave a high degree of mobility to the Spanish artillery. This was a decisive factor, even against the Chinese, as the Portuguese of the Pearl River Delta realized.

Mexico-Tenochtitlan fell in August 1521, when Tomé Pires, having been dismissed, had embarked on the interminable road back to Canton. It was not so much the relative superiority of the Spanish as the political fragmentation of the Mesoamerican world that decided the fate of this part of the globe. To which must be added its extreme immune fragility faced with the pathologies originating in the Eurasian part of the world. Not a hardened empire, lacking a bacteriological shield, the people of Mexico would never succeed in getting rid of their visitors.

The Clash of Civilizations

The fall of Mexico and the disintegration of the Indian societies seem self-evident today, and the fact that the first encounters went badly for the Spanish gets forgotten. The chronicler Díaz del Castillo had terrible memories of the expedition of 1517: 'Oh, how painful it is to discover new lands, and especially to do it in the way we did! It is impossible to understand unless you have endured terrible ordeals'.[35] Hernán Cortés, with his 500 men and score of horses, plus 100 sailors,[36] faced the Indian populations of Mexico who numbered some 20,000,000. This was fewer than the 150,000,000 of Ming China, but still a huge number. In one of those *pesées globales* – or 'weighings-up of the world' – of which he was a master, Pierre Chaunu pointed out that Middle America had as many people as North China, and that the America of the High Plateaus as a whole, with its Andean and Mesoamerican 'empires', as many as the whole of China.[37] The immoderation I have often remarked on here is in part explained by this massive difference. It characterizes the whole of this history, which provides one of the most spectacular and most dramatic examples of the collision of worlds; and of a collision that ended in a clear victory for the Europeans.

What the West chiefly remembers of this clash of civilizations is its brutality: the Spanish, far inferior numerically, went on the rampage against the Indians, who needed time to get used to fighting warriors on horseback, breathing the smell of gunpowder and hearing the thunder of cannon. The black legend puts so much emphasis on the cruelty of the Castilians that it overlooks the ferocity with which numerous indigenous societies resisted the conquistadors. It exaggerates the rapidity of the conquest, forgetting its slow start, makeshift nature and failures. The fall of the city of Mexico, in August 1521, did not immediately sound the death knell of the pre-Hispanic world and herald the birth of Spanish Mexico. It was generations before the country was Hispanicized and Westernized. The settlers had to face much resistance and many hardships. Added to which, the frequency of intermarriage had unexpected and unpredictable results, which would prevent the local societies from sinking into oblivion or turning into clones of settlements in Castile.

Nevertheless, it remains the case that the seizure of the Mexica capital marked the beginning of the long process of capturing the American continent which would attach this part of the world to the Iberian, European and then Western camp for centuries. By this fact, it was a continental event. But it was more: the conquest of Mexico was a crucial stage in Iberian globalization; it began the integration of the societies of the American continent into a Spanish Empire which extended into the four quarters of the globe. It was also part of a race to the Asia of China and spices, and by this fact, too, an event of global significance.

Many reasons have been advanced for the collapse of the Indian societies: the diplomacy of Cortés, skilled in exploiting divisions among the enemy and his own men; his pragmatism; the superiority of Spanish weapons; and above all the first ravages of the illnesses brought from Europe. Iron got the better of copper, before a missionary and destabilizing Christianity devoted itself to the destruction of the routine of the ancient idolatries and the establishment of new ones. These are all good reasons, which we may also observe in operation in other parts of the American continent in subsequent decades.

Compared with the brilliance of the conquest of Mexico, the embassy of Tomé Pires can seem a sorry affair, even a non-event. It is an episode forgotten by world historiography, known, at the very most, to the narrow circle of historians of Portuguese Asia. Not only was the embassy a fiasco, but it seems to have had no consequences. There was no effective penetration of China, no conquest or colonization, even less Christianization, certainly nothing comparable to the massive impact of Iberian globalization. Perhaps the West only remembers the clashes which succeeded, like those in the Americas.

How are we to explain such contrary fates, apart from the contexts outlined above? Differences in the men and in the national images come at once to mind. Tomé Pires, royal factor, merchant and acute observer of the business world, was no Hernán Cortés, that turbulent spirit, happy warrior and skilful politician. Added to which, the Castilians are traditionally seen as born conquistadors and the Portuguese as traders. Yet there are many features common to both nations: a love of discovery and a thirst for wealth, incontestable mastery of the sea, the ability to overcome significant numerical inferiority, the effectiveness of their weapons, the support of rear-guard bases (Cuba as well as Malacca) and even the presence of exceptional warriors. Albuquerque, conqueror of Goa, Malacca and Ormuz, who has been compared to the great captains of Antiquity, was the equal of Cortés.[38] And there is another, more surprising, point in common: the letters of Vieira and Calvo reveal that the Portuguese, too, had the intention of conquering and colonizing a part of China, which was where, in the event, they were caught in a trap.

The Portuguese attempts to approach China were rendered null by the Chinese reaction. If we are to explain such contrasting fates, we need to look also for differences in the adversaries and terrains. The Portuguese were paralysed, reduced to silence and then destroyed. They were never able to gain control of the situation created by their landing, whereas one gets the impression that it was the contradictions in the Mesoamerican world that catapulted the conquistadors into the forefront of American history.

8

Naming the Others

Where had the visitors to China come from? Their weapons suggested to the educated Chinese the hypothesis of an Asiatic origin. According to the *Yue-chan ts'ong-t'an*:

> the kingdom of the Fo-lang-ki is to the south of the Kingdom of Java. These two kingdoms use firearms of a similar form, but the firearms of the Fo-lang-ki are large, those of Java are small. The people of the country use them with great skill, and with the small ones they can kill a sparrow. When the Chinese use them, if they are not careful, they take off several fingers, or cut off a hand or an arm. Firearms should be long; if they are short, they do not shoot far. The bore has to be round and smooth; if it is bent or rough, the projectile does not leave straight. Only the people of Tong-kouan make them of the same design as the foreigners (*fan-ren*); those that are made elsewhere are often [too] short, and unusable.[1]

A Strange Forgetfulness

To seek a Javanese origin for the Fo-lang-ki was surely to display a remarkable amnesia. Europeans, and not only Marco Polo, had visited China from the thirteenth century until the beginning of the fifteenth. In the fourteenth century, the pope had even sent an embassy from Avignon to the court of the Great Khan of Cathay, led by the Franciscan Giovanni de Marignolli; it had arrived in May or June 1342. The Chinese annals remember the great horses brought as a present from the *Fou-lang*. When the *Yuan che* refers to Marignolli's

delegation, it calls the country from which the papal envoys had come
Fou-lang. Early in the next century there is a reference in the Ming
annals on Calicut[2] to double-edged sabres that are called *fou-lang*.
In spite of this written evidence, memories of these direct or indirect
contacts seem to have faded by the beginning of the sixteenth century.
The collection of Ming ordinances says nothing about the country of
the foreigners or about an earlier visit. Nor is there anything in the
reports of the expeditions of the admiral Zheng He (1371–1433),
who had reached the coast of East Africa. It is no wonder the Chinese
authorities were perplexed.

So it was by attaching the name of their cannon to the foreigners
that the Chinese authorities baptized them Fo-lang-ki. They gave
them a name whose Arabic and Persian origins they had forgotten,
and which the Portuguese, familiar with the term, transcribed as
Franges or *Frangues*.[3] This is not to say that the Chinese were indifferent. The Chinese sources speculate at length as to the location of
the mysterious country: was the kingdom of the Fo-lang-ki situated
in the southwest of the Ocean, not far from Malacca? Or was it, as
suggested above, south of Java? Might it be a new name for the
country of Lambri, northwest of Sumatra, or for the country of P'o-
li?[4] Did the Fo-lang-ki come from islands populated by cannibals?
Thus, in China, instead of reviving the term *Fou-lang*, according to
tradition, to translate *Farangi* or *Frangi*, *Fo-lang* prevailed. It was
probably a phonetic transcription that caused *Fou-lang* to change
into *Fo-lang*. This was not without consequences, because *Fo* meant
Buddha and *Fo-lang* could also be understood as 'Boys of the Buddha'.
As the Buddha was originally from India, this interpretation was
appropriate for a people who had arrived from the west. The different
meanings given to *Fo-lang* both further obscured things and added
new dimensions: it was possible to read 'Boys of the Buddha', but
one could also hear 'Wolves of the Buddha', which was peculiarly
suited to a people renowned for their ferocity in battle.

Yet Peking was well informed about the Portuguese presence in
South-East Asia, especially their recent and violent settlement in
Malacca. To this was added the ubiquitous gaze of the Chinese diaspora, which at a very early date included one man who had left for
Lisbon. The junks which frequented the ports of South-East Asia and
got as far as the ports of India did not only carry merchandise. They
relayed news and rumours which the Muslim sailors spread from the
Indian Ocean to South-East Asia. And the followers of Islam who
frequented these seas had good reason to disseminate a sinister image
of their Christian rivals and warn their Chinese partners, who had
also often converted to Islam long ago.

For more substantial information about the Fo-lang-ki, we need to refer to the *Kouang-tong t'ong-tche* of 1535 and the *Hai-yu* of 1537, in the section devoted to Malacca. Later still, the history of the Ming Dynasty includes a brief historical notice:

> The Fo-lang-ki are close to *Man-la-kia* [Malacca]. Under Zhengde they settled on the territory of Malacca and expelled the king. In the thirteenth year they sent an ambassador *kia-pi-tan-mo*, with others, to offer in tribute products of their country and to request a seal of investiture. Their name was then known for the first time...These people hung around for a very long time without leaving, robbing travellers and even seizing little children so as to eat them.[5]

The appearance and physique of the foreigners was the subject of much comment. The Chinese sources describe the Portuguese as people who were 'seven foot high, [with] a long nose and a white colour and an oriole's beak',[6] or with 'a hooked nose and cats' eyes, curly beards and reddish hair'. Korean sources venture a comparison with their Japanese neighbours: 'These people, whose physiognomy recalls that of the Japanese, wear clothes and eat things which are not very civilized'.[7] It is all extremely vague. The Portuguese may have tried to impose the words 'Portugal' and 'Portuguese', possibly as early as 1534 and certainly in 1565, when they claimed to be called 'P'ou-tou-li-kia', but it made no difference.[8] They remained Fo-lang-ki, a name whose origin seemed of little interest to the educated Chinese.

Castilan! Castilan!

The commercial and diplomatic network all around China was in no way comparable to the meagre sources of information available to the societies of Central America. Nevertheless, by 1517, that is, by the time of the first encounter, the Iberians were called by their name: it was with cries of 'Castilan! Castilan!' that the Maya of Yucatán received the Europeans, asking them if they came from the place where the sun rose.[9]

From the beginning, the invaders were given an origin and a name, and this time it really was their name, *Castellanos*. As the conquistadors had to say this name frequently in Indian hearing, it was no doubt one of the first words of Spanish that the latter had reason to remember. The attention they paid to everything would later make a deep impression on the Franciscan chronicler Motolinía: 'These people watch and are remarkably observant'.[10] *Castellano*, which became, in Nahuatl, *Caxtilan*, was systematically used to indicate the foreign origin of the animals and objects introduced by the Spanish: a horse was called *Caxtillan mazatl* ('Castile deer'), a European ship was a *Caxtillan acalli* ('Castile boat') and similarly with paper, which became *iztac Caxtillan amatl* ('white Castile paper').[11] This is not to say that the Indians had any idea what the country they were told about was like: *Castilan* was for them as vague as 'Frank' was for the Chinese and Malays. In the Mesoamerican world, you did not belong to a country or a continent but to a city state, the *altepetl*, such as Tlaxcala or Mexico-Tenochtitlan.[12] Thus *Castilan* referred to a hypothetical place which bore this name. In fact this idea was by no means foreign to the Iberians, who frequently identified themselves by their place of origin: Cortés was first and foremost a man from Medellín. However, the name *Castilan* was also associated with the East, with the Orient and the rising of the sun. This could suggest a superhuman origin. That the Portuguese passed in China for people of the West (= of the Buddha) and the Spanish in Mexico for sons of the East is striking testimony to the pincer movement the Iberians were then trying to execute on the world.

At the time of the discovery of Mexico, Europeans had already been present in the Caribbean for some twenty years. There may have been sporadic contacts between the coasts of Mexico and Central America and the Antilles, as shown by the travels of the Indian from Jamaica who was found by the Spanish on the Mexican coast, and who acted as an interpreter for them. There were certainly rumours in circulation regarding the presence in the Caribbean islands of unknown visitors, their huge ships and, no doubt, their predatory habits. In 1502 Columbus had met off Honduras a boat as long as a galley, laden with merchandise and with Indians who covered their bodies and faces 'in the fashion of the Moors of Granada'.[13] This encounter had made a deep impression on Columbus, but probably an even deeper one on the passengers in the Maya boat. This may explain the intuitions of the pilot Alaminos, confided to Hernandez of Cordoba, a friend of Las Casas: 'As for this western sea, below the island of Cuba, he had a feeling that there must be some very rich country there'. Further, shipwrecked Spaniards washed up on the beaches of Yucatán, where they had been reduced to slavery, must have had many opportunities to tell their masters about their compatriots. As for the Mayans who had seized them, they in their turn had had plenty of time to observe the strengths and weaknesses of those they had not sacrificed. The Europeans who had survived had become more or less Indianized, so much so that one of the shipwrecked Spaniards preferred to remain on the indigenous coast and employ his knowledge in the service of the battle against the invaders.[14]

However, information did not circulate only along the coasts of the Gulf of Mexico and the Yucatán Peninsula. It is likely that the people of Mexico-Tenochtitlan had received news from the eastern sea by the beginning of the sixteenth century. Political and commercial links meant that goods, persons and news from the dependent lordships or the turbulent lands that gave onto the Gulf of Mexico and the Caribbean Sea penetrated deep into the country. Powerful Nahua merchants, the *pochtecas*, conducted a long-distance trade which brought them into contact with the Mayan peoples and the tropical coasts. We know they took advantage of this to spy on behalf of the Triple Alliance and that they were close to those in power. The speed with which Moctezuma was informed of events on the coast of the Gulf when the fleet of Narváez arrived there testifies to the efficiency of the information networks of the Triple Alliance.

It is the loss of the indigenous sources and the Indian and colonial rewriting of history that has created the impression that the Spanish invasion took the local societies by surprise, with the result that they crumbled under the double shock of the unexpected and the unpredictable. This could also, of course, help to explain their inexplicable defeat and minimize the errors made in dealing with the conquistadors.

Lastly, even if there had been no shipwrecked sailors on the Mexican coasts, the expedition of Cortés hardly came like a bolt from the blue. It followed two earlier attempts (1517–18), which had given the Indians the time and the means to appreciate the threat which hung over them, and hence to prepare. When the soldiers of Cortés landed on Mexican soil, they did not suddenly emerge from nowhere, and they generally got the reception they deserved.

Barbarians or Pirates?

Fo-lang-ki, Castilan: in both China and Mexico, the other who came from elsewhere, the alien, that is, the Iberian, thus received a name. However, these names defining a people and a region, quite apart from the fact that they remained extremely opaque, represented only one element and one stage in a much more complex process of identification. This did not proceed with the same urgency in each case. For the Chinese, the Fo-lang-ki were only one set of unrefined visitors among others, whereas the Indians of Mexico felt a pressing need to understand the aggressor who had invaded them, and who would soon crush and then transform them. Indeed, it can be argued that the Mesoamerican societies seem always to have retained a place for the other, which would explain why it was so much more difficult for them to close ranks and protect themselves than for the Celestial Empire.

For the Chinese and the Mexicans, the Portuguese and the Spanish incarnated the unknown and the mysterious. Their nature and the meaning of their arrival were much debated. They were also interpreted in ways which give the impression of matching each other when they tried to make of the sudden arrival of the foreigners a long foretold and deeply dangerous event. For the Mexicans, the Spanish might be the descendants of an exiled prince who had come to reclaim his own.[15] For the Chinese, traditions of obscure origin put them on their guard against a predicted invasion which would destroy their country.

Other reactions derived from the store of beliefs and experience in each country. In China, no one knew where precisely the Portuguese had come from and no one remembered the Europeans who, centuries before, had visited the Empire of the Yuan, the predecessors of the Ming. It was decades before the veil would be lifted on the mysterious origin of the Fo-lang-ki. However, there was another form of knowledge that was acquired through direct experience of and familiarity with the intruders. In the eyes of the Chinese, as Vieira and Calvo explained, the Portuguese belonged to the category of foreigners; hence they were savages (*fan-ren*). Savages, as far as the Portuguese could tell, meant those who did not belong to 'God's land', and who therefore 'knew neither God nor land'.[16] This word – *fan-ren* – was also used for a criminal, a delinquent, a culprit, who desecrated, infringed and transgressed. The Portuguese were men like the Chinese, but of an inferior and disreputable species, rather as the *barbaroi* had been for the Greeks, who accused them of bestial practices, in particular eating human foetuses.[17] Cruel, ferocious and intellectually inferior; a whole string of denigratory adjectives belittled the foreigner and strengthened their conviction of an innate superiority.

Paradoxically, faced with an attitude like this, the Portuguese were on familiar ground. They and the Chinese were alike in feeling a deep distrust for people who lived outside their own world, whether Christian or sinicized; except that in this case it was the Iberians who were the barbarians, and the others who saw them as from an inferior world. This was hardly a novel situation for the Portuguese of Asia. They were constantly encountering societies that were comparable with their own, when they were not in many ways superior, in power or in capacities. The sailors of Lisbon shared the precarious fate of travelling people; they were everywhere transitory unknowns, often put in a difficult situation or a position of inferiority, especially by their Muslim rivals.

The Portuguese were barbarians, therefore, but barbarians in possession of certain assets. However uncivilized they were in Chinese eyes, they were also people who sailed in swift boats and were equipped with massive firepower, hence capable of deploying sophisticated technologies in the military sphere. Were they beyond redemption? In Canton the visitors had been instructed in Chinese customs and the emperor had viewed their errors indulgently. However, their image grew steadily worse as the Chinese got to know them better.

When they landed, the terrible reputation of the sailors of Lisbon had preceded them. The authorities in Canton and then Peking knew that they had seized Malacca in 1511 and that they had behaved like petty tyrants on the Chinese coast. Even in Peking, the Portuguese, badly brought up and arrogant, had proved unbearable: 'They wrangled about the right of precedence'.[18] The Malay ambassador at the court of Peking, Tuan Muhammed, did not pull his punches: 'The *Franges* thieves came to Malacca full of energy and in large numbers, they seized the land, they destroyed and killed many people, they robbed some and took others prisoner, and the survivors were totally dominated by the Franges.'[19] The mandarins would demand that Malacca be returned to its legitimate lord, pointing out that this country was under Chinese protection.

The Malays were not the only ones to air their grievances. Censors from the Canton region complained to the Minister of Rites. The intruders faced a barrage of criticism.[20] These foreigners had not paid taxes on the merchandise they had landed on the island of Tunmen, off Canton; they had prevented the men from Siam from paying taxes and barred their access to trade; they had captured and sequestered the junks of other merchants; they maintained many armed men and bombards. They had even carried out an execution to maximum publicity. The Portuguese presence was shockingly visible: 'They had a stone fortress with a tiled roof, surrounded by artillery and well stocked with weapons'. Perceived as threatening strangers, the new arrivals deceived no one. They were spies who had come to settle on the land of other people, as shown by the famous *padrões*, the dressed stones which the sailors from Lisbon erected everywhere they went. The judgement of the Chinese authorities was damning: 'They were robbers' and murderers. The Fo-lang-ki were not only barbarians, then, but also pirates and spies,[21] according to the sentences pronounced against them in December 1522. The executions and the fate meted out to Tomé Pires could hardly have further degraded the Portuguese. Yet the condemnation would go further.

Nevertheless, in spite of all these accusations, justified or not, for the Chinese who wanted to grow rich with the aid of new commercial partners, the 'barbarous foreigners' were valuable and necessary interlocutors with whom one could do business. On the one hand was the official discourse, the reasoning of learned men rigid in their convictions, and the xenophobic propaganda designed to justify the closure of the country; on the other, the generally accepted interests of numerous commercial lobbies and of the unfortunate people who were dependent on trade with the foreigners for a living.

Divine Monsters

It was the same in Mexico. The groups who wanted to manipulate the Spanish intervention did not see the Castilians in the same light as the Mexicas anxious to get rid of them at all costs. It is difficult to know what the first indigenous reactions were. Who were these Spanish who had suddenly appeared on the coast? Were they men, people like the Indians, *tlacatl*? Or common people, *macehualli*? Or people of high birth, lords, once again *tlacatl*? Were they all-powerful forces, as it were like Huitzilopochtli or Ehecatl, in which case it was then again the word *tlacatl* that should be used?[22] Another word was preferred, which distanced the new arrivals from Indian humanity. Just as the indigenous peoples of the Antilles had taken the sailors to be people who had come from heaven, and before the Peruvians likened them to the *viracocha*, the ancient Mexicans made their inconvenient visitors into divine creatures.

According to the European and Indian sources, the Spanish were taken for 'gods', *teteo*, rendered as *teules* in Castilian. The Indians likened them to supernatural creatures, or creatures from a super-natural space, hence to potentially dangerous visitors from a world over which the indigenous peoples, as 'inhabitants of the surface of the Earth', had in principle no control. Even the weapons of magic to which the Mexicas resorted proved ineffective. In a society which paid great attention to reverential forms, the register of the divine settled a question left unclear by the novelty of the situation: *teotl* – *teteo* in the plural – provided an elegant way of addressing creatures who had no place in the local hierarchies because they were not part of the indigenous society. How else to speak to these creatures who could not be treated as 'natural' lords than by calling them *teules*?

Logically, the divine Spanish were housed in sanctuaries which the Indians called *teocalli*, 'god-house', or *teopan*, 'where a God is'.[23]

Teotl refers to an Amerindian conception of the divine of which our words 'God' and 'divinity' convey only a very approximate version. Some of the Spanish realized at an early stage that *teotl* could mean both 'God' and 'Devil'. This word was also used to indicate disturbing powers, whose behaviour was unpredictable and uncontrollable, and was even applied to the human beings deemed to incarnate them on earth in rituals and celebrations. The chronicler Bernal Díaz del Castillo tells a story which illustrates how well the conquistadors had learned to exploit this double meaning. So as to impress the Indians, Cortés decided to send the horrible Heredia, a blind Basque with a limp, a repulsive heavily scarred face and a long beard, with instructions to fire his musket off several times in the woods. He explained: 'I am doing this so they will believe we are gods, or so we live up to the name and reputation they have given us, and as you have an ugly mug, they will believe you are an idol'.[24] A *teotl* was also a candidate for human sacrifice, a 'divinized' victim, ready for eating. The Indians who were lucky enough to capture Spaniards would certainly have remembered this.

For the Mexicans, the foreign invasion actually happened, whereas for the Chinese it remained only a fantasy or an abortive attempt. In Mexico the visitors settled in for the long term. They were not people who could be expelled or physically eliminated. So it had to be said what these 'gods' had come to seek on Indian soil; and even to end up by presenting their invasion as an event both predicted and inevitable so as to explain the sequence of mistakes, errors of judgement and indecision that had led to the defeat. The attitude and words attributed to Moctezuma by Cortés in November 1519 express resignation and abdication in the face of the fulfilment of destiny in a way that is rather too sudden to be wholly credible. Nevertheless, they prefigure the arguments made necessary by the fall of Mexico and the occupation of New Spain, once it had become essential to provide a meaning for the invasion and a justification for the defeat.[25]

Once victorious and masters of the country, the invaders gradually passed from the category of *teules* to that of *tecuhtli*, or lords. This was sometimes against their will, as the missionaries recalled: 'Some foolish Spanish were offended, they complained and waxed indignant against us, saying that we had taken away their name... and they did not realize, poor wretches, that they had usurped a name which belonged only to God'.[26] Until then they had been delighted with the name they had been given, which they had made their own and which they had Hispanicized as *teules*. The word continued in use for many years, before colonization finally brought the invaders of Mexico back to earth.

Hell is Other People

The Indians of the New World were barbarians – on this point the Europeans were as categorical as were the Chinese with regard to the Portuguese. The Portuguese did not use the word 'savage' or 'barbarian' of the Chinese, but the Spanish freely used both adjectives of the Indian peoples of America, thus justifying the regime to which they proposed to subject them.

Since Antiquity we, that is, the Greeks, the Romans, the Christians, the Europeans and then Westerners in general, have been in the habit of calling other peoples 'barbarians'. For the Greeks the gulf was one of language and lifestyles, for the Christians one of religion, for the Europeans of the Renaissance and the Enlightenment one of technical, military and cultural inferiority, with race successfully breathing new life into this distinction in the nineteenth century. The word 'barbarian' became such an all-purpose word that it could be applied even to Europeans as, for example, when Machiavelli denounced the intrusion of foreigners onto the soil of his homeland.

During the course of the sixteenth century, in the wake of Iberian globalization, Europeans found themselves face to face with most of the great civilizations of the planet and with myriads of people who had long been described as primitive. In the New World the Spanish and the Portuguese both used and abused the word 'barbarian' (whereas they generally presented themselves as *cristianos*),[27] introducing distinctions which were more than just stylistic exercises because they influenced the relations between the colonizers and the colonized.

On the Spanish side, the debate developed throughout the first half of the sixteenth century; it involved jurists such as Juan López de Palacios Rubios, theologians such as Francisco de Vitoria, humanists such as Ginés de Sepulveda and the major figure of the Dominican Bartolomé de Las Casas. Were the Indians of the Caribbean slaves by nature because they were barbarians? Where should one place the Indians of Mexico and Peru, whose towns, trade, crafts and religions displayed so many marks of civilization, but whose many deplorable practices – human sacrifice, cannibalism, even sodomy – consigned them to barbarity? Were the Indians of America men who were still children, and thus in need of more education? Or were they subhuman, *homunculi* destined to labour in the service of civilized people? The discovery of America provided not only situations in need of urgent resolution but food for thought over the longer term, whether it be to criticize the notion of barbarity as unjust or too vague, or to adapt or refine it on the basis of experience on the other side of the Atlantic. The debate had its high points, such as the junta of Burgos, in 1512, which saw the first attempts to define the rights and obligations of the Indians; the discovery of the civilizations of Mexico in 1517; the teaching of the Dominican Vitoria at Salamanca between 1526 and 1539; and the controversy between Las Casas and Sepulveda in 1550.

The Chinese were absent from this debate. They appeared in the writings of Las Casas, but only under the name by which they were known in Antiquity – the 'Seres' – and on the basis of information dating back to this distant period.

Naming the Indigenous Peoples

Both the Chinese and the Mexicans tried hard to name their visitors. They in their turn had to face up to the same problem. The term 'barbarian' did not win universal acceptance, but the word 'Indian' was settled on from the beginning, and once and for all. The Spanish needed to name the natives of the New World, which they did in the conviction that Asia was nearby, long before they realized they had discovered a new continent. 'Indians' prevailed, therefore, as if the populations discovered by Columbus belonged to one of the Indies of the Ancients. In fact the Greeks had not invented anything either. The name India derived from a word in ancient Persian, Sindhi, which indicated the Indus. The word passed from Greek to Latin.

While they recycled a classical word that might equally well have been applied to those who lived on the shores of the Indian Ocean, the Spanish learned of the existence of the Chins from the Portuguese. The latter, and the Iberians in general, spoke of the Chins even before they had landed on the coasts of the Celestial Empire. The Spanish book published in Salamanca in 1512, *The Conquest of the Indies of Persia*, refers to 'the Chins who are people close to Malacca, who wear leather boots and who are white like Christians. They do not eat with their hands but with highly scented wooden sticks'.[28] However, Chins was simply a name taken over by the sailors from Lisbon. It, too, came from the Persian, which had taken it from the Sanskrit. In other words, we continue to call the inhabitants of the Celestial Empire and the autochthonous people of the New World by words of Persian origin, without always being aware of the role this great civilization played in transmitting them. And as we have seen, the word *Franks*, from which came the word *Frangi*, then the word *Fo-lang* which the Chinese associated with the Portuguese, also came through Persian.

Thus the encounter of the Iberians, the Indians and the Chinese obliged all of these interlocutors to give each other names, not only to give but to receive. However, the process was not limited to pinning stereotypes on the enemy, because it was necessary to be able to speak of the others using terms that were locally understood, hence familiar to the indigenous populations. So the Spanish attempted to assimilate a huge Indian terminology intended to take full account of the linguistic, ethnic and cultural diversity of the local societies: the people of Mexico immediately appeared under the name of Colhuas, 'Indians from Culua',[29] which had been given them by the tributary peoples of the *altiplano*. Cortés quickly learned that the 'natives of Tascalteca' – the Tlaxcaltecs – were the traditional enemies of the Mexicas, and so on. This did not prevent the conquistadors from abandoning the name Anahuac in favour of 'New Spain', as Cortés explained in his second letter, of October 1520.[30]

In other words, the act of naming the other took many forms: it was possible to borrow from an ancestral baggage rooted in a reductive dualism (barbarians/Christians, barbarians/Han), to have recourse to words taken from the language of the peoples concerned (Culua, Castilan) or to invent a category (*teules*, Sons of the Buddha) and attach it to the observed reality; that is, to obliterate under a cliché or opt for ethnographic precision and respect for the usages of the other. Traditions die hard, given that we still speak of 'Indians' when we refer to the indigenous populations of America, or of 'Aztecs' – which is hardly any better – to indicate the Mexicas of Mexico-Tenochtitlan. Only the word 'barbarian' has been banished from our scientific jargon, thanks to political correctness and cultural relativism.

In the same way, long use has validated the words 'China' and 'Chinese', of Persian origin, although the Portuguese in the area had quickly learned that China was called 'Kingdom of Dõ', that is, of Than ('that which is unlimited'), the name given them by the Japanese.[31] All through the sixteenth century the Portuguese and the Spanish debated the best way of referring to the inhabitants of the Celestial Empire. Like 'Indians', 'Chinese' would prevail. Only the expression 'Occidental Indies', that is, the *Indias occidentales* of the Spanish, has fallen out of use, except in the English form, the West Indies, for the Caribbean islands.

Naming the Intruders

Identifying did not only mean assigning a geographical origin and nature to the new arrivals; it also involved designating individuals. It meant putting names and titles to faces using models which varied according to the civilization and country. The various Chinese sources, including the *Shilu* of the Ming,[32] speak of the *kia-pi-tan-mo* who was the leader of the mission. They gave the title borne by Peres de Andrade (*capitão mor*)[33] to Tomé Pires and made it the name of a person, a practice current in South-East Asia. The term 'captain', in its Italian or Portuguese version, passed through several languages of India and Insulindia, then through Chinese to reach Japanese. So we should hardly be surprised if the Nahuas did the same. When they referred to Hernán Cortés, they, too, called him *capitan*, and this term is also found in the mouths of Sahagún's informants and those of the authors of the *Cantares*, the indigenous songs of the colonial age.[34]

The names were not always stable. The Chinese sources reveal changes which show that the intentions and the identity of the Portuguese posed problems. Tomé Pires, called *kia-pi-tan-mo*, could become *Huo-chê Ya-san* – it was by this name that he was presented to the emperor in Nanking – for reasons that it is difficult to understand.[35] Perhaps he chose of his own accord to assume a name with Muslim resonance – like Khôjja Hassan – which would sound more familiar to Chinese ears? For their part, the Indians did not hesitate to Indianize Spanish names: one of Cortés's men, Rodrigo de Castañada, became *Xicotencatl*,[36] and Pedro de Alvarado *Tonatiuh*, the sun, because of his abundant fair hair. But, as military prowess demanded, the Castilian soldiers received prestigious titles.

In Canton, once they had been thrown into prison, the Portuguese lost even their names and their titles. Tomé Pires, at first dignified with the title of 'great captain ambassador', was demoted to the status of *kia-pi-tan-mo*,[37] '*capitão mor*', when the ambassador ceased to be seen as such and the envoys were stripped of the rank they had been accorded. For reasons of bureaucratic inertia, Cristovão Vieira was landed with the name of the notary he replaced, Tristão da Pinha: 'Because that was what was already written in the books of the mandarins, that was what they called me'. It was not easy to transcribe the Portuguese names into Chinese. Vasco Calvo became *Cellamen*: 'They all had names which did not correspond because [the Chinese] could not write them and because the Chinese did not have letters which were written, their letters are letters of the devil'.[38] The Spanish fared scarcely better with the indigenous names. What was different was that in Canton it was the Chinese who wrote from the position of victors, whereas in the New World it was the Castilians.

Cannibal Indians and Man-Eating Portuguese

In the eyes of the Chinese, the Portuguese were no more than pirates. It was rumoured that they were guilty of cannibalism perpetrated on young children. These stories spread terrifying images which seem disproportionate in relation to the shock caused by the irruption of 'uncivilized' people, that is, people unacquainted with Chinese mores.[39] While the denunciations did not come explicitly from the Chinese authorities, they seem to have been used as a way of keeping the population well away from these disturbing visitors. Consequently, the Portuguese were reported to steal children, whom they then 'ate...roasted'.[40]

The Portuguese sources recorded this dreadful accusation, but disguised it, the copyist having had the idea of substituting the word 'dog' for the word 'child'. The Chinese texts went into more detail. It was the practice of the intruders to steam the children in metal receptacles before skinning them alive and then cooking them slowly.[41] In his *Decades of Asia*, João de Barros repeated this rumour and even tried to explain it: 'For people who had never heard of us, we who were the terror and fear of the whole Orient, it was easy to believe these things, and as for us, we believe the same thing of them and of other distant nations about which we know almost nothing'.[42]

When people talk about cannibalism in the sixteenth century, it is always the New World that springs to mind, thanks to Montaigne and numerous other texts which described or pondered anthropophagic practices.[43] The accusation of cannibalism has a crucial place in the exotic image the Europeans constructed of the new populations, in justifications of the conquest and, as an indirect result, in the mirror critique of European society. Attacked, despised or defended (it was Montaigne who said 'I think there is more barbarity in eating a man alive than eating him dead'),[44] the Indians remained a perennial subject of European speculation, distant figures in a discourse in which they could be made to say anything you wanted. Whatever was said about them, these Indians never for a moment questioned the position of those who observed them.

With China, it was the other way round. This time it was not tribes remote in time and space that were at the receiving end of the accusation, but the Europeans themselves.[45] The Portuguese were not only barbarians, but lovers of human flesh. Did the Chinese perhaps take a malicious pleasure in, so to speak, returning to sender the prejudices the Portuguese had brought with them?[46] In this case, however, there were no mitigating circumstances: nothing, not religion, not rituals, not even the warrior ethic, could justify the behaviour of the Europeans. Nor was there, as far as I can see, a single voice on the Chinese side to dismiss this foolish nonsense as it deserved.

Portuguese Invisibility, Castilian Exhibitionism

These prejudices and rumours confirm that the origin of the Fo-lang-ki long remained for the Chinese a nebulous subject. No one knew the whereabouts of the country these people had left behind; no ancient author had spoken of it. Nor was the story of their arrival any clearer.

A surprising text, patiently deconstructed by Paul Pelliot, mixes many accounts of embassies to Peking, all of which ended badly. It makes the envoy Houo-Tchö Ya-san (*Khôjja Asan*) a Chinese in the service of the Portuguese, or even the Portuguese ambassador himself. It is as if the Chinese memory confused men and events at will, assuming, that is, that the event in question was worth bothering about! The new arrivals were quite probably not easy to identify. The Portuguese were surrounded by Asiatics of various origins, they married Asian wives, they often passed themselves off as merchants from that part of the world, in particular Siam, and they were treated as such – when, that is, they were not taken for Chinese. This discretion made communication easier. It seems to have suited everybody; it avoided raising questions to which there was no easy answer and which, at the end of the day, mattered little in a world where money and business ruled. Globalization has no use for ethnographical precision.

In Mexico, by contrast, the invaders repeatedly explained who they were and who had sent them in order to accentuate their difference, and above all make an impression on their interlocutors. The defeated Portuguese would soon learn how to move inconspicuously along the coasts, making use of secret bays, quiet, wooded shores and sheltered anchorages. Their Spanish cousins, by contrast, set about rebuilding Mexico in their own image, and in the image of how they dreamed New Spain should be.

9

A Story of Cannon

The *fo-lang-ki*, who made them?
...

Their thunder terrifies at a hundred *li*,
 and the brigands' courage deserts them
...

The *fo-lang-ki*, who made them?

Wang Yangming[1]

It was in 1519, the same year that Cortés landed in Mexico, that the Chinese philosopher Wang Yangming composed this elegy for the lord Lin Kien-sou. Wang Yangming is today seen as a key figure in the history of Confucianism. His thinking dominated the Chinese intellectual scene in the sixteenth century, in particular through his *Enquiry on the Great Learning*.[2] However, neither his reflections on the 'innate moral' nor his propositions on the unity of the principle and the mind stopped him from leading a political career and serving the empire, fighting against the armed bands. This intellectual could write: 'The great man is he who considers the world as a single family and the country as a single person...all men are his brothers...Be at one with the ten million.'[3] He was also a man of action who led repressive campaigns in the name of the emperor; it was during one of these that he composed a short tribute to the mysterious *fo-lang-ki*, who were so singularly effective against the brigands and rebels, in a private elegy entitled *Paper in memory of the fo-lang-ki*.[4] The sage who had been given the task of putting down the uprising of the prince Tchou Tch'en-hao had sought the help of the lord Lin

Kien-sou. 'It was then the sixth moon, and the heat was cruel; many people had died of sunstroke on the road. The lord sent two servants bearing provisions who, using the side roads, braving the heat, marched day and night for over three thousand *li* to get them to us.' After his success, he thanked the lord Lin for having had the idea of getting cannon of the *fo-lang-ki* type made and for sending him the formula for gunpowder together with provisions to assist him in this difficult campaign.

The Artillery of the Invaders

It is hard to imagine those who were defeated at Tenochtitlan singing a similar refrain. The crushing of the Mexicas and their allies is traditionally associated with the firepower of the Castilians. On both sides of the Pacific, in very different circumstances, the deadly weapon of the Iberians, the cannon, proved decisive thanks to its destructive power. The Chinese called them the 'cannon of the Franks' (*fo-lang-ki*) and the Nahua Indians called them 'fire trumpets' (*tlequiquiztli*); the harquebus became *xiuhalcapoz*, the '*alcapoz* of fire', a phonetic transcription of the Castilian word *arcabuz*. In Nahuatl, *tlequiquiço* began to be used for anything that could fire projectiles: harquebuses, bombards, cannon.[5] The difficulty of handling these weapons, added to the shortage of gunpowder and ammunition, greatly restricted their effectiveness on the battlefield, but it is nevertheless clear that they added greatly to the shock effect of the Europeans.

It is more surprising to realize that the Chinese feared the Iberian cannon as much as the Indians, even though it was they who had invented gunpowder and artillery. We need only remember the naval battles between the Chinese and the Portuguese, and the firepower of the Iberian vessels armed with light cannon. The Portuguese 'do not know how to fight on land; they are like fish: as soon as you take them out of water or the sea, they die';[6] positioned high up on their ships, however, they were formidable. According to an imperial censor:

> The Fo-lang-chis are most cruel and crafty. Their arms are superior to those of other foreigners. Some years ago they came suddenly to the city of Canton, and the noise of their cannon shook the earth...Now if we allow them to come and go, and to carry on their trade, it will inevitably lead to fighting and bloodshed, and the misfortune of our South may be boundless.[7]

The manoeuvrability and mobility of their firepower made it as devastating in the Pearl River Delta as in the Lake of Mexico.

Chinese Piracy

What was to be done about the Iberian cannon? Our Portuguese informant Cristovão Vieira explains that the Chinese, appreciating the superiority of the Portuguese weapons, had managed to obtain their secret.[8] They may have taken advantage of defections from the enemy camp. This is suggested by a story Vieira tells. In 1521, realizing that the situation was deteriorating, Pedro, a Christian Chinese who was sailing with Diogo Calvo, jumped ship, together with his wife, and went back to the place 'he came from'. There he hid until he could obtain a safe conduct from the mandarins in exchange for information about the Portuguese forces in Cochin and Malacca and a commitment to manufacture gunpowder, bombards and galleys. The two galleys he built were never put to the test, because the mandarins decided they consumed too much timber. They chose instead to send him to Peking to exercise his skills as an artificer in return for a living allowance. Someone must have told Vieira that he was making cannon in the distant northern capital.

The Chinese sources are more informative, but they are at variance with the Portuguese.[9] They, too, talk about a Chinese, Ho Jou, who had been singled out by the emperor, but this man held a different position and he was sent to Nanking, not to Peking like the Pedro of Cristovão Vieira.

> There was the assistant of the [surveillance] station (*siun-kien*) of Paicha, of the sub prefecture of Tong-kouan, Ho Jou, who boarded the ships of the Fo-lang-ki for the purpose of collecting customs dues. It was there that he saw some Chinese, Yang San, Tai Ming and others, who had lived in that country for a long time and were thoroughly conversant with the methods for building ships, casting cannon and manufacturing gunpowder. [Wang] Hong instructed Ho Jou to send men secretly to these [ships], on the pretext of selling wine and rice, who would secretly join up with Yang San and others and command them to return to civilization,[10] on the promise of a substantial reward. In the end they joyfully accepted and it was decided that Ho Jou would that very night secretly send a boat which would pick them up and take them to land, and that he would carefully check the truth [regarding their technological skills]; lastly, he instructed them to make [cannon] of the same design.

We learn from what follows that it was thanks to these cannon that, in 1522, Wang Hong drove out the Portuguese, and that on this occasion 'he seized more than twenty [Portuguese] cannon, large and small'. Wang Hong was convinced of the effectiveness of the Iberian artillery. He explained, later, when he had become First Minister:

> The reason the Fo-lang-ki were so extremely dangerous was solely due to these cannon together with these ships. As for the destructive power of the cannon, no weapon since Antiquity has been superior. If we use them to drive back the barbarians [of the north] [that is, the Mongols], guarding the walls will be easy. I ask that a model should be sent to each frontier so that they can manufacture them on the spot to repel the barbarians. The emperor approves this; so far, we have used many of these [cannon] on the frontiers.

While it is unarguable that the Chinese took advantage of the clashes with the intruders to copy Portuguese techniques, the arrival in the empire of the *fo-lang-ki* cannon very probably preceded the arrival of the Portuguese. It was in 1519, as we have seen, that Wang Yangming wrote of the destructive machine of the *Fo-lang*. If the *fo-lang-ki* cannon were already known in Fujian at that date, and if it was already known how to make them, the inhabitants of that region must have had time to familiarize themselves with the new weapon. This is confirmed by a reference dating from 1510. In that year more than a hundred *fo-lang-ki* cannon were used against the brigands of the province. In other words, the foreign cannon had not had to wait for the Portuguese to arrive in China. The Chinese had begun by knowing about the machines (*ki*), they had called them the 'engines of the *Fo-lang*' (*fo-lang-ki*) and then, a few years later, given this same name, *Fo-lang-ki*, to the intruders, retaining the final character *ki*, so identifying the people from Lisbon with the weapon they had brought with them.

How are we to explain the fact that the Portuguese cannon appear to have arrived in China all on their own? The circulation of words may offer some clues. We know that, around 1500, Babur, founder of the dynasty of the Grand Moghols, called the weapons of the Portuguese *farangi*. This word of Turkish origin then passed into Telugu and then into Malay. It is reasonable to conjecture, therefore, that it was Malayan intermediaries who had introduced the first cannon into China, and this even before the seizure of Malacca (1511).

A Cannon for the Hereafter

How did the Mexicans react to being fired at by cannon and harque-buses? The deafening noise, the reek of gunpowder and the devasta-tion made such an impression on the Indians of New Spain that they could never afterwards speak of the events of the conquest without some reference to the invaders' weapons. The illustrated account left by the informants of the Franciscan Bernardino de Sahagún in the mid sixteenth century contains many images depicting cannon and harquebuses, at rest or in use.[11] Other codices of the colonial era also emphasize their presence. They were later commemorated at great festivals, when, in town squares, Indians danced and sang the praises of those who had fought during the Spanish invasion. Their songs, or *cantares*, described the siege of Mexico[12] in a sort of hallucinatory incantation, and memories of firearms loomed large in these ephem-eral resurrections of the past: 'It thunders and thunders from out of a turquoise harquebus, and the vapour rolls...'[13]

The *cantares* also preserved the memory of episodes in which the Mexicas of 1521 appeared not as cannon fodder but as brave men capable of turning a situation around. We see this in a song with the title *Tlaxcaltec Piece* in which the battles that accompanied the siege of Mexico are refought. To the sound of accelerating drumbeats, Mexica warriors hurled themselves into the dance to confront their traditional enemies from Tlaxcala or Huejotzingo, at that time allies of the Spanish. The great lords reappeared before the astonished eyes of the colonial, Indian, Spanish and Métis audience. It was at this point that the great Mexica captain Motelchiuh, 'the Eagle who is our bulwark, the Jaguar who is our bulwark', suddenly materialized, his arrival signalling the renewal of the offensive and the (temporary) retreat of the Spanish: 'And when they had captured the artillery of the conquerors, Rabbit cried "let the dance begin! Hey! men of Tlaxcala! Hey! men of Huejotzingo!"'[14] For Motelchiuh and his men, come to disarm and even to destroy the 'conquerors' (*tepehuanime*), this was the hour of the Lords and the time of the dances of thanks-giving, in the frenzy of the battles incarnated by Rabbit, the God of all drunkenness.

It was a brief respite. The song went on to describe the arrival of the Castilians in their brigantines, who surrounded the Tenochcas and the Tlatelolcas, followed by the capture of Cuauhtemoc and the headlong flight of the Princes onto the lake, to the sound of the thunder of firearms. In the middle of the sixteenth century, thousands of leagues from China, at the heart of Mexico City, youthful colonial capital of the New Spain, indigenous nobles danced, clad in their finest feathers, and voices chanted to the rhythm of drums:

> It thunders and thunders from out of a turquoise harquebus, and the vapour rolls...
> All the Mexican princes go off through the water.
> Tenochcans are surrounded, Tlatelolcans are surrounded.[15]

The reference in this song to the seizure of the cannon helps us to make sense of Book 12 of the Codex of Florence.[16] This story, written in Nahuatl more than thirty years after the events it describes, and based on the evidence of survivors of the battles against the Spanish, is one of the richest surviving indigenous accounts of the conquest and the seizure of Mexico.

It is indefatigable in its descriptions of the devastation inflicted by the Spanish artillery.[17] It depicts the ravages of the Spanish cannon installed on the brigantines as they crisscrossed the lake. Taking advantage of their great mobility, the gunners chose their targets carefully and destroyed them by starting fires, which wiped out whole districts. But the besieged Mexicas did not give in. They soon learned how to avoid the bullets and cannon balls. They devised new tactics: 'Seeing this, the Mexica began to draw back and protect themselves from the artillery, going zigzagging with the canoes, and also when they saw that they were about to fire one of the cannon, they crouched down in the canoes'. The Nahuatl text is more vivid than the Spanish translation of the Franciscan Sahagún: 'when they saw that the big gun was about to go off, everyone hit the ground, spread out on the ground, crouched down'.[18] Another tactic was to force the Spanish prisoners to fire on their fellow Spaniards, though this did not always go according to plan. When one crossbowman refused to play this game and fired into the air, the Indians reacted by hacking him to pieces 'with great cruelty'.[19] The episode says less about the anger of the Indians than their inability to handle the Castilian weapons.

It was in this that the real inferiority of the Indians consisted. The informants of Sahagún described one of the Castilian breakthroughs in detail:

> The Spaniards fired the heavy cannon they had with them at that building that was there, and with the thunderous sound and smoke those who were below took fright and began to run away...they took the cannon further ahead in the direction of the square of Huitzilopochtli, where there was a large round stone like a millstone...

The Spanish were then forced to withdraw when Mexica reinforcements arrived in canoes: 'Indians skilled with canoes came and landed; they began to summon other people to prevent the Spaniards' entry'. It was at this point that some Indians seized the Spanish cannon: 'The Indians took it from there and threw it into the water at the place they call Tetamaçolco, which is near the mountain called Tepetzinco, where the baths are'. The Nahuatl version emphasizes the fury of the Indians who had dragged the cannon from the sacrificial stone.[20]

How should we interpret this action on the part of the Indians? Tamazolin means 'toad' in Nahuatl, so Tetamazolco can be translated as 'Stone toad'. This toponym indicated a place on the banks of the lake of Tetxcoco where the boats the priests guided to the whirlpool of Pantitlan berthed. At the feast of Etzalqualiztli, in honour of the gods of rain, or *tlaloque*, priests went to the edges of Pantitlan, and threw into it offerings of human hearts: 'the water began to churn, it made waves and foamed'. Once they had returned to Tetamazolco, the priests took a ritual bath. We know a little about this sacred place.[21] During the celebration of the goddess Xilonen it was customary to sacrifice a woman who wore the ornaments of the goddess: 'They said that she was her image'. Before she was put to death, she was taken to offer incense to the 'Four Directions'. One of these four points was Tetamazolco, 'where they made offerings in homage to the four signs of the account of the years': *acatl*, reed; *técpatl*, flint; *calli*, house; and *tochtli*, rabbit. Tetamazolco corresponded to the direction of the east, to Acatl, to the colour red and to the masculine. One can hardly fail to associate the eastern origin of the piece with the direction marked by Tetamazolco, the red East.

What was so extraordinary about these places was that they materialized four points of transition between the human and the divine worlds. Through them passed the four pillars of heaven, or the four sacred trees, or the four *tlaloque* which sent the rain 'from the edges of the Earth'. These were the routes taken by the gods and their forces to arrive on the surface of the Earth: the divine influences radiated from these trees, as did the flame of destiny and time.

> These routes thus connected the place of turquoise (the sky) and the place of obsidian (the subterranean world) to produce in the centre, in place of the precious green stone (the surface of the Earth), time, change and the war of the two fluxes.[22]

So the Mexica priests made haste to dispatch the Spanish cannon into the other world. Far from trying to copy, or if preferred, 'pirate' it, the Indians got rid of it by sending it to other abodes where it might constitute an offering of choice and never again harm the defenders of Mexico.

A Technology of the Past

Should we at this point take up the familiar refrain of the invincible technical superiority of the Europeans as compared with the Amerindians still living in the Stone Age? The indigenous account recalls another episode in the siege of Mexico, the story of the catapult:

> And then those Spaniards installed a catapult on top of an altar plat-form with which to hurl stones at the people. And when they had it ready and were about to shoot it off, they gathered all around it, vigor-ously pointing their fingers, pointing at the people, pointing to where all the people were assembled...The Spaniards spread out their arms, [showing] how they would shoot and hurl it at them, as if they were using a sling on them...But the stone did not land on the people, but fell behind the marketplace...Because of that the Spaniards there argued among themselves. They looked as if they were jabbing their fingers in one another's faces, chattering a great deal.

The Nahuatl recreates the Indian view:

> And the catapult kept returning back and forth, going one way and then the other; bit by bit it righted itself. Then it could be seen clearly that there was a stone sling at its point, attached with a very thick rope (*tomauac inmecatl*). Then because of that they named it a 'wooden sling' (*quauhtematlatl*).[23]

The failure of the catapult – *el trabuco*, or trebuchet – used by the Spanish against the Tlatelolcas gainsays the impression of Indian impotence and panic in the face of Spanish weapons. Sahagún's informants also revealed that fear was not a prerogative of the Indians, who were quite capable of terrifying their enemies. The *cihuacoatl* (councillor) Tlacotzin exhorted his men to use the insignia of Huitzilopochtli, a long spear with an obsidian point, because this was the 'envoy of Huitzilopochtli', sent to terrorize the Spanish: it was the 'fire serpent, the fire drill'. Then the quetzal-owl launched into the attack 'with the quetzal feathers waving. When our enemies saw him, it was as though a mountain had fallen. Every one of these Spaniards was frightened; he intimidated them'; it was as if they saw something other on the standard.[24] This did not stop the town from falling into the hands of the Spanish and their allies.

With the conquest, the Indians moved quickly from the age of obsidian and copper to the age of iron and steel. The time lag was huge but it was quickly made up. They then overcame the disadvantages that had been partly responsible for their defeat with remarkable speed. The Spanish introduced the art of the blacksmith into the towns and the countryside, iron replaced the local copper and the indigenous craftsman quickly learned how to manage the anvil, the hammer and the bellows. Iron was called *tliltic tepoztli*, 'black copper', and steel *tlaquahuac tliltic tepoztli*, or 'hard black copper'.[25] A string of new words was invented to name the new tools and objects which became part of everyday life: axes, saws, nails, scissors, iron chains and threads, anvils, hammers and much else. All were based on the root *tepoztli*, copper, long the Indians' chief metal.

Words for Saying It

One might have expected the Indians to proceed in a similar fashion when it came to naming the weapons of the victors, given that they owed much of their terrifying efficiency to the new metals. This was not the case. The Indians invented many words to describe the Iberian weapons and the way they were used, but they set about it differently. For a firearm they hit on *tlequiquiztli*, or 'fire trumpet', a word which seems to have been coined at the time of the conquest. In the word *tlequiquiztli*, *tletl* meant fire and *quiquiztli* was a seashell or a horn made out of a conch-shell which the priests made resound from the tops of the temples. The Nahua Indians here opted for visual and acoustic references which associated the strange object with ritual contexts, since the shell and fire played a part in numerous religious celebrations. The word *tlequiquiztli* quickly became the core of a range of neologisms relating to firearms, ranging from gunpowder, called 'fire-trumpet earth', to the harquebus, or 'hand fire trumpet'.[26] These verbs and nouns ignored the new metal from which these objects were made, preferring to privilege the indelible imprint of the first impression made by the explosion bursting out of a tube.

The Chinese, who had long been familiar with gunpowder, already had a word for it and for the thing itself: 'cannon' was *tch'ong*. There was no cause for them to be surprised at the strangeness or the operation of the Portuguese weapon, except for its extreme destructiveness. It was not the object that needed to be identified, but its provenance. So they called it *fo-lang-ki*, 'machine of the *Fo-lang*'. The character *ki* (or *chi*)[27] referred to the concept of the device as a motor force, agent or mechanism; but *ki* also indicated ingenious method, strategy, artifice. *Fo-lang* referred to the foreign origin: the Portuguese cannon was the 'machine of the *Fo-lang*'. This label served to distinguish the object from the traditional cannon, but also acted as a reminder that its presence was the result of a borrowing, a rapid and successful appropriation. At the beginning of the sixteenth century, as noted above, the Portuguese cannon appeared in India before spreading throughout South-East Asia and being adopted by the Chinese. The reference to the Franks attaching to these cannon passed from one language to another. But in China, as we have seen, instead of *Fou-lang* to translate *Farangi* or *Frangi*,[28] it was *Fo-lang* which stuck. *Fo* indicated the Buddha and, as he had originated in India, this interpretation confirmed that these killing machines had arrived from the West. It remained to establish the link between the cannon and the new arrivals. This was done after the naval defeat of the Portuguese in 1522: 'the royal troops obtained cannon which were called *fo-lang-ki*'.[29] In other words, the European cannon had arrived first and received a name before the Portuguese themselves. They were doomed to bear the name of their weapons, *fo-lang-ki*. But a name was not enough to clarify the geographical origin and identity of the foreigners, a point to which I will return in the next chapter.

Even if they were alike in connecting the irruption of the Iberians to their powerful artillery, the Indians and the Chinese reacted in different ways. In Mexico, the Indians thought of seashells and trumpets, in China the experts spoke of a machine. It would be easy to oppose the archaism of Indians stuck fast in a ritual and visual sphere to the modernity of the Chinese, enamoured of machines and technical innovation. It was not so straightforward, however, because both interpretations, Mexican and Chinese, were based on the idea of an instrument intended to produce a powerful sound. The machine prevailed with the Spanish and the Chinese. The Amerindians did not possess cannon, just as they were without the wheel, the cart and the sailing ship. Nevertheless, all these machines and devices led to the invention of a large number of indigenous words adapted to the new order of things.[30] For to connect worlds was first to find the words to speak of them; and to name them was already to domesticate them, even if it was impossible to appropriate them.

10

Opacity or Transparency?

Your vassal and others have had the opportunity to deal with [the Portuguese] and they have found that they are very open people.
Lichao Shilu, Korean source

Our intention [is] to cherish those who come from far away.
Emperor Zhengde, in Yu Ruji, *Libu zhighao*, 1620

Were the Chinese, the Portuguese, the Spanish and the Mexicans capable of communicating with each other from the beginning? Or were the separate worlds so impermeable that the Iberians had to struggle to form links with the populations of the regions in which they landed? It is precisely when societies are brought into contact that it becomes possible to ask questions about both the opacity that separates them and the affinities that emerge; these questions are as valid in relation to the Iberians as to the Chinese or the ancient Mexicans.[1]

The Iberian Experience

The European invaders seem to have had no difficulty in communicating with their Asiatic or Amerindian hosts. In its everyday manifestations, with all its improvisations, makeshifts, confusions and approximations, communication as we understand it here has little to do with the sort of intellectual confrontation which would imply acknowledging that cultures are incommensurable. The Iberians and their partners were not explorers of the mind. They were constantly faced, however, with problems of adaptation and survival which made frequent exchanges with the surrounding populations a necessity.

The major effort was required, of course, on the part of the new-comers, who knew nothing about China or Mexico. The ease with which they landed and established themselves, negotiated, accumulated information and generally got a feel for the country is quite disconcerting. Both the Portuguese of Tomé Pires and the Castilians of Cortés often give the impression of having been in their element. They were surprised when they needed to be, and though both the countries and the situations in which they found themselves had plenty to occasion surprise, they rarely showed signs of disarray or disorientation. Amazement in the face of the unexpected pulled them up short and made them think, and then usually revert to what they had already seen or knew. Thus the splendour of the city of Mexico or of Canton elicited parallels with familiar cities such as Lisbon, Venice or Granada. The Iberians constantly domesticated the reality of others.

It is as if the opacity of the opposing worlds, though it is to us undeniable, was not for them an insurmountable obstacle. It was not, at any rate, one of their main concerns. But complete understanding has never been a necessary prerequisite of communication. All that is needed is to understand enough to achieve one's goals. No one wanted or even contemplated engaging in an ethnography of the other, which would have been totally anachronistic. This explains the uncertainties of the Chinese with regard to the Portuguese, the dogmatic judgements of the Castilians with regard to the Indians, and the various stereotypes ('divinities', barbarians, bandits, etc.) which laid down rough-and-ready markers that made it possible to fix the respective roles and put the encounters in a context.

It is true that the actors in these dramas were not ordinary men. According to the chronicler João de Barros, Tomé Pires 'was not a person of high quality, because he was only an apothecary...but for such a trade he was the cleverest and the most skilful it would be possible to find...so eager was he to investigate and to know things, and in everything he had a lively mind'.[2] Nor was Tomé Pires an isolated case. In Malacca the Portuguese give the impression of having immediately felt to be on an equal footing with the Chinese merchants. The governor Afonso de Albuquerque had plenty of opportunity to observe those who frequented that great port and he was lavish in his praise. According to João de Barros, 'in his exchanges with them, he saw that they were noble, civilized men, knowledgeable in all the sciences, and with nothing of the barbaric behaviour of the other nations of India'.[3] The nature of the relationship established with the Chinese was felt to be exceptional, and it was this that was remembered, nearly forty years later, when Barros published his chronicle.

Nor did the activities of Cortés in Indian territory seem to have encountered any major obstacles; so much so that one is left with the impression that it was not so much the indigenous potentates as his compatriots, the henchmen of the governor of Cuba or even some of his own companions, who made life difficult for him. There is nothing in the sources to encourage philosophizing on the subject of the incommunicability of the opposing worlds. This is not to say, of course, that there were no differences between the peoples or the societies, but that the general tendency was to build bridges – more or less solid, more or less peaceable – so as to allow at least a minimum of coexistence and exchanges. In specific situations the Iberians had a deep conviction that they understood what was before them, when in reality they were either over-interpreting or distorting what was explained to them; but mistakes, misunderstandings, short-cuts and approximations of this sort are often the basis, and some-times the motor, of the links people form with each other.

For the Castilians and the Portuguese, Mexico and China were comprehensible worlds. You could begin by approaching them indi-rectly (as Tomé Pires tried to do in his *Suma oriental*) or you could learn, so to speak, on the job. This might mean, at first, drawing on what you knew, such as the Islam of Granada, to make something that was too disconcerting seem less so (as Hernán Cortés did when he saw and described a Mexico covered with mosques). It was because the Iberians were in both cases sure they had grasped the essentials that they could construct projects of conquest and colonization. How can we forget the way Cortés systematically gathered and exploited all the information he could get his hands on before extracting the quintessence (often what was 'politically correct') to be relayed to the Peninsula? La Malinche was not his only source of information. Cortés knew how to make both his allies and his victims, such as Moctezuma and the indigenous princes, first-rate informants. When the Mexicas tried to lure the Castilians into the trap of Cholula, it was the Tlaxcaltecs who 'decoded' the situation for Cortés's benefit: 'The people of [this town] said that this was a trick'.[4] Tomé Pires, too, manipulated his sources, and the *Suma oriental* shows that he was just as capable as Cortés of constructing a synthesis – a synthesis that would interest large numbers of European experts once it had been translated into Italian and distributed by the Venetian Ramusio.

Both men knew how to play the diplomatic card, officially and to the end like Tomé Pires, or tactically and in opportunist fashion like Cortés. It was in the fifteenth century, that is, just before the period which is our concern here, that the Europeans perfected their diplomatic practices, honed their formal documents and became more aware of the differences in conception and style existing both among and around them.[5] The growth of relations between the different parts of the world was facilitated by this new tool, diplomacy, which the Courts of Latin Christendom had developed between them and also with the Muslim worlds. The Portuguese in Africa and Asia had already acquired the habit of dealing with extra-European powers, and the Castilians were not far behind. The war of Granada had brought them face to face with the masters of the Maghreb and the Mamelukes of Egypt, while the Court of Castile, at the very beginning of the fifteenth century, had dispatched an embassy to Tamburlaine. The envoys of King Henry III had returned not just with a diplomatic success but with an extraordinary account which reveals observational gifts worthy of the best Italian ambassadors of the Renaissance.[6]

The examples of Pires and Cortés show that rules already existed but that they did not always suit the country visited. In the eyes of the Portuguese, the Chinese seemed to be obsessed with respect for convention: 'In these matters, they were extremely touchy'.[7] This explains the efforts to learn and to adapt, but also the inevitable frictions. It did not help that neither Pires nor Cortés were career diplomats. Only the former had experience of dealing with foreign powers, and then only in the context of establishing commercial relations.

It is diplomacy that explains the presents collected by Cortés, which he described in detail in his first letter and sent to the Emperor. The Mexican jaguars which crossed the Atlantic would have joined the lions and leopards presented by the princes of the Maghreb if the long voyage had not reduced them to a sorry state. Similarly, Cortés drew attention to the presents he gave to Moctezuma: a cup of Venetian glass, a 'necklace of pearls and cut glass'[8] and clothes of velvet, even if the latter did not come from the emperor but were the captain's own. It was important to know how to give, and to give without stint, even if it was equally necessary to improvise, so as to receive fittingly in return.

Diplomacy also explains the importance attached to audiences and ceremonials of reception. Cortés earned his at the gates of Mexico, but Pires, quarantined in Peking, had to make do with a private audience in Nanking. It was in the fifteenth century that ambassadors learned to adapt to local customs; as did Pires, who seems not to have ruled out the idea of prostrating himself before the emperor, and even Cortés, depicted by the Indian painters of the Codex of Florence arrayed in the feathers sent by Moctezuma:

> Then they took out the ornaments that they carried and put them on Captain don Hernán Cortés, outfitting him with them. First they put on him the crown and green-stone serpent earplugs...and around his neck they put the plaited green-stone neckband with the golden disc in the middle...and they gave him, placing it on his arm, the shield with gold and shells crossing...[9]

Written communication played an increasingly important role in the fifteenth century, both within Christendom and in relations with Byzantium and the Muslim worlds. This was clearly the case between Portugal and China; I have already referred to the letters carried by Pires. One might think that this dimension would be lacking in the case of Mexico, in the absence of alphabetic or ideographic writing, but this was not quite the case. Cortés kept introducing it and he assured the emperor that the agreements reached with the indigenous lords had all been formalized in writing.

Diplomacy was a way of making peace – or war. The Castilian *requerimiento*, which enjoined the indigenous peoples to accept the emperor's suzerainty, can be interpreted as a diplomatic instrument intended to avoid bloodshed, but which left only one possible response. In a way, the absolute determination of the Chinese authorities to deal solely with those tributary states which recognized the supremacy of the ruler of Peking amounted to very much the same thing: only total allegiance on the part of the supplicants was acceptable. Such attitudes left little space for notions of equality or reciprocity. The representatives of the sovereign in question must still at all costs avoid their master losing face. Cortés, by his own telling, constantly harped on about the greatness of Charles V, albeit the emperor was totally unknown in Mexico. Pires was ready to accept anything except that his king should bow before the emperor of China. There was some room for manoeuvre, but it did not extend beyond the instructions issued to the emissary; it was impossible for Pires to negotiate the return of Malacca.

Were relations any easier in the Mediterranean, between Muslims and Christians? For exchanges to take place, both sides were reduced to exploiting the 'judicial flaws' in their respective systems.[10] As for Cortés, who in any case lacked any official mandate, he was so successful in massaging the facts that it is difficult to know how far, in reality, he explained to his hosts what allegiance to Charles V implied.

It is a sign of the importance acquired by diplomacy in the sixteenth century that Cortés was so insistent on mimicking the forms and the acts. Cortés presented himself to Moctezuma as his emperor's ambassador and did this so successfully that he ensured, for some months at least, a sort of temporary immunity for his men and his allies.

The Intermediaries

The linguistic obstacle, which might have impeded further progress, was quickly circumvented by the use of intermediaries charged with the task of transmitting the intentions of the Europeans and the reactions of the local population. For their first expedition, in 1517, the Spanish had no one they could rely on. On the second expedition they were accompanied by two Mayan Indians from Cape Catoche, Melchorejo and Juliano; they then met an Indian woman who spoke the language of Jamaica, which was close to that of Cuba and understood by the conquistadors. During the course of this expedition they encountered a third local man who became an interpreter in his turn, probably for Nahuatl. Nevertheless, many things were still accomplished 'by signs'.[11] For the third expedition, the future conquistadors at last had the advantage of effective intermediaries, who helped them to bridge the gap separating the two worlds: la Malinche, another local woman, and a shipwrecked Spaniard, Jerónimo de Aguilar. La Malinche translated the Nahuatl of the Mexicas into Mayan, Aguilar translated the Mayan into Castilian. Eventually the beautiful Indian la Malinche became sufficiently proficient in the language of Cortés to speed up communication and dispense with the intermediary of Mayan.

In China, Pires had access to contacts and knowledge acquired throughout Asia. The Portuguese embassy left Malacca accompanied by a group of translators, probably Chinese or *jurabaças*. In Canton they had ample time to acquire a few key basics before reaching distant Peking. The months of waiting in the great port were put to good use learning the rudiments of Chinese, and the slow pace of their dealings with the imperial capital gave them the opportunity to study the people around them and learn something of local customs.

In both Asia and America, the Iberians recruited their translators from among the local population or from Europeans who had 'gone native'. In Mexico, there seem not to have been any professional interpreters, though it is likely that the *pochteca* merchants resorted to local correspondents for assistance in their dealings. In any case, faced with the Europeans, they could only reclaim the indigenous interpreters trained by the Spanish or, in Yucatán, take advantage of the services of Jerónimo de Aguilar, a Spaniard who had been taken captive by the Mayas. There was nothing comparable to the teams of translators who owed their existence to the longevity and intensity of relations between China and South-East Asia. By contrast, both the Andalusian Aguilar and the Indian la Malinche had to learn on the job.

In Asia and America alike, the interpreters were crucial inter-mediaries and it was on them that communication initially largely depended. Both misunderstandings and failures occurred. We need only remember the affair of the letters carried by Tomé Pires. As we have seen, Pires arrived in Peking equipped with three letters: the first, which was sealed, was from King Manuel; the second was the work of Fernão Peres de Andrade, the military leader of the expedition, and had been translated into Chinese by the interpreters; the third was from the 'governors of Canton'. The first letter was directly at odds with the second. In the latter, the translators had made the words of the captain of the expedition conform to Chinese traditions: the king of Portugal appeared as a vassal deferring to 'the Son of God, Lord of the Earth'. There was nothing like this in the letter from Manuel, which, while displaying every diplomatic courtesy, was in no way an act of submission. The Chinese minister immediately demanded an explanation. The Portuguese anger towards the interpreters only made things worse and the resulting confusion ended in the rejection of the embassy by Peking. We might see this as an error of translation, thus reintroducing the question of incommunicability. One Chinese source, the *True Chronicle of the Emperor Wuzong*, even seems to suggest this: 'The affairs of the barbarians are contradictory, this cannot but be a cause of concern to us'.[12] I see it rather as Chinese perception of the real ambiguities which surrounded the Portuguese embassy. The imperial authorities understood that they were facing equivocal and suspect schemes. They could read the behaviour of the Portuguese well enough to be increasingly distrustful of them.

Looked at more closely, the scandal caused by the translators did not spring from some difficulty or error of translation from one world to another. On the contrary, it derived from an attempt at intelligibil-ity on the part of the interpreters, even if it was, in the eyes of the Portuguese, 'politically incorrect'. They themselves explained this. How could they be faithful to the letter of King Manuel when they had not had access to it (it had been closed and sealed, no one could read it or open it)? How were they supposed to have known what was in it? Why, therefore, in the circumstances, not put the Portuguese into the only form compatible with the diplomatic usages of the

Imperial Court, 'according to Chinese custom...according to the practice of the country'?[13] What else could they have done? So the behaviour of the translators was not the result of an error regarding the meaning of a message of which they were ignorant. It sprang, rather, from a desire to adapt to the Chinese way of seeing things, even if it was contrary to the intentions of the Portuguese negotiators who ended up wrong-footed by the translators' initiative. The latter had had no reason, even less right, to turn the king of Portugal into a willing vassal of the emperor of China.

To the contretemps caused by the death of the emperor had been added a terrible diplomatic faux pas. Already suspicious, the Chinese authorities viewed with deep disfavour foreigners who not only refused to comply with the ancestral customs but who had presented a letter in Chinese whose contents they made haste to disavow. From that point the embassy of Tomé Pires was doomed; it was 'false' in the same way as the letter and the foreigners were suspected of imposture and trickery. 'It seems to them all that we had entered China in a fraudulent manner to have a look at the country and that the difference between the letters was a matter of deception'.[14] The letter from Manuel was burned. The new administration dismissed the foreigners and the Portuguese were stuck in Canton, deprived of all diplomatic status; worse, they stood accused of espionage.

Portuguese logic compromised the embassy of Tomé Pires, even though he had been informed, well before setting foot in China, of the hair-splitting nature of Chinese etiquette and the limits Peking diplomacy imposed on relations with the outside world. He had probably underestimated the strength and deep-rootedness of imperial pretensions. Added to which, in China, the translators were assumed to be in league with the foreigners and the repression suffered by Tomé Pires and his companions was in no way exceptional. These translators of dubious origins – the empire had little liking for the Chinese diaspora – were often accused of acting on behalf of their employers and breaking the laws designed to close the country off. In Mexico, the translators, who were constantly improvising, reacted in different ways, subject to a shifting balance of power. Some of them, tired of being manipulated by the Castilians, fled and returned to the indigenous world. Others, confident of being on the winning side, became dedicated accomplices of their masters, like la Malinche, keen to serve the interests of Hernán Cortés. In both Mexico and Asia, women played a role as intermediaries and partners – sexual as well as political or commercial – which should not be underestimated, even if the sources, whichever they are, are always discreet on this subject.

Dealing with Difference

In Mexico, the Castilians and the Indians did not see the differences between them in the same way. The European/Amerindian dichotomy only makes sense to us. Used to placing themselves vis-à-vis the Muslims of Granada or the indigenous peoples of the Caribbean, the intruders generally presented themselves as Castilians or as Christians.

For the inhabitants of Mesoamerica, it was very different. For them, the Castilians must have come from a city state, or *altepetl*. They were not perceived as the people of a country or a continent or of a distinct religion. In relation to the invaders, furthermore, it was very rare for the natives to define themselves globally as 'we people', *nican titlaca*.[15] Lacking any context or information, they often reduced to local norms, hence de-singularized, the new things they observed. Thus a catapult became a *quauhtemamatl*, a 'wooden sling'; a horse became *mazatl*, a 'deer'; a harquebus a 'hand fire trumpet', and so on. Anything new was tamed and absorbed, contrary to the impression given by conquest historiography. As noted above, though the venture of Cortés can appear from the European side as a clash of civilizations, this was not initially the case for the inhabitants of Mesoamerica. It was only with hindsight, with the entrenchment of colonial society, the devastation of exploitation and epidemics and the campaigns of Christianization, in short, in a situation of no return, that the defeated societies realized a page had forever been turned, at their expense.

The Castilians, for their part, quickly – and even with some relief, after the 'barbarity' of the islands – recognized the presence of towns, fortresses, merchants and religious buildings, the latter soon described as 'mosques'. What struck them most was not so much the different religion in itself as a range of very visible types of behaviour which they saw as incompatible with Christian practice: idolatry, cannibalism and human sacrifice. These were spectacular deviations, all of a religious nature, which provoked feelings of extreme repulsion in the invaders. Officially, that is, in the version sent to the Spanish court, they behaved in an impeccably orthodox manner: Cortés took risks, he smashed the idols and demanded that they be replaced by Christian images, he refused to touch the flesh of the sacrificed and fought against this practice.

Far from the authorities of metropolitan Spain, however, the reality was very different. Cortés made a show of battling against cannibalism, but had to tolerate it among his indigenous allies, just as he was obliged to shut his eyes to their idolatrous practices. He was left with no option but to manage, as we would say today, certain differences that he was in no position to eliminate; in other words, to accept them so as not to endanger his policy of forming alliances with indigenous groups. The thresholds of tolerance operating in the Christian kingdoms of the Iberian Peninsula were transported to Mexican territory and adjusted to the shifting balance of power. True, Muslim practices were at this period still tolerated in the kingdom of Granada and in other regions of Spain; we are still some way from the hardening of attitudes that marked the second half of the sixteenth century.

As we have seen, the Amerindians also tried to define and master the difference they noted in their visitors by making them *teules*, with all the ambivalence with which this word was charged. It is difficult to penetrate further, given that the indigenous evidence, gathered after the defeat, colonization and Christianization, is extremely biased. From the sparse evidence that survives for the initial period, it would seem that the Mexicas lumped together the Castilians and their indigenous allies, whom they saw, en bloc, as the implacable enemies of the Triple Alliance. It was some time before the inhabitants of Mesoamerica got used to the category of *Indios* with which they were landed by the victors, and also before they could grasp the extent of the distant world covered by the name *Castellanos*.

In China the Portuguese were also alert to the differences they observed among their hosts. Since they had left home, whether on the coasts of Africa, the shores of the Indian Ocean or in remote South-East Asia, they had constantly been exposed to all sorts of differences, like those noted by Tomé Pires in his *Suma oriental*. Their sensitivities and their attentiveness seem sharper than those of the Castilians of the New World, largely because they were much better informed by their interpreters and because they were travelling in parts of the world which had been in contact for millennia. The things, the people, the situations and the contexts were much more immediately readable than in Mexico. And while it is reasonable to speak of the greater flexibility of the Portuguese, this was to a large extent due to the position of weakness in which they found themselves vis-à-vis the kingdoms and societies they encountered. This was most notably the case in China, where they were in a precarious situation. Here, the question of difference and of the other was brought up by their interlocutors more than by the Europeans.

For the Chinese, unlike the Indians of Mexico, the world was divided into the Chinese and the barbarians; and the Portuguese were barbarians of the very worst sort. It was the visitors, therefore, who found themselves in the hot seat. It was their difference which was at issue and on which the Chinese constantly harped. They forced the Portuguese to see their singularity as a perpetual handicap, a limitation which was not only a product of ignorance of their customs but a clear sign of a state of barbarity and of an inferior condition. For example, when the Portuguese ships carrying Tomé Pires arrived within sight of Canton, the crew thought they were doing the right thing by firing artillery salvos and unfurling their flags on the pretence that this was the Portuguese custom, and that the Chinese had done the same in Malacca.[16] They may well have acted in good faith, but the Cantonese panicked and the city authorities had to remind the Portuguese that such bad manners were unacceptable in China. From that point the Portuguese were obliged to familiarize themselves with a 'Chinese style', with habits and ways of behaving about which they knew nothing and which their hosts struggled to inculcate in them. For long months they were coached in Canton, without it ever being quite clear whether they had been installed in the great Mosque or in a Buddhist temple. The Chinese authorities never stopped telling their visitors that they, the Chinese, were superior to them. They were confident that the local opulence and wealth would impress them. The Portuguese were not stupid. They were well aware that the calculated slowness with which the Chinese authorities treated the embassy in Canton was a strategy designed to dazzle them with 'the majesty and pomp of their persons'.[17]

Not all the Chinese were so particular. The ignorance and the casualness of the Portuguese may have shocked the provincial administration, but they seem to have amused the emperor, who came to the visitors' defence. It is true that Zhengde took a malign pleasure in thwarting his bureaucracy and that he manifested an exceptional openness of mind. The emperor, who had built the 'House of the Leopards' to escape the straitjacket of the Forbidden City, surrounded himself with Tibetan Buddhist monks, strolling players from Central Asia, Mongol and Jurchen bodyguards and Muslim clerics. Having acquired the rudiments of the Mongol and Tibetan languages, he enjoyed conversing with the Mongol and Muslim ambassadors, and also dressing up in their clothes and tasting their cuisine.[18] His interest went so far at one stage for him to observe the alimentary prescriptions of the Koran. His watchword was 'cherish those who come from afar'.[19]

The Portuguese benefited from the emperor's curiosity about foreign worlds and it emerges even more clearly what a serious blow his death was for them. Korean observers in Peking were just as interested as Zhengde. They found the visitors particularly 'open', expressed astonishment at their clothes 'made of goose feathers' (in reality, of velvet), remarked on their use of ruffs and noted the beauty of their books, written in another fashion: 'they seemed to contain veritable phrases of proverbial type...they were of extremely high quality, without parallel'.[20]

Deciphering the Societies

In general, the Iberians felt they had sufficiently understood the specific features of the societies they had discovered to be able to analyse them and identify their weaknesses. We should be careful not to judge the depth of their understanding on the basis of the success or failure of the project of conquest and colonization, despite the temptation to link the victory of Cortés to the strength of his analysis and attribute the Portuguese failure to a political and social myopia. Are we really to believe that the Castilians understood the Mexican world better than the Portuguese understood that of China?

The criteria for success seem to me to be highly questionable. True, the Spanish and the Portuguese missed some crucial aspects, but nothing suggests we would be better equipped today faced with the China or the Mexico of the twenty-first century. The Iberians were able to grasp certain aspects of the societies they invaded, identify dynamics and contradictions and assemble what seemed to them enough information to develop a project of conquest and colonization; and in the Spanish case they successfully put this into practice. They did this by taking advantage of local alliances which they had actively sought, as any invader would do today. And it was not for nothing that the Portuguese were accused by the Chinese authorities of engaging in espionage.

At a deeper level, one senses the beginning of the emergence of a 'global sphere', that is, a world-wide space in which all circulations and all encounters became possible and in which the necessary bases for regular exchanges were being put in place. Any number of 'middle grounds'[21] materialized in the most diverse parts of the planet, where religions and civilizations intersected. The China of the Portuguese and the Mexico of the Castilians only added further spaces to the oecumene the Europeans knew. Each on its own part, but simultaneously, these zones experienced the first tentative moves towards a global synchrony which put the different parts of the world, one after the other, on the same wavelength.

11

The Greatest Cities in the World

A Terra da China hé de muitas cidades e fortalezas, todas de pedra e quall. A cidade omde o rei estaa chama se Cambara. Hé de gramde povo e de muitos fidallgos, de imfidos cavallos. [The land of China has many cities and fortresses, all of stone and lime. The city where the king is is called Cambara. It has a big population and many noblemen, and innumerable horses.]

Tomé Pires, *Suma oriental*

Esta gran ciudad de Temixtitan está fundada en esta laguna salada... Tiene cuatro entradas, todas de calzada hecha a mano, tan ancha como dos lanzas jineta. [The great city of Temixtitan is built on the salt lake... There are four artificial causeways leading to it, and each is as wide as two cavalry lances.]

Cortés, *Segunda Carta*

One of the most insidious ways in which the Iberians and then the rest of Western Europe took over the world was to put into words, maps and images the territories they explored or colonized. Victory or disaster, the two Iberian projects were aimed at two regions of the world that were destined to loom large on European horizons. They have left us our first portraits of China, of Mexico and of their cities. This dual entry onto the world stage, not concerted but simultaneous, as shattering for Mexico as it was unobtrusive for China, marked a crucial stage in the advent of a world consciousness and a global *imaginaire*.

Geography or the Art of Espionage

Thanks to the *Suma oriental* of Tomé Pires and to a handful of texts of lesser importance, China narrowly beat the Mexican New World in making an appearance in the writings of Europeans. In fact it was the unfortunate Pires who first produced a portrait of Ming China worthy of the name, just when the Portuguese and the Italians were beginning to frequent the Chinese coast. But Pires wrote his book before he had been to China.

Captivity in Canton allowed Vasco Calvo and Cristovão Vieira to gather a large amount of information, but their curiosity was hardly welcomed by their hosts, who became reluctant to let them go. Like Tomé Pires, these two men had enough facts and figures to present an overall picture of China. First, they offered a short administrative and economic geography. They describe fifteen provinces and two capitals, Nanking and Peking, of which they give the respective latitudes, noting that the second ranked higher than the first; a coastline dotted with towns; a circulation that was largely by river, the roads being generally less safe; and the absence of sea navigation between the North and South 'to stop the country becoming known'.[1] It was by water that Nanking was linked to Peking, which received most of its food from the south of the country. They concentrated on the three southern provinces, Guanxi, Guangdong and Fujian – those, obviously, of most interest to the Portuguese and which they knew most about. Separated from the other twelve provinces by mountains, they were connected only by two 'very steep and difficult' roads. The description of the area round Canton, of the town itself and of the coast from Hainan Island to the Pearl River Delta was intended to prepare the ground for a Portuguese invasion. When, along with Calvo and Vieira, we observe that all the arsenals were concentrated around Canton, and that the sea was the umbilical cord of the province, we can understand why they believed there was no possibility of resistance to a maritime attack by the Portuguese, if once they enjoyed naval superiority. These observations among others justify the Chinese accusation that their foreign visitors were engaged in espionage. And this is, indeed, how we should interpret the letters of Calvo and Vieira.

The agricultural and mercantile wealth of the province of Canton made it one of the most prosperous in China. The taxes levied on imported goods filled the coffers of the sovereign and the mandarins. The province produced 'cordage, linen, silk and cotton cloths'. Pearls were fished and areca palms cultivated – 'the best thing there is in the country of China'.[2] It was even the only region in the country where there were iron ore deposits. This metal was used to make 'pots, nails, weapons and everything else of iron'. Skilled craftsmen, as was well known, were plentiful and could be exported like any other merchandise: 'from here four or five thousand men may be taken every year without the country suffering'.

The judicial and administrative system seems to have held few secrets for Vieira and his companion. Months spent shuttling between prison and the courts had familiarized them with the mysteries of the Chinese bureaucracy. They describe in detail the hierarchy of the mandarins, the distribution of power and the allocation and circulation of officials; they explain the constant and unpredictable changes and even career structures. Vieira drew very negative conclusions which are in sharp contrast to the praises which European observers continued to lavish on China: there was corruption everywhere, the judges thought only of filling their own pockets, they neglected the common good and they exploited the population to the maximum extent: 'The people are treated worse by these mandarins than by the devil in hell'. A bad administration is the sign of a bad government and a loss of control. The population was sinking irrevocably into criminality and banditry, to the point where revolts were counted by the thousand in the regions situated at some distance from the rivers, where the forces of law and order were concentrated. The repression was of extreme brutality if we are to believe their descriptions of the punishments and penalties, from the most cruel to the least mutilating, alongside which the practice of banishment, the equivalent of the Portuguese *degredo*, seemed extremely lenient.

Next they turned to the army and defence. Everything in this sphere seemed overrated to the Portuguese. The leaders? The men in charge were on the margins of the bureaucracy, 'knight mandarins', who had no judicial powers except over the men they commanded. They were reprimanded for trifles and treated no better than peasants. The soldiers? They were often criminals whose sentence had been commuted into banishment to a remote province. Weapons? They spoke briefly about cannon: 'Before the arrival of the Portuguese they had no bombards, but [cannon] of one type only...which are not up to much'.[3] The population was unarmed and the soldiers had to hand their weapons back to the mandarins when they were not in use. Defence, fortifications, the resistance of the walls and the guarding of the ramparts and gates were all described in minute and critical detail.

What about the Chinese fleet? It consisted largely of the junks of pirates conscripted to the service of the Crown after an agreement reached with the mandarins of Canton. The crews were made up of 'second-rate, low types', all pressed into service, most of them very young and lacking experience. After the storm of 1523, which had destroyed most of the ships, it could be assumed that the town had only its ramparts to defend it. There was nothing to fear from that quarter.

What about the condition of the peasantry? They were overburdened by taxation, forced to sell their land and their children. When not summoned to perform personal services for the mandarins, they were exploited in the hostelries used by travellers and high officials. They were left with nothing to live on after the tax collectors had called. If they refused to pay, their goods were confiscated and they were thrown into prison. In these circumstances, they chose to comply, ready to endure all sorts of humiliations: 'Faces pressed to the ground, they listened and watched the mandarin as if he was someone who threw lightning bolts'. The net result? The people were plunged into misery. They were thrown into prison for trifles: 'Everyday, they arrest many people and let a few go; they die of hunger in the prisons like beasts'. Centuries before the arrival of Mao, the movements of the Chinese were subject to extremely strict controls. It was out of the question to travel more than twenty leagues from home without a permit from the mandarins. The permit had to be paid for, and bore the name and age of the person concerned. Anyone found without this document, which was easy, because there were spies everywhere, was arrested, accused of banditry and harshly punished.

It was not much, but it was at the same time a lot for a first encounter. The analysis was visibly dictated by the idea that a conquest was feasible and even necessary. However, our authors also revealed an omnivorous curiosity and remarkable resourcefulness. The picture painted by Calvo was based on a Chinese document he had managed to procure: 'I have a book of the fifteen provinces with for each province how many cities, market towns and other places it contains, all thoroughly treated, together with the form of administration which exists everywhere and for everybody, with the towns and their situations'. Calvo gives us in passing some indication of his methods: in prison and sick, he learned to read and write Chinese, and he had the assistance of a translator, whose name he prudently withheld, to exploit the book in question. This book also included a map of the area governed by Canton: 'it shows the rivers, the cities, of which there are ten, with the name of each one at the foot of the page'. Calvo notes at least ten *villas*, 'each one ten times larger than the town of Evora', and he calculated at some fifty or sixty leagues the distance between the islands of the Delta and Canton.

This portrait, not unimpressive for a first attempt, brings together both written and cartographic information of Chinese origin; it provides an overall view of the country with more detailed information about the region and the things they had actually seen and occasional comparisons with the towns of metropolitan Portugal: Canton 'was of the same type as the town of Lisbon'.[4]

The Greatest Cities in the World

Within the space of little more than a year, the Iberians discovered Mexico-Tenochtitlan (November 1519) and Peking (December 1520). As they travelled through the countrysides of China and the Mexican *altiplano*, they came across other cities, some of which were also capitals: Nanking in the case of the Celestial Empire, Tlaxcala in that of Mesoamerica. From Peking to Mexico the Europeans had to contend with the singularity of the worlds they entered, and which they knew might at any moment swallow them up. The accounts of the Iberians are exceptional, because they had to confront in their own way, which was not that of the theoreticians of the town such as Alberti or Dürer, many of the great urban models which were then present on the planet: the Chinese city, the Mesoamerican city, the Iberian city with, always in the background, the Arabo-Andalusian city. We have no Asiatic or Amerindian view of the European town; the inhabitants of Mesoamerica and China had to imagine the Portuguese or Spanish town as the double of an *altepetl* or a Chinese town. At best, a few merchants of Canton or Fujian knew the Portuguese settlements in Malacca – as it happened of little consequence, the new arrivals from Lisbon having scarcely had time to establish themselves after their recent conquest (1511).

These were no ordinary encounters. Mexico-Tenochtitlan was not yet the capital of Mexico but it was the principal city of the Triple Alliance, the confederation that controlled most of the *altiplano* of a territory which extended from the Atlantic to the Pacific shore. It has been estimated that Mexico-Tenochtitlan had a population of some 250,000 at the time of the Spanish arrival. It was incontestably the metropolis of the Americas; which it remains today.[5] Built to an orthogonal plan, clearly showing the influence of Teotihuacan, arranged according to cosmological principles and oriented according to the points of the compass, the city had grown in an original manner around an enormous ceremonial centre, which had replaced the main square traditional in Nahua cities. The *Templo mayor* stood at the heart of the sacred enclosure, which it dominated from its great height, and from which radiated avenues that divided the city into four quarters.

Whereas Mexico-Tenochtitlan had been founded at the beginning of the fourteenth century, the origins of Peking are lost in the first millennium before Christ. The Peking of the Ming was at the centre of an immense empire which extended from the Mongol frontiers to the Indochinese Peninsula and from Central Asia to the shores of the China Sea.[6] It was after an eclipse of more than half a century that Peking had recovered the position occupied by Dadu, the 'Great Capital', centre of Mongol power since the second half of the thirteenth century. Dadu was the Khanbalikh described by Marco Polo; it had a population in his day of at least half a million. In 1420, with the intention of subjecting Asia to a Sinocentric order, the Emperor Yongle decided to restore the ancient Mongol capital to its former glory.[7] He gave it the name it bears today, Beijing, 'capital of the North'. Peking then appeared as the materialization of an ideological project to exalt Confucian values; it incarnated a political project aimed at the centralization of power and a strategic need to counter the threat from the north. In the middle of the sixteenth century the town had reached the size that it retained until the beginning of the twentieth century. It is today the second city in China after Shanghai.

If the centre of Mexico-Tenochtitlan – hence centre of the world – was marked by the *Templo mayor*, the centre of Peking was the 'Purple Forbidden City'.[8] The name of the Forbidden City, *zi jin cheng*, refers to Ziwei, the Pole Star, where the supreme deity had his palace, at the apex of the vault of heaven. The city realized a synthesis of the cosmology of the yin and the yang; it bore the imprint of the neo-Confucianism according to which the Prince was the Sage par excellence reigning under heaven. A cosmic centrality of this type, Chinese or Mexica, was totally lacking in the case of Valladolid, the city of the Spanish court, or even Granada, ancient Nasrid capital. Rome and Jerusalem, both a long way from Spain, constitute the nearest, but still remote, equivalents in Christian Europe.

What did the Iberians understand of these Chinese or Mexican cities? Essentially, what they saw from the outside, that is, the mass of human beings they contained, the wealth and commodities they promised, the military force and even potential threat they represented. Not all the Castilians and Portuguese were literate, but those with even a smattering of classical education knew that the city was the touchstone of a civilized society. To live in towns was to reveal that one belonged to the 'nations endowed with intellect and reason'.[9] The *ciudad* was the *res publica*, the chief locus of all social life, as

Aristotle had explained, and as Bartolomé de Las Casas would reiterate in all the debates about the Indians of America.

The Dominican Las Casas used this hoary old argument to defend the rationality of the inhabitants of the New World. He was the first to paint a panoramic picture of the pre-Columbian cities of the Americas, from those of Cibola in North America to the Cuzco of the Incas and the ruins of Tiahuanaco.[10] In the sixteenth century, when people thought about American man, they thought about the city. At the opposite pole from the Noble Savage, wholly contrary to the sylvan clichés associated with our vision as Europeans, Las Casas defended the image of an urban Indian, an Indian of cities:

> These people lived in society as rational men in large agglomerations which we call towns and cities...And these were not small affairs, they were large and admirable cities, complete with large buildings, adorned in many places, and some were larger and better than others, just as men of reason can differ amongst themselves.[11]

This vision of the city served not only to elevate Mexican society to the level of the societies of the Ancient World, but also to propel Chinese society into the highest ranks of humanity.

Like Lisbon, Or Like Salamanca...

The arrival of the Spanish off the coasts of Yucatán immediately marked a step change in relation to the island world they had so far encountered.

> From the ships, we saw a large agglomeration which seemed to be about two leagues from the coast and, as we saw that it was a town of some importance, and as we had seen nothing like it either on the island of Cuba or on Hispaniola, we called it Great Cairo.[12]

It was the capital of the Mamelukes that provided a point of reference, a town that would be described, just over a century later, by the Scot William Lithgow, as 'the most admirable city on earth'.[13] This touch of African exoticism, for Cairo was not Granada, or Salamanca, or Venice, which would serve as foils, shows that a threshold had been crossed in the expedition of 1517.

The existence of towns changed the course of the Castilian discoveries. The visitors saw, at last, a world that reminded them of the one they had left. In the settlements along the coast they found merchants and priests. This urban life was irrefutable proof of a civilized population: 'They are such an orderly and intelligent people that the best in Africa cannot equal them'.[14] The first agglomerations they discovered were the Mayan cities of the Yucatán, initially on Cape Catoche, on the northeastern point of the Yucatán Peninsula. A fortnight later, at Campeche, the Castilians saw from their ships another *pueblo*, 'apparently quite large'. There they found 'very big buildings, which were the oratories of their idols, well constructed of stone and lime'.[15] It was only during their third expedition (1519), and after a march of several months into the interior, that the conquistadors encountered the cities of the *altiplano* before eventually reaching Mexico-Tenochtitlan.

In his first letter (July 1519) Cortés speaks only of *pueblos* (that is, villages), although some were 'large and well organized'. In his second letter he introduces the categories of *ciudades* and *villas*, both to indicate the agglomerations he is supposed to have mentioned in his 'lost' letter and to describe those he had encountered on the road leading to Mexico: Cempoala, Nautecatl, Tlaxcala, Cholula and of course the star of the expedition, Mexico-Tenochtitlan, systematically described as that 'great city'.[16] The Castilians also discovered many *villas* and *fortalezas*, though seemingly not drawing a clear distinction between the two.[17] This fluid terminology was not simply a response to the size of the new settlements they were finding. It gives the impression that Cortés would now stop at nothing to give his discovery the aura of an exceptional event. Thus even a place of such minor importance as Iztaquimaxtitlan was praised to the skies, with its 'some three or four leagues' extent of built-up land' and 'a better fortress than any to be found in the middle of Spain'.[18]

Lastly, Cortés recorded *aldeas* and *alquerías*, which were much smaller in size.[19] The Arab heritage was as influential as the Latin tradition in determining what he saw: *ciudad* and *villa*, at the top of the scale, might refer back to Latin and the Roman occupation, but *aldea* and *alquería* were words of Arab origin, vestiges of long centuries of Muslim domination. He usually offered a population estimate for the towns: Texcoco, one of the capitals of the Triple Alliance, was supposed to have 'as many as thirty thousand inhabitants', while towns of lesser importance were usually attributed with between 3,000 and 4,000 inhabitants.[20] If need be, he noted some striking feature of the urban topography: in the case of Iztaquimaxtitlan, Cortés contrasted a downtown and an uptown, the inhabitants of the latter having 'very good houses' and seeming 'somewhat richer than those living in the valley', close to the river.[21]

Overall, the picture was very positive. To Cortés, Mexico had no cause to be jealous of Spain: 'On their journey these Spaniards passed through three provinces with very beautiful lands and many towns and cities and other communities in great numbers, and with so many and such good building that they say in Spain there could be none better'. The inevitably subjective comparisons the invaders were so ready with – with Burgos or Granada or Seville or Cordoba or Salamanca – were generally to the advantage of Mexico. The conquistadors usually kept to the towns of Castile and Andalusia, with which they were more or less familiar, but occasionally they referred to cities in Italy, which some of them had seen, or even more remote capitals of which they had heard tell, like those of the Ottoman Empire and Mameluke Egypt. This gives us some indication of how the Castilians imagined and conceived the town in the sixteenth century in a situation in which they were forced to put their impressions into words and constantly to assess and interpret what they saw. Thus the town of Tlaxcala seemed to them 'much larger' and to have 'many more people' than Granada; kept constantly supplied with foodstuffs, it had a market 'where each and every day upward of thirty thousand people come to buy and sell', and where all was 'as well laid out as in any square or marketplace in the world'.[22]

Was this the beginning of a world consciousness? There was no doubt an element of rhetorical flourish, but it is also clear that the very fact of comparing the Mexican towns with the cities of Europe, Asia and Africa meant that global horizons were replacing Iberian and Mediterranean horizons in the way they were thinking. This shift reveals that America, conceived in its Mexican and then in its continental form, gave a crucial impetus to the emergence of a world consciousness. This differentiated it from China, which was added to an Asia that they had already known, or felt they had known, for a long time. Ming China simply added one more piece to the jigsaw; Mexico added the piece that had been missing for a conception of the totality of the globe and the piece that revealed to the West all its human and civilizational density, through, precisely, the town.

Another way of approaching the Indian towns was through the singularity of the political forms they contained. Tlaxcala very quickly attracted Cortés's attention because it was the seat of an oligarchic power that was almost like that of the 'states of Venice or Genoa or Pisa', whereas Mexico and Texcoco were ruled by monarchs. For all these reasons the town was an essential marker: the Indians, as we have seen, identified themselves by the city to which they belonged; this made perfect sense to someone like Cortés, who, as noted above, was first and foremost in his own eyes a man from Medellín (Estremadura). And the fact of naming the Tlaxcaltecs or the Culuas meant that the indigenous peoples emerged from the indistinct, anonymous mass, lacking any history, that was implicit in the word *Indio*. The city state was central to the geopolitics of Mesoamerica and this was something Cortés was quick to grasp.

With Mexico-Tenochtitlan, goal of the long march through the country, a final quantitative and qualitative threshold was crossed. The city fascinated the Spanish even before they entered it. How could they not be struck by the site of the town, built in the middle of a lake, in a valley dominated by two great volcanoes? The Mexican authorities pulled out all the stops to ensure that the splendour of Moctezuma's capital impressed their visitors from the start. So their first contact with the town had both a spectacular and a political dimension. Access roads, movable bridges, straight, wide streets, often with canals running alongside, palaces and 'mosques' all made a deep impression on the new arrivals. The staging of the welcome for Cortés offers further proof of what the spectacular demonstration of power could achieve in the Mesoamerican world.

It was only later that the invaders appreciated the economic importance of Mexico-Tenochtitlan. The markets would inevitably attract invaders so greedy for gold and riches. The largest of them, which seemed to be as big as the town of Salamanca, was used by more than 60,000 people and subject to strict regulation; each aisle was devoted to particular products, here medicinal plants, there fruit and vegetables, further on game, further still earthenware vessels.[23]

The Portuguese writings contemporary with the arrival in China lack much of the suggestive power of the letters of Cortés for reasons we already know. The letters in which we may assume Pires, in similar fashion to Cortés, described his stay in Canton, his reception in Nanking and his arrival in Peking are lost, as are the drawings he is known to have made.[24] We are left with the prison letters of Vieira and Calvo. They drew on oral testimony, maps and even written documentation of Chinese origin, like the 'book of the fifteen provinces' discussed above.[25] They describe a large number of things they had seen in the case of Canton and its surroundings. But these were 'things seen' from prison: the Portuguese gaze at the towns may have been much better informed than that of Cortés, but it was constantly and oppressively restricted by the Chinese authorities. It offers an analysis which came from inside a Chinese town, whereas Cortés's view of Mexico was as if from above, panoramic, whether from the foothills of the volcanoes as they first arrived in the valley or from the summit of the *Templo mayor* which towered over the city.

Canton was the first city the Portuguese entered, and hence the one they knew best. Time and enforced inactivity made things easier. It was months before the embassy received authority to set out, first for Nanking and then Peking. The Portuguese were left with ample leisure to observe the various places in which they stayed and the countryside through which they travelled during their long journey of several thousand kilometres. As with Mexico, the existence of towns loomed large in their view of the new realities. The urban density fascinated the visitors; the closer the settlements lay along their route, the more impressed they were. The size and beauty of the Chinese towns struck the Portuguese wherever they went.[26] In their case, the comparisons were Portuguese (Lisbon, Evora) or, occasionally, Indian (Calicut). However, they kept pointing to a significant difference of scale: Canton, a more than middling town, was the same size as Lisbon, and the small towns through which they passed had populations ten times as large as Evora.[27]

'Peking is the capital, where the king by law resides'.[28] The Portuguese, always keen on geographical coordinates, calculated the position of the town at 38° or 39° north latitude. They noted the strategic importance of the Chinese capital in relation to the Mongols: 'It is found at the extremity of the country, because they are at war with peoples called Tazas [Tartars]'; they also noted its Mongol origins and its dependence on Nanking and the rest of the country, which supplied it with foodstuffs: 'the region has no rice because it is cold and produces little... [it has] no timber, no stone, no brick'. Peking was correctly perceived, therefore, as a political capital and strategic base facing the northern frontier, which posed the greatest threat to China.

It was the chronicler João de Barros who synthesized all the information collected by the first visitors to Canton:

> What makes the city more beautiful is the arrangement of the houses, because the city has two roads which intersect and which end in four gates out of the seven which serve the town; these roads are as straight as a die, so that if you stand at one of the gates you can see the one opposite. The other streets are laid out according to these two arteries; in front of the door of each house a tree has been planted, which keeps its leaves all year round and which gives shadow and coolness. The trees are planted in such an orderly way that if you stand at the foot of one of them you can see in a row the feet of all the others.[29]

Barros, who claimed to know more, promised the rest for the books of his *Geography*, sadly now lost.

As in Mexico, the Chinese towns were classed into *ciudades* and *villas*, but the first Portuguese observers also felt the need to introduce local categories such as *chenos* (from *xian*, prefecture) to distinguish the most important agglomerations, those which the Chinese placed above cities.[30] The Portuguese would continue throughout the sixteenth century to employ local categories, taking note of the explanations given on the spot by their informants and drawing on Chinese literature.[31] They counted the towns. The province of Canton alone had thirteen cities, seven prefectures and a hundred *villas*. They pondered the rank each one held; and then realized that the hierarchy of small and medium-sized towns was based not on their demographic importance but on the existence or absence of fortifications and administrative functions.[32]

The distinction between the Chinese elites and the exploited masses was a leitmotif running through all the Portuguese analyses. It was imprinted on the physiognomy of the town, and that of Canton in particular. The city had a popular quarter, consisting of houses constructed of timber, 'with walls of wattle and daub, into which whole families were crammed',[33] with, elsewhere, the temples, the administrative palaces, the houses of the mandarins and many prisons which constituted veritable micro-societies. We may conclude that the Portuguese registered in particular the extremes, or simply that visitors come to trade and spy were not notably well equipped to engage in urban sociology.

The Gaze of the Conqueror

The Chinese towns were primarily approached from an economic and military standpoint. This was particularly the case with the towns of Guangdong and above all Canton, which had a monopoly of relations with foreigners and external trade. The geographical and topographical situation of this emporium was studied with especial care because the visitors envisaged its imminent occupation.

The Portuguese gaze was thus, like that of Cortés, the gaze of the spy and the conqueror, preoccupied with military matters. So the Chinese towns appeared as cities surrounded by ramparts, decked out with monumental gates, but without a fortress. The Portuguese who had managed to walk on the ramparts of Canton had taken note of the length of the walls. They had counted the towers, of which there were ninety, 'which served as bastions'. They had estimated the number of soldiers in the garrison: 'it had on a permanent basis three thousand men who guarded the gates of the town, supervised by captains'.[34] How was the town to be kept once it had been taken? The Europeans soon spotted 'a little flat hill pressed up against the wall in the north part', which could be made into a small fortification. From it, the whole town could be controlled without difficulty.[35] In the centre of Canton they could use the landing stage of the mandarins to construct a second fortified structure and so hold the whole town in a pincer movement. One may imagine that Cortés and his men had similar considerations in mind each time they walked through Mexico-Tenochtitlan.

On the other side of the Pacific the conquistadors were subjecting the Mexican cities they visited or attacked to a similar gaze. The lines of defence, the height and length of the ramparts,[36] the resistance of the building materials and embankments and the strategic points were all carefully studied and evaluated just like the forces of the enemy and their defensive capacity. It was important not to miss anything that might either hinder the progress or facilitate the breakthrough of the Europeans. They deconstructed whichever town was in front of them all the more attentively in that they knew their lives and the fate of the expedition depended on it. It was the same with the Portuguese, who sent all sorts of strategic information to their compatriots in Malacca in the hope that they would soon come to rescue them from the prisons of Canton.

The Posthumous Triumph of the Aztec Capital

The death of the Portuguese ambassador Tomé Pires, the limited circulation of the letters sent from Canton, the loss of many of them and the discretion inevitably surrounding the Portuguese discoveries all help to explain why this first image of China never impressed itself on the reading public in the Old World. Tomé Pires may well have visited and spent time in Peking, but it was its predecessor, Khanbalikh, capital of the Mongols, and Cathay, visited by Europeans in the thirteenth and fourteenth centuries and described at length by Marco Polo in his *Travels*, which continued to hold sway in the minds of Europeans.[37]

Ming China failed to make its mark on the intellectual horizons of the Renaissance. It is as if a diplomatic and military fiasco turned into a media disaster. This was to the advantage of China's image. The exasperated descriptions, negative judgements and unflattering analyses offered by Vieira and Calvo made almost no impact in the short run, leaving the field clear for continued praise for the commercial, political, intellectual and artistic grandeur of China. In any case it was only in the second half of the sixteenth century that a few Jesuits and the Augustinian Gaspar da Cruz caused this perpetual object of admiration and fascination to become lodged in the European *imaginaire*. Is this to say that the first impression was forgotten for ever? Not entirely. The negative image of Calvo and Vieira was rediscovered decades later, as if China had another side, a dark and disturbing side, of a nature to justify an early intervention.

The huge impact made by the expedition of Cortés is in sharp contrast to the relative silence surrounding the Portuguese expedition to Peking. The wide circulation of Cortés's letters in Europe and the intervention of the humanists and painters – Albrecht Dürer was in raptures over the treasures of Mexico exhibited in Brussels – familiarized the whole of Christendom with the splendours of Indian Mexico and the city of Mexico-Tenochtitlan. Cortés went to great lengths, even sending a sketch, to establish the great city in the minds of the Spanish of the Court and then of the educated population of the Old World. The plan of Tenochtitlan, published in Nuremberg in 1524, added illustration to the texts. It probably inspired Dürer's speculations on the subject of the ideal city in the treatise on fortifications he published three years later in that town. The representation of Mexico, a combination of indigenous elements and European re-readings, thus played a part in the gestation of the modern city and of a modernity born of the meeting of worlds and clash of civilizations.

Much splendour, not a little sensationalism and an all-round valorization of the conquest eventually created an unforgettable image that would be imprinted on the European memory for centuries. It is impossible here to recall all the elements which Cortés supplies, on page after page, and which have formed our Americanist and Mexicanist vision: the arbitrary delimitation of territorial space, New Spain or Mexico; an emblematic metropolis, Mexico-Tenochtitlan; the emphasis on the Mexicas at the expense of their neighbours, allies and adversaries, which has persisted in our fixation on the 'Aztecs'; the idea that there was an 'Indian religion', with its places of worship or pyramids, its great festivals and its human sacrifices; the treasures sent to the emperor; and, lastly, the ambiguity of the gaze directed at a sumptuous civilization, whose exoticism fascinated, but which was destroyed without compunction.

After Cortés, the Iberians and then the Europeans as a whole saw Mexico as a society frozen in time, torn between a prestigious pre-Hispanic past and a colonial history bent on destroying whatever had survived of ancient times. It is in this context that we continue to see America and Mexico today and it is to the conquest of Cortés that we owe our contemporary gaze. Today, crucible of *métissages* of every sort, rebuilt from top to bottom by the colonizers, subject to every wave of Westernization, and modernity, the Mesoamerican *altepetl* has become one of the urban giants of Latin America. Mexico has joined Peking and Canton in the club of the megalopolises of a globalized world. Nevertheless, we never imagine Mexico as we imagine the great Chinese cities which escaped colonization. The early sixteenth century, another history of which I am sketching out in this book, was crucial in this.

The appeal of Mexican America faded only in the face of the interest aroused by the Ottoman Empire. Hindu India, which had caught the imagination of the Ancients and their medieval heirs, had scarcely more success than the China of Pires. Once again the dates coincide: in 1520 the kingdom of Vijayanagar, a country as extraordinary as ancient Mexico, welcomed a Portuguese horse trader who left a vivid description of it. But it was not until the chroniclers João de Barros and Jerónimo Osório took it up that it entered the established repertory of European orientalism, though without ever arousing the same fascination and interest as the Ottoman Empire, the Mogul Empire, China or Japan.[38] The Mexican New World was perceived as something very different from just one more page added to the atlas of the known world: it was the missing piece which made it possible at last to think the globe in its totality, and a piece the Europeans took good care not to allow to escape.

12

The Time of the Crime

But when states are acquired in a province differing in language, in customs, and in institutions, then difficulties arise; and to hold them one must be very fortunate and very assiduous... it is better to be impetuous than circumspect; because fortune is a woman and if she is to be submissive it is necessary to beat and coerce her.

Machiavelli, *The Prince*[1]

What better way to do this than 'establish settlements in one or two places; these will, as it were, fetter the state to you'?[2] In 1513, having been banned from Florence, Machiavelli pondered the best way of conquering and holding on to territories. His reflections were principally focused on the European states but they did not exclude more remote lands, African or Asian, 'differing in language, in customs, and in institutions', as he was also interested in the Turkish monarchy and the ancient East. It was only a few years after the publication of *The Prince* that the question of conquest and difference was posed in the most direct and most pragmatic way for the Iberians. In Asia and in America they were confronted with the triple challenge of understanding, 'acquiring' and 'holding' new societies. To understand, to conquer and to retain; or rather to understand in order to be able to conquer and retain, because to get it wrong was every time to risk losing one's life. Far from the shores of Spain and Portugal, far even from the familiar context of the Latin Mediterranean and the Ancient world, Cortés, Pires, Vieira and Calvo were probably the first Europeans to think politics outside the Christian–Muslim world. They would for this reason have taken their place alongside the author of *The Prince*, had centuries of Eurocentrism not purged modernity of its 'exotic' peripheries.

The Art of Dismantling Societies

What was the best way of confronting populations about which nothing was known, which were different in many respects, clearly civilized and as large as those of China and Mexico? How to overcome the obstacles of numbers, distance and unpredictability? The Spanish and the Portuguese had to face the same problems and the same challenges at the same time. To begin with, without realizing it, they followed Machiavelli's advice: to 'establish settlements in one or two places; these will, as it were, fetter the state to you'. Arriving by sea, they quickly constructed bases on the shore so as to maintain direct links with the outside world, Cuba in the case of the Spanish, Malacca in that of the Portuguese. The foundation of Villa Rica de la Vera Cruz, in July 1519, and the construction of the fortress and gibbet of Tunmen, in 1518, were the concrete consequences of this policy. It was here that Pires and Cortés stored material and men to safeguard their rears before embarking on the long marches that would take them into the heart of the two 'empires'.

It remained to be seen whether political wisdom – the *virtù* of Machiavelli – would prevail over the hazards of fortune and the unpredictability of circumstances, without the need to use brute force. As regards *virtù*, the Portuguese and Castilians were alike. The similarities at tactical and strategic level, the convergence of objectives and the ambiguity inherent to both enterprises (were they diplomatic missions, reconnaissance operations or preparations for conquest?) revealed both to be skilful operators. Their mobility and adaptability and the speed with which they reacted in the face of the unknown and the unforeseen gave them a huge advantage. As regards fortune – this was how Machiavelli referred to circumstances, fate and chance – the Chinese realities proved much more intractable than the Mexican.

The Iberians were convinced, like Machiavelli, that they should exploit the divisions among the enemy in order to get the better of them and that they would need to use force to achieve their objectives. This meant identifying the disagreements and conflicts dividing the societies they discovered and gradually penetrated. Cortés quickly realized the benefits to be reaped from the resentment created by the domination of the Triple Alliance. He banked on the fragmentation of the country, less on the 'ethnic' or 'cultural' differences – never of course referred to in these terms – than on the weakness of the recent hegemony which, he claimed, was based on threats, blackmail and the brutality of the armies. To explain the ascendancy of the Mexicas over their indigenous vassals by the 'fear'[3] they inspired was also, by the same token, to deny their legitimacy and justify a future resort to force, that is, conquest. It was Cortés's aim to neutralize the fear of Mexico-Tenochtitlan and turn Moctezuma's vassals into subjects of the emperor by systematically encouraging transfers of obedience, through force or negotiation. Impressed by the firepower of the intruders, many Indian cities went over to the enemies of the Triple Alliance, which was not at that point perceived as the Spanish camp, even less that of the victors. All Cortés then needed to do was put men, cannon and horses at the service of his new allies 'against the Culuans, their enemies and ours'.[4]

He still had to deal with the unexpected and ensure that fortune favoured him by subjecting it to his will and lucidity, that is, by demonstrating Machiavellian *virtù*. From start to finish, and all along the way, Cortés gives the impression of one in control of events, turning situations around and dealing successfully with one crisis after another. His journey, which he presents as having passed off almost without a hitch, would have made him a remarkable disciple of Machiavelli had he not constructed himself, all on his own, thousands of kilometres from Europe, as he overcame all the problems posed by his discovery.

In China, things were very different. The Portuguese failed to adapt to circumstances in the same way. Vieira and Calvo tried to analyse Chinese society. Their vision was dualist: the 'people' (*povo*) faced the mandarins just as in Machiavelli the *popolo* opposed the great (*grandi/nobili*). The Chinese people were exploited: 'the people are very poor and ill treated by the mandarins who govern them'. They were silenced by fear: 'the people are so subdued and so fearful that they dare not open their mouths'. Such a regime drives people to rebel against the government in power: 'Everyone longs to rise up and for the Portuguese to arrive'.[5] In Machiavelli, too, it was popular hatred that destabilized the prince: 'The best fortress that exists is to avoid being hated by the people'; if 'the people hate you', you arouse their 'enmity' and risk being driven from power.[6] The Portuguese of Asia were unaware that Machiavelli had made this opposition, a recurrent feature in *The Prince* and the *Discourse* and the main driving force behind the political mechanisms he analysed. It was, however, a commonplace of the Middle Ages,[7] and the Portuguese chronicles, such as that of Fernão Lopes, did not hesitate to describe the role played by the people against the lords or to evoke 'the conflict of the small against the great'.

The Portuguese people had emerged as an actor in its own right during the accession, in 1385, of the Master of Aviz, the future John I, as if the popular origin of the new dynasty, hence royal power, was perfectly obvious.[8] It is hardly surprising, therefore, that such ideas should have accompanied the Portuguese on their travels in Asia, or that they should discover them in Canton. Like Machiavelli, the prisoners of Canton were convinced that by supporting the 'people' against the great it would be easy for them to seize power. But the 'great' that Vieira and Calvo had to deal with were not nobles but a body and an institution on a scale unimaginable either to Machiavelli or to those nostalgic for the Roman Empire: the Celestial bureaucracy. This is one reason why the Portuguese analysis of the situation in China was exactly opposite to that of Cortés, and why it was mistaken. In China the enemy to be brought down was the product of a bureaucratic machine without parallel in Western Europe, the mandarins; in Mexico, more classically, it was a coalition of lordships dominated in the recent past by the Mexicas. It remained the case that in both China and Mexico the Iberians intended to take advantage of the fear inspired by those in power.

The Portuguese kept pointing out the fragility of mandarin domination and the rampant exploitation of the masses. They assumed that the latter were ready to rise up at the least sign of weakness on the part of the authorities. 'They keep quiet while being desperate for change because they are exploited to the highest degree possible, and even more than that'. The arrival of the Portuguese forces could not fail to produce a state of shock that would degenerate into chaos: 'These cities will quickly rise and the majority of people will begin to steal from each other and kill each other because there will be no one to rule them nor anyone to obey, because the mandarins will either be killed or put to flight'. All the visitors from Malacca would need to do was take advantage. They would be welcomed as liberators by a people pushed to the limit. In a word, and Vieira kept repeating this in a variety of ways, the people 'do not like their king', they are full of hatred against the mandarins and they long for the changes that will bring them freedom.[9]

In each case we see the Iberians ready to play the role of redresser of wrongs. In Mexico, Cortés hoped to exploit the political fragmentation by relying on the lordships hostile to the Triple Alliance, that is, the city states, and occasionally on the internal divisions between lords and people.[10] In China, it was the social conflict, not to say 'class struggle', which was supposed to bring about the fall of those in power and deliver victory to the invaders. It is revealing that the Portuguese spoke constantly of the 'people', and that they saw them as forced to endure living conditions they regarded as intolerable.[11] With only a little exaggeration, we may contrast the Spanish in Mexico, plunged into a feudal war, pitting lordship against lordship, where they thought only in terms of vassalage and transfers of suzerainty, to the Portuguese imagining they were fomenting a popular war of liberation.

It was in this spirit that Vieira even contemplated drawing up a proclamation, 'to declare freedom for everyone in the country'.[12] It was not the first time he had used this word. But what sort of freedom was he talking about? It would be tempting to liken it to the 'independence with regards to tyranny' that Machiavelli and the Florentine humanists spoke about, if we were better informed about the Portuguese political thinking of the period. Free are the people who have rid themselves of a tyrannical government.[13] In any case, what could be easier, in China, than to mobilize a population ready to give itself to the first comer: 'They have no loyalty...either to the king, or to their father or to their mother, they are content to follow whoever is strongest'.[14] Such an assessment may seem surprising given the aura of power surrounding Ming domination. It is easier to understand if we remember that, after Malacca, the Portuguese had been in regular contact with Chinese dissidents and with coastal populations accustomed to breaking the law in their dealings with pirates and smugglers.

What was to be done with the master of China and the *tlatoani*? The question arose in both Canton and Mexico. For months Cortés negotiated with Moctezuma before getting him at his mercy and trying to use him to quell the rebellion in Mexico. For the Portuguese the person of the Chinese emperor was never directly challenged. The court of Peking was too distant and virtually inaccessible, appearing only as a shadowy presence behind the Cantonese authorities and the provincial bureaucracy. Nevertheless, the Portuguese contemplated making the Ming emperor a dependant of Lisbon, which was, we should not forget, the first choice offered to Moctezuma.

How did they come to underestimate the capacity to react of societies numerically so infinitely superior? In the minds of the Iberians, the weakness of the enemy, whether Chinese or Mexican, was not simply a product of circumstances. The establishment of Chinese and Mexica rule was considered too recent or too contested for its bases to be sufficiently solid. This weakness was then seen as a structural given. They assumed it was experienced as such by the populations in question. By Moctezuma's own admission, the people of Mexico saw themselves as strangers come from elsewhere: 'They were not natives of this land'.[15] As for the Chinese, they were alleged to have a 'deep fear of losing the country' because, according to the Portuguese, their right of possession was highly suspect.[16] The visitors were quick to attribute to their enemy the unease and the bad conscience of those who know themselves to be politically weak. But while the perception of Mexica power was reasonably accurate, given that they really were a group recently established on the *altiplano* and that their legitimacy was contested, the reading of the Chinese past remains puzzling, unless they saw only the youth of the Ming Dynasty – in existence for only a century and a half – and its difficulties on the northern frontier.

The Advantage in Arms

The weakness of Chinese society was also attributed to the defects in its armed forces, so grave that the Portuguese enjoyed envisaging the conquest as a blitzkrieg. With a handful of ships and a few hundred men, they would topple the house of cards. It was the same in Mexico, on condition, that is, that they moved faster than the Mexicas; Cortés must at all costs tip the balance of power in his own favour by preventing further adhesions to the Triple Alliance,[17] and by neutralizing or winning over unstable loyalties; he must strike hard before Mexico-Tenochtitlan recovered the upper hand and before his indigenous allies realized the threat the Spanish posed.

The weakness of the local armies, in spite of their sheer numbers and the constant replenishment of their ranks, amazed the Iberians. This was expressed differently in China from in Mexico. The Chinese were not, on the whole, a people who knew how to fight: 'From birth to death, they have nothing in their hand but a knife without point to cut their food'. The ordinary people had no weapons, no swords, no arrows; all they could do if they were threatened was bury their meagre possessions.[18] In case of war, they barricaded themselves in their houses and eventually surrendered to the victor, whoever that might be. The Portuguese had learned to distinguish between the army and the Chinese people. In Mexico, by contrast, all the natives were ready for war. They proved formidable adversaries in hand-to-hand fighting. However, and this was a serious disadvantage, they had no metal weapons, no horses and no artillery.

The firepower of the European artillery had a similar effect on the local population in both Mexico and China. Their panicky reactions strengthened the Iberians' sense of their own superiority, even if the fear demonstrated was greater than the damage done. The Spanish chronicles contain innumerable descriptions of the scenes of terror caused by the guns of the conquistadors. It is more difficult to imagine that the Chinese were equally badly shaken by the Portuguese cannon: 'They put their finger in their mouth amazed at such a powerful thing, by reason of being a people that have no stomach'. The Chinese people were deficient in courage, of this the Portuguese had no doubt.

What, then, was the point of the Chinese army, because professional army there was? Its main purpose was to hunt down brigands and put down popular uprisings. Its firepower left much to be desired: 'They fire arrows, but not to much effect'.[19] Troops were recruited from among men who had broken the law and been banned from their province, who made very mediocre soldiers. Vieira and Calvo saw them as the equivalent of Portuguese *degredados*, criminals who had been exiled far from the capital. There were between 13,000 and 14,000 soldiers, 3,000 of them in Canton. But it would need at least 40,000 to resist one single Malabar warrior! The Chinese soldiers were like women, with their effeminate airs: 'There is nothing in their stomach, all they knew how to do was shout'.

The Mexican fighters were a very different matter. True, it was very much in the interests of Cortés and his companions to exaggerate the courage of their enemy so as to increase their own glory, whereas the Portuguese, by contrast, set out to minimize the valour of theirs so as to convince Lisbon and Goa that they could confidently invade China. Both the Spanish and the Portuguese were well aware that the armies they encountered were formidable in numerical terms; however, they were convinced that their own tactical and technical skills, together with their courage, were enough to hold at bay or put to flight the masses they confronted.

Plans for Conquest

Same cause, same effect – or almost. The revolt of Mexico against the conquistadors and the punishment inflicted on the Portuguese of Canton led the Iberians to envisage the military conquest of the territories which resisted them. Both were now convinced that they were justified in resolving by force a situation that had become intolerable. The 'cruelty' and the 'deceitfulness' of the mandarins, who had gone out of their way to pillage the Portuguese ships, and the supposed treachery and uncontrollable fury of the Mexicas, the death of Moctezuma being the last straw, together with the daily insecurity in which they lived, made a military solution seem an urgent necessity to the Iberians. In the case of Cortés, such a solution was all the more natural in that, in his mind, or rather under his pen, war was simply an inevitable and deserved consequence, a resumption of control together with an act of legitimate defence: '[the country] will shortly be restored to the state in which I held it before'. What better way of presenting the imminent conquest to Charles V in the best light?

The Portuguese of Canton were equally well able to advance such an argument because they had for some years enjoyed a degree of peace and freedom of action on the island of Tunmen. By their account the conquest would be an act of revenge for the trials endured by the embassy and for the promises made but not kept; it was also a way of punishing the execrated mandarins and, most of all, of keeping alive their hopes of emerging from the jails of Canton. The Portuguese believed that they were still in a position to influence a train of events which was in reality out of their control. From now on, faced with an implacable and 'monstrously' iniquitous enemy, whether in Mexico or Canton, there could be no question of retreat, even if care had to be taken not to make any mistake that might, in the words of Cortés, 'enrage those curs still further and give them the courage and daring to attack those who may follow after'.[20]

How to move into the attack? The second letter of Cortés and the letters of Vieira and Calvo revealed the plans that were being hatched in the minds of these apprentice conquerors. In the Spanish case Cortés had the good luck – always luck – and the means to carry out his programme. In the Portuguese case, the plans would remain a dead letter. In both cases the letters reveal the state of mind, goals and intentions of the Iberians in the short and medium term. It is as if we are able to catch in the act a bunch of criminals planning a job. But when the target of the crime is China or Mexico, the 'job' assumes the huge scale and inordinate and unprecedented dimensions which Peter Sloterdijk has associated with European modernity: 'We begin to see modern times, taken as a whole, as a period in which monstrous things are brought about by human perpetrators, entrepreneurs, technicians, artists and consumers...modern times are the age of the monstrous created by man'.[21]

The 'time of the crime' would soon arrive, but now the crime or attempted crime would have a global resonance. This was not like the Italian wars, or even like the confrontations resulting from the barbarian incursions and the Ottoman advance. Here the perpetrators were Iberian and it happened at the same time though some thousands of kilometres apart.

Expelled from Mexico in October 1520, Cortés's first thought was of replenishing his army. He needed to do this with all possible speed, drawing on the Spanish reinforcements based in the Caribbean islands. He sent four ships to Hispaniola (San Domingo) 'to bring at once horses and men to aid us', with the idea of acquiring four more to bring back 'horses, arms, crossbows and powder' and everything necessary for a conquest. True, the enemy was to be feared not only because they were numerically superior, but because they possessed fortified towns and fortresses and seemed determined to exterminate the 'Christians' and drive them out of the country. With the reinforcements sent from Cuba and Hispaniola, Cortés pondered the idea of returning to Mexico, laying siege to the city and capturing it, confident he would be able to manage this 'shortly'. He had already taken the initiative of constructing 'twelve brigantines with which to cross the lake'. They were built in separate parts so they could be carried overland on the backs of men before being 'swiftly assembled on arrival'. While waiting, the construction of a fortress and the founding of a *villa de Españoles* at Tepeaca ensured the safety of communications between the Gulf of Mexico and Cortés's camp.[22]

The Portuguese in Canton had to be content with planning their conquest from the 'infernal prisons'. It remained the dream of captives longing for revenge and tormented by their impotence. It inspired letters written in appalling conditions, concealed from the Chinese, unknown even to the servants who looked after them. 'I cannot write more, as my hand is covered in sores which have suddenly appeared', notes Vasco Calvo at the end of his first letter, sent from the 'prison of the provincial judge'. 'My body is afflicted with pain and suffering', he added, 'and it is impossible for me to write with one of our pens, but only with the Chinese brush which stops me from shaping the letters better'.[23]

Nevertheless, Vieira and Calvo imagined this conquest unfolding according to a scenario as implacable as that pursued by Hernán Cortés in Mexico. The project must have been constantly going round and round in their heads. These men kept the present at bay by throwing themselves into a future for which they desperately longed. They knew very well that in the event of a Portuguese attack and defeat their lives would be at risk. But was this so very different from the recently expelled, defeated and pursued Cortés, as he pondered his fate after the disaster of the *Noche Triste*? His second letter to Charles V (October 1520) did not yet have the ring of a triumphal and triumphant literature, written after the event, in all the elation of success. He and his men had been within an ace of death in the revolt of Mexico, and if the Indian populations could profit from their flight, that would be the end, none of them was in any doubt, not only of their dreams but of their lives. As written up by Cortés and by the Portuguese, the projects of conquest were also appeals for help addressed to sovereigns who were too far away.

The Portuguese conquest would be limited to the province of Canton and the coasts of southern China. The invasion of the latter is briefly considered, but more as a way of convincing Lisbon of the viability of a more restricted intervention than as a realistic objective. They would begin by seizing control of the Pearl River Delta and by destroying as many enemy vessels as possible. As nothing had been achieved with 300 men (an allusion to the failure of Afonso de Mello in 1522), it would need an extra 200 or 300 men to take the small towns situated on the islands of the Delta (Nanto or another even better), search and sail up the rivers, destroy all the fustes and everywhere put the Chinese on the back foot. They would set fire to the river banks 'to clear everything so that our artillery will be able to operate and the Chinese cannot stay there to shoot their arrows at us by hiding behind the houses'; and for good measure: 'they must burn them to clear everything so that not a single house remains'.

Everything was described with meticulous attention to detail, from the deployment of the artillery, by way of the choice of a landing site (near the principal port of Canton), to the use of three artillery pieces to destroy two gates overlain with copper.[24] In only half a day, and with a favourable wind, they should reach Canton that same evening. South of the town they would find enough in the way of fish, rice and meat to feed 20,000 men. Between Nanto and Canton, at Anung-hoi, which had a harbour sheltered from the wind, there was sufficient stone to build a fortress as large as that of Goa. The fleet brought by the Portuguese would undertake the cleansing of the rivers of the Delta. The mandarins would have no alternative but to surrender, unless they chose to evacuate the town and take flight. Canton would fall into the hands of the Portuguese.

Let no one imagine that the enterprise would demand huge resources; any more than the conquest of Mexico, which was achieved without reinforcements from Spain. For Calvo, a mere thousand men would suffice. With a single Portuguese galley, the town would be brought to its knees. Vieira, greedier for men, or perhaps more realistic, estimated the forces necessary at between 2,000 and 3,000 men. Once inside the city, they need only pillage the palaces of the mandarins, which were chock-a-block with gold, silver and merchandise. They would take that of the Grand Treasurer *pochenci*, which housed the Royal Treasury (*fazenda do rei*), and then the prison of the governor of the prefecture of Canton (*conchefaa* or *chanchefu*), not forgetting two other 'factories'. This treasure hunt envisaged by the Portuguese recalls a famous episode in the sack of Mexico, when the Spanish tried desperately to get their hands on the indigenous jewels that had been thrown into the waters of the lake. The Portuguese would also seize the stores of rice, which would be sold to the inhabitants, who would be famished because the town would have received no provisions since the beginning of hostilities. Some of the rice would be distributed in the form of wages to the men working on the fortresses it was proposed that the occupiers would build; care should be taken to pay them more than the mandarins had done but it would not cost Lisbon a single real.[25]

Nevertheless, the conventions would be respected. Before embarking on hostilities a message, a *recado*, would be sent to the authorities of Canton through the intermediary of a 'little kaffir Negro', whose miserable fate one can only imagine. This was the equivalent of the *requerimiento* which the Spanish employed in America; it would refer to the unjust treatment of Tomé Pires and denounce the attacks carried out against the property, vessels and soldiers of the Portuguese. If the ambassador was not allowed to return, or if the response was too tardy, the retaliation would be pitiless.[26] The tone was similarly threatening in both Mexico and China.

The Time of the Crime – Or War with Fire and Sword

The Portuguese and the Spanish knew that the best way of imposing themselves by force was to terrify the local populations. The men of Cortés never tired of describing their skill in this sphere, beginning with the acts of barbarism committed in the first confrontations with the Indians of Tlaxcala. At Izucar, a little later, '100 temples and shrines, well fortified with towers...were [all] burnt'.[27]

The Portuguese were equally determined to engage in war with fire and sword, à la Cortés, so as to 'instil fear in the Chinese'. 'From the outset, o Lord, let them all go through fire and sword, because this is what the enemy deserves from the word go'.[28] Nanto, at the mouth of the Pearl River, 'must be destroyed...it must be taken and burned in its entirety, everything should be devoured by the flames, this is what the people who live there must expect'.[29] The Portuguese would carry out 'acts of great destruction leaving absolutely nothing behind, so as to terrify the people'. They would resort to scorched earth tactics: 'Not a single Chinese thing would escape burning'. They would set fire to all the ships that could not be turned into vessels of war. And they would adhere to a policy of which the men of Cortés would have approved: 'Let the war be waged without pity wherever this is possible'.

The activities of the Portuguese forces would be such a powerful deterrent that the people would no longer fear the cruel mandarins. To keep the Chinese forces at bay, all that was needed was to 'show them their teeth'. The Portuguese had total confidence in their fire-power: 'These people have no means of defence, they only have to hear the roar of a bombard for them to come to our hills to hear what the Portuguese intend to do'.[30] Nevertheless, it was still neces-sary for the operation to be carried out as quickly as possible so as to leave the provincial authorities with no time to marshal their resources or receive reinforcements.

Post-war Canton

The occupying forces would keep Canton under their control by building two fortresses. So that the city would be under Portuguese artillery, they would first build a fortified enclosure to the north of the town. The pagodas nearby would provide excellent building material; as in Mexico, the destruction of pagan sanctuaries was par for the course. A second fortress would complete the operation. It was to be built on the edge of the sea, at the landing place of the mandarins. The number of soldiers installed in the garrison and their relief every three to four months – all was spelt out and counted. The occupying troops would oversee the closing of the gates of the city. In each quarter, 'night watchmen' would be recruited locally and made responsible for the surveillance of the inhabitants, 'because that was the custom, and they would be given drums taken from the houses of the mandarins'.[31]

The fortresses could be built in a few days thanks to the dressed stone, timber and lime that was found everywhere and, above all, the plentiful local labour force. The Portuguese gave much thought to this matter. The Chinese masses were likely to provide docile, skilled, cheap labour, and they must be sure to take advantage of this. They envisaged this whole small world flocking to the aid of the Europeans – 'a hundred thousand of them will come' – in order to build galler-ies, galleasses, fustes and, why not, as in Mexico, brigantines. The custody of the gates, their closure at night, the distribution of the Portuguese garrisons, the supervision of the town – they thought of everything, and it was all considered, reconsidered and endlessly discussed by Vieira, Calvo, Tomé Pires and others during their interminable time in captivity. Everything must be done at top speed: 'It will need less time to do than to write'.

How to control the region? The Portuguese of Canton envisaged building small forts in the towns they occupied. To hold the coast and the offshore islands, they would build a fortress in every important settlement, while some 5,000 Portuguese would control the 'sounds'. Other small forts would watch over the cities built on the banks of the rivers. All these forts would receive garrisons of fifty men brought from India and given the task of collecting taxes from the local population: 'They will all have jobs and they will all be rich, and this will all be done in the fashion of the country'. They should make as few innovations as they could get away with. As far as possible they should conform to local custom, to the 'style of the country'. The ordinary people should continue to kneel before the authorities, so as not to fall into bad habits, and delinquents should still be flogged at the drop of a hat, 'because these people are bad'.[32]

They would leave the king of China alone, as long as he was reasonable and agreed to hand over, every year, a ship loaded with silver, so as not to see the disturbances spread to his other provinces. This was to subject him to the suzerainty of the man the Chinese called 'the King of thieves', Manuel of Portugal. It was also, as we have seen, what the Castilians had initially offered to Moctezuma in Mexico when they had proposed that he recognize Charles V. These extraordinary pretensions on the part of the Europeans confirm that the time of the crime had well and truly begun at the two extremities of the globe.

The Colonial Project

The conquest would be profitable in both the short and the medium term. The region of Canton seemed likely to be a goose that would lay golden eggs: 'The country is of such importance and it offers such profits'. At a rough guess, the city would render 50,000 taels of silver, and the small towns between 20,000 and 30,000 each. The towns of the Delta alone would provide significant revenues. The ginger found there in large quantities and the 'very fine' cinnamon would fill the holds of the Portuguese ships. Canton, 'such a beautiful and populous city', would in the end cost the Crown a good deal less than Goa. 'Nowhere in the world would they find such a rich land to conquer, and the stronger our presence there the greater the wealth we will extract'.

War and the cessation of external trade would spread chaos throughout China. In reaction to the slump caused by the invasion, the province of Canton would rise up, and the interior would follow suit.[33] Vieira was aware of the tension created by the imperial decision to close the region to foreigners and he saw the Portuguese intervention as the precipitating factor that would cause the collapse of the Celestial Empire. The porcelain and silk factories of the interior would be quick to see the advantages of dealing with and working on behalf of the Portuguese.

The aims of the Portuguese went well beyond simple predation. Calvo imagined a systematic exploitation of the region's resources within the broader context of Portuguese Asia by opening 'another *casa da India*' in China, by sending gold and silver to India if it was needed there and by exporting raw materials, 'copper, saltpetre, lead, alum, oakum, cables, all the iron [possible], ironmongery and pitch'. If Portuguese India was in need of ships, 'galleys, galleons and ships' could be built on the spot, using Chinese timber, carpenters, who 'breed like vermin', and all sorts of craftsmen. No demands would be made on the local Portuguese. They would open a 'great factory' for the pepper of Pazem, Pedir (Sumatra), Patane and Banda, with a monopoly for the Crown. It would instantly fill up with Chinese merchandise which would bring in huge profits.[34]

Once the region was under control, they would expand the sphere of operation of the Portuguese 'presence'. From the province of Canton they would attack Fujian with a fleet of forty ships, crewed by between 600 and 700 men. This province would in its turn become a dependency of Lisbon, to which it would send each year at least one cargo of silver; the ideal would be to share the resources of the country equally, half to the king of Portugal, half to the conquerors. Everybody would gain: 'We will obtain another India, just as profitable and for a long time; the more people there are, the greater the profits and the firmer the control of the country, and in this way the Portuguese will become extremely rich, so suitable is the country for this purpose'. Once the 'government of Fujian' had been brought to heel, they would push on to the Ryukyu Islands. This archipelago, which had long traded clandestinely with the Chinese coast, and which was one of the great commercial platforms for the whole of the region, possessed wealth in gold, copper and iron as well as being a great purchaser of pepper.

The Portuguese were as yet unaware that the Ryukyu Islands were the port of another regional power, Japan, the Cipangu of Marco Polo and Columbus. By gradually occupying the whole southern Chinese coast, the Portuguese would be re-establishing contact with a group of merchants who had been accustomed to visit Malacca before the arrival of the Portuguese and who has since retreated to Patane.[35] In other words, the prisoners in Canton were envisaging and planning for total control of the trade of the China Sea. This is probably what Manuel of Portugal had had in mind and what the Portuguese had wanted to set in motion by imposing their law on the Siamese when the latter had tried to approach Canton.

Last but not least, the export of skilled labour to Portuguese India – or the delocalization of labour, if we may be forgiven the anachronism – opened up other tempting prospects of the further integration of the Canton region into Portuguese Asia. The Portuguese were already imagining their ships transporting Chinese craftsmen to the ports of the Indian Ocean: 'Carpenters, masons, smiths, tilers, sawyers and all the crafts with their wives'.[36] They were not so lucky in Mexico, where the Spanish had to train the indigenous workforce to make them into smiths, weavers and bakers before they could start exploiting them as they saw fit.

The Hard Apprenticeship in Colonization

Whether Chinese or Mexican, the towns, once conquered and in part destroyed, were to receive the imprint of the victors. They must be adapted to the military, commercial and political needs of the Europeans. The Iberians proposed everywhere to remodel the urban fabric, taking advantage of the destruction caused by the fighting. They were equally determined in both places to dismantle the indigenous temples and palaces, which would provide material to construct fortresses in Mexico and Canton. In Mexico, where the conquerors had evangelical designs of a sort quite foreign to the Portuguese in China, they intended to use the stone of the 'mosques' to build Christian churches.

The new building, carried out with the aid of large quantities of forced labour drawn from the defeated population, did not involve a radical transformation of the indigenous town into a European city. In the case of Canton it was explicitly to India that the Portuguese looked for a model for one of the two fortresses they proposed to build: it was to be based on that of Calicut, which had been built in 1513 with the agreement of the local sovereign.[37] In the case of Mexico the decision by Cortés to make it the capital of New Spain militated against a policy of total demolition, even though the Indian metropolis had suffered badly during the siege and even though the victors were determined to leave their mark.

This decision should rightly occupy an important place in urban history, since not only did age-old traditions, European, Asiatic and Amerindian, face and confront each other, but, at least in America, this situation produced something entirely novel, that is, the colonial city imposed by Europeans. The urban projects of the Portuguese would remain virtual; Canton survived intact, unaware of the fate that had been planned for it. Peking got rid of its visitors, whereas the Spanish seized Mexico, entered a pile of rubble and embarked on its reconstruction. The war had done incalculable damage. The weeks of siege had exposed the city's infrastructure, its streets, residential quarters, palaces and pyramids, to Spanish gunfire and cannon. The agony of the Mexica city included the extermination of its defenders and the exodus of those who survived. The fall of Mexico-Tenochtitlan inflicted a terrible blow to the Indian psyche.

However, the Mexica *altepetl* had a second life by inspiring a new model, the colonial city, which was replicated, in a variety of forms, from one end of the continent to the other. The Spanish were not content with fortifying areas within conquered sites for their own use, as the Portuguese had intended to do in China, or with remodelling them at will, as they did in Mexico. Rather, they built new towns according to a systematic programme of occupation which involved ensuring that each region would be a province suitable for colonization; Cortés 'looked to see what sites there were on which to build a town', and 'to lay out the town and to build a fort'.[38]

By building new cities the conquerors introduced a toponymy of European origin which coexists to this day with the indigenous toponyms: Puebla de Los Angeles, Valladolid de Michoacan, Antiquira de Oaxaca, etc. However, these colonial creations were only the tip of the iceberg of a massive appropriation of land, men and nature: it was this that created Latin America.

It should not be thought that the Iberians had only *conquista* and diplomacy in their armoury. My comparison here is of two examples which are antithetical both in the countries concerned and in the results obtained. It forces us to relocate success in the West in the context of failure in the East, and vice versa. It is only in this way that we can obtain a global view of this phase in Iberian globalization. The last years of the fifteenth century and early years of the sixteenth were a time of trial and error and of achievements almost as varied as the lands the Castilians and the Portuguese visited; the disastrous experience of the Spanish in the Caribbean is well known; Africa is another story.

Since 1489 the Portuguese had established relatively peaceful contacts with the Kingdom of Kongo, bringing this country under the suzerainty of Lisbon. There had been no invasion, no war, not even any tribute, but a series of links marking the superiority of Lisbon over that 'barbarous province'.[39] The alliance with the European king and the preaching of Christianity went hand in hand with a sort of 'didactic colonialism',[40] an acculturation without tears, the education of the elites in the metropolis and a material, technical, military, judicial and administrative upgrading of the African kingdom. In this, the spread of writing was crucial. On the ground, however, the excesses of the Portuguese in Africa, more interested in making slaves than in 'civilizing' the Kongo, and more disposed to smuggle weapons than set an example to the natives, eventually sabotaged this colonizing project. Nevertheless, the king did not renounce Catholicism and in 1539 wrote to Paul III to submit in everything to the papacy.

The example of Kongo is as different from that of China as it is from that of Mexico: neither fiasco nor conquest but the tortuous paths of corruption and business, with, in the background, a Catholicized elite. Once again, the early sixteenth century made a lasting mark on relations between Europe and the rest of the world. There was more to Portuguese Africa than the Kongo, but this single example is enough to remind us that, between the Amerindian West and the Asiatic East, there was Africa, also of huge importance and not only as an exporter of ivory and slaves. It is for historians and their ever fewer readers to learn to appreciate the diversity of the situations, the singularity of the trajectories and the complexity of the links which already made them inseparable.

13

The Place of the Whites

The place of the Whites was already marked by absence within systems of thought based on a dichotomous principle that at each stage forces the terms to become double, so that the creation of the Indians by the demiurge necessitated the creation of non-Indians, too.

Claude Lévi-Strauss, *Story of Lynx*

China and Mexico infiltrated the European *imaginaire* in the first half of the sixteenth century. Was the opposite also the case? Or are we faced with a feature specific to Latin Christendom, and one of the conditions of European modernity, that is, the putting into words, pictures and maps of the rest of the world? In fact it is much harder to evoke the images of the Iberian countries that were formed by the Chinese and the Mexicans, assuming, that is, that any were. The Asiatics and the Amerindians asked questions about the nature of their visitors and their country of origin, but they were at a disadvantage compared with the Europeans, who had travelled halfway round the world with the express intention of discovering new lands, new peoples and, even more, new wealth.

The Vision of the Vanquished

The Indians who were dispatched to the Iberian Peninsula in the sixteenth century would form a concrete idea of Latin Christendom. And those who remained in Mexico, once evangelized and Hispanicized, would learn to visualize the country of their conquerors;

the availability of books and maps, and conversations with the Spanish, would give them access to all sorts of facts and ideas about the other side of the Atlantic. But no trace survives of anything resembling a conscious and systematic effort on their part to acquire information about, or describe, these distant lands. In the seventeenth century the writings of the educated Indian Chimalpahin, whenever they concern Europe, are simply lifted from works that had passed through his hands. In particular he drew on the information that the German printer and cosmographer Heinrich Martin had made available to readers in New Spain.[1] In other words, no Indian has left us with their personal vision of Spain or of the Old World, and whatever views they formed have remained without any written posterity, dooming the European gaze to remain without an Indian counterpart.

There are ways, however, by which we may gain at least a partial view of this *imaginaire*. The *Cantares mexicanos* are poems in Nahuatl which reproduce, in a colonial version, the creative output of pre-Hispanic bards. They are full of striking images, some of which, exceptionally, evoke pontifical Rome, a Rome that has been Indianized, and where palaces are painted with golden butterflies.[2] In Mexico, Spanish festivals represented, in theatrical or allegorical form, Mediterranean and Oriental lands such as the island of Rhodes and Jerusalem. And the funeral of Charles V saw the staging of many episodes of European history. On the basis of these fragments and fleeting glimpses, we can just about imagine what might have constituted the Indian vision of the country of the invaders. But there is a huge gulf between the idea that another world existed in the Levant and a direct, empirical and physical knowledge of the heartlands of Christendom. This is not to suggest that the Europeans had visionary abilities lacking in the others. But the Indians of the Renaissance lost the battle of the gaze. They were without the means to construct or transmit an image of their own world to the Europeans – with few exceptions it was missionaries or Castilian chroniclers who took on this task; added to which it is still we who have the power to create clichés and impose them on the rest of the world. It is not so much that a Mexico of beaches and gastronomy has today supplanted the imagery developed in the sixteenth century, further narrowing our field of vision. It is still – but for how much longer? – the West which fixes the image of the other, often with the ready connivance of the other in question.

Did the Chinese have any particular desire to know more about their visitors? The context here was diametrically opposite. The Indians – attacked, invaded and colonized – had every reason to want to know their aggressors. Not so the Chinese. The repercussions of the Portuguese episode were simply not comparable to the crisis brought about by the Spanish conquest. The official sources of the Celestial Empire reveal a certain curiosity, but this never developed into an obsessional desire to know, write about or give an account of so as to understand. As we have seen, the Chinese looked at the intruders and physically described them, emphasizing their size, the colour of their skin, the shape of their noses and eyes and their head and body hair.[3] They speculated about their geographical origins, and credited them with a number of barbarous habits, even invoking cannibalism.

This is not much, it might be thought, for a first contact with the Iberians. It was enough, however, for intruders who were regarded as no more than common pirates. We may hypothesize, nevertheless, that the Chinese of Canton and Peking, and the Emperor Zhengde in Nanking, must on many occasions have asked their visitors to describe Portugal and the world from which they came. But if written evidence of this survives, it has not reached the West, or at least nothing that might have helped to lay the foundations of a body of knowledge about Europe and Portugal. The other Chinese, the ordinary people of the coastal districts, the Chinese of the diaspora and officials seeking to profit from the transit of any visitors, must have learned just enough to engage in trade, relying on a few basic notions which rendered superfluous, even unhelpful, any deeper knowledge. The majority of the Indians of Mexico probably had a similar, hardly unexpected, approach to the things and the people. Not every European was a spy or a nascent ethnologist.

Barbarian Pressure

The limited nature of official curiosity was probably a consequence of the way in which the Chinese court dealt with foreigners and the status it accorded them. The Portuguese had come from a country that was unknown to the Chinese and that did not figure in their list of tributary states. Relations between China and the external world were strictly codified. Even the *Suma oriental* of Tomé Pires, written before he had set foot in China, had noted this.

To send an ambassador to Peking, it was necessary to have the requisite credentials, that is, be among the kingdoms recognized as vassals of the Son of Heaven. Then tribute had to be paid, which was what opened up the possibility of commercial exchanges. It was still necessary for Peking to accept both the ambassador and the tribute.

The peculiar Chinese practice of linking diplomacy and trade allowed for no alternative in case of rejection. Other than, for those in a position to do so, opting for war and going in person to seize the goods to which access had been refused by the Chinese court.

It was not only foreign visitors from the south who were treated with such suspicion. Relations with China's northern neighbours, Mongols and other nomads, were a constant cause for concern: due to their turbulence, no doubt, but also because the Imperial government proved to be incapable of adopting a clear policy and sticking to it. For a large part of the fifteenth century Chinese policy towards the Mongols and the nomads of the north was characterized by endless equivocation, which owed more to faction fighting in Peking than to the search for an adequate response to the threats on the frontier. As we have seen, the problems of the Portuguese had as much to do with machinations at court as with any appreciation of what the new arrivals represented.

In the middle of the fifteenth century, the defeat of Tumu, northwest of Peking and not far from the Great Wall, proved disastrous for the Ming Dynasty. The capture of the Emperor Zhengtong dealt a blow which might have proved fatal. The Ming were forced to abandon any attempt to control the world of the steppe. Their military prestige never recovered. From then on the army was China's Achilles heel, as first the Portuguese and then the Spanish had more than one occasion to discover.

After the disaster of Tumu, and for the first time since the accession of the Ming, the steppe of Ordos, in the Loop of the Yellow River (today in Inner Mongolia), fell into the hands of the Mongols and became central to the 'military debate' which developed round the construction of huge defensive lines, among which was the Great Wall of the Ming. This fortification, begun in 1474, required a workforce of 40,000 and cost a million silver taels. In the second half of the fifteenth century, the moves towards the unification of the Mongol tribes and the rise of the kingdom of Turfan, to the west, introduced new threats in the north of the country, while the court remained divided as to what measures to adopt. In 1488, Batu Mönke, a descendant of Genghis, proclaimed himself Khan of the Yuan, Dayan Khan, and embarked on the unification of all the peoples of the steppe. Twenty years later he eliminated his rival Ibrahim, then, between 1508 and 1510, took possession of Ordos and entrusted it to the command of one of his sons.[4] In 1520, a grandson of Batu, Bodi Alagh, received the title of Khan, while two other descendants established themselves firmly in the Loop of the Yellow River. They all attacked an empire which refused to be part of their trading system. It was at this period that the Portuguese were contemplating the conquest of southern China.

In Peking the defence of the frontiers had eventually become both a focus and a pretext for political battles, to the point where any long-term strategy was a secondary consideration. The construction of defensive lines remained, in principle, the only possible point of agreement between the factions. Nevertheless, the proposal of the Minister of War, Yu Tzu-chun (died 1485), along these lines was opposed by the eunuchs, who were able to get the building works stopped. For some fifty years major projects were virtually abandoned in favour of only sporadic operations.

The emperor Zhengde proclaimed his support for the reconquest of Ordos, but the project fizzled out, the construction of new walls being preferred, though little was actually done. When the emperor decided to resume the offensive, his troops won a victory over the Mongols, in 1517, south of Datong.[5] But it made little difference. Things were hardly better under his successor Jiajing (1522–67). In 1540, the government was still wavering between attempting reconquest or temporizing and compromise.

An Aversion to Foreigners

To compensate for the weakness or indecision of imperial rule, what was needed was a powerful first minister or army leader capable of imposing tough solutions and applying them in a sustained fashion. The problems were many. How were the 150,000 men it was estimated in 1472 would be required to clear the frontier and defeat the enemy to be assembled and provisioned? This would mean emptying the capital and bringing in troops from other parts of the Empire. How was the fear instilled by the nomadic horsemen, capable of putting to flight thousands of far from hardened Chinese soldiers, to be overcome? The exploitation of the local population, recruited for the building works and taken away from their farms, raised numerous other problems. And, most of all, how were the funds needed to maintain the interminable lines of fortification, constantly under attack from erosion and bad weather, to be obtained?

To these problems were added the way in which those in the upper ranks of government perceived the foreigners of the north. The educated classes were traditionally hostile to any rapprochement with the barbarians. Remote from the frontiers, and especially in the Chinese south, the gulf between the Chinese and the Mongols appeared immense. The quest for Confucian rigour in the academies of the south went together with a deep aversion to the barbarians. It was made a question of ethics, and ethics was the basis of the state. This attitude, which was part of an idealist and idealized vision of the world, hence indifferent to all forms of realpolitik, reached its apogee at the time of the Song. In periods of dynastic weakness, this retreat to within China, sometimes called 'Chinese culturalism',[6] tended to intensify and crystallize. It helped to bolster the criticism by the educated officials of whatever government was in place whenever it seemed indecisive or unsure of itself.

There was also the more mundane problem of the xenophobia triggered by the nomads. Ignorance and contempt for the world of the steppe was widespread, even though, paradoxically, the disaster of Tumu (1449) had provided striking proof of the military superiority of the barbarians. Others, more familiar with the nomads of the north, suspected that the plans for conquest were impracticable and that only a commercial opening up offered the possibility of a stabilization of relations between the two parties. They called for a resumption of the policy that had been instrumental in creating the glory days of the Tang Dynasty, the Yuan and even the first Ming. But those in favour of a treaty and compromise were never sufficiently influential to make their views prevail. They were sometimes seen as traitors, whose machinations would result in a peace shameful for China. Zhengde's successor, the Emperor Jiajing, detested the Mongols. He believed it was so humiliating and so intolerable to engage in relations with the barbarians that he demanded that the character *Yi* (= barbarian) be reduced to an insignificant size.[7] He was still too young at the time of his accession to demonstrate a similar hatred for the Portuguese, and it was the man who had engineered his ascent to the throne, the prime minister Yang Tinghe, who took on the task of getting rid of the Portuguese embassy. But the anecdote is suggestive of a hostile climate of which, rightly or wrongly, foreigners often bore the brunt.

So every attempt by the Mongols to establish diplomatic and commercial relations with the Empire was doomed to failure. Chinese diplomacy was caught in a vicious circle. The flat rejection of the Chinese authorities offended the nomads, who were reduced to self-help in the form of even more razzias. The transformation of a rebuffed embassy into a *casus belli* was also common – as the Portuguese would discover to their cost.[8] So was the execution of foreign envoys.[9] This sort of response could cost the Empire dear. In 1448, it was the failure of the embassy of the Mongol chief Esen that sparked hostilities and precipitated the Ming army into the rout of Tumu.

It was not easy to be received in Peking. In 1462 Bolai, the leader of the Tatars, sent a mission of 300 persons, which the court rejected on the pretext that it was too large. The following year, an embassy 1,000 strong suffered a similar fate. The Portuguese envoys were by no means the only ones to suffer the consequences of imperial defiance. In the north, missions were accepted by Peking until 1506, but then suspended in the years that followed. This led inexorably to a resumption of the razzias which provided Baty and the Mongols with the goods they were unable to procure by any other means. Much later, in 1550, the Khan of the Mongols, Altan Khan, sought in his turn the favour of bringing tribute according to Ming protocol; like his predecessors, he was met with a flat refusal. The pretext chosen by the court was that his letter had not been written in Mongol, so it was not possible for its authenticity to be established. We are inevitably reminded of the difficulties experienced by the Portuguese. After much procrastination, all relations with the Mongols were forbidden. When, in 1553, Altan Khan sent six ambassadors, all six were thrown into prison and four of them lost their lives. Once again, we see a very similar scenario to that which had defeated the Portuguese.[10]

So if indeed there was a 'clash of civilizations', it is only from the perspective of a global history that the expression can be truly understood. The Portuguese were not driven out because they were Europeans or Christians or even cannibals, but because the current Chinese administration was deeply hostile to foreigners and barbarians. True, the people from Malacca and Lisbon had values, knowledge and interests which all derived from Latin Christendom. But it is clearly not the fact that they purveyed these, consciously or unconsciously, that caused the clash. More important was a political conjuncture which had revived within the bureaucracy a tradition of rejecting foreigners. And this was a consequence less of a militant xenophobia than of an inability to engage in fresh thinking on the part of the administration and an idealized image of relations with the external world.

The nomads of the north who had taken refuge around Lake Kokonor were regarded by the Chinese as pirates. The real pirates, meanwhile, were scouring the South China Sea. Since time immemorial the coastal regions had been subjected to raids or to even more destructive campaigns.[11] Japanese, Koreans and Chinese organized bands which engaged in a variety of trading ventures which were as profitable as they were illegal, and they had no hesitation in penetrating far into the interior for the purpose of pillage. In the fifteenth century, the rise of maritime trade in the East Asian seas was accompanied by an increase in piracy and numerous other clandestine activities. The organization of a war fleet, the reinforcement of the armies in the maritime provinces, the hunting down of pirates and the restrictions the imperial administration attempted to impose on the circulation of men and ships – all were in vain. Results were achieved only on the northern frontiers. The official prohibition on maritime trade, in 1525, simply led to a fresh upsurge of piracy and smuggling.[12]

These failures might have been expected to raise questions about the ban itself, but the conviction that here, too, there must be no compromise with the barbarians was too deeply rooted. Once again any serious discussion of foreign policy invariably lapsed into an internal debate between 'corrupt traitors' and 'irreproachable servants'. On occasion, lessons learned in the south were applied in the north, as when Portuguese cannon, or copies of Portuguese examples, were used to strengthen the defences on the Mongol frontier. In reality, the length of the coastline, the extent of collaboration at every level of the population and the lure of gain meant that the situation was beyond control. Like so many others, the Portuguese took advantage of this to gain entry to China. But in the end, and not without reason, they were bound to be seen as no different from the thousands of pirates who were such a cause for concern among those who ruled the Empire.

The Portuguese had nevertheless come close to slipping through the net when the distrust and distance cultivated by the Chinese government in situations of this type was revived. It only needed the death of Zhengde for everything to turn to dust; the new team made haste to profit from the vacuum created by the death of the emperor by eliminating the favourite Jiang Bin and his clique, who had supported the Portuguese. The new alarmists from Malacca and Canton did the rest.

The rejection of the intruders was thus not exceptional and their diplomatic failure was wholly predictable, given that they were unlikely to make any impact on the factions at court or on the conception of the world to which the educated Chinese clung. When we remember that about the same time, in 1520, there was a deterioration in relations with Japan, a kingdom known since the dawn of time, and that in 1521 a Japanese embassy pillaged the town of Ningbo, where it had landed,[13] the Portuguese episode comes to seem even less remarkable. What appears to us, seen from Europe, as a first official contact, which was how it was viewed by King Manuel, was for the Chinese little more than a simple matter of piracy. The apparent myopia of the Chinese brings home to us how great a distance the Celestial Empire was determined to maintain with regard to its visitors, and how limited was its curiosity about them.

What Place for the Alien?

Faced with aliens, which is what the Iberians were, did everything turn on the degree of closure or openness? Should we contrast inward-looking and clear-headed Chinese with open-minded and ingenuous Mexicans? On the face of it, the Indians of Mexico had no more reason to be 'open' than the Chinese, and their reactions were neither monolithic nor fatalistic, but they had no way of appreciating the scale of the danger that threatened them. They were quick to realize the destructive capacity of the invaders but they were in no position to grasp the forces they had behind them or the motives that inspired them, even less the bacteriological bombshell about to explode on their soil.

The ease and rapidity with which Mexico, Central America and then South America fell into the hands of the Spanish confirms the scale of this misjudgement. The Spanish – *Castilan* or *Teules* in Mexico, *Viracochas* in the Andes – were never seen for what they were, until it was too late. The error was general. The indigenous allies of the Spanish, who had been indispensable to the conquest of Mexico, were as mistaken about the Castilians as were the Mexicas. They were all of them caught unawares by a situation they were never able to get a hold on, which they had no information about and which was without precedent.

The impact of the 'aliens' on the upper ranks of the Chinese government was very different: the emperor, the mandarins, the ministers and the eunuchs were not spontaneously closed to the new arrivals, as the welcome received by Pires shows, but they had an experience and a conception of the barbarians which gave a context to and significantly limited the effects of the contact and the damage it might do. A foreigner was a barbarian, and a barbarian was a threat. What could be more logical? A host of rules, principles, prejudices and unhappy experiences, together with diplomatic inertia, protected the empire from external worlds. Added to which, in the circles of power, was the influence of neo-Confucian values. By contrast, the Amerindian societies were without any standpoint from which they could appreciate the lethal threat their visitors represented or reduce their impact by normalizing them. Further, they lacked any sort of bureaucratic machine that might have slowed down, blocked or neutralized the

intruders: Tomé Pires had to sit it out for months in Canton; Cortés
literally charged into Mexico.

Lastly, far from systematically discrediting the aliens, the Mexican
societies tried to interpret them in a way that would make it possible
for them to be incorporated into their own local history. The idea
that the foreigners were in fact returning home confused the issue
and defused resistance. The Mesoamerican societies, and probably
Amerindian societies in general, had always allowed a place to the
other.[14] For Claude Lévi-Strauss, Amerindian dualism 'draws its
inspiration...from an openness to the Other, an openness that very
visibly manifested itself during the first contacts with the Whites,
even though the latter were impelled by directly opposite motives'.[15]
Cannibalism may even, on closer examination, be simply a physical
way of integrating the other, the intruder, the enemy, into oneself.
And this faculty is not entirely irrelevant to the proliferation of all
forms of *métissage* triggered by colonization in the north and south
of the American continent.

The Chinese reaction, of normalization, rejection and extirpation,
was not without consequences for the forms of European expansion.
It obliged the Portuguese to develop a more oblique way of approaching China, developing a different form of contact, in collaboration
with various Asiatic partners, who helped them to circumvent the
barriers and prohibitions put in their way. It was all the easier for
them to become what the Chinese wanted, that is, pirates in troubled
waters, because this was an identity with which they felt perfectly at
home. The Indians of Mexico, meanwhile, defeated, colonized and
Christianized, learned how to be the survivors of a lost civilization.

14

To Everyone Their Own Post-War

Digamos que esta tierra como otra Egipto, en ella el agua fue converttida en sangre de aquella cruel enfirmedad. [Let us say that that land [is] like another Egypt, where water was changed into blood from that cruel illness.]

Motolinía, *Memoriales*

[Antonio de Faria] se embarcou sem contradição nenhuma & todos muyto ricos e muyto contentes & con muytas moças muyto fermosas que era lastima velas yr atados cos murrões dos arcabuzes de quatro em quatro de cinco em cinco e todas chorando e nossos rindo e cantando. [[António de Faria] embarked without encountering any opposition and all were very rich and very content, accompanied by a lot of pretty young girls who it was piteous to observe when you saw them march tied four by four with the wicks of harquebusses; they wept while we laughed and sang.]

Fernão Mendes Pinto, *Peregrinação*

The Portuguese failure in Canton drew a dividing line between Asia and America. On one side was a New World which would give its raison d'être to the West, and whose wealth, population and spaces would be ruthlessly exploited; on the other was Imperial China, which would absorb much of the silver extracted from the mines of America by the defeated Indians and African slaves.[1] The fate of the two shores of the Pacific was now linked, as the Iberians had laid down the economic and political bases for a massive decanting of precious metal. The history of the colonization of the New World would have China always in the background, America would be a constant presence in that of modern China. This is obvious to us, with the benefit of hindsight, but was not obvious to contemporaries. In the 1520s the mines of America had yet to be discovered; the Iberians were trying to take over the world, but without really knowing what they would find or what they would do with it. The Amerindians, defeated or allies of the Spanish, were entering into a chaotic post-war, while the Chinese authorities were already beginning to forget the *Fo-lang-ki*.

The Brothers of the Coast

Failure in China forced the Portuguese Crown to adopt a different approach. The dreams of Manuel the Fortunate gave way to the pragmatism of John III,[2] who distanced himself from his predecessor. There was no question now of an official embassy or of plans for conquest, even less open war. It seemed a much better prospect – but was there really any choice? – to let the Portuguese merchants pursue their own personal initiatives and build relationships with their Asiatic peers, allowing a gradual return to the coasts of China. All talk of occupation or of periodic raids on the southern provinces was abandoned in favour of personal contacts, discretion, even secrecy, bribes and hoping for lucky breaks. Attempts were made to improve relations with the merchant communities throughout the region. Patani, in Malaysia, appeared to offer an excellent base for launching into this peaceful 'Reconquest'; it was frequented by merchants from Siam, Malaysia and Asia who were familiar with the shores of Fujian, and it was where one could meet Chinese merchants and establish friendly relations with profitable deals in mind.

The Portuguese had to contend with a number of factors which they had no choice but to accept: the presence of the *wokou* pirates, defectors from the empire, Japanese or other, who had some support in the coastal villages and were often hand in glove with the Chinese merchants of the diaspora and the coast;[3] the existence of an imperial fleet which was far superior to anything the Portuguese could muster; and the constraints imposed by the closure of the country – an officially non-negotiable policy, though it could be circumvented. It was in this context that relations were gradually resumed during the course of the 1520s and strengthened over the two subsequent decades. Guangdong was abandoned in favour of Fujian, much further to the northeast, in response to pleas from the Chinese of the coasts, with whom contact was being resumed.[4] A Luso-Asiatic interloper society developed, characterized by swift sorties, fleeting appearances and extreme mobility, active all along the coast, a distance of hundreds of kilometres, and taking advantage of welcoming islands, isolated ports, complicit peasants, unobservant coastguards and corrupt mandarins.

The Portuguese latched onto this pre-existing network. They did not innovate but were content, soldiers, sailors and merchants, to be the first Europeans to infiltrate this economic world, developed over the years by Chinese and Muslim merchants.[5] The perspective of conquest leading to colonization, which had been the desperate hope of terrified prisoners, was superseded by the pragmatic management of an everyday life in which risk, precariousness and dreams of fabulous wealth were the order of the day. The Portuguese had to learn how to deal both with the mandarins of the coasts and with the 'robbers of the seas' and – why not? – blend in with the latter. What else had they been, in the eyes of those Chinese judges who had described them as 'petty thieves'?

Fernão Mendes Pinto's masterpiece, *The Voyages and Adventures*, is the best guide to this milieu as seen through European eyes. The ease with which one of the book's heroes, Antonio de Faria, changes partner, replacing the pirate Quiay Panjão, after his untimely death, with another Chinese, Similau, a man of the same ilk, speaks volumes as to practices which Mendes Pinto defends in one striking sentence: 'Antonio de Faria was by nature curious, but nor was he entirely devoid of greed'.[6] Three maritime provinces of southern China were involved: Guangdong, Fujian and Zhejiang.[7] Fujian and Zhejiang were most important until the 1540s; Guangdong dominated in the following decade; Macau became the chief Portuguese base from the mid sixteenth century.

In principle the imperial administration prohibited all trade with foreigners. In practice the situation was extremely variable. The foreign presence was dependent on a range of individuals, factions, lobbies and interest groups, with shifting and often contradictory preoccupations. How was it possible for the size of the empire, the integrity of its frontiers, the susceptibility of the mandarins, the greed of the merchants, the rise of the coastal towns and the prosperity of maritime trade to be reconciled? In the face of the great merchants of the three regions concerned, of the provincial administrations and of the government departments of Peking, the Portuguese constantly manoeuvred to make a profit amidst events they could not control.

The coteries at the Imperial Court remained unpredictable. As we have seen, they had frustrated the embassy of Tomé Pires. In Canton and in the maritime provinces the military commanders tended to approve the closure of the frontiers, whereas it was in the interests of the men of the sea to ignore it; the provincial judges, meanwhile, preferred to see which way the wind blew, fluctuating between 'understanding', laissez-faire and hostility. By tradition and by conviction, the educated Confucians were far more inclined to mistrust the barbarians than the merchants, who had traded with the people of Siam, Malacca and South-East Asia for centuries. In China itself the economic rivalry between cities and coastal regions further complicated the picture. It goes without saying that the great merchants of Canton were not always in accord with their fellows of Fujian and Zhejiang, with whom they were in fierce competition; the foreigners had to learn how to turn this to their own advantage.

On the coasts of Zhejiang and Fujian the Chinese merchants ignored the law and developed contacts with the foreigners at will. The Chinese sources are informative about such masters of smuggling as Zhou Lan, Wang Zhi and Lin Xiyuan. Wang Zhi, a pirate and merchant from Zhejiang, who always maintained close links with Japan, operated on the coasts of all three provinces until his execution in 1559. Lin Xiyuan is a more intriguing figure: educated, a former mandarin and master of a considerable fleet, he had remained close to the provincial administration, where he had friends who helped him to control the provision of supplies to the Portuguese ships which docked illegally.[8] For the Chinese authorities, they were all 'boors', as were two other smugglers, Li Guangtou of Fujian and Xu Dong of Anhui, who were based in Shuangyu, near Ningbo.[9] These Chinese were afraid of nothing, escaped from the provincial prisons if need be, held at bay the expeditions launched against them, attacked the patrols of the fleet and even captured military leaders, who were released in return for substantial ransoms. The abduction of famous and wealthy persons became such a flourishing business that the administration had to put a price on the head of the gang leaders to get rid of them. Which speaks volumes as to the violence and brutality which prevailed in these societies of 'brothers of the coast', or mafias before their time.

Predation and Asianization

These Chinese traded alongside foreign merchants, all – with the exception of the Portuguese – Asiatic, some of them Muslims, who were alike in seeking a profit. Success went to those who established the best relations with the Chinese administration, entered into beneficial partnerships with influential merchants or, as we have seen, joined forces with well-armed pirates, Chinese, Malaysian or Japanese. The Portuguese who accompanied Mendes Pinto and whom he described were among them; it was a clever man who could draw a clear line between trade, smuggling and piracy.

The raids in which the Portuguese joined left vivid memories in the mind of Mendes Pinto, which no edifying criticism – the book was published long after the author's death – could altogether suppress: Antonio de Faria 'embarked without encountering any opposition and all were very rich and very content, accompanied by a lot of pretty young girls who it was piteous to see when you saw them march tied four by four with the wicks of harquebusses; they wept while we laughed and sang.'[10] The sack of a Chinese town, decided on the spur of the moment, was lovingly described: they were to have half an hour, no more, for reasons of security, but the pillaging went on for over an hour and a half and Antonio de Faria had to set fire to the town to get his men to return to the boat. 'Within a quarter of an hour, everything had burned so fiercely that it was as if one was in hell'.[11]

We are poorly informed about this clandestine (perforce) and secretive (by nature) society, unless we take Mendes Pinto's *Voyages and Adventures* for what it is, that is, not so much a faithful chronicle of Portuguese activities in the China Sea as an engrossing glimpse into the shady world of the coasts and a mine of information on *mentalités* and behaviour. Following in the tracks of a sixteenth-century Indiana Jones, we discover, in the course of short, readable chapters that maintain the suspense, an astonishing way of life. The dates and figures – which Mendes Pinto does not skimp – may be wrong, and the story of the Portuguese exploits may be interspersed with pious observations, but we are presented with situations and practices that we know only through the writing and the sensibility of this particular author.

One dynamic stands out at once from the succession of adventures with which the author enthrals his readers: though never ceasing to be themselves, the Portuguese had of necessity to merge into the landscape. From the moment of their arrival in the Indian Ocean, the influence of their Asiatic surroundings had been impossible to resist. In the China Sea, this Asianization went a stage further. How could they remain immune when they were in daily contact with Indians, Malaysians and Chinese; when they learned the local languages; when they became familiar with toponyms and climatic phenomena such as typhoons; when they associated with women of every origin; when they got caught up in the mysteries of regional politics; and most of all when they accepted that they were not running the show but simply partners in a mercantile scene which had not waited for their arrival to become prosperous and which had nothing to learn from them.

The way they were received facilitated this transformation at every turn. In South-East Asia they were presumed to be Asiatic, including by the Chinese. In the Annals of the Monarchy of Malacca and Johor, the Portuguese became 'white men from Bengal';[12] in China they were assumed to have come from Malacca or Siam;[13] elsewhere, the king of Portugal was thought to be one of the sultans of South-East Asia. Rather than get bogged down in long explanations (who were they? where did they come from? what were they looking for?), the Portuguese themselves often preferred to pass themselves off as merchants from Siam, or let it be believed they were Chinese.[14] It was easier to conduct their affairs inconspicuously – money has neither smell nor origin – than launch into lessons in geography, ethnography or history that would only have complicated matters and aroused suspicion. This was a game at which the Portuguese excelled; to the point where the Nguyen Kings of Cochinchina would always distinguish the people of Macau from the other Europeans, granting them privileges they allowed only to Asiatic merchants.[15] In the version presented by Mendes Pinto, Tomé Pires was not executed in Canton but lived out his days in the Chinese interior, complete with wife and children. This anecdote, which is very unlikely to be true, is nevertheless revealing as to the state of mind of, and pressures weighing on, the Europeans. To merge into the Asiatic scenery, that too was a destiny!

Asianization was furthered by the weak institutional presence of the Portuguese in the region. They were concentrated in the vicinity of Goa and in the Indian Ocean. Once past the island of Ceylon, practically left to themselves, the Portuguese were in no position to Lusitanize their hosts, even if such an idea had entered their heads. In this part of the world, the Asianization conceived as wholesale adaptation to the receiving milieus gave birth to a new 'colonial' model, the foundation of Macau.

A Mestizo Island

The setting is an island called Liampó in spring 1542 or, to be more precise, a channel between two islands, not far from the Chinese city of Ningbo, in the southeast of Shanghai province.[16] It was here that merchants of every origin put in, in order to offload their merchandise and load up their ships with Chinese products. It is thought to have been the harbour of Shuangyu, where the Portuguese began to gather in the early 1540s, once it had been turned into a base by a Chinese smuggler from Fujian, Deng Liao. The Portuguese did not arrive alone. It was the Xu brothers who brought to Liampó merchants from Patani and Malacca as well as the Portuguese, the barbarian *Fo-lang-ki*. A few years later, in 1545, still according to the Chinese sources, Wang Zhi, an associate of the Xu brothers, attracted some Japanese smugglers into this society.[17] They were probably not the first.

The Portuguese, who were far from dominating these communities, had to accommodate to all the groups gathered here for the same purpose. There was plenty of mixing, but it was a mixing subject to the ways of life, beliefs and traditions of South-East Asia, an Asia of smuggling and piracy. In any case, reading Mendes Pinto we observe a remarkable similarity between all these people. He describes exchanges and movements which made these coastal islands not simply buffer zones but zones where worlds met. Beyond the control of Lisbon or Goa, on the margins of the Chinese Empire, the Portuguese colony insinuated itself into the ancient economic circuits on which it battened before eventually imposing itself as the chief intermediary in Sino-Japanese trade. The idealization and pride which shows through in the pages of the *Voyages and Adventures* speaks volumes as to the appeal of this way of life and the nostalgia for it that Mendes Pinto still felt. Yet he never glosses over the tensions or the eruptions of violence, as if they were an integral part of the daily life of these adventurers. They might raid a Chinese town one day, hire its dancers and singers to celebrate a famous prize or bloody victory the next.

Did this phase end with the settlement in Macau in 1554?[18] It is clear that the sedentarization of the Portuguese and the rise of a community they dominated, in this case without any rivals, changed the rules of the game. Though Macau insisted on asserting its independence. It was a local initiative, on the margins of the *Estado da India* and the port authority of Malacca (Lionel de Souza in 1554), which laid the foundations of this establishment, which was negotiated directly with the mandarins of Canton. In constant dialogue with the Chinese authorities, Macau practised a diplomacy of the frontier and of survival,[19] which developed autonomously, constantly on the lookout for shifts in imperial policy or dynastic overthrows, always attentive to regional changes and ready to reach agreements with the Japan of the Tokugawa, Siam or Cochin China. In many respects, the 'Macau formula' was heir to the years of smuggling and clandestine activity which had followed the disaster of Canton.

The liquidation of the Portuguese embassy in Canton did not end the European presence in the region. The Portuguese made a major contribution to facilitating the entry of Ming China into a world economy which extended in the sixteenth century from Lisbon to the Pacific Ocean. But the European retreat had opened up paths which involved neither conquest nor colonization, and which ultimately made the Chinese masters of the game. By brandishing the threat of an official prohibition of all trade, Peking disposed of a formidable weapon for influencing supply or demand, while on the coasts large numbers of the subjects of the Celestial Empire engaged in trade of every description.

Chaos in Mexico

Things were very different in the Mexico of Cortés. Here, the first ten years of conquest was a time of chaos and of trial and error. The Castilian victory gave rise to problems without precedent. How were the millions of Indians and the hundreds of thousands of square kilometres which had fallen into their hands to be subjected to a few thousand Spaniards? How were these myriads of pagans to be integrated into a Catholic Empire? No one had any idea what sort of society would emerge from the ruins of the conquest and the collapse of Mexica domination. The Spanish had emerged from the *reconquista* of Spain from the Moors, and they had embarked on a colonization of the Caribbean islands with disastrous consequences for the indigenous populations, but the challenges which they faced in Mexico bore no relation to these earlier experiences: the size of the indigenous population, the huge continental – as opposed to merely island – space, the nature of the societies and the role to be allowed to the indigenous elites – everything was uncertain.

First, however, it was the chaos created by the war and the fall of Mexico City that the victorious Spanish had to face. In the 1520s nothing was as yet decided. I have discussed elsewhere the evidence for the chaos consuming Mexico – political, social and human, but also economic and religious.[20] The government was destabilized, the war had devastated the countryside, epidemics were decimating the population. This was not a classic post-war situation. It was impossible to return to what had been, to restore the old order. Nor was it possible to rely on a programme of reconstruction launched from the metropolis or the Caribbean. There was no recipe for transforming the Mesoamerican societies into colonial societies; all the modernity of Machiavelli would not have sufficed.

The invaders had to establish forms of exploitation and domination adapted to local conditions; they had to design a policy of evangelization; they had to make institutions of Hispanic origin function on a quite different scale from the original, drawing on anything that might serve locally to build a new order, eliminating anything that seemed likely to be detrimental. At a very early stage, even before the country had been conquered, Cortés had suggested to the Crown that Mexico be given the name New Spain. Like the kingdom of Granada, which had fallen in 1492, the Indian country had to be subjugated and Christianized. There was no other way of imposing these changes than to put in place institutions, powers, beliefs and values, forms of urban life and an agrarian landscape of Castilian and European origin. The need to select and then export to Mexico a whole arsenal of practices, customs and traditions that had developed on the other side of the ocean made it necessary constantly to weigh up what was essential to the salvation of a Christian and to the profitability and efficiency of Castilian domination. Any error, local or metropolitan, risked wiping out the precious Indian labour force, as had happened in the islands, infuriating the settlers who were indispensable to any durable settlement and putting at risk royal power and relations with the Caribbean islands. The colonists had to invent what came to be called Westernization. It was a huge programme. To impose Castilian law, based on Roman law, to apply the prohibitions of canon law, to teach alphabetic reading and writing, to spread the use of the Latin mass, marriage in church and auricular confession, and a host of other more prosaic activities, such as metalworking, drinking wine and wearing shoes – all this was 'Westernization'.

In principle, there could be no question of the Spanish compromising; Christian beliefs were non-negotiable, hence the systematic imposition of Christianity and the war on idolatry. It was impossible for the defeated to reject the political control, which implied a situation of total dependence on the part of the Indians with regard to their victors; even less to reject the economic domination, which involved systematically bleeding the country, as far as this could be done. This is not to say that the Spanish simply imposed what they were, or that they remained immune to any influence from the societies they took over. The intruders had to adapt to the food, the languages and the climate, with its alternating dry and rainy seasons. For the colony to be viable, they needed to know how and when to make compromises and adjustments between the European elements they had introduced and Indian realities.

It was necessary, too, to reckon with the resistance and habits of the local populations. The Indians were never passive recipients.

Everything that was received or imposed was gradually reinterpreted, amended and sometimes radically transformed. In reality, the frontier between what was negotiated and what not seems much less clear-cut than at first appears. The Europeans were inevitably changed by their encounters, as were many of the institutions, values and habits they introduced or imposed. The 'shock between civilizations' was not simply a matter of eliminations and substitutions. The confrontation between persons and societies gave rise to *métissages* in the most unexpected areas. And the repercussions of Mexico's colonization cannot be ignored today. These *métissages* involved for the first time people who were natives of three continents. So this was not just a Westernization, but a decisive stage in the history of the globe and of globalizations.[21] Colonization, Westernization, an intermixing of persons and mindsets: this was what China escaped on a lasting basis in 1522.

Americanization and Asianization

Though to some extent anticipated in the Caribbean islands, the massive operation of exporting the medieval *ancien régime* to new lands was the first large-scale colonizing venture undertaken by a European country. No European kingdom had until then faced the task of administering such vast and distant lands. The occupation of the Caribbean had confronted the Spanish with conquests of modest size, where they had always been within reach of their ships and faced with rapidly reducing populations. In the case of Portuguese Asia, the *Estado da India* and its capital Goa (since 1510) were tiny in comparison with Mesoamerica. The difference was immeasurably greater once the Spanish had added South America – from Colombia to Patagonia – to Mexico and Central America.

Was there not, nevertheless, over and above the processes of Westernization and *métissages*, or rather as a result of these two dynamics, a sort of Americanization, counterpart of the Asianization experienced by the Portuguese? Yes, as long as the term 'Americanization' is not taken in its most common sense, which is today that of the influence exercised by the United States on the rest of the world. The American experience transformed the people concerned, not least the Europeans. This was first because they had left their ancestral homes behind and were forced to build new homes thousands of leagues away from Old Spain. A family that had some of its members living in America was no longer the same as a family that had for generations remained in Europe, in familiar surroundings. The trans-oceanic extension of family relationships, the re-focusing in an unknown and non-Christian land, the habit of mobility, successive phases of pulling up sticks and of putting down roots – all this changed people. As did American space, which was not simply disproportionately larger than the space in which they had originally lived; Indian time, which was no longer that of the ancestral celebrations of their country of origin; and coexistence and intimacy with indigenous women. All of these and many other novelties affected the behaviour of individuals, probably without them realizing it, eventually transforming the lives and sensibilities of the new arrivals. Added to which was the advantage that all victors, even the most humble, enjoy in relation to the defeated locals, that element of social and economic superiority which they would have hoped for in vain in the Castile or Basque country of their birth.

Americanization meant social promotion and recognition for many Europeans. At best it was the assurance of belonging to the dominant sector in society; at worst it gave access to a range of advantages they had failed to find in the Old World. Asianization could also bring wealth and recognition to the Portuguese, but accompanied by a high degree of risk and an only marginal integration, never unrivalled domination.

The Secrets of the South Sea

In the distance, behind the mountainous slopes and the wooded hills, there stretches as far as the eye can see an immense mirror of silver, the Ocean, that great legendary Ocean, of which many had dreamed but which none had seen, the Ocean which had been vainly sought for many years, by Christopher Columbus and those who came after, the Ocean which bathed the shores of America, India and China.

Stephan Zweig, *The Tide of Fortune*

La voluntad que yo de vuestra majestad conocí de saber los secretos de este mar del Sur.

Hernán Cortés to Charles V, 1532

Was China now out of reach for Europeans? Our story could stop here if we believed that all idea of conquest was definitively abandoned at the beginning of the 1520s. This would be to forget that the Portuguese were not the only Europeans to take an interest in the Far East, and that the colonization of America and the history of Asia are linked.

The China of the First Voyage Round the World

On one point European observers were agreed. Magellan's voyage, in the words of Maximilian Transylvanus, had made it possible to 'get closer to China'.[1] The expedition had not landed on the Chinese coast, but, on one island after another, Magellan's sailors had found numerous traces of the Celestial Empire.[2] After Magellan's death, his sailors had fallen on the Chinese junks;[3] at Bacchian they had found cloth of gold and silk. And from Borneo had come coins that were pierced in the middle so they could be strung; on one side they had 'the four marks which are letters of the Great King of China'. From information gathered in the ports of the region they learned of a country governed by 'the greatest King in the world, Santhoa Raja', in reality the Ming emperor Zhengde. His immense power was said to extend over all the lords of India Major and India Minor.[4] They imagined him at the head of an opulent court, living amidst his wives and his guards in a palace with innumerable rooms. The sailors heard talk of a great port, Guantau (Canton), and of two capitals: Namchin (Nanking) and Commihala (the Khanbalikh of Marco Polo). The country was attractive, even reassuring with its 'white and [decently] clothed' inhabitants, who 'ate off a table'. However, it was not necessarily easy of access since the seal of the Emperor was necessary to enter China. Some Spaniards sold as slaves to Chinese merchants after the massacre of Cebu may even have set foot in the Middle Empire.[5] Throughout the 1520s the Moluccas, with China in the background, were in the Castilians' sights.

The Attempts from Spain

The Spanish Crown was not put off by the failure of Magellan's expedition. The year 1525 was an auspicious one for Charles V: his victory at Pavia on 24 February sealed his military and political supremacy in Europe, and the king of France, Francis I, was his prisoner.[6] Charles was anxious to add the Spice Islands to his list of achievements. On 24 August 1525 he appointed Fray Garcia Jofre de Loaisa, commander of the Order of St John, captain of a fleet of eight ships which was dispatched to take possession of the Moluccas, to establish a permanent settlement in the islands and assure its government.[7] The indications are, however, that Loaisa planned also to go to Japan. After passing through the Strait of Magellan, a bark separated from the squadron and sailed due north; it reached New Spain and informed Cortés of the aims of the expedition. But Loaisa died on the voyage, and the captains who succeeded him also perished, one after the other. Only a single ship landed in the Moluccas, where its arrival was enough to sow confusion, 'because the Moors of the Moluccas are very attached to the Castilians'.[8] The Portuguese in Asia were not ready to forgive the Spanish for the special relationship they enjoyed with their Muslim competitors.

Still in 1525, another expedition set out for the Moluccas with the aim of 'discovering Eastern Cathay'.[9] Financed by the rich merchant Cristobal de Haro and commanded by a Portuguese, Estevan Gómez, it left from La Coruna but sailed in a northwesterly direction, seeking a passage to the Pacific somewhere between Florida and the 'land of Cod'. Gomez got as far north as Nova Scotia and returned with a few slaves. So impatient was Spain to gain direct access to the Moluccas that news of his return was greeted by frenzied excitement. Word spread that his ship was loaded with *clavos* (cloves), whereas what it actually carried was *esclavos* (slaves).[10] La Coruna was never to become the Atlantic terminal of a new spice route, carved out through the ice fields of the Far North.

In April 1526 the *piloto mayor* Sebastian Cabot sailed from La Coruna at the head of an expedition consisting of three naves and a caravel. Again, it headed southwest. Far from reaching the Moluccas, however, or even entering the Pacific Ocean, Cabot contented himself with exploring the delta of the Rio de la Plata. On his return to Spain, in 1530, he was prosecuted and imprisoned for disobedience, though he later obtained an imperial pardon. Meanwhile, the idea of a Northwest Passage continued to arouse intense interest. It explains the resumption of the exploration of Florida in 1527, under the command of Panfilo de Narvaez, but this expedition was a disaster.

The Second Life of Hernán Cortés

Since 1521, the conquest of Mexico and access to its Pacific coast had changed the name of the game. New Spain was bathed by an immense sea, the South Sea, 'to be discovered, conquered and settled', and the shores of Mexico provided a natural base for voyages to the Moluccas. The continental obstacle had been circumvented. The indefatigable Hernán Cortés was soon so firmly convinced of this that, in 1522, he occupied the region of Jalisco and Zacatula on the Pacific coast.[11] His third letter held out all the tantalizing prospects opened up by the exploration of the South Sea: 'He believed he could import by that route the drugs of the Moluccas and Banda and the spices of Java with less difficulty and less risk'.[12] His fourth letter (October 1524) proposed the occupation of the Spice Islands and a voyage to China. But he was forced to curb his impatience and wait for two years and the failure of Loaisa before, in June 1526, from Granada, the emperor gave him a free hand and instructed him to send his ships in search of the survivors. This rescue expedition was also given the mission of collecting the fifty or so survivors of the expedition of Magellan who had sailed on the *Trinidad*. It only remained for Cortés to discover the route leading from New Spain to the Moluccas.

In the interim he had been left with plenty of time to explore the Mexican coast; he had to choose the best sites for ports, lay claim to them and establish arsenals, stocked with the necessary tools and materials for the construction of many ships. Cortés did not stint himself: he assembled material from Spain and skilled workers for his shipyards. The conqueror of Mexico was sufficiently rich and enterprising to build himself a flotilla on the Pacific and to nurture intercontinental ambitions. Warned of the passage of the expedition of Loaisa by the bark which had broken away, Cortés immediately speeded up the construction of his ships. He was convinced that the Moluccas were easily accessible from New Spain, as he explained, in May 1527, in a letter addressed to the king of Cebu: 'We are so close and we can make contact in so short a time'. He was thus the obvious choice to send ships to the rescue of the Spaniards of the Moluccas, and there were many, in both Mexico and Seville, who were not unhappy to see his formidable energies diverted towards the dangerous ocean.

The Pacific quickly became a family affair. Cortés made haste to place at the head of the expedition his cousin Alvaro de Saavedra y Cerón to whom he gave precise instructions (May 1527): he was to sail straight for the Moluccas without stopping at other islands or lands except 'to make contact and draw up an account of the things found there'. These instructions reveal how the conquistador had morphed into a maritime entrepreneur. However, he was still driven by the same desire for order and efficiency: there was to be no blasphemy aboard ship; gambling for money was tightly restricted; no women were allowed on board, 'because they habitually cause problems in groups of this type'; there was to be no conflict with the indigenous populations ('do not importune them or irritate them; on the contrary, seek to please them'), nor any contact, at any price, with the wives of the natives. Saavedra was to avoid confrontation with the Portuguese fleets, gather as much information as he could and, most important of all, collect spice plants which could be acclimatized in Spain.

The captain who had conducted the conquest of Mexico in such masterly fashion proved an accomplished diplomat when he made overtures to the rulers of Cebu and Tidore. In the case of the former, he asked forgiveness for the excesses committed by Magellan, 'for having unleashed war and discord on you and your people'. As

Cortés explained, God had properly punished him: 'Our Lord and Creator of all things allowed him to pay for his disobedience by dying in the way he did, in the wrongful action committed against the wishes of his Prince'.[13] Thus, in only a few words, the famous navigator was executed, relegated to the dustbin of history, his succession appropriated – a little hastily – and Cortés himself erected into an impartial interlocutor. Cortés remained a manipulator without equal, oblivious of the fact that he too had quite recently acted 'against the wishes of his Prince'. To the king of Tidore he addressed thanks for the welcome offered to the survivors of Magellan's expedition, together with promises of aid and military assistance 'to defend and protect your lands and your person against the attacks of your enemies'.[14] Cortés even professed himself disposed to receive his envoys 'so that they may see New Spain'. The conquistador proclaimed the very best of intentions, in line with the emperor's orders, quite prepared to assume control of the affairs of the other half of the globe.

Saavedra left from Zihuatanejo on 31 October 1527, provided with letters which Cortés addressed not only to the king of Tidore but also to Sebastian Cabot, Gómez de Espinosa and the survivors of Magellan's expedition. Saavedra first reached the Marshall Islands (Rongelap). Once past the Archipelago of the Ladrones (the Mariana Islands), the Spanish disembarked on an island where they were greeted by cries of '*Castilla! Castilla!*'. In February 1528 the flotilla reached Mindanao, where it rescued a Spaniard from the expedition of Loaisa. It was from him that they learned that other prisoners, who had accompanied Magellan, had been sold by the people of Cebu to Chinese merchants. On a neighbouring island, some sailors who had organized a mutiny against Loaisa were recovered, before being punished in Tidore.

Saavedra estimated the distance between the island of Gilolo and New Spain at 1,500 leagues.[15] He eventually landed at Tidore on 27 March 1528, where there languished a Spanish garrison of 150 men under the command of Hernando de la Torre. The latter gave Saavedra a letter for Cortés, seeking his assistance. The small troop, which possessed a couple of dozen cannon, was waging a pitiless war against the Portuguese of the region. Saavedra came to his aid, seized a galiot and killed its Portuguese captain. Portugal and Castile might be at peace in Europe and America, but on the other side of the world they fought relentlessly. We see an exotic and distant consequence of European expansion, of which colonial rivalries would provide many more examples over the centuries. It was also a precocious political and military manifestation of the trends activated by Iberian globalization: the transfer onto a world stage of a phenomenon that had been local or continental.

After this, the expedition degenerated into fiasco. On 12 June 1528 Saavedra decided to sail for home with a cargo of 60 quintals of cloves. The first attempt, sailing eastwards, failed, made impracticable by winds and currents. They turned back and, having passed the Admiralty Islands, the Bismarck Archipelago, the Caroline Islands and the Mariana Islands, and after several months at sea, at last reached Tidore, where they executed the Portuguese prisoners, who were beheaded, quartered or hanged. The Castilians were not notably more soft-hearted than the Chinese.

In May 1529 Saavedra tried a second time to return to New Spain. He bore south and once again reached the coasts of New Guinea. En route the Spanish added to their knowledge of the Pacific by discovering the Pintados (the Visayan islands, in the middle of the Archipelago of the Philippines); they probably also reached the north of the Archipelago of Hawaii. Saavedra gives us a first description of the natives of the Pintados. From their faces and their size they seemed to be descended from the Chinese, but these were 'degenerate' Chinese: 'As they have been there for such a long time, they have become so savage that they no longer have any religion or sect and they do not raise any animals'.[16] The winds were stubbornly against them. In October 1529 Saavedra's death at sea caused dismay amongst what remained of the expedition.

Did this voyage achieve anything? The Spanish had learned more about the Pacific Ocean and were beginning to explore islands and coasts: Carolines, Islands of Papua (near Gilolo), Admiralty Archipelago and others. This was enough to make another attempt to cross the immense ocean tempting. In fact Saavedra was more than merely a hired hand of Cortés. He nurtured projects which, retrospectively, were likely to be of real concern to the Portuguese of the Moluccas: 'He hoped to persuade the emperor to open a passage from sea to sea through Golden Castile and New Spain', making a dash for 'the land and isthmus of Panama', where he could unload his cloves, which would be transported in carts to Nombre de Dios, 'where there were the naves of Castile'. He even projected four possible itineraries across Central America.

This link between the Moluccas and the Canaries, by way of the Pacific and the Atlantic, promised an enormous saving of time since, on the Pacific side, the route would run between the Equator and the Tropic of Cancer.[17] It would no longer be necessary to sail round the Cape of Good Hope, go through the Magellan Strait or follow a hypothetical northern channel off Newfoundland. Once again Iberian globalization emerges as a maritime globalization: it inspired the network of oceanic routes which encircled the globe and disseminated the idea that one could equally as well travel from one part of the world to another by sailing north, south, east or west. As they familiarized themselves with the Pacific Ocean, the Spanish, even more than the Portuguese, were faced with the challenge of grasping the globe in its entirety.

The Ambitions of Cortés and World Consciousness

It is easy to see why Cortés was so interested in the Moluccas. The conquistador could hardly stand aloof from a source of wealth which was then the focus of all European and Asiatic greed. He knew that, with his Pacific ports, he was uniquely and ideally positioned; this was not a chance to be missed. But 'the thirst of the conquistador to discover the South Sea' was also a product of the global projection Cortés gave to his enterprises: he saw himself as the architect of a universal and providential empire. He articulated this in a letter to the companions of Sebastian Cabot in May 1527: 'I am much interested in these regions, I wish to see them under the imperial sceptre and I put my trust in Our Lord, convinced that in our time we shall see his Majesty King of the world, because it was not without reason that God permitted the discovery of such numerous and extensive lands'. The same mindset and the same obsession are visible in a letter sent in May 1527 to the distant sovereign of the islands it was hoped to reach and occupy: God 'in his bounty has wished that [Charles V] should be emperor of the world and he to whom all the other princes recognize pre-eminence and authority'.[18]

Between the Pacific Ocean, New Spain and imperial Europe there appeared a vast new space which impressed itself on people's minds even before it was translated into institutions – sign of the globalization which in future encouraged people to think not only of circulation but also of power on a world scale, that is, on the scale of the seas crossed by the sailors of Magellan.

Globalization implies synchronization. Was it by chance that, on the other side of the ocean, the imperialism of Cortés was in accord with a European dream which expected the Emperor Charles V to restore universal concord? The Old World was at this period teeming with eschatological expectations. People were not content simply to wait for the Emperor of the Last Days or to experience for the umpteenth time the repercussions of medieval Joachimism. Was it not Erasmus himself who called on Charles V to establish peace between peoples, and the Chancellor Mercurio di Gattinara who devised his image as universal emperor? And whom do we find among the councillors of Gattinara but Maximilian Transylvanus, he who had described the expedition of Magellan in his book *De Molluccis*,[19] and was probably one of the first Europeans to grasp the global significance of this voyage. If, after the victory of Pavia over the king of France, Charles V appeared as 'master of the world', the coronation in Bologna in 1530 seemed to justify all those who hoped for the advent of an era of universal peace under the aegis of the new Augustus.[20]

Never, probably, had the ambitions of the conquistador and his master been so close. Cortés took advantage of this. In a letter sent from Texcoco, one of the old capitals of the Triple Alliance (October 1530), he pandered to the emperor's curiosity in words that might equally well apply to himself when he referred to 'Your Majesty's desire to know the secret of these regions'. Two years later he renewed his assault in very much the same terms: 'I know very well just how much your Majesty wishes to know the secrets of this southern sea'.[21] Yet the formula was at the same time fairly cautious. There was no talk of future conquests, he spoke only of the Pacific and its mysteries, that is, of a simple desire to know more about a space that was in principle a dependency of Spain. We know only too well, however, what such curiosity meant in the case of Castilian soldiers.

The prudence of Cortés was in no way anodyne. He could not but be aware that, since April 1529, by the Treaty of Zaragoza, the emperor had officially renounced his claims on the Moluccas in return for substantial cash compensation from John III of Portugal. It was obvious that among the secrets of the South Sea was that of the routes which led from Mexico to the Moluccas and to China, and back. In October 1529 the conquistador had obtained capitulations which granted him access to the whole extent of the Spanish Pacific. This was some consolation for a man who had hoped to become viceroy of New Spain but been forced to make do with the title of Marquis of the Valley of Oaxaca, which carried with it, in principle, some 23,000 indigenous vassals. Cortés was to 'discover, conquer and settle whatever islands were found in the South Sea of New Spain and all those he might discover to the west'. Since Columbus and Magellan, the West had continued to be an endless source of fascination. Just as Mexico had succeeded the Antilles, now the Pacific succeeded Mexico.

The Moluccas thus disappeared, in principle, from the list of lands to be conquered, but not East Asia, whose coasts were believed to join up with those of New Spain in the northern Pacific. But a major obstacle stood in Cortés's path: the seas which bathed the 'government of Nuño de Guzmán' in New Galicia, and were therefore part of the Mexican Pacific, were forbidden to him. Also excluded from the capitulations were those lands which lay in the government of Florida granted to Pánfilo de Narváez. To which Cortés responded with insatiable demands: he dared to ask for a twelfth of the wealth to be discovered in the South Sea for himself and his descendants, in compensation for the considerable investment required to pursue his explorations. This demand was not met, but he managed to get jurisdictional rights of first instance in the discovered lands.

'The Obstacles Placed by the Devil'[22]

A difficult situation awaited the conqueror on his return to New Spain, where he came up against the hostility of the authorities, who forbade him to enter Mexico. In 1530, Cortés had at his disposal, in principle, five ships ready to weigh anchor, but in his absence the Audience of Mexico had ordered the arrest of the man in charge of the shipyard, seized the material destined to fit out the ships and cut off his supplies of indigenous labour. It did not take much to block the exploration of the Pacific. For almost a year the Spanish craftsmen had been unemployed and the 'ships practically lost'. Many had left the shipyard, all of them demanded their unpaid wages. Cortés was appalled: 'They have made me lose more than twenty thousand castillans [a gold coin] that I had spent on the construction and fitting out of the five ships'.[23] In spite of his losses, and in spite of the 'diabolical' obstacles put in his way by the first Audience, Cortés went ahead with his plans. All the more so as, in 1531, a *real cédula* had reminded him of his commitments and given him two years to launch the fleet intended to explore the Pacific, in default of which the capitulations would be defunct.

It is possible that the orders signed by the Empress Isabella in 1530 and 1531 had more immediate objectives than the exploration of the Pacific, and that they were primarily designed to keep Cortés away from the capital of Mexico at a time when, on the ground, the conflict with the first Audience seemed about to explode. This is not to say that the Spanish Crown did not make haste, after signing the Treaty of Zaragoza, to reassert its rights over the Pacific, and did so with what was to hand, that is, the fortune, vessels and ports of the man who had wanted to become the master of New Spain. Honour your promises: Cortés rebuilt his fleet. By 1532 he had a caravel at Tehuantepec, two brigantines at Acapulco and two other ships under construction. Indian porters, or *tamemes*, shuttled back and forth between Cuernavaca and the coast to bring 'supplies and equipment for the brigantines'. If we add the five vessels abandoned in the shipyards during his absence, Cortés was then in possession of a fleet of nine or ten ships.

In 1532 in New Spain, that is, ten years after the conquest, not everyone was experiencing the same difficulties as Cortés. The ventures of discovery were going full steam ahead and attracting an increasing number of Spanish who were no longer able to live off the land. The former president of the Audience, Nuño de Guzmán, was feverishly busy in his province of New Galicia, where he built a brigantine so as to launch in his turn into the exploration of the South Sea. For his part, Pedro de Alvarado, governor of Guatemala, was preparing 'nine seaworthy ships', which were to be fitted out in July. It was even beginning to be felt that he was spending too much time on maritime matters. Lastly, in Florida, there was still no news of Pánfilo de Narváez, who had set out in search of the famous Northwest Passage.

But it was Cortés who was the target of the Audience. It demanded that the Crown confiscate the caravel and the two brigantines of the conquistador, against whom it was at that point pursuing a lawsuit.[24] Cortés reacted in his usual fashion, that is, he forged ahead notwithstanding. In June 1532, his cousin Diego Hurtado de Mendoza sailed from Acapulco, site of one of the conqueror's arsenals. He had two ships under his command, the *San Miguel* and the *San Marcos*, bought by Cortés from Juan Rodríguez de Villafuerte. Diego sailed up the coast for some 200 leagues, taking care to avoid the lands of Nuño de Guzmán. He reconnoitred the shores of Colima and Jalisco. One of his ships returned southwards and its crew was massacred in the Bay of Banderas (Nayarit). The other, commanded by Hurtado, sailed north, but 'no more was heard of him or his ship, and he was never seen again'.[25] Cortés blamed this failure on the second Audience, which had done everything it could to sabotage the preparations for the voyage and hinder the provisioning of the vessels. These spokes in his wheels confirm that the Crown and the colonial authorities were in league to exhaust the energies and wealth of a conqueror who was too troublesome and who had never inspired confidence. Viewed from this perspective, the Pacific looks more like a decoy brandished in front of the conquistador than an objective to be seriously pursued. Failures at sea could only eat away at the aura of invincibility surrounding Cortés, without endangering a New Spain which had other things to worry about.

At the end of 1532 Cortés prepared a new expedition. It led to the discovery by Hernando de Grijalva of the Revillagigedo Islands, situated just over 300 kilometres from the tip of Lower California. Of the two ships, one returned home safely but the other fell into the hands of Nuño de Guzmán, the rival established in New Galicia.

The Crown then made the decision to give its support to Pedro de Alvarado and grant him all Pacific expeditions. But Cortés persisted, and demonstratively. In April 1535 he himself took command of a flotilla of three ships which carried some 300 Spanish men plus thirty women. He set sail from Chametla and landed at the southern end of the peninsula of Lower California in the Bay of Santa Cruz. Famine hit the soldiers and sailors: 'Of the soldiers who were with Cortés, twenty-three died of hunger and disease; of the rest, many were sick and they cursed Cortez, his island, his sea and his discovery'.[26] The survivors were eventually repatriated to the continent.

By this time the Spanish and the Portuguese were no longer the only ones searching for spices and China. In 1534 the French Jacques Cartier set out in search of the Northern Passage, 'to bring back to France the spices and drugs of the Indies'.[27] He found only one land, which he called New France, 'provided with resources, villages and well populated'. The conquest of Peru also transformed the situation for Mexico. The South Pacific was now within direct reach of the Spanish. In 1536 Francisco Pizarro and his men, surrounded by Indians, appealed for help to the governor of Guatemala, Pedro de Alvarado. The letter came into the hands of the viceroy Antonio de Mendoza, who entrusted the rescue mission to Cortés, who had returned to Acapulco. He leapt at the chance to dispatch two vessels, one commanded by his majordomo Hernando de Grijalva. The expedition was given two objectives: to take provisions and gifts to Pizarro, and to explore the South Pacific as far as the ... Moluccas. In fact, instead of returning to New Spain, Grijalva's ship set sail for the west. Aided by the Portuguese pilot Martim da Costa, the major-domo of Cortés followed the line of the Equator as far as the Christmas Islands and reached the Gilbert Archipelago (Los Pescadores). But Grijalva was killed by his own sailors and the mutineers eventually abandoned ship. In 1538 the Portuguese António Galvão rescued a handful of survivors who had fallen into the hands of the indigenous population.

Did this amount to a total failure? This was probably true for Cortés. But it was in the 1530s that the Castilian Crown gained possession of a large part of the American Pacific shore; which might, one day, turn the great ocean into a Spanish lake. And metropolitan Spain had never lost interest in the South Sea. In 1535 a small expedition, consisting of two ships and 200 men, left Seville headed, it would appear, for the Moluccas or China. It was led by a man who knew the region, Simão de Alcaçova, a Portuguese who had explored the Moluccas and even accompanied the expedition of Fernão de Andrade to China. Charles V had instructed him to verify the limits laid down by the Treaty of Tordesillas. The attempt was no more successful than its predecessors. Having tried to sail through the Strait of Magellan, and dropped anchor in Patagonia, one ship mutinied and the other chose to return to San Domingo and ultimately Spain.

The ball was back in Cortés's court. Four years later, in July 1539, he embarked on his last expedition. Three ships left Acapulco with the intention of exploring the coasts of Lower California and, as always, finding a practicable route to the East. The ships sailed deep into the Gulf of California, continued down the Sea of Cortez, doubled Cape San Lucas and sailed up the length of the Pacific coast as far as Cedros Island. However, on their return, at Huatulco, one of the two ships was seized by the authorities of New Spain. Apart from reconnoitring the Californian coast, they had nothing very remarkable to report: 'They brought news of no land which was worth the effort. A lot of fuss about nothing. Cortés believed he would discover on this coast and in this sea another New Spain'. The ageing conquistador had to admit defeat. But when he left one last time for Spain, Cortés still had five ships with which he hoped to resume his explorations.

For the conquistador, the balance sheet was negative overall; he had spent a large part of his fortune, 'two hundred thousand ducats' according to one estimate. According to his biographer, 'no one had ever invested with such passion in similar enterprises'.[28] It was this that had caused Cortés to quarrel with the viceroy Antonio de Mendoza and sue his king. His tenacity shows that, in his mind, the conquest of the Pacific was inseparably linked to that of Mexico. It is significant that the man who had taken the risk of seizing Tenochtitlan had immediately wanted to press on in the Pacific; his trajectory gives the impression not only of a perpetual headlong rush, always further west, but also of a taste for investment on the other side of the sea, even in unknown lands. We see the beginnings of a European modernity in which an insatiable quest for profit and a projection into space and the future were combined.

The Baton Passes to the Viceroys

This was a modernity not unfamiliar to the Crown. On his arrival in New Spain, in 1535, the representative of Charles V, the viceroy Antonio de Mendoza, proposed to take charge of the Pacific expeditions, reserving the monopoly of these ventures to his prince. The monarchy intended to make its law prevail in the colonial society which had emerged from the years of chaos following the conquest. Besides, the time had come to make a fresh start. The definitive departure of Cortés for Spain, where Nuño de Guzmán had already arrived, and the deaths of Pedro de Alvarado in 1541 and of Hernando de Soto the year after had removed all those who might reasonably have claimed to lead the discoveries and clamour for the profit.

The explorations resumed, under strict control. In March 1540 Mendoza sent Vasquez de Coronado to reconnoitre the north of New Spain. The viceroy then appropriated the fleet of Pedro de Alvarado. In 1542 he dispatched some of it to explore California and the rest, under the command of his brother-in-law Ruy López de Villalobos, in the direction of the Spice Islands. This fifth expedition towards the Moluccas consisted of 370 men, including one survivor of the voyage of Magellan, Ginés de Mafra, and a few Augustinian monks. López de Villalobos reached Mindanao in February 1543, then the island of Luzon and the archipelago of the Philippines before colonizing – or attempting to colonize – Sarangani. An attempt to return to New Spain ran into difficulties, like its predecessors. Exhausted and famished, the survivors of the expedition reached Tidore, from which they made another attempt to discover a return route. In 1545 they took possession of 'New Guinea', so-called because its inhabitants resembled those of the African Guinea, but they were unable to get back to New Spain. This made five failures in a little over twenty years:[29] Gonzalo Gómez de Espinosa in 1522, Saavedra in 1528 and 1529, Bernardo de la Torre and Ortiz de Retes in 1543 and 1545. In all, 143 men managed to return to Spain by way of the Indian Ocean, but not López de Villalobos, who had the privilege of dying at Amboyna in the arms of St Francis Xavier. He is credited with having explored the Carolines and Palau, and above all with reconnoitring the Philippines. Bit by bit the immense Pacific Ocean was being Hispanicized. But Iberian sailors had not yet sailed from east to west.

Yet the appeal of Asia had never seemed so strong. In 1531, Martín of Valencia, one of the Franciscan apostles to Mexico, toyed with the idea of abandoning New Spain in favour of living among the inhabitants of the shores of the Pacific. In 1549, there was much talk of the leaders of the religious orders leaving for Asia. Money and liturgical vestments were dispatched to the Dominican Domingo de Betanzos. The voyage did not take place and the objects were distributed among the convents of Mexico, Puebla and Oaxaca. In March 1550, after two cedulas issued in Valladolid in June and September of the previous year,[30] the voyage to the 'Spice Islands' was cancelled. In 1554 the archbishop of Mexico, the Franciscan Juan de Zumarraga and the Dominican Betanzos once again contemplated fitting out a ship that would take them to Asia. It was the second viceroy of Mexico, Luis de Velasco, who persuaded Philip II to resume the expeditions. In 1559 he was given the order to build ships to cross the ocean. They were not to enter the Portuguese zone, and they were to discover a return route with the assistance of an Augustinian, Fray Andrés de Urdaneta, who was regarded as the great expert on Pacific affairs. The Basque Miguel López de Legazpi, notary and ordinary alcalde of the city of Mexico, was appointed to lead the fleet.

The initiative of the viceroy, the resort to the monk Urdaneta and the appointment of López de Legazpi once again gave New Spain a prime role in the conquest of the Pacific and Eastern affairs. However, the viceroy died before the expedition had been able to leave. When, finally, some years later, in the autumn of 1564, the expedition set out, it was amidst huge enthusiasm, as recorded by a contemporary witness:

> A large number of people were recruited and as many captains as were needed were appointed. It was widely reported that they were leaving for China, *la grita era que iban a la China*, and it was this that made many people join, and it was in this way that they assembled a very fine fleet thinking that they were going to China, without taking account of the power of this country and of their own small number if compared with the large number of its inhabitants.

The volunteers were disillusioned when, once at sea, López de Legazpi informed them that the expedition was simply heading for the Philippines.[31]

16

China on the Horizon

The Simple man: You're looking for people? You're leaving for
China?
Divine love: That's what one does, Innocent one, for the Divine
Country.

Fernán González de Eslava, *Coloquio Segundo hecho
a la jornada que hizo a la China Miguel López
de Legazpi*, 1565

In the second half of the sixteenth century, some sixty years after
the events discussed above, the conquest of China was back on the
agenda. Or rather, a group of Spaniards, in league with some
Portuguese and energetically led by a Jesuit, spent several years trying
to get one of the greatest powers of the age, the Catholic Monarchy,
to launch its forces against the 'kingdom of China'. In Manila,
Macau, Mexico and Madrid, the Jesuit justified his military projects,
gained supporters and stirred up hatred. Once again, however, the
Chinese war would not take place. The warmongers got no further
than Macau and nothing for their pains. This non-event would
scarcely merit a mention were it not for the fact that it was an extreme
manifestation of a pressing interest in China and marked the transition in certain quarters from conquest to what may properly be
called colonial war. It also reflected how the New World was beginning to see itself and assert itself with regard to Asia, even before
the shipment of American silver to China forged crucial links with
the East.

The Way is Clear

If China emerged on the horizons of the Spanish empire, it was because the thorny question of the return voyage had been settled since 1565. It was an expert in Pacific navigation, the Augustinian Andrés de Urdaneta,[1] who had taken the initiative of sailing north in search of winds favourable to the return to America. After 130 days at sea he landed at Acapulco in October 1565, putting the Philippines and China on Mexico's doorstep. Urdaneta had accompanied Saavedra in the discovery of the Philippines in 1528. The new link was celebrated in the Mexican theatre: in 1565 Fernán González de Eslava devoted his *Second Colloquy* to this feat.[2] Whatever the reasons that caused Eslava to depict the departure for the East, it is clear that it was a topic that fascinated people in Mexico and in the rest of New Spain. The China evoked by the poet was the Philippines, now within sailing distance, but also, beyond the archipelago, the Celestial Empire. The *Colloquy* operates throughout at two levels, that of an earthly and that of a celestial voyage. When the Simple Man speaks of China, Divine Love replies 'Divine Country'; when the Simple Man refers to the discovery of the famous return route, Divine Love continues: 'It is now sure, the crossing from earth to heaven'; when the Simple Man describes the gold chains and the cinnamon brought back from Asia, Divine Love evokes the treasures which await 'he who flies towards heaven'. It was not by chance that the crossing of the Pacific, with its endless ordeals on a ship that was entirely at the mercy of Providence, and its promise of temporal and spiritual riches, was put on the same plane as the ascent to heaven. It is because this globalization was being played out on the ocean that it transformed the voyage into an ordeal which led to the Other World as well as to other worlds. We find in later works the same exaltation of the departure 'for China',[3] always endowed with a mystic dimension and always combined with more mundane preoccupations: 'O Lord, take me to China!' exclaims a woman who is forbidden to wear silk.

So from 1565 the voyage to China was on the agenda. In July 1567, Legazpi proposed to Philip II that galleys be built 'to sail up the coast of China and trade with the mainland'.[4] One is irresistibly reminded of the way in which, Mexico-Tenochtitlan barely conquered, the ships of Cortés prepared to cross the Pacific. News of Urdaneta's return had a huge impact. It was not only that the Pacific Ocean had been conquered, it was the very position of the New World that had been transformed. For the Spanish settlers of New

Spain the periphery they occupied had swung towards the centre. In Seville the commentators had a field day: 'The people of Mexico are extremely proud of their discovery; they now regard it as given that they are at the centre of the world'.[5] This shift was soon visible on maps that divided the world round the north–south axis provided by the American continent.

This reordering of world space echoed the hopes of the missionary circles who placed their hopes of a reformed Christianity in America. The most intrepid, at their peril, even prophesied that Europe would fall into Turkish hands and that the centre of gravity of Roman Christianity would shift to the New World. We are far from that in the sixteenth century when the writ of the Iberian metropolis and Tridentine Rome ran in every sphere. This did not prevent the fixation on the return route from encouraging the colonial elites to turn their attention towards an empty – thus up for grabs – space that was rich in both known – the spices of the Moluccas – and potential resources that might be extracted from China or Japan or perhaps from a continent, a fourth or fifth part of the world, that was still to be discovered.

The Line of Demarcation

In fact this space was no longer quite free. It was Portuguese or Castilian, depending on whether you started from Lisbon or Seville. Since the end of the fifteenth century geographers and cosmographers had debated where exactly to place the line dividing the world between the Crowns of Castile and Portugal. In 1529 the Treaty of Zaragoza temporary settled the matter in favour of the Portuguese. But the continued exploration of the Pacific in subsequent decades had revealed that the Crown of Castile had never fully renounced its rights to this part of the world. In 1566, one year after the opening of the Manila–Acapulco route, experts had been summoned to Spain to debate the issue yet again. Among them were scholars and cosmographers of the first rank, such as Alonso de Santa Cruz, Pedro de Medina, Francisco Falero, Jerónimo de Chaves, Sancho Gutiérrez and Andrés de Urdaneta. The cosmographer Sancho Gutiérrez was categorical: the Anti-meridian passed through Malacca.[6] This put China in the Castilian half. The Augustinian Diego de Herrera, passing through Mexico in 1570, said the same. And so, six years later, in 1576, did the governor of the Philippines, Francisco de Sande.

Nothing is more revealing as to the ambitions of Madrid than the *Geographía y descripción universal de las Indias* (1574), the work of

Juan López de Velasco, cosmographer and chronicler of the Indies.[7] This summa, which remained in manuscript until the sixteenth century, reveals that at this point, for the Crown of Castile, the West Indies was not restricted to the American continent. It also included 'the Ponant islands, those of the Moluccas that are called the Spice Islands, the Philippines, Japan, the Ryû Kyû, New Guinea and the Solomon Islands'. Where did that leave the famous line of demarcation between Spain and Portugal, subject of so much polemic and so much envy?

For the Spanish this line ran through Malacca and the middle of Sumatra 'according to astronomical observations made with care'. There follows a crossed-out passage which seems to identify the author of this claim, a 'man knowledgeable in mathematics, Spanish by nation and resident in the Philippines for many years',[8] clearly Urdaneta. A map, the first to be made of the Western Pacific, is unequivocal about this division: the latitudes are remarkably accurate, but the longitudes are designed to bolster Spanish claims.[9] López de Velasco had sufficient honesty, however, to note that this was not the opinion of the Portuguese, who situated the line much further to the east, on the island of Gilolo, 'leaving on their side the islands which they call the Moluccas and everything which is found between them and Malacca'. No doubt the enormous distance between these regions 'at the end of the world' and Spain explains these uncertainties, but they were in any case soon dissipated. The coast of China marked the western limit of the 'Indias del Poniente'. One senses that the *Geography* of López de Velasco anticipated a settlement favourable to Spain, should the Spanish have the opportunity once again to set foot in Asia. He did not hide the gaps in his knowledge, which were perhaps only temporary: 'of the coast of the mainland which extends as far as China and the numerous islands which are found in these parts, I will say nothing in particular because until now they have been owned by the Portuguese, so one finds little information about them in the papers of the Council of the Indies'.[10] 'Because until now (*hasta ahora*)' they have been owned by the Portuguese...

It was at this point that the Spanish revived their claims to the Moluccas. Why stay true to an agreement that no one any longer respected? The Portuguese had been unable to resist the temptation to build a fort at Ternate, contrary to their commitments; the Castilians had ultimately settled in the region, colonizing the archipelago of the Philippines, which appeared to be within the part ceded temporarily to Portugal. In any case, as we have seen, the junta of experts had in 1566 tried to restore order to the Spanish maps, in spite of the protests of the king of Portugal.

The *Geography* of Velasco had also noted the Iberian forces present in this part of the world. At the time there were only 'four agglomerations of Spanish and Portuguese', in all a good 500 Europeans, and indigenous peoples everywhere, but 'they are not very numerous and their numbers are decreasing as a result of the ill-treatment and problems caused by conquests and new discoveries'. Above all, the *Geography* gives the impression that a confrontation between the two Crowns could not be far off. The Portuguese of the islands numbered between 300 and 400, not counting those there simply to trade. They had two fortresses in the region, including that of Malacca. The Castilians had a potential ally, the king of Tidore, where they had previously had a fortress. And then there was Malacca, 'through which passed the demarcation', a place of major importance which traded with Java, Timor, the Moluccas, Borneo, Bengal and China.

It was not by chance that this geography of the New World, compiled in 1574, takes us across the Pacific, thousands of kilometres from America. Not only did it revive ancient claims, but it was compiled at a time when the Crown of Spain was beginning to speculate about the dynastic future of Portugal and its empire. Were they, in the absence of direct Portuguese heirs, about to fall into the hands of Philip II? Finally, it is a reminder that the West Indies was far from having broken its ties with the East Indies.

Where does China fit in? The geography also contains a surprising 'Chorography of the coast of China'.[11] The information came from the Philippines thanks to the commercial relations between Manila and the Chinese and the members of the Society of Jesus, who were well informed about this part of the world. López de Velasco was convinced that China belonged to the 'demarcation of the kings of Castile...even if until now no one has discovered or taken possession of it in the name of the kings of Castile'. We should note the use, once again, of the expression 'until now (*hasta ahora*)', which, coming from a Spanish pen, suggested a whole programme. Yet López de Velasco knew of what he spoke: as regards what was said of the Chinese, 'until we are better informed, we take it as given that China is the greatest kingdom in the world'. There followed a variety of information about distances, the division into fifteen provinces and the city of Peking (Paquia), seat of the 'royal court', that is, the capital; and also about the population: the Chinese were 'people of white colour, both men and women, vain and very cowardly, vile and effeminate'.[12] The country exported silks, precious furniture and coloured and gilded porcelain. It attached great value to silver, which it lacked. The population was not armed, the soldiers made poor warriors and the empire's troops did not know how to use their artillery. But the Chinese knew how to read and write, they had 'schools of science' and they had even had printing houses for a long time. To crown it all, López de Velasco sketched a 'Hydrography of China', which was fairly brief and unsatisfactory but 'which might assist in the discovery of and entry into these provinces'.[13]

The *Geography* circulated only within the administration, and the Spanish reader without access to circles of power had to wait until 1577 to learn all about China. It was then that the first work in Spanish devoted to the Middle Empire appeared, the second of this type published in Europe, coming after the treatise of Gaspar da Cruz (Evora, 1570), the *Discourse on the navigation made by the Portuguese to the kingdoms and provinces of the Orient and the information available on the grandeur of China*.[14] Its author, Bernardino de Escalante, was a Galician and the language of Camoens presented no difficulties to him. While en route from Galicia to Seville he stopped at Lisbon, where he collected all sorts of information about the East. He met some visiting Chinese and freely plagiarized the treatise on China of Gaspar da Cruz. He even consulted a map of China in the possession of the chronicler João de Barros and he was the first to print ideograms in a book published in Europe. Bernardino de Escalante thought in terms not of the conquest but rather the Christianization of China, which was to him an urgent necessity.

The Spiritual Deal of the Century

For in Spain it was by no means only the experts, the administrators and the reading public who were interested in the East and in China. For many churchmen the Christianization of China emerged as the (spiritual) deal of the century. From 1565, for prospective missionaries, the religious conquest of the Philippines and the islands of the South Sea was an urgent task – but not necessarily their ultimate objective. The Augustinians, pioneers in the evangelization of the archipelago, were the first to see it as a starting point rather than a cul-de-sac buried deep in the Pacific. The letter sent by Diego de Herrera to Philip II in 1570 sketched out immense vistas: 'Very close to Cebu are lands so extensive and so rich, and which belong to Your Majesty, such as China, the Ryû Kyû, Java and Japan'.[15] They 'belonged to Your Majesty', in the sense not of potential conquests but of spaces it was incumbent on the king of Castile to Christianize. Could there be a more exalted programme?

Mexico was not to be outdone. In 1578 the capital of New Spain sumptuously celebrated the reception of relics sent by Rome to the Jesuits. The roads were adorned with statues and decorated with inscriptions. A triumphalist watchword was flavour of the month:

> Goa will give Japan, and Mexico China
> Bones of saints and exceptional men.[16]

It was a means by which the Jesuits of Mexico could take out an option on the evangelization of China, which was in principle reserved to their Portuguese brethren in Macau. But the spiritual appeal of the Middle Empire extended beyond the narrow and well-informed circles of the clergy of the capital. An *ensalada* (medley) sung by the people in Mexico during the Michaelmas festivities contains the idea that to go to China was also, to some small degree, to go to heaven:

> He who wishes to depart for the Great China on high
> Must quickly understand that it is time to prepare
> It is the great general Michael who tells us this
> He who must guide all the faithful to the great kingdom.[17]

Once again China suggested something never suggested by the New World or Africa: a troubling proximity between heaven and earth. Centuries later it would inspire in Paul Claudel this ecstatic vision: 'that endless bustle of silks and palms and naked bodies, all those banks alive with human fry, more populous than the dead, and awaiting baptism'.[18]

Meanwhile, the all-powerful Moya de Contreras, inquisitor, archbishop and viceroy of Mexico, had also become interested in China and the Chinese. In October 1583 he was delighted at the establishment of an Audience in Manila, all the more so in that the Philippines were within the sphere of influence of New Spain, and thus a Mexican outpost in the Far East. He took advantage of this to invoke the 'friendship we should cultivate with the Chinese so as to know more about their vast kingdoms which in various ways the Divine Majesty has reserved for the human Majesty because it has arranged for them to be surrounded by his subjects and his vassals'. This was, it must be said, a very intrusive friendship, given that the word 'surrounded' (*cercados*) was a military term which might equally well be rendered by 'besieged' or 'encircled'. True, Moya de Contreras had a hardly favourable opinion of the Chinese: they were 'extremely greedy people who run after all sorts of profits'.[19] But they were commercial partners with whom it was prudent to maintain good relations; even if it meant buying their mercury, which might reach the Mexican market more cheaply than the mercury of Spain, or 'giving them large quantities of silver', or even gold, like that exchanged in Manila for Chinese goods.

An Advanced Base

Whatever the intentions of the Spanish of Castile or of Mexico, nothing could be done without the establishment of an advanced base in the Far East. The Philippines provided what they had never managed to procure in the Moluccas. As we have seen, the project was first launched by Luis de Velasco, then taken over and carried to a successful conclusion by the Audience of Mexico. The programme was restated in September 1567 by the governor, López de Legazpi: 'These islands must be conquered, settled and placed under the authority of your Royal Crown'.[20] But the archipelago was not an end in itself: 'It is our intention to carry on with pacification, settlement and discovery in the island of Luzon and in the islands which are closest to China, such as Japan, the Ryû Kyû and the island of Cochin [China]'.[21]

The conquest of the Philippines was a catalyst for all sorts of interests attracted by Asiatic prospects. *China is near*, to quote the title of a famous film,[22] geographically, spiritually and economically. Near enough for pressure groups to emerge in Mexico, Manila, Lima and Macau, which included members of the ecclesiastical hierarchy, missionaries, officials of the Crown, great merchants and adventurers.[23] In Mexico, the Velasco family, which numbered in its ranks two viceroys of Mexico and an impressive number of hangers-on and henchmen, had transmitted a taste for all things Asiatic from generation to generation, since the Viceroy Luis, in the mid sixteenth century, had re-launched the conquest of the Philippines. Other viceroys followed suit, like Almansa, who, in 1572, proposed sending an expedition to explore the coast of China, and even Moya de Contreras. The governors of the Philippines were convinced that the survival of the Spanish establishment depended on its relations with the Middle Empire. The fabulous trade envisaged with China, with all it implied in the way of contraband, clandestine cargoes and hidden profits, fired the imagination. Hopes focused on the galleon from Acapulco which, every year from 1565, connected the Asia of the Philippines to Mexican America.[24] The Spanish of Lima only had to join these groups when the prospect of exporting the silver of Potosi to China offered Peru the hope of massive profits.

17

When China Awakes

La guerra con esta nación es justísma por librar personas miserables que matan y toman hijos agenos para estupros [The war with that nation is most just because it frees wretched persons who kill and take other people's children to abuse [them].]

Francisco de Sande to King Philip II, 1576

El hacer guerra aunque sea justa, es cosa de muchos y grandes daños y males... Y si es injusta y ilícita, demás de la grave ofensa de Dios, trae cargos irreparables de restitución. [To make war, however just it may be, entails many serious hurts and evils... And if it is unjust and illicit, apart from being a grave offence against God, it brings burdens impossible to repay.]

José De Acosta, *Parecer sobre la guerra de China*, 1587

It still needed someone to take the plunge and call for conquest. This happened in June 1569 when, from the Philippines, and even before the imminent occupation of the island of Luzon, the factor Andrés de Mirandaola made a plea for China to be conquered.[1] It was the Augustinian order, however, intent on keeping the Christianization of the Celestial Empire to itself, which issued the most resounding war cry. That same year one of its most prominent members in the region, Martín de Rada, put the conquest of China firmly on the agenda. This country, he said, had abundant resources but was not a true military power. With a solid base from which to set out – Manila, obviously – and even only a modest army, its conquest was perfectly achievable, notwithstanding its great size, its wealth, its high level of civilization ('gran policía') and its fortified towns ('much larger than those of Europe').[2] The furious Mexican assault still preyed on people's minds, although in Spain the page of conquest had officially been turned and the preferred term, at least on paper, was the euphemistic 'discovery'. The views of Martín de Rada had all the more effect in that he was an expert who knew of what he spoke: a cosmographer and mathematician, he had been educated in Salamanca and Paris. Added to which, he wielded the moral authority conferred on him by his struggles on behalf of the Indians of the archipelago. It was thus, in a sense, the 'Las Casas of the Philippines' who was calling for war against China; as if to remind us that, in the Iberian world, Indophilia and imperialism went hand in hand.[3] Not all the missionaries dreamed only of conquest, it should be said. Some, in particular the Franciscans, envisaged a peaceful penetration of the Middle Empire, but all their efforts, of necessity clandestine, came to nothing.

Why War Against China?

There were many reasons. First, as we have seen, the conversion of China had continued to create vocations both in Spain and in America. So the race was on, a race the Augustinians hoped to win at the expense of their Spanish rivals, who were mostly Franciscans, and of the Portuguese Jesuits of Macau. Further, locally, the colonization of the archipelago had proved something of a disappointment. The Philippines had not lived up to the invaders' expectations, materially or spiritually. Expansion towards China offered a way forward which might resolve local difficulties as well as salve consciences. There were similarities with the conditions which had led the Spanish of Cuba to set out for the Mexican coast.

It was against this background that the plans for an invasion were developed. In July 1570 the governor López de Legazpi explained that in choosing Manila, hence the island of Luzon, rather than Cebu, as the site of the capital of the archipelago, the Spanish had borne its proximity to the Chinese coast in mind, with a view to an 'extension' of the domination of the Philippines. Two years later it was decided to make a start, and an expedition intended to reconnoitre the coast of China and take possession was hastily mounted. The expedition was cut short by the death of Legazpi. In July 1574 the interim governor of the Philippines, Guido de Lavezaris, revived the question of expansion by sending a general map of China to Philip II, together with a map of the coasts of China and the Philippines which exaggerated their proximity. The hawks did not consist only of missionaries and governors. That same year a royal official came up with a plan for conquest, notable for its wild optimism. The warmongers were joined by local conquistadors like Juan Pablo de Carrión, who was already touting the conquest of China in return for the grandiloquent title of Admiral of the South Sea and of the Coast of China.[4] Another protagonist was also demanding a pioneering role in the affair: Juan Bautista Román, the royal factor in the Philippines. However, an opportunity to establish commercial and diplomatic relations with China emerged. It was based on the notion of waging a joint war against the pirates, but it was short-lived. Yet the Spanish had been close to acquiring a Chinese base in Fujian, on the model of Portuguese Macau. In the event Castilian apathy and ill will exacerbated Chinese susceptibilities, eventually creating an explosive situation and a total impasse. This revived the hopes of the interventionists, who included the new governor Francisco de Sande (1575–79).

Even more strongly than his predecessors, the doctor Sande pressed for war. Trained in law at the University of Salamanca, Sande had held a series of positions in Mexico, successively *alcalde del crimen* (1568), fiscal and auditor. An implacable servant of the Crown, he had demonstrated his talents against the son of Cortés, accused of plotting, and against the Chichimec Indians, who raided the frontiers of New Spain. His successful career later took him from the Philippines to Guatemala (1593–6) and then to Santa Fe de Bogota (1596–1602), where he presided over the Audiences. He was thus an expert in colonial affairs who might reasonably be expected to be well informed as to the capacity of the Catholic Monarchy to wage war, and even to know better than most what opportunities for expansion existed in this part of the world. 'The expedition to China poses no problems and will cost little money...The Spanish will arrive unpaid, armed at their own expense and recruited according to their services; they will pay their travel costs and be content'. In June 1576 he openly advocated the conquest of the 'Kingdom of Taybin' on the basis of information supplied by Martín de Rada: it would be 'of the greatest importance for God's service...because China has a population of six million, whose tribute brings the king more than thirty million.'[5]

It was a tempting target: 'the very smallest province contains more people than New Spain and Peru put together'.[6] Sande even came up with a war plan. 'Six thousand men armed with lances and arquebuses' were to be recruited, with the necessary ships, artillery and munitions; they would be joined by the pirates and the Japanese of the region. They would seize the Chinese province they reckoned would be most profitable and they would make sure they had mastery of the sea. The conquest of a maritime province would determine the ultimate victory, but this was dependent on the support of the Chinese people, who were so visibly oppressed and so worn down by poverty that they would rise up against their masters. 'The judges, the authorities and the king engage in acts of tyranny such as have never been seen'. There need be no scruples, this was a war 'as just as could be', both because it would liberate a nation which lived plunged into vice and because China lay, according to the Treaty of Tordesillas, on the Castilian side of the line of demarcation. Here, more than fifty years on, we find the Portuguese project repeated virtually word for word by Sande, though no direct connection can be established between the writings of the prisoners of Canton and the boastful words of the governor of the Philippines.

Sande introduced a new argument which would soon be turned against the Iberians: 'The sea ought to be free, according to the common law, and the Chinese make their law prevail there, massacring and robbing those who risk entering their waters'. To justify his project, the governor produced a description of China full of wild exaggeration: hordes of good-for-nothings, troops incapable of fighting, a disastrous artillery, crass ignorance ('they know neither how to read or to write'), generalized venality. The Chinese 'are idolaters, sodomites, highway robbers and pirates'. We are far from the flattering portraits the Chinese usually inspired. A just war had to have its reasons and the Chinese themselves provided them: 'However well you treat them, every day they give you a thousand reasons to undertake a just war'.

It should not be presumed that Sande was content with China. He also envisaged attacking Borneo, and even the Sultanate of Aceh, to counter the expansion of Islam. The governor of the Philippines already saw himself as the leading light in a vast project for expansion that would marry commercial and crusading interests. Sande was in fact only one spokesman of an anti-Chinese lobby which also included the former governor Guido de Lavezaris and all those who already imagined themselves masters of China. In 1578 the Philippine group received the support of another person of importance, the doctor Diego García de Palacio, member of the Audiences of Guatemala and then Mexico. His plan was equally expeditious. With 4,000 men sent from Guatemala, six galleys and stocks of bronze to manufacture whatever cannon proved necessary to the enterprise, the Spanish would be able to reduce the kingdom of Taybin.[7] Interested in China and the Philippines, García de Palacio claimed to be a military expert, and proved it by publishing a treatise on the subject in Mexico in 1583.[8] He was also, which was no disadvantage, an expert in maritime affairs, as is shown by his *Nautical Instruction*, published two years later, also in the capital of New Spain. So the only author from the Americas to have published works of war and navigation in the sixteenth century was also one of those who argued for conquest. It was as if it was enough to be able to discourse on the functioning of firearms or the art of ship-building, or to have dealt with the incursions of the piratical Francis Drake, to decree the fate of China.

So the idea of attacking the Celestial Empire was a local initiative, in the sense that it originated in the Philippines and New Spain. Contrary to the anachronistic clichés which depict a Spanish metropolis obsessed with pursuing its global expansion, it was the periphery that urged the crime and it was the Peninsula that reined it in. Through, for example, the voice of Bernardino de Escalante, the first Spanish author to have written about China, and also the first to have put into print his rejection of all armed intervention. He based himself on the *Relation* of a captain, Diego de Artieda, who was convinced that conquest was impracticable and against common sense: it was equally impossible either to fight innumerable armies – 'this king can commit three hundred thousand men to the campaign and two hundred thousand horsemen' – or to cope with such interminable sea journeys.[9] Philip II reacted to this battle of the experts by, in April 1577, categorically rejecting any idea of conquest. It was not even to be talked about; on the contrary, relations of 'warm friendship' were to be developed with the Chinese.[10] The Council of the Indes expressed itself at a loss to understand how anyone could contemplate invading a gigantic kingdom protected by five million men who were as well armed as the Europeans.

In 1580, Madrid was instead thinking of sending an embassy to the Emperor Wanli. Strangely, just like all the plans for war, this project, which had been entrusted to the Augustinians, fizzled out. It is as if the Catholic Monarchy was unable to make up its mind what attitude it should adopt towards the Celestial Empire. We have already observed the rigidity of the China of the Ming in its relations with the external world. It seems that the other giant of the age, the Empire of Philip II, was equally confused, torn between local dreams of conquest, irenic opportunism and bureaucratic procrastination. This time the failure of the embassy was not the fault of the Chinese. It was the viceroy of New Spain, the count of la Coruña, who blocked the expedition. He insisted on consulting his predecessor, who had left for Peru, on questioning Sande, who had returned from the Philippines, and on hearing the procurator of the archipelago, who was then passing through Mexico. The experts were throwing their weight about yet again. They were of one accord that the expedition should be delayed. The Augustinian Juan González de Mendoza, the chosen ambassador, the magnificent gifts and the letters of Philip II intended for Wanli never reached their destination.[11] It was not so much that the war party triumphed in the New World as that the path to peace seemed perpetually strewn with pitfalls. The affair demonstrates, if demonstration were needed, that Spanish America was now in a position to impose its views on the Crown on a matter of such importance as peace with China.

The War of the Jesuit

The partisans of a war lacked a favourable opportunity, a spokesman and an ideologist. They got the first of these in 1580 with the union of the Crowns of Castile and Portugal under Philip II. This created one of the greatest empires in history, as Madrid, Lisbon, Antwerp, Brussels, Milan, Naples, San Domingo, Mexico, Lima, Manila, Malacca, Goa and Luanda were all brought under the rule of one prince. The Catholic Monarchy now had a presence in all four quarters of the globe.[12] Its resources were hugely increased, and it demonstrated by its very existence that a universal domination could be global. It demonstrated politically the extent of Iberian globalization, which meant that a European event, in this case the invasion of Portugal, had an immediate impact at the other side of the world (Macau, Malacca, Manila) and might even cause serious concern to neighbouring countries, in this case China, which normally cared little about what was happening outside their own world. The Spanish of Manila seized on it as the longed-for opportunity to resume their expansion in South-East Asia and towards China, even if the union of the two Crowns, in principle, stipulated that the two empires should remain separate entities.

While the intellectual elites of Portugal were still reeling from the shock of the annexation,[13] the Spanish of Manila found the ideologist for their battle in the person of Alonso Sánchez. This Jesuit, who had entered the order in 1565, had spent time in New Spain and Puebla, where he was for a time director of novices. The governor of Manila, who had developed the port of Nueva Segovia, northeast of Luzon, with the prospect of an attack on China in mind, decided in March 1582 to send Sánchez to Macau to inform the Portuguese and the Jesuits of that town of Philip II's accession to the throne of Portugal.[14] It was during this journey that Sánchez became aware of the importance of the Portuguese position: to occupy Macau was already to have a foothold in China, this port being 'of the very greatest importance for what His Majesty might intend to do in the kingdoms of China'. For Sánchez, this voyage was primarily an opportunity to make direct contact with this country. He returned with an unfavourable impression of the Chinese he had met and of the region through which he had travelled, but above all with an overwhelming conviction that conquest was inevitable.

In Macau he had to persuade the Portuguese of the benefits of the union of the two Crowns, while at the same time urging discretion so that the news did not reach the Chinese. The idea that the Europeans of Macau and Manila were now subject to the same king was likely to cause some anxiety to the Celestial bureaucracy. The Portuguese of Macau had been tolerated by the Chinese administration of the province as long as they respected certain rules, provided them with an income and appeared militarily inoffensive. It was advisable that they should not be encouraged to rethink this policy by news of the union of the two Iberian Crowns. Sánchez was equally disinclined to tolerate the clandestine landings of the monks of the Philippines. It was necessary at all costs to avoid incidents which would be blamed on the Portuguese of Macau and which would complicate the plans for invasion and conquest. He was also determined to see that the Christianization of China was entrusted exclusively to the Jesuits and carried out in accordance with conditions laid down by him. He believed he could count on the assistance of some of the local Jesuits and of the Portuguese who were trading wholly illegally with Manila.[15]

The Intolerable Insolence of the Chinese[16]

Why make war on China? This time it was not the jurists or royal officials who argued for armed intervention, as in the 1570s, but two members of the ecclesiastical establishment of Manila, the Jesuit Alonso Sánchez and Bishop Domingo de Salazar,[17] who were determined to justify a war. They claimed to have the support of the governor and of local notables such as the royal factor Juan Bautista Román and even, according to Sánchez, the tacit agreement of the Italian Jesuits who had entered China, among whom was the celebrated Matteo Ricci.

Their argument was simple. It was essential to go to war in order to bring about the conversion of China. The duty of evangelization justified the intervention, as it seemed impossible to make any headway through 'peaceful' preaching. The Chinese were allergic to the latter, for many reasons. In the first place they were a people puffed up with pride:

> They do not wish to believe and do not wish to hear that there are people who know anything other than them; they will not allow anyone to teach them anything and they think there is no other truth than their lies, and as for us, they consider us all to be barbarians and animals, people without law, without reason and without government. When they have a stranger in their town...they play with him as they would with an animal; this is what happened to us when we were among them, at least what we looked like, having to keep mum without knowing how or being able to defend ourselves...They are very sarcastic and very wily, very arrogant and very intolerable.

So the Chinese mocked not only strangers who were unable to speak their language properly but also the God the missionaries preached. What troubled Sánchez, apart from the open antipathy, not to say xenophobia, he sensed all around him and his compatriots, were his ordinary daily contacts. Even the curiosity of the Chinese crowds upset him:

> The people were so intrusive and they were so amazed to see, among other things, the material of the cloak I was wearing, the one I normally wear in Spain, that they practically killed each other for a chance to see it and touch it with their hands. To the point where, in the end, they tore it and they carried off two pieces more than half an ell in size without either I or any of my companions even realizing it, so large was the crowd milling around us.

Sánchez returned from his short stay in China with a whole string of prejudices.

There were other obstacles to conversion. The 'greed' of the Chinese was 'insatiable', 'in particular for silver, which is their god'. But Sánchez found they had many other failings, including gluttony, not to speak of their disgraceful morals. In accusing them of 'the great indecency and dissipation of the sin against nature', Sánchez was simply conforming to an old Iberian reflex, which was quick to raise the spectre of sodomy whenever it needed to justify the annihilation of an enemy. From this to affirming the superiority of the Europeans and the absolute necessity of forcing the Chinese people to listen to the missionaries was but a short step. The Chinese would become malleable once they had to reckon with a power stronger than them. This was the discourse that had long been applied in the case of the Indians of America. And Sánchez already imagined the Chinese, once conquered and converted, embarking on the study of Castilian, 'like children in school'.

However, there was another and even more formidable obstacle. For Sánchez, Chinese was an incomprehensible language:

> It was God's will that there should be between them and us a wall in the form of a language that is different from ours and so obscure that even among them there are no other studies nor any apprenticeship in letters than to study from infancy their characters or their signs which are said to number more than eighty thousand.

The study of Chinese was so time-consuming that it became intellectually impoverishing, because it made it impossible to learn other languages 'or other sciences of the natural and supernatural things and also the laws and moral issues'. Sánchez was quick to detect the hand of the devil: 'The devil invented so as to warp their judgement and alienate their spirit that what a child learns in a year or a year and a half, they spend a lifetime doing'. The complexity of this language, which had nearly 100,000 letters, was beyond understanding, and its pronunciation, which involved 'the lips, the throat, the palate and the nose', caused endless difficulties. Though it had never seemed to present an insuperable barrier to the Portuguese, Sánchez saw the Chinese language as an anti-Christian weapon. From an obstacle to communication, it became an obstacle to preaching.[18]

Might the use of interpreters be a way of getting round this obstacle? This was problematic, 'because to use an intermediary seemed to the Chinese a risible process, and it was madness on the part of anyone who risked it'. Sánchez explained that during his travels in China he had been obliged to employ a translator 'who knew a little Portuguese and no Castilian'. Added to which, though he does not admit it, the Spanish were always extremely reluctant to use the Portuguese language. The Chinese authorities were consequently irritated at not being able to understand him, and when Sánchez tried to find out what was happening by questioning his translator, he was immediately accused of seeking to manipulate him. When the interpreters were local, they were never trustworthy: 'We know that they are not in the habit of speaking the truth, on the contrary, they pride themselves on telling lies, mocking us and inventing nonsenses'. It must have been one of these interpreters who presented the Castilians as 'bad people who go to rob foreign kingdoms and kill their natural rulers, and who seize any country they enter'. It is rare to read outside Europe such a critical and convincing description of Spanish expansion. It is even rarer to see Iberians physically facing such attacks and reporting them back to Madrid. Sánchez did not understand, or claimed not to understand, that what the Chinese interpreters feared most was provoking the wrath of the mandarins; but it was also, for the Spanish, a way of blaming them for the difficulties put in their way by their interlocutors.

So to the unease provoked by contact with crowds of people, by the mockery and lack of respect of the onlookers and by evil morals was added the confusion of being 'lost in translation'. This was what Sánchez experienced every time he was unable to understand 'what they said to him, or where they were going, or where they were taking him, or when they were mocking him or when they were deceiving him'. In reality, misunderstandings and irritations were simply an expression of the deep distrust of the local authorities, who had few illusions about their new visitors: 'We were supposed to be robbers and Castilian spies who had come to learn about the language and the local ports'.

Another criticism of China was that it was a kingdom closed to the outside world. The Chinese fleets let no one enter, 'even if you arrived because you had been diverted or said that you had come to trade or other things by means of which kingdoms customarily communicate with each other'. The laws of China decreed the death penalty, life imprisonment or a whipping for anyone who dared to enter the kingdom. The case of Macau was probably an exception, but it was a very fragile one. The Portuguese of Macau constantly feared the worst, being put to death or suffering persecution which would force them to leave the country and diminish the revenues for the Crown. Murders and unexplained disappearances were a regular phenomenon in the city: 'Every day, people known in the town of Macau go missing and it is taken for granted that they have killed them'. The risk of a Portuguese exodus to India was real, with incalculable consequences for the faith: 'The Christianity of Japan would be as good as lost, because its survival depends on what reaches it each year from this town.'

The missionaries, especially the Jesuits, would be the first victims of this closing down: 'The Chinese have never allowed the Jesuits to enter the town, or to build a house there or a church, or to preach the holy gospel, and when someone has attempted this, they have had him whipped'. To this hostility was added the terror which the provincial authorities sowed so as to prevent any conversion, otherwise 'countless people would come to hear the Gospel'. It was no longer possible to count the instances of harassment and humiliation endured by the preachers, who were made to kneel and press their faces to the ground. The interpreters, for their part, never dared to translate anything that touched on matters of the faith and conversion. If they so much as dressed in the Western style or wore Christian symbols they were whipped and treated as traitors to king and country. For this Jesuit, the obscurity of the language, the intellectual backwardness and the closure combined to create an extremely hostile environment, at the opposite pole from the civilizing virtues of Christian charity.

'The Path to War'

For all these reasons, the conversion of China would have to be achieved by force. The experts were agreed: 'Everyone who knows these people and who has been to China considers it is mad to think that one can convert them amicably'. In other words, there was 'another path, different from that of the primitive Church, which has already been followed in New Spain and Peru, where Christianity is now as well-established as in Spain; and in these Philippine islands the same path is being followed'.

True, no war was without its down side, but 'the ravages, the evils and the devastation which are associated with conquests' should not constitute an obstacle. The ways of the Lord are inscrutable: 'God may permit these things...', as we have seen in the 'legitimate' conquest of Portugal. 'Might those who went to preach the Gospel in the wake of the soldiers' be uneasy about the justice of their battle? Sánchez dismissed such worries out of hand, invoking 'the well founded right which Your Majesty has to conquer...these kingdoms of China'. This right applied to any other pagan country, 'as all the scholars who are in these parts and who have a stake in the matter believe'. From a specific case, that of China, we have moved to the affirmation of an outright and unqualified right of conquest, as long as the enemy was not Christian.

The weakness of the Chinese forces was a further argument in favour of military intervention. First, the ordinary people did not have the right to bear arms. Second, the numerical argument did not hold water. What nonsense the enemy spouted! According to Bishop Domingo de Salazar, the Chinese 'rulers trust so entirely in the abundance of people in this kingdom that they laugh when the Spanish tell them they will subject them, because they say that, even if all they have in the way of weapons to defend themselves are the corpses of the soldiers, they will make a rampart of them which will prevent anyone from getting in'. To which, the self-confident Bishop retorted: 'But these barbarians have had no experience of what the Spanish can do, they do not realize that all it needs is a few arquebusiers in their ranks to put millions of Chinese to flight'. The Spanish of the Philippines seemed to be dreaming of re-enacting the conquest of Mexico.

The Jesuit Sánchez and Bishop Salazar preferred to talk numbers, in particular how many men would be needed for the enterprise, and the efficacy of an armed intervention; they banked on a lightning raid putting the Chinese troops to flight. Local support would soon be forthcoming. They would benefit from the assistance of the oppressed population, ready to put themselves under the protection of a Christian prince so as to escape the tyranny of their masters. The 'opinion polls' could not lie! In fact, Sánchez had been 'secretly informed of the general desire to liberate themselves from so great a wretchedness and subjection, because they were treated not like free men but worse than slaves'. We might well be hearing the arguments of Calvo and Vieira, prisoners in Canton, sixty years before.

Sánchez and Salazar discussed logistics, too. They would investigate 'the place where it would be best to enter [China] and the provisions that could be got ready to support the people who would come'. The governor of the Philippines later sent a relation in which he estimated at 8,000 the number of Spanish troops necessary for the conquest, and the size of the fleet at a dozen galleons. Whereas the royal factor proposed the more ambitious figure of 15,000 soldiers;[19] though the rector of the Jesuit College of Macau would be content with 10,000, who should include 2,000 Japanese enlisted with the aid of the members of the Society who lived in the archipelago.[20] The Japanese were potential allies not to be disdained, because 'they are great enemies of the Chinese and they will make haste to enter this kingdom at the same time as the Spanish'. And, to put this initiative into action: 'The best way would be for Your Majesty to request the general of the Society to instruct the religious of this order who are in Japan to tell the Japanese what they ought to do in this matter'.[21] The Japanese alliance was taking up an idea put forward by the governor Francisco de Sande in 1576. Nor did they forget the contribution of the indigenous Filipinos, who were numerous and effective, just as, long ago in Mexico, the Spanish had turned to the Tlaxcaltecs, who had served Cortés and his men so well. Lastly, the rector of the Jesuit College of Macau offered his own services and those of his brethren Matteo Ricci and Michele Ruggieri to collect 'in secrecy' all sorts of strategic information. The war on China was not an end in itself. One senses the emergence in the minds of the bishop, the Jesuit and the governor of a vision of an Iberian rule destined to be exercised over the whole of this part of the world.

Once again we are confronted with the 'monstrosities' of Peter Sloterdijk, with an unbridled ambition which now seemed no longer ready be satisfied with America and the Pacific.

There was little point, in these circumstances, in following the diplomatic route or losing time by sending a gift, as had originally been planned: 'It is beneath the dignity of the grandeur of the king to send a present to such a barbarous and arrogant king, who would not only not receive it, but would despise it when he saw it and would not even allow the person who brought it to see him in person'. There could be no question in future of tolerating 'the casualness and the arrogance manifested by his viceroys and his governors who were unable to imagine that there existed anywhere else in the world a prince who might equal their king'. To diplomacy, they unashamedly preferred the sound of cannon fire: 'Here, the sound of drums and artillery will be as sweet and as useful as there the voice of the preachers'.

When China Awakes

Every day that passed worked against the Castilians. Sánchez and Salazar were firmly convinced of this. The Portuguese, according to the Jesuit, bore a heavy responsibility for the awakening of China. Unlike the Castilians, they had not waged war:

> They have little taste for it and make even less effort, as we see all over India, where they possess only the beaches for giving and taking, bartering and trading in their lairs and their fortresses; may we be pardoned, but they have done more harm to Christianity than any other people, because they have awakened this whole world and instructed it in arms and the arts of war by introducing an artillery and an arquebuserie more powerful than those of the people of the region. These same Portuguese admit today that in the beginning, with a single ship, they put to flight sixty or seventy ships of the pagans, but that now, when they fight one to one, the others defend themselves very effectively, attack them and often defeat them.

Which led him to conclude: launch an attack while there is still time! 'China is still asleep, but with their relations with the Portuguese and the rumours which reach them about the Castilians, and which make their ears tingle, they will awake, and they are people, from what we have seen, who are all endowed with minds, ingenuity and remarkable resources'. The theme of the awakening of China, which would be taken up by Napoleon and many others after him, is thus almost as old as the connection of the Europeans to this part of the world. It is a leitmotif in all the writings of Sánchez. 'This is what everyone who knows them says: even if now they are still asleep, if they wake up, if they begin to have suspicions and if they prepare, they will be lost to the faith for all the reasons we have explained, but also because of the huge number of these people who are like a swarm of locusts on land and sea'.

This was confirmed by Bishop Domingo de Salazar: the Chinese have 'until now been a people asleep, who could not believe that bad things could come to them from this side'. All their efforts had been directed towards the side of the Tartars. Their fleets had so far been used only to drive back the Japanese and the Chinese pirates, but watch out if the country's authorities began to suspect something! 'If their eyes are opened as to what is being prepared for them, the invasion will be more difficult than it would be now, when they are not on their guard'. So a preventive strike, at the earliest opportunity, was urgent! In the interests of surprise, they must be discreet. So not a word to the Chinese of Manila, or even to the pope – who, in any case, had no say in the matter, 'because the Roman Church has left this responsibility to the kings of Spain'. This was a reminder of the right of patronage enjoyed by the Castilian kings over all of the monarchy's Catholics. Thus was Rome excluded by the representative of the Society of Jesus and by the bishop of the Philippines. In fact this attitude is hardly surprising; it is wholly in accord with the Castilian policy which, with the support of the Iberian universities, had deliberately shut the papacy out of global affairs.

Another facet, by contrast, does surprise, when we remember the origin and the obligations of the Jesuit Sánchez: not a word of all this was to reach the ears of the general of the Society. These precautions reveal the transition from a global *imaginaire* of power (let us also remember Cortés opening up the vast horizons of Mexico, the Pacific Ocean and the Spice Islands to the Emperor Charles V) to its enactment on the ground. This raised a variety of problems. Who should decide the fate of China? Was it the bishop of Rome, with his universal competences? Or was it the Society of Jesus, with its global sphere of activity? Or the ruler of the Catholic Monarchy? In which case, was it the king of Castile, Philip II, or the sovereign of Portugal, Philip I, who should intervene in this part of the world? The Manila initiative disregarded bureaucracies and power mechanisms rendered obsolete by the perspectives opened up by the globalization introduced by the Iberians. Nor was it only the conduct of the enterprise that posed problems. Space and time were still far from having been mastered. Sánchez and Salazar struggled to hurry on the Crown, although they knew it took years for information and decisions to circulate between Manila and the metropolis.

Something So New...

So Sánchez decided to go to Madrid to plead the cause of war. He would present himself both as ambassador of the Philippines and as the expert entrusted with handling an affair he summarized in a sentence: 'the right which Your Majesty has to conquer China...or, put more cautiously, to ensure that the Chinese receive preachers who may spread the gospel in total freedom and security'. He had good reason to feel uneasy. He might proclaim the support of Manila and Macao, but he suspected that his position risked conflicting with the ideas then prevailing in the metropolis. To present himself as the champion of the periphery – 'of the things which are so far away' – was to prepare to confront a government incapable of fully appreciating the importance of what was happening in 'countries so remote'. He was of the opinion that things ought to be decided primarily 'according to the views and decisions of those who have some understanding of things here [in the Philippines], and not only according to what was debated in the schools over there [in Spain]'. This tension between centre and periphery was by no means exceptional in the empire of Philip II. It reveals once again the extreme difficulty of putting into practice a global strategy adapted to the scale of the Catholic Monarchy. With distance, the gravity of situations seemed reduced and the urgency decreased.

But Sánchez was preparing to encounter a very different and much more formidable obstacle. The idea 'that one might conquer kingdoms unknown to the scholars of these parts of Europe' risked causing offence. It was 'such a new thing that it must appear as a sort of provocation'. It was a 'new language...and new meant over there [in Spain] that it was not talked about and it was not understood'. In what way did this language risk conflicting with the doctrine generally taught in Spain?

At first sight, the bishop and the Jesuit tried to avoid any head-on clash by locating themselves within the Iberian theological and juridical tradition. The teaching of Francisco de Vitoria and the University of Salamanca,[22] and the great debates such as those between Bartolomé de Las Casas and the humanist Ginés de Sepulveda, had led to the formulation of a number of principles intended to regulate the relations between peoples or, to be more precise, between the Castilians and other nations.[23] The debate had focused on the right of the

Crown of Castile to conquer the New World. In the middle of the sixteenth century China was not yet an issue; Bartolomé de Las Casas had not even mentioned it in his universal summa, the *Apologética historia sumaria*. However, at the end of the century the debate shifted to the Middle Empire. It had changed continent and enemy, and this was certainly one aspect of the novelty evoked by Sánchez. There could be no question now of claiming that the pagans were slaves by nature (Sepulveda) or that they were children who had to be taken in hand (Vitoria), so obviously was this contradicted by the Chinese realities observed and described by the Spanish and the Portuguese. However, this was not the only new element introduced by the warmongers of the Philippines.

For Francisco de Vitoria, who continued, long after his death, to dominate the debate, war could only be justified in the case of open aggression. Neither religious difference nor the desire for conquest and military glory could provide grounds for European intervention. There could be no question of attacking sovereigns on the pretext that they were not Christians. True, the principles of free circulation and free preaching were inviolable. It was therefore legitimate to fight a just war against those who tried to restrict them. But Vitoria had hedged in any intervention with strict conditions, which Sánchez and Salazar roundly ignored. A few years after Vitoria, in 1546, Melchor Cano had even argued that the *jus predicandi* could not give any right of ownership over the property of secular princes; the Indians had remained free subjects. In the middle of the sixteenth century, though they never managed to reverse the course of events, the attacks of Las Casas on the cruelties of the conquest and his defence of the rights of the Indian inclined theologians to be mistrustful of the consequences of an armed intervention and to ask searching questions about the reasons which might motivate it.[24]

There were discordant voices, of course, like that of the humanist Ginés de Sepulveda, or of Bishop Vasco de Quiroga, who in 1552 defended the thesis that it was not only perfectly legitimate, but obligatory, to make war on the Indians.[25] By this period, however, Quiroga made no attempt to conceal the fact that the contrary opinion was more widely held and publicly asserted. It was the ideas of Vitoria and those influenced by Las Casas which persisted in university circles. In the second half of the sixteenth century, masters of the school of Salamanca like Bartolomé de Medina, Domingo Báñez and Juan de la Peña were imbued with them, whereas the doctrines of Sepulveda were greeted with general hostility.

Sánchez and Salazar already knew this. If, from Manila, they proclaimed the right of free circulation and the freedom to preach as a way of justifying military intervention in China, it was because they wished to give their project a veneer, a 'Vitorian' gloss. They claimed also to be ready to provide juridical proof of the obstacles put by the Chinese in the way of the propagation of the Gospel and the free circulation of the Spanish. Indeed, it was for this purpose that the bishop had conducted a formal enquiry, but one from which he had prudently excluded the Chinese and also the Castilian and Portuguese opponents of the project. In other words, they did everything possible to influence public opinion, gain the support of the Crown and give the impression that they were seeking to respect the principles of Salamanca. They were no doubt quietly calculating that there was always, in any case, a gap between theory and practice and that, bearing in mind the distance, this 'spin' would be enough. Sánchez and Salazar knew that the use of force in moderation was acceptable when the right to preach was obstructed, even if, with Báñez, peaceful forms of intervention were always to be preferred. But it remained possible to resort to force to remove the impediments put in the way of missionary activity, because it was important to defend the 'right of people' to hear preaching.[26]

It was this gap that the Manila-based partisans of war against China hoped to exploit. Yet it was a very narrow gap, if one rereads how the theologians of Salamanca defined the room for manoeuvre allowed to non-Christians. For Peña, if they were all in accord, the infidels had the right to refuse to hear the preachers. They could not be forced to come and listen to them. For Báñez, the use of violence and war was absolutely forbidden when the infidels were not subjects either of the pope or of a Christian prince.

What happened on the ground? Did the grand principles of the university theologian simply serve to mask less orthodox practices, as Salazar and Sánchez believed? It is undeniable that many compromises were necessary between the demands of the theologians, the legal rules and the pressure of the settlers. The laws of the Crown defined the conditions of military intervention or *entrada*. After the *juntas* of Valladolid (1550–1) and the official suspension of conquests, the peace option seemed to have won the day, though the use of force was never categorically excluded.[27] So in 1558, after the failure of his brethren in Florida, a Dominican, Domingo de Santa Maria, denounced *entradas* carried out without military support. It is not without relevance that among the members of the expedition had been one of his co-religionists and companions in misfortune, Domingo de Salazar, future bishop of the Philippines. Nevertheless, in general, the missionaries were opposed to the armed solution. In 1583, some Franciscans from Jalisco in Mexico asserted that the difficulties the preachers encountered were 'because they went about in the company of soldiers'.[28] In that same year the Franciscan Gaspar de Ricarte was fiercely hostile to the idea that 'the ministers of the gospel should be permitted to go in the company of men of war to preach the gospel among the infidel barbarians'. Such a notion was in his eyes 'heretical, rash and scandalous'.

For its part, the Crown sought a happy medium. The *Instrucción* of 1556 to the viceroy of Peru authorized the use of force in specific circumstances, 'without causing more harm than is strictly necessary', against, for example, those who prevented preaching and conversion or in order to overcome the resistance of indigenous lords. In 1573, the ordinances of Juan de Ovando spoke of pacification, and not of *conquista*, while making preaching the ultimate purpose of the discoveries and *poblaciones*. There was an insistence, therefore, on the desirability of choosing peaceful means, though without precluding the assistance that could be provided by small escorts to protect the results of the mission.[29]

The War with China Will Not Take Place

These Philippines projects remained just that. Sánchez might well plead his cause in Spain, but the war with China did not take place. For this, there were many reasons. The distances between the Philippines and metropolis were huge, whether one crossed the Pacific or the Indian Ocean. Any exchanges, any round trips, hence any decision making, came up against the hazards of navigation, storms, shipwrecks, mutinies, unforeseen events and the interminable length of the voyages. The principal elements of the dossier took two years to travel from Manila to Madrid. A simple journey by the bishop or the Jesuit to the court presented serious difficulties. A prelate, in principle, did not leave his diocese without the authorization of the prince, and to procure such an authorization it was first necessary for the request to travel halfway round the world, and the same was true of the response. Simply getting bogged down was thus the principal enemy of enterprises of this sort, and Sánchez had few illusions with regard to the success of a negotiation in Spain. It was technically extremely complicated to organize from Manila and Macau an enterprise which required management from Madrid and crucial logistical support from New Spain. The means for Iberian expansion did not match its ambitions. Yet the war lobby was not lacking in grandeur of conception. It was capable of imagining a redistribution of the cards in this part of the world, in collaboration with a European metropolis. It remains the case that it was hardly possible to seize China in the same way that Mexico had been conquered.

Even more serious, the reasons put forward by Manila – the closure of China and the persecution of the missionaries – were flatly contradicted by the welcome offered by the Chinese authorities to the missionaries of the Society of Jesus. The bishop and the Jesuit had no luck: not only was their argument largely based on a partial and tendentious view of the Chinese reaction, but it collapsed with the arrival of the encouraging news sent from Canton and the interior of the province by Matteo Ricci and Michele Ruggieri. In September 1583, these two men obtained for the second time permission to settle in Zhaoqing, the provincial capital. The Italian Jesuits even nurtured hopes of getting as far as Peking. In that same year the idea of a peaceful embassy gained ground once again, even if accompanied by some dubious ulterior motives. The embassy was to help to 'understand the country, its forces, its customs and its character, with a view to advising Your Majesty should it be found opportune to lead, now or in the near future, such a remarkable enterprise'. Bishop Salazar saw this as a way of testing the intentions of the Chinese authorities on the question of preaching and the concession of a commercial enclave.[30] Like other such attempts, it came to nothing. What remained was the desire of the Italian Jesuits and Rome to undermine Castilian ambitions in favour of a more specific and more targeted penetration: no more than a handful of Jesuits, a sustained effort to merge into the background and adapt to the Chinese way of life, and a one-step-at-a-time policy.

All that was needed, to complicate even further the task of the war party, was dissension between Manila and Macau. Some of the inhabitants of the Portuguese enclave looked amiss at the way the Spanish of the Philippines were taking control of the destiny of the whole region by trying to short-circuit the favoured relations which had developed between Macau and Chinese authorities. Rampant commercial growth was even more to be feared, because Manila now had access to the silver extracted from the mines of the New World in such quantities that Chinese prices risked going through the roof. There was another fracture running through the Society of Jesus. While the rector Francisco Cabral supported Sánchez and the military project, the Italian members, Valignano, Ruggieri and Ricci, did everything to hold on to their privileged access to the Chinese interior; they had the approval of Rome and of the general, Acquaviva, who it had been hoped to exclude from the enterprise.

In Mexico, in 1587, it was the Jesuit José de Acosta who was given the task of neutralizing Sánchez. Acosta had played a major role in the rise of the Society of Jesus in Peru, and he enjoyed increasing authority in matters of evangelization. The task of demolishing the arguments of Sánchez and of explaining why it was out of the question to wage war on the Chinese fell to him. In doing so he was expressing the official opinion of the Society. Sánchez was absolutely forbidden from any further mention of the project. This put a damper on Mexican ambitions in China, which had been all the more hopeful in that the viceroy himself, Archbishop Moya de Contreras, in 1585, had been attracted by the arguments of Sánchez and the support they enjoyed.[31] The debate between the two Jesuits raised the question of the relations of the Church with the other half of the world, or, to be more precise, it revealed the extent to which the challenges of Mission (how far it should be extended, at what rate and by what means?) and political and economic interests made it necessary to perceive the world in its totality, which Acosta expressed as *universo mundo*. It is significant that it was primarily in Mexico that it was decided how a Catholic monarchy based in Madrid and Rome was supposed to lay out its cards in South-East Asia.

In the end European realities won the day at the expense of the two men in the Philippines. The negotiations conducted by Sánchez in Madrid coincided with the arrival of news of the fleet. The defeat of the Invincible Armada in August 1588 put a stop to any idea of an attack on China. The massive losses sustained off the coasts of England made it as unthinkable as grotesque to send a fleet and assistance to the China Sea. 'Looked at with a very human caution, the circumstances do not lend themselves to a negotiation with the king'.[32] There was no longer any question of an attack. The war with China would not take place.[33]

Conclusion: Towards a Global History of the Renaissance

The King: Thus this sea where the sun is setting – the glittering expanse,

...

The daring eye of my predecessors ranging over that sea, their finger imperiously pointed out the other shore, another world.

Paul Claudel, *The Satin Slipper*

The galleons of Manila...are only one thread, of huge importance, certainly, if difficult to quantify, in a dense and infinitely complex web of relations and exchanges which had Manila at its heart, and which had a strategy that did not stop at Acapulco...but at Manila incidentally, at Mexico significantly, and at Macau, China, the Indies and the shores of Atlantic Europe.

Pierre Chaunu, *Le Pacifique des Ibériques*

The war with China did not take place in the sixteenth century. 'All those banks alive with human fry, more populous than the dead, and awaiting baptism' described by Paul Claudel would avoid Christianization and colonization. It was much later, in 1840, that a European war broke out – the Opium War. Admiral Elliot would then realize the long-ago dream of the friends of Pires and Sánchez by making himself master of the Pearl River Delta, establishing an insular base, sailing up the river and attacking Canton. The town was bombarded and had to be ransomed. Hong Kong passed into British hands. A humiliated China submitted to European demands. But it was never, strictly speaking, colonized.

All this was still well in the future in the sixteenth century. The Portuguese and Spanish dreams of conquest had simply been whistling in the wind. While the New World was subjected to a systematic colonization and its wealth exploited in every conceivable way by the Iberians, and while Christianity triumphed over idolatry, China experienced unprecedented prosperity, behind frontiers that were once again half open. Trade enriched the merchant class. Silver flooded in from Japan before arriving from Manila and Macau. The Middle Empire was never wholly untouched by what happened beyond its frontiers, especially in the China Sea. But it was on conditions it set, and at a tempo it dictated, that China was connected to the rest of the world, and the rest of the world to China, through the globalization of exchanges. The connection was complete at the end of the sixteenth century, when American silver began to flow into the Celestial Empire. All paths now led, not to Rome but to Peking. Directly by the Pacific route, or by taking the Atlantic and then Indian Ocean route, silver reached Chinese coffers. So it was neither conquest nor conversion, even less economic dependence, that linked China to Europe, but circuits that went right round the world and connected its different parts. Not only would Spain never attack China 'before it awoke', but, by its exploitation of American mineral deposits and establishment of a colonial society and a system of forced labour, it may be argued that it put much of its energies at the service of the Middle Empire, and that it deserved its gratitude. The Spanish of the Americas, who exchanged the silver of Potosi, usually illegally, for costly Asiatic merchandise, found this to their advantage. In the Andes and in Mexico the indigenous and African workers were unaware that they toiled deep in the mines not only for their European bosses but also for the Chinese merchants who hoarded the precious pesos of Mexican silver.

The opening-up of the world thus took place in synchronous but antithetical fashion. Fully to appreciate this, it is still necessary that we abandon the tired old frameworks of a national, colonial and imperial history, which are an obstacle to a global approach.[1] As will have become clear, a global history is not the same thing as a history of European expansion, even when it is focused on the European dimension of the globalizing process. I have rejected Eurocentrism not, as is common across the Atlantic, in the name of a narrow ethic of political correctness, but for sound intellectual reasons. The urgent necessity of understanding the world that surrounds us today can only be achieved by sweeping away the time-honoured frameworks within which what remains of historical memory still operates. They have become obsolete and archaic, they are stifling and they lead ultimately to a presentism whose perverse effects have been well described.[2]

A global history of the Renaissance helps us to reinterpret the Great Discoveries by restoring links which European historiography has either been ignorant of or passed over in silence. It makes it easier for us to escape the simplistic schemas of otherness, in which history is reduced to a confrontation between them and us, and enables us to substitute far more complex scenarios: global history shows that there are not only victors and vanquished, and that the dominant may also be the dominated in another part of the world. A global history enables us to reassemble the pieces of the global jigsaw disassembled by national historiographies or fragmented by poorly conceived micro-history. It encourages us to delocalize our interests and our problematics. In my earlier book, *What Time is it There?*,[3] I began with a survey of the Catholic Monarchy of Philip II, that worldwide empire born of the union of the Crowns of Spain and Portugal, and a recapitulation of all the places it occupied in every part of the globe. I then proceeded to a discussion of the real and virtual relations maintained by Islam and the New World in this context. A global history ought to pay proper attention to Africa, because it was there that the first large-scale colonial experience was developed, with the blessing of the papacy, and because this continent continued to provide slaves to the newly conquered America while retaining its old strong links with the worlds of the Indian Ocean. Nor should we forget that it was in Africa that the Portuguese celebrated the tragic coming together of the slave trade and Christianity.[4]

I have spoken of a global history of the Renaissance because history cannot be written without a standpoint – one does not write history from Sirius – for risk is of drowning in the generalities of a world history. A detour via global history and connected histories always leads back to square one. To relocate local history and the history of Europe in broader horizons is not only to resize it, but also to return to the particularities of this part of the world; and to simple questions that deserve serious consideration: it was the Iberians who visited America and China, never the other way round.

To focus on these particularities also reveals a fracture that is probably as damaging to our knowledge of the past as the Eurocentrism that is so justly decried. Sixteenth-century Europe was not the same as Northern Europe. The men who discovered Mexico and China, like their promoters, were for the most part Iberians and Italians. We need to keep always in mind the importance of Southern Europe and the Mediterranean and the massive impact of the Catholic sixteenth century on the history of Europe and of the world. We should never forget the role played by the Roman Church and by Mission, so often passed over in favour of English and Dutch expansion, vehicles of the northern manifestations of the Reformation, when there was a spiritual and even mystical dimension to the global mobility which gripped the Europeans.

Modernities

In an earlier book, *Les Quatre Parties du monde*, I suggested that to go on describing the appearance of modernity in exclusively European, even worse Italian, French, English or Dutch, terms is exceptionally limiting. The increasing number of interactions with the great religions and civilizations of the globe fostered countless human experiences and these gave rise to other forms of modernity, hidden away on the peripheries, among the Europeans but also among all those who had contact with them, willingly or not.

In this book I have analysed European modernity in two other ways. First by demonstrating the true scale of Magellan's revolution, which, as Peter Sloterdijk has shown, was just as important and probably more critical than the Copernican revolution. A global history of the Renaissance cannot ignore this. With and since Copernicus, the Earth has revolved round the sun; with Magellan it was European people and European capital that began to revolve round the Earth. This had an immediate impact on sailors, merchants, financiers, princes and chroniclers; it made the sea and the movement of men and capital the motor of all circulation and of all the new opening-up. There could be no globalization without Magellan's circumnavigation, whereas it was perfectly possible to connect the four quarters of the globe and administer a universal monarchy while still believing in the old cosmic schemas of Aristotelian origin.

The history of the world cannot, however, be reduced to the history of Europeans. Magellan was killed at Mactan, an island in the Philippines; Cortés failed in his projects in the Pacific. The cargoes of spices would never cross the South Sea to reach Europe via the Americas, and on at least two occasions the Iberians abandoned their plans to attack China. Asia, and most notably China, did not fall to the Europeans, who were forced to draw the appropriate lessons. They no longer, as in Brazil or the rest of the Americas, had the upper hand in every confrontation with populations of savages, good for little else than to be conquered, massacred or exploited. The war with China did not take place. Not only did the Iberians feel powerless and out of their depth, except on the plane of salvation, and not only were they forced, Portuguese and Spanish alike, to endure the insults heaped on them by the Chinese, but they ended up by erecting into a model the power which had crushed them with its arrogance. They were fascinated by Chinese greatness – political, economic and cultural. The history of relations with China from the middle of the sixteenth to the beginning of the eighteenth century was that of an intellectual construction in which the elites of western Europe never ceased to see themselves. Things were very different in Mexico, quickly relegated to the great warehouse of dead civilizations, a land of unthreatening exoticism, good at best for eliciting pity or lamentations.

A Westwards Turn and the Birth of the West

In the second half of the sixteenth century the Pacific and its eastern shores, including that of China, came within the sightlines of the Spanish empire. The West Indies – in Spain they did not speak of the American continent – was the counterpart, extension and outpost of the East Indies, which lay on the other side of the South Sea. But the unknowable immensity of the Pacific and the impossibility of seizing China or colonizing Asia made it necessary to fall back on the New World and to separate it from the rest of the Indies. America, gradually and irreversibly colonized by the European powers, turned to the east and forged close ties with the Old World. Together these two formed what has come to be called the West; a concept and then a reality that only a global history can satisfactorily explain.

The gestation of the Euro-American West is inseparable from failure in China and later in Japan. This blocked the westward turn initiated by the expeditions of Columbus and Magellan, which had reversed a trend of more than a millennium. It had been known since Antiquity that the Earth was round and that it was a globe. Aristotle himself had observed that it was theoretically possible to reach distant India by taking a westward route. But this would have meant crossing an ocean whose waters and winds were unknown to pilots, and having access to ships capable of covering such vast distances. The West remained for the Ancients an unreachable horizon. This hardly changed in medieval Europe, which kept its eyes fixed on the East: Paradise, the Holy Land, Jerusalem, the tales of Antiquity, the memory of the Crusades, the Mongol invasions, the threats of Mameluke and Ottoman Islam, the fabulous wealth of India and a host of other factors combined to make the East object of all hopes and all greed, and all hatred when confrontation with Islam was at issue. Even the

Portuguese conformed to this tropism because, though their vessels sailed first towards the South Atlantic, they still favoured the route towards the East and to the India of the Ancients. Once past the Cape of Good Hope it was the East which beckoned for the exhausted and frozen sailors.

With Christopher Columbus and Magellan, they began to head West. The direction of European circulation was now reversed. True, this made no immediate difference. The discovery of the Antilles did not transform the customary image of the West as an oceanic solitude dotted with a handful of quickly decimated islands, and what the first circumnavigation of the globe revealed above all was that the western route was long and horribly dangerous. It claimed the lives of Magellan among others. Another discovery, central to this book, irrevocably marked the emergence of the West on European horizons. This time it was not long-distance travel. After 1517 Europeans realized that there existed, on the mainland, astonishing societies with ways of life that seemed close to those of the Old World. With the discovery of Peru and the empire of the Incas, the existence of another world, overlooked by the Bible and by the Ancients, was finally accepted. As far away as Istanbul contemporaries realized the extraordinary nature of this discovery and, as Muslims, the scandal of a conquest which had handed to the infidel, that is, the Christians, a far from negligible sector of humanity. An anonymous chronicler of the Ottoman court, around 1580, urged the Sultan to make up for lost time and remove these new lands from the Christians so as to make Islam prevail.[5]

So the West ceased to be simply a direction, an inaccessible point given up to 'illusion and madness' (Claudel).[6] It materialized, and it became what it would for a long time remain: a promised land for the missionaries, a source of wealth to be pillaged freely, a laboratory where people struggled to reproduce a nascent Europe and a space as welcoming to emigrants as it was a living hell for the Blacks of Africa. For some Catholics the new Indies seemed likely to be the future of the Christian world. Providentially spared by Islam and Protestant schism, densely populated by a new humanity, the Indians, these lands offered Catholicism perspectives which a corrupted Europe, threatened by the Turks, seemed no longer to provide. On the Protestant side, in the seventeenth century, there were dreams of a Puritan America, an American Palestine purified of the savages who populated it. It is hardly necessary to recall the way in which, over the centuries, the Americas became the hope of generations of Europeans who set out to seek on the other side of the Atlantic the survival and future they were denied in the Old World. In the nineteenth century the rush to the West was simply reviving the appeal acquired by the countries of America before the West itself became synonymous with liberty, the spirit of enterprise and finally the Atlantic Alliance and anti-Communism. As opposed to an ancient, despotic, languid and decadent East, the West gradually emerged as the motor of modern civilization and the cradle of modernity. To which we should add that the idea of Europe – as it is familiar to us today – was forged alongside the emergence of the New World, which makes it easier to understand why the destinies of these two parts of the globe are inseparable: if the Americas have been shaped by Europe, Europe has in its turn, since the Renaissance, been enriched, constructed and reproduced by projecting itself to the other side of the Atlantic, through the links it has forged with the different parts of the new continent. It is through New Spain, New Granada, New England and New France that the countries of Europe performed their dual role of predators and 'civilizers'. These are all good reasons to conclude not only that the change of direction so brilliantly initiated by Columbus far surpassed in significance the islands and the coasts he discovered, but also that it was the resistance of China that defined the contours of the West.

Failure in Asia and the impossibility of conquering China made the Pacific into a boundary between worlds, a huge gulf between East and West. And America was for a long time chained to the Old World, as Philip II explained in *The Satin Slipper*:

> And that shore of the world which wise men long ago gave up to
>   illusion and madness, –
> From that shore now my Exchequer draws the vital gold which here
>   gives life to the whole machinery of State and pushes out on all
>   sides, more thickly than grass in May, the lances of my squadrons!
> The sea has lost its terrors for us and keeps only its wonders;
> Yes, its moving surges are scarcely enough to break up the broad
>   golden highway which binds the two Castiles,
> On which hurry to and fro the double file of my trading ships.
> Carrying thither my priests, and my warriors, and bringing back to
>   me those barbaric treasures teemed by the sun...[7]

Notes

Introduction

1. Paul Claudel, *Le Soulier de satin* (Paris: Gallimard, 1997), p. 15; trans. Fr. John O'Connor as *The Satin Slipper or The Worst is Not the Surest* (London: Sheed & Ward, 1932; repr. 1945), p. xxvi. The play was made into a film in 1985 by the Portuguese director Manoel de Oliveira, and performed at the Edinburgh Festival in 2004 and in New York in 2010.
2. Claudel, *Satin Slipper*, p. 30.

Chapter 1

1. Jean-Michel Sallmann, *Charles Quint. L'empire éphémère* (Paris: Payot, 2000), p. 100.
2. David M. Robinson, 'The Ming Court and the Legacy of Yuan Mongols', in David M. Robinson (ed.), *Culture, Courtiers and Competition: The Ming Court (1368–1644)* (Cambridge, MA: Harvard University Press, 2008), p. 402, quoting *Chugjong taewang sillok*.
3. Timothy Brook, *The Confusions of Pleasure. Commerce and Culture in Ming China* (Berkeley/London/Los Angeles: University of California Press, 1998), p. 144.
4. Ibid., p. 146.
5. Robinson, 'The Ming Court', p. 401.
6. Shen Defu (1578–1642), *Unofficial Gleanings from the Wanli Era*, in Timothy Brook, *The Troubled Empire. China in the Yuan and Ming Dynasties* (Cambridge, MA: Harvard University Press, 2010), p. 13.
7. Barend J. ter Haar, *Telling Stories: Witchcraft and Scapegoating in Chinese History* (Leiden: Brill, 2006).

8. Michel Graulich, *Moctezuma* (Paris: Fayard, 1994); Susan D. Gillespie, *The Aztec Kings. The Construction of Rulership in Mexica History* (Tucson, AZ: University of Arizona Press, 1989).
9. The Italians Vivaldi, Spontini, Paisiello and Galuppi, the Bohemian Myslivecek and the German Graun.
10. Jacques Gernet, *Le Monde chinois* (Paris: Armand Colin, 1972).
11. That is, equivalent to six Mesoamericas: Brook, *Confusions of Pleasure*, p. 95.
12. Jean-Michel Sallmann, *Le Grand Désenclavement du monde, 1200–1600* (Paris: Payot, 2011), pp. 556, 561.
13. Ibid., p. 118.
14. Ibid., pp. 128–9.
15. Ibid., p. 92.
16. Ibid., p. 132, quoting the case of the library of Qui, a councillor of the emperor Hongzhi.
17. Timothy Brook, 'Rethinking Syncretism: The Unity of the Three Teachings and their Joint Worship in Late Imperial China', *Journal of Chinese Religions*, 21 (1993), pp. 13–44.
18. Anne Cheng, *Histoire de la pensée chinoise* (Paris: Seuil, 1997), p. 533.
19. *Atl*, water, was opposed to fire (*tlachinolli*) and sky (*ilhuicatl*), whereas 'divine water' (*teoatl*) meant war: see Frances Karttunen, *An Analytical Dictionary of Nahuatl* (Austin, TX: University of Texas Press, 1983).
20. Ross Hassig, *Comercio, tributo y transportes. La economía política del valle de México en el siglo XVI* (Mexico: Alianza Editorial Mexicana, 1990), p. 111; and see pp. 112–13 and note 43, for a comparison with China, a territorial empire.
21. Ibid., p. 117.
22. Inga Clendinnen, *Aztecs: An Interpretation* (Cambridge: Cambridge University Press, 1991), p. 117.
23. Ibid., p. 131.
24. Ibid., p. 268.
25. But note the originality of the interpretations of Inga Clendinnen (*Aztecs*) and Christian Duverger (*L'Esprit du jeu chez les Aztèques* (Paris: Mouton, 1978) and *L'Origine des Aztèques* (Paris: Points Seuil, 2003)), which are of exceptional value in aiding us to appreciate Mesoamerican difference.
26. Louise M. Burkhart, *The Slippery Earth. Nahua–Christian Moral Dialogue in Sixteenth-Century Mexico* (Tucson, AZ: University of Arizona Press, 1989).
27. Clendinnen, *Aztecs*, p. 251.
28. Cheng, *Histoire de la pensée chinoise*, p. 40.

Chapter 2

1. Miguel León-Portilla, *Le Livre astrologique des marchands, Codex Fejérvary-Mayer* (Paris: La Différence, 1992), pp. 19–21.

2. There were Chinese living on the Ryu Kyu archipelago, Siam, Champa (a kingdom east of Cambodia), Malacca, Sumatra, Brunei, Java and the Philippines.

3. Patrick Boucheron (ed.), *Histoire du monde au XVe siècle* (Paris: Fayard, 2009), p. 625.

4. Ibid., p. 628.

5. Timothy Brook, *The Confusions of Pleasure. Commerce and Culture in Ming China* (Berkeley/London/Los Angeles: University of California Press, 1998), p. 123.

6. Marsha Weidner Haufler, 'Imperial Engagement with Buddhist Art and Architecture', in *Cultural Intersections in Later Chinese Buddhism* (Honolulu, HI: University of Hawaii Press, 2008), p. 139, quoted by David M. Robinson, 'The Ming Court and the Legacy of the Yuan Mongols', in David M. Robinson (ed.), *Culture, Courtiers and Competition. The Ming Court (1368–1644)* (Cambridge, MA: Harvard University Press, 2008), p. 407.

7. Owen Lattimore, *The Inner Asian Frontiers of China* [1940] (Boston, MA: Beacon Press, 1962).

8. Hugh R. Clark, 'Frontier Discourse and China's Maritime Frontier: China's Frontiers and the Encounter with the Sea through Early Imperial History', *Journal of World History*, 20, 1 (March 2009), p. 9 and note 13 on the meaning of Zhongguo.

9. Ibid., p. 6.

10. Alfredo López Austin and Leonardo López Luján, *El pasado indígena* (Mexico: FCE, 1996), p. 188.

11. Christian Duverger, *L'Origine des Aztèques* (Paris: Points Seuil, 2003).

12. Miguel León-Portilla, *Toltecayotl: Aspectos de la cultura náhuatl* (Mexico: FCE, 1980), p. 28.

13. López Austin and López Luján, *El pasado indígena*, pp. 187–90.

14. Clark, 'Frontier Discourse and China's Maritime Frontier', p. 20.

15. Billy K.L. So, *Prosperity, Region, and Institutions in Maritime China: The South Fukien Pattern, 946–1368* (Cambridge, MA: Harvard University Press, 2001).

16. Ibid., p. 125. The Ming established three offices for the reception and control of embassies arriving on Chinese soil.

17. One pirate was accused of killing babies and of force-feeding the bodies of the husbands he had killed to their wives under threat of being cut into pieces: see Clark, 'Frontier Discourse and China's Maritime Frontier', p. 25.

18. Toribio de Benavente, called Motolinía, *Memoriales o libro de las cosas de la Nueva España y naturales de ella*, ed. Edmundo O'Gorman (Mexico: UNAM, 1971), p. 214.

19. Ottavia Niccoli, *Profeti e popolo nell'Italia del Rinascimento* (Bari: Laterza, 2007), trans. Lydia G. Cochrane as *Prophecy and People in Renaissaince Italy* (Princeton, NJ: Princeton University Press, 1990), pp. 61–88; Timothy Brook, *The Troubled Empire: China in the Yuan*

and Ming Dynasties (Cambridge, MA: Harvard University Press, 2010), pp. 13–23.
20. David W. Pankenier, 'The Planetary Portent of 1524 in China and Europe', *Journal of World History*, 20, 3 (September 2009), pp. 339–75.

Chapter 3

1. For a global overview, see Pierre Chaunu, *Conquête et exploitation des Nouveaux Mondes (XVIᵉ siècle)* (Paris: PUF, 1969).
2. Pedro Mexía, *Historia real y cesárea* (Seville: 1547), quoted in Xavier de Castro et al., *Le Voyage de Magellan (1519–1522). La relation d'Antonio de Pigafetta & autres témoignages* (Paris: Chandeigne, 2007), vol. 1, p. 23.
3. For a synthesis of the early period, see Giuseppe Marcocci, *L'invenzione di un impero. Politica e cultura nel monde portoghese (1450–1600)* (Rome: Carocci Editore, 2011), pp. 45–58.
4. João Paulo Oliveira e Costa, 'A coroa portuguesa e a China (1508–1531): do sonho manuelino ao realismo joanino', in António Vasconcelos Saldanha and Jorge Manuel dos Santos Alves (eds), *Estudos de história do relacionamento luso–chinês, séculos XVI–XIX* (Macao: Instituto Português do Oriente, 1996), pp. 15–16.
5. Sanjay Subrahmanyam, *The Portuguese Empire in Asia, 1500–1700: a Political and Economic History* (London/New York: Longman, 1993), p. 70.
6. Francisco Manuel de Paula Nogueira Roque de Oliveira, 'A construção do conhecimento europeu sobre a China', doctoral thesis (Geography), Autonomous University of Barcelona, 2003, pp. 185–6.
7. Castro et al., *Voyage de Magellan*, vol. 2, pp. 889–90, quoting Maximilianus Transylvanus. It was said that 'Malacca and the great gulf [of China]' belonged to the Crown of Castile and that the Portuguese had crossed the demarcation line; though there was less certainty about Malacca, 'the great gulf and the Chinese people approached the limits of the navigation of the Castilians'.
8. Oliveira, 'A construção do conhecimento europeu sobre a China', p. 24.
9. Castro et al., *Voyage de Magellan*, vol. 1, pp. 20–21.
10. Ibid., pp. 57, 70.
11. Ibid., vol. 2, p. 780: 'from the Antilles to China, the lands do not form a single continent'.
12. Ibid., p. 918.
13. Ibid., p. 938.
14. Cristobal Colón, *Textos y documentos completos*, ed. Consuelo Varela (Madrid: Alianza Editorial, 1982), p. 170.
15. Ibid., p. 173.
16. Serge Gruzinski, *What Time is it There? America and Islam at the Dawn of Modern Times*, trans. Jean Birrell (Oxford: Polity, 2010).

Chapter 4

1. John Larner, *Marco Polo and the Discovery of the World* (New Haven, CT: Yale University Press, 1999), p. 142.
2. Juan Manzano y Manzano, *Los Pinzones y el descubrimiento de América* (Madrid: Cultura hispánica, 1988), vol. 1, p. 40; Larner, *Marco Polo and the Discovery of the World*, pp. 143–4.
3. This would be the Latin text now in the Columbine Library of Seville.
4. Bartolomé de Las Casas, *Historia de las Indias* (Mexico: FCE, 1986), vol. I, p. 217.
5. Ibid., pp. 217, 219, 227.
6. Ibid., pp. 257–8.
7. Marco Polo's book also circulated in a Catalan version. Did Columbus have access to this Aragonese Marco Polo before his first voyage? There is nothing in the *Diario* transmitted to us by Las Casas to suggest this. It is true that the Dominican, who blithely confused Marco Polo and Paolo Toscanelli, taking one Polo for another, is not always reliable and his silence is not conclusive.
8. Larner, *Marco Polo and the Discovery of the World*, p. 149.
9. The humanist Conrad Peutinger received his notes on the Portuguese voyages, which formed the *Manuscrito de Valentim Fernandes* (Staatsbibliotek of Munich). See *Códice Valentim Fernandes*, ed. José Pereira de Costa (Lisbon: Academia Portuguesa da História, 1997).
10. He was also the author of a 'Description of the West Coast of Africa', based on the stories of Portuguese sailors. See Georges Boisvert, 'La dénomination de l'Autre africain au XVe siècle dans les récits des découvertes portugaises', *L'Homme*, 153 (January–March 2000), pp. 165–72.
11. Anselmo Braamcamp Freire, 'Inventário da guarda–roupa de D. Manuel I', *Archivo histórico portuguez*, vol. 2, Lisbon, in Francisco Bethencourt and Kirti Chaudhuri, *História da expansão portuguesa* (Lisbon: Círculo de Leitores, 1998), vol. 2, p. 535.
12. Rui Manuel Loureiro (ed.), *O manuscrito de Lisboa da 'Suma oriental' de Tomé Pires* (Macao: Instituto Português do Oriente, 1996), p. 145.
13. Armando Cortesão (ed.), *The Suma oriental of Tomé Pires and the Book of Francisco Rodrigues* (London: Hakluyt Society, 1944), vol. I, pp. 117–27 for what follows.
14. Loureiro, *O manuscrito de Lisboa da 'Suma oriental' de Tomé Pires*, pp. 194–5.
15. Ibid., p. 197.
16. Ibid., p. 200.
17. Francisco Manuel de Paula Nogueira Roque de Oliveira, 'A construção do conhecimento europeu sobre a China', doctoral thesis (Geography), Autonomous University of Barcelona, 2003, p. 414; Duarte Barbosa, *Livro das cousas da India*, ed. with the title *O livro de Duarte Barbosa* by Maria Augusta da Veiga e Sousa (Lisbon: Ministério da Ciência e da Tecnologia, 1996); *Suma oriental of Tomé Pires*, pp. 290–322.

18. Letter from Cochin, 15 November 1515, published by Marco Spallanzani in his *Giovanni da Empoli: mercante navigatore fiorentino* (Florence: Spes, 1984), pp. 202–3.
19. Oliveira, 'A construção do conhecimento europeu sobre a China', p. 396.
20. His version of Marco Polo was republished twice more before his death in 1509 (and again in 1518 by Juan Varela). Santaella drew on Fernandes for his cosmographical prologue, but used a Venetian original which he accompanied with the *India recognita* of Pogge. A modern edition by Juan Gil was published in 1987 (Madrid: Alianza Editorial). See Henry Harrisse, *Biblioteca Americana vetustissima* (repr. Madrid: 1958), vol. 1, pp. 130–4; Donald L. Lach, *Asia in the Making of Europe* (Chicago, IL: University of Chicago Press, 1994), vol. 2, p. 164.
21. *Libro de las maravillas del mundo* (Valencia: Jorge Costilla, 1521).
22. Peter Martyr d'Anghiera, *Décadas del Nuevo Mundo*, ed. Edmondo O'Gorman (Mexico: José Porrúa e Hijos, 1964–5), vol. 1, p. 387.
23. Bernal Díaz del Castillo, *Historia verdadera de la conquista de la Nueva España*, ed. Joaquín Ramirez Cabañas (Mexico: Porrúa, 1968), vol. 1, p. 45.

Chapter 5

1. Peter Martyr d'Anghiera, *Décadas del Nuevo Mundo*, ed. Edmondo O'Gorman (Mexico: José Porrúa e Hijos, 1964–5), vol. 2, p. 439.
2. Ibid., vol. 1, pp. 429–31.
3. Ibid., p. 425.
4. Marcel Bataillon, 'Les premiers Mexicains envoyés en Espagne par Cortés', *Journal de la Société des américanistes*, new ser., 48 (1959), p. 140.
5. Peter Martyr d'Anghiera, *Décadas del Nuevo Mundo*, vol. 1, pp. 425–6.
6. Michael D. Coe, 'The Royal Fifth. Earliest Notices of Maya Writing', *Research Reports on Ancient Maya Writing*, 28 (Washington, DC: Centre for Maya Research, 1989).
7. Peter Martyr d'Anghiera, *Décadas del Nuevo Mundo*, vol. 1, p. 427.
8. Exhibited in Spain, the collection of objects accompanied the Court on its return to the North. It was in Brussels in the autumn of 1520, where it was admired by Albrecht Dürer.
9. Anselmo Braamcamp Freire, 'Inventário da guarda–roupa de D. Manuel I', *Archivo histórico portuguez*, vol. 2, Lisbon, in Francisco Bethencourt and Kirti Chaudhuri, *História da expansão portuguesa* (Lisbon: Círculo de Leitores, 1998), vol. 2, p. 535.
10. T.C. Price Zimmerman, *Paolo Giovio: The Historian and the Crisis of Sixteenth-Century Italy* (Princeton, NJ: Princeton University Press, 1995); Laura Maffei, Franco Minonzio and Carla Sodini, *Sperimentalismo e dimensione europea della cultura di Paolo Giovio* (Como: Società Storica Comense, 2007).

11. Paolo Giovio, *Historiarum sui temporis tomus primus* (Paris: Michaelis Vascosani, 1553), fol. 161r; Joseph Needham, *Science and Civilization in China*, vol. 5: *Chemistry and Chemical Technology*, part 1, Paper and Printing, by Tsien Tsuen-hsuin (Cambridge: Cambridge University Press, 1985). The Chinese were said to have invented xylography six centuries before the West, and typography four centuries before. But there was also in the sixteenth century a bold spirit (Gilbert Génébrard, *Chronographie*, 1580) who claimed that printing had been brought back by Cortés from Mexico-Tenochtitlan.

12. Prosper Marchand, *Histoire de l'origine et des premiers progrès de l'imprimerie* (The Hague: 1740), p. 64.

13. Robert Wauchope (ed.), *Guide to Ethnohistorical Sources: Handbook of Middle American Indians*, vol. 14, part 3 (Austin, TX: University of Texas Press, 1975), pp. 235–6; Otto Adelhofer (ed.), *Codex Vindobonensis Mexicanus I* (Graz: Akademische Druck- u. Verlagsanstalt, 1963); Jill Leslie Furst (ed.), *Codex Vindobonensis Mexicanus. 1: A Commentary* (New York: Institute for Mesoamerican Studies, 1978).

14. Peter Martyr d'Anghiera, *Décadas del Nuevo Mundo*, vol. 1, p. 426.

15. Nancy Bisaha, *Creating East and West. Renaissance Humanists and the Ottoman Turks* (Philadelphia, PA: University of Pennsylvania Press, 2006).

16. Paolo Giovio (1483–1552) was one of the first collectors of objects from the New World. For his *Museo*, see Laura Michelacci, *Giovio in Parnasso: tra collezione di forme e storia universale* (Bologna: Il Mulino, 2004).

17. For Ludovico di Varthema as a Renaissance traveller who did not belong to the world of humanism, see Joan Paul Rubiés, *Travel and Ethnology in the Renaissance: South India through European Eyes, 1250–1625* (Cambridge: Cambridge University Press, 2000), pp. 14 and passim.

18. The correspondence of the chronicler Fernandez de Oviedo with his Venetian interlocutors continued the work of Peter Martyr d'Anghiera: see Antonello Gerbi, *La natura delle Indie nove. Da Cristoforo Colombo a Gonzalo Fernández de Oviedo* (Milan: Riccardo Ricciardi, 1975).

19. Francisco Manuel de Paula Nogueira Roque de Oliveira, 'A construção do conhecimento europeu sobre a China', doctoral thesis (Geography), Autonomous University of Barcelona, 2003, p. 398.

20. Four Portuguese manuscript copies of this text and six in Spanish survive today: ibid., p. 40; *O livro de Duarte Barbosa*, ed. Maria Augusta da Veiga e Sousa (Lisbon: Ministério a Ciência e da Tecnologia, 1996).

21. Oliveira, 'A construção do conhecimento europeu sobre a China', pp. 394, 402. A modern edition of the letter appears in Spallanzani, *Giovanni da Empoli*, pp. 131–85.

22. Oliveira, 'A construção do conhecimento europeu sobre a China', p. 402.

23. Hernan Cortés, *Cartas y documentos*, ed. Mario Hernández Sánchez-Barba (Mexico: Porrúa, 1963); Hernán Cortés, *Letters from Mexico*, ed. Anthony Pagden (New Haven, CT/London: Yale University Press, 1986).

24. Benjamin Keen, *The Aztec Image in Western Thought* (New Brunswick, NJ: Rutgers University Press, 1971), p. 67.
25. *Isolario di Benedetto Bordone. Nel quale si ragiona di tutte l'isole del mondo, con li lor nomi antichi & moderni, historie, fauole, & modi del loro vivere, & in qual parte del mare stanno, & in qual parallelo & clima giaciono. Ricoretto, & di nuouo ristampato. Con la gionta del Monte del Oro nouamente ritrouato* (Venice: 1547).
26. Frank Lestringant, 'Fortunes de la singularité à la Renaissance: le genre de *l'Isolari*', *Studi Francesi*, 28, 3 (1984), pp. 415–46; *Le Livre des Îles: Atlas et récits insulaires de la Genèse à Jules Verne* (Geneva: Droz, 2002).
27. Manfredo Tafuri, *Venice and the Renaissance* (Cambridge, MA: MIT Press, 1989), pp. 152–3.
28. T'ien-tse Chang, 'Malacca and the Failure of the first Portuguese Embassy to Peking', *Journal of Southeast Asian History*, 3, 2 (1962), p. 54.
29. Raffaella D'Intino, *Enformação das cousas da China. Textos do século XVI* (Lisbon: Imprensa nacional, Casa da Moeda, 1989), p. 5. This date is debatable, but it seems highly unlikely that it was ten years later: Donald Ferguson, *Letters from Portuguese Captives in Canton, written in 1534 and 1536* (Bombay: Education Society's Steam Press, 1902); Ernst Arthur Voretzsch, 'Documentos acerca da primeira embaixada portuguesa à China', *Boletim da Sociedade Luso–Japonesa*, 1 (Tokyo: 1926), pp. 30–69. See also the bibliographical introduction and presentation of new sources of Korean origin in Jin Guo Ping and Wu Zhiliang, 'Uma embaixada com dois embaixadores. Novos dados orientais sobre Tomé Pires e Hoja Yasan', *Administração*, 60, 16 (2003-2), pp. 685–7.
30. Ibid.
31. With the exception of Portuguese scholars, notably the works of Rui Manuel Loureiro; see 'A China na cultura portuguesa do século XVI. Noticias, imagens, vivências', doctoral thesis, 2 vols, Lisbon, Faculty of Letters, 1995; *Nas partes da China* (Lisbon: Centro Ciéntifico e Cultural de Macau, 2009).
32. João de Barros, *IIIᵃ Década da Asia*, part 2, books 6, 7 (Lisbon: 1563); Fernão Lopes de Castanheda, *História dos descobrimentos e da conquista da India pelos Portugueses* (Coimbra: 1552–61); Gaspar da Cruz, *Tractado em que se contem por extenso as cousas da China* (Evora: 1569); Fernão Mendes Pinto, *Peregrinação* (Lisbon: 1614). For these texts, see D'Intino, *Enformação das cousas da China*, pp. XXX–XXXI.
33. Miguel León-Portilla, *Vision de los vencidos: crónicas indígenas* (Madrid: Historia 16, 1985).
34. See Bernardino de Sahagún, *Historia general de las cosas de Nueva España* (Mexico: Porrúa, 1977), vol. 4, trans. Angel María Garibay (English trans. in James Lockhart, *We People Here: Nahuatl Accounts of the Conquest of Mexico* (Los Angeles, CA: University of California Press, 1993).

35. There remain, however, massive differences between the two corpuses: the Chinese texts are independent of the Portuguese, the Mexican accounts reproduce the reactions of the vanquished, Christianized and Westernized elites.

36. I have drawn on the sources listed by Paul Pelliot in 'Le Hoja et le Sayyid Husain de l'histoire des Ming', *T'oung Pao*, 2nd series, vol. 38, 2–5 (1948), pp. 81–292; the *Ming-che*, commissioned in 1645 and officially completed in 1739, after several revisions (ibid., p. 198); the *Che lou* of Tcheng-tö (= Zhengde), which several times refers to the Portuguese embassy; the biography of Leang Tch'ouo (*Nan-hai hien tche*, 36, 20b); the *Houang-Ming che-fa lou* (cf Tcheng Sing-lang, H1, 397), from which the *Ming-che* borrows; the *Houang-Ming siang-siu lou* (with preface of 1629); the *Chou-yu tcheou-tseu low*, 9, Sb, and the *Ming-chan tsang* (first half of seventeenth century).

37. Pelliot, 'Le Hoja et le Sayyid Husain de l'histoire des Ming', p. 11. As suggested by his Chinese name (*Houo-tchö*), a transcription of the Arabic Khôjja, he would be called Khôjja Asan.

38. Ibid., pp. 196–7.

39. According to Pelliot, Khôjja Asan had a Muslim name and he is mentioned in the biography of a personage of Cantonese origin, Leang Tch'ouo. The Muslim from central Asia, Sayyid Husain, had a son-in-law who was also called Khôjja. Recent research has suggested he was of Chinese origin: see Ping and Wu, 'Uma embaixada com dois embaixadores', p. 690, n. 32.

40. Ibid., p. 164. For the history of the Ming, see *Ming shilu*, Shizong, *juan* 545, ed. Academia Sinica (Taiwan: 1963–8), in Jorge Manuel dos Santos Alves, *Um porto entre dois impérios. Estudos sobre Macau e as relações luso–chinesas* (Macao: Instituto Português do Oriente, 1999), p. 19, n. 7.

41. See León-Portilla, *Vision de los vencidos*; Nathan Wachtel, *La Vision des vaincus. Les Indiens du Pérou devant la conquête espagnole* (Paris: Gallimard, 1971), trans. Ben and Siân Reynolds as *The Vision of the Vanquished: the Spanish Conquest of Peru through Indian Eyes, 1530–1570* (Hassocks: Harvester Press, 1977).

Chapter 6

1. Xavier de Castro et al., *Le Voyage de Magellan (1519–1522). La relation d'Antonio de Pigafetta & autres témoignages* (Paris: Chandeigne, 2007), vol. 1, p. 45.

2. Pierre Chaunu, *Conquête et exploitation des Nouveaux Mondes (XVIe siècle)* (Paris: PUF, 1969), p. 137.

3. Bernal Díaz del Castillo, *Historia verdadera de la conquista de la Nueva España*, ed. Joaquín Ramirez Cabañas (Mexico: Porrúa, 1968), vol. 1, p. 43.

4. Ibid., pp. 51, 57.

5. Ibid., pp. 52, 48.
6. Ibid., pp. 60, 73. According to Las Casas (*Historia de las Indias* (Mexico: FCE, 1986), vol. 3, p. 204), Velazquez had forbidden Grijalva to '*poblar*'.
7. Díaz del Castillo, *Historia verdadera de la conquista de la Nueva España*, vol. 1, pp. 67, 70.
8. Ibid., pp. 63–4.
9. Armando Cortesão (ed.), *The Suma oriental of Tomé Pires and the Book of Francisco Rodrigues* (London: Hakluyt Society, 1944), p. XXVII.
10. João Paulo Oliveira e Costa, 'A coroa portuguesa e a China (1508–1531): do sonho manuelino ao realismo joanino', in António Vasconcelos de Saldanha and Jorge Manuel de Santos Alves (eds), *Estudos de história do relacionamento luso-chinês, séculos XVI–XIX* (Macau: Instituto português do Oriente, 1996), p. 21. In 1519, Lisbon considered organizing trade from India by establishing a Cochin/Canton/Cochin route which would take over the trade between Malacca and the Chinese port: ibid., p. 25.
11. Luís Filipe F.R. Thomaz, *De Ceuta a Timor* (Algés: DIFEL, 1994), p. 196.
12. Sanjay Subrahmanyam, *L'Empire portugais d'Asie, 1500–1700. Une histoire économique et politique* (Paris: Maisonneuve & Larose, 1999), p. 103.
13. *Suma oriental of Tomé Pires*, p. XXIII.
14. Oliveira e Costa, 'A coroa portuguesa e a China', pp. 20–21; *Suma oriental of Tomé Pires*, p. XXV.
15. Díaz del Castillo, *Historia verdadera de la conquista de la Nueva España*, vol. 1, p. 82.
16. Introduction by Anthony Pagden, in Hernán Cortés, *Letters from Mexico*, ed. Anthony Pagden (New Haven, CT/London: Yale University Press, 1986), p. LI.
17. The *Carta das novas*, which foretold the imminent fall of two cities, was published in June 1521: Thomaz, *De Ceuta a Timor*, p. 200.
18. Pierre Chaunu and Michèle Escamilla, *Charles Quint* (Paris: Fayard, 2000), p. 143.
19. Karl Brandi, *The Emperor Charles V. The Growth and Destiny of a Man and of a World* (London: Jonathan Cape, 1939), p. 134, quoted in Chaunu and Escamilla, *Charles Quint*, p. 179.
20. Magellan was supported by Cristobal de Haro, a shipowner of Antwerp. In Portugal, this agent of the Fugger financed clandestine voyages before being expelled by Manuel. He came to an agreement with Fonseca, Bishop of Burgos, who presented the project of Magellan to Charles V: Nancy Smiler Levinson, *Magellan and the First Voyage around the World* (New York: Clarion Books, 2001).
21. Castro, *Le Voyage de Magellan*, vol. 1, p. 49.
22. An island east of Tanzania.
23. Oliveira e Costa, 'A coroa portuguesa e a China', p. 133.

24. Martín Fernández de Figueroa, *Conquista de las Indias de Persia e Arabia que fizo la armada del rey don Manuel de Portugal*, ed. Luis Gil (Valladolid: University of Valladolid, 1999), p. 46.
25. Paul Pelliot, 'Le Hoja et le Sayyid Husain de l'histoire des Ming', *T'oung Pao*, 2nd series, vol. 38, 2–5 (1948), p. 87, n. 9; T'ien-tse Chang, *Sino-Portuguese Trade from 1514–1644: A Synthesis of Portuguese and Chinese Sources* (Leiden: E.J. Brill, 1934; New York: AMS Press, 1973).
26. Raffaella D'Intino, *Enformação das cousas da China. Textos do século XVI* (Lisbon: Imprensa nacional, Casa da Moeda, 1989), p. XXVI, n. 61.
27. For the Chinese reception as seen by local sources: Gu Yingxiang, *Jingxuzhai*, published by Wan Ming in *Zhongpu Zaoqi Guanxishi* (Peking: Documents for the Social Sciences in China, 2001), pp. 29–30.
28. Pelliot, 'Le Hoja et le Sayyid Husain de l'histoire des Ming', p. 97, n. 19. The chronicler João de Barros speaks of a 'solemn feast with great lamps'.
29. Ibid., p. 113, n. 47; Jin Guo Ping and Wu Zhiliang, 'Uma embaixada com dois embaixadores. Novos dados orientais sobre Tomé Pires e Hoja Yasan', *Administração*, 60, vol. 16 (2003-2), p. 692.
30. Pelliot, 'Le Hoja et le Sayyid Husain de l'histoire des Ming', p. 92, n. 12.
31. Ibid., p. 93, n. 14.
32. Cortés, *Letters from Mexico*, p. 50.
33. Díaz del Castillo, *Historia verdadera de la conquista de la Nueva España*, vol. 1, pp. 72, 73, 78, 82. Authorization to 'conquistar y poblar', with the title of *adelantado*, was granted at Zaragoza on 13 November 1518 and reached Velázquez in spring 1519. Cortés took with him 200 of Grijalva's men: Pagden, in Cortés, *Letters from Mexico*, p. LIV.
34. Cortés, *Letters from Mexico*, p. 23.
35. Peter Gerhard, *A Guide to the Historical Geography of New Spain* (Cambridge: Cambridge University Press, 1972), p. 360.
36. Díaz del Castillo, *Historia verdadera de la conquista de la Nueva España*, vol. 1, pp. 151, 139, 149, 152.
37. José Luis Martínez, *Hernan Cortés* (Mexico: FCE, 2003), p. 179.
38. Ibid., p. 180.
39. Pagden, in Cortés, *Letters from Mexico*, p. XX.
40. Peter Martyr d'Anghiera, *Décadas del Nuevo Mundo*, ed. Edmondo O'Gorman (Mexico: José Porrúa e Hijos, 1964–5), vol. 1, pp. 423, 431.
41. Raffaella D'Intino, *Enformação das cousas da China. Textos do século XVI* (Lisbon: Imprensa nacional, Casa da Moeda, 1989), pp. 27, 31, 38.
42. Ibid., pp. 31, 36.
43. According to the biography of Ho Ngao in the *Chouen-tö hien tche*, in Pelliot, 'Le Hoja et le Sayyid Husain de l'histoire des Ming', p. 95, n. 15. It is possible that the Chinese demand for exotic products – in particular amber – was so strong that the provincial authorities chose to bend the rules and allow passage to missions not anticipated by the

official texts and outside the usual periods: see Jin Guo Ping and Wu Zhiliang, 'Uma embaixada com dois embaixadores', pp. 693–5.

44. Ibid., pp. 179, 97, n. 20.
45. Executed 11 July 1521 on the orders of Jiajing: see Pelliot, 'Le Hoja et le Sayyid Husain de l'histoire des Ming', p. 16, n. 95; Guo Ping and Wu Zhiliang, 'Uma embaixada com dois embaixadores', p. 697, n. 67, p. 699.
46. Pelliot, 'Le Hoja et le Sayyid Husain de l'histoire des Ming', pp. 178, 182.
47. Díaz del Castillo, *Historia verdadera de la conquista de la Nueva España*, vol. 1, p. 151.
48. Martínez, *Hernan Cortes*, p. 208; Peter Martyr d'Anghiera, *Décadas del Nuevo Mundo*, vol. 2, p. 442 (who gives the number of *tamemes* as 1300).
49. Cortés, *Letters from Mexico*, pp. 57–8.
50. Peter Martyr d'Anghiera, *Décadas del Nuevo Mundo*, vol. 2, p. 423.
51. Díaz del Castillo, *Historia verdadera de la conquista de la Nueva España*, p. 207.
52. Martínez, *Hernan Cortes*, p. 216; Andrés de Tapia, *Relación sobre la conquista de México* (Mexico: UNAM, 1939), pp. 67–8.
53. Peter Martyr d'Anghiera, *Décadas del Nuevo Mundo*, vol. 2, p. 455; Cortés, *Letters from Mexico*, p. 72.
54. Lope de Vega made this the subject of a play.
55. Marcel Bataillon, *Varia lección de clásicos españoles* (Madrid: Editorial Gredos, 1964), pp. 314–17, 325–8.
56. Cortés, *Letters from Mexico*, p. 63.
57. Ibid.; Pagden, in ibid., p. XXVII.
58. Cortés, *Letters from Mexico*, p. 63.
59. Peter Sloterdijk, *Essai d'intoxication volontaire, Suivi de L'heure du crime et le temps de l'oeuvre d'art* (Paris: Pluriel, 2001).
60. Rui Manuel Loureiro (ed.), *O manuscrito de Lisboa da 'Suma oriental' de Tomé Pires* (Macao: Instituto Português do Oriente, 1996), p. 197.
61. Jean-Michel Sallmann, *Charles Quint. L'empire éphémère* (Paris: Payot, 2000), pp. 94–5.
62. Cortés, *Letters from Mexico*, p. 47.
63. Some striking images suggest the size of the towns: the city of Tlaxcala appeared larger than Granada, whilst its government resembled that of the great Italian cities, Venice, Genoa or Pisa: Cortés, *Letters from Mexico*, p. 68.
64. D'Intino, *Enformação das cousas da China*, p. 21.
65. The letter was discovered by Donald Ferguson in 1910 in a volume of the BNF with the title *Historia dos reis de Bisnaga. Crónica de Bisnaga y relación de la China*.
66. Peter Martyr d'Anghiera, *Décadas del Nuevo Mundo*, vol. 2, p. 452; Cortés, *Letters from Mexico*, p. 55.
67. This was a demand that the enemy submit to the representatives of the Crown of Castile.

68. Cortés, *Letters from Mexico*, pp. 50, 49, 81, 59, 62.
69. Ibid., p. 69.
70. Ibid., pp. 69–70.
71. Ibid., pp. 75–6.
72. Ibid., pp. 77–80.
73. Ibid., p. 69.
74. D'Intino, *Enformação das cousas da China*, p. 7.
75. *Fragmentos do Archivo do Torre do Tombo*, maço 24, fols 1–4, published by Ernst Artur Voretzsch, 'Documentos acerca da primeira embaixada portuguesa a China', *Boletim da Sociedade Luso-Japanesa*, 1, Tokyo, 1926, pp. 50–69.
76. T'ien-tse Chang, 'Malacca and the Failure of the First Portuguese Embassy to Peking', *Journal of Southeast Asian History*, 3, 2 (1962), pp. 52–3.
77. In 1283, Alfonso X of Castile wrote the famous *Book of Games* (*El libro de ajedrez, dados e tablas*).
78. Draughts already existed in Spain and with the name – 'Women's game' – given it in many countries today; see Lorenzo Valls, *Libro del juego de las damas, por otro nombre el marro de punta* (Valencia: 1597). See also Harold Murray, *A History of Chess* (Oxford: Clarendon Press, 1962).
79. Díaz del Castillo, *Historia verdadera de la conquista de la Nueva España*, vol. 1, p. 301.
80. *Xoxolhuia*, 'lie deliberately': Rémi Siméon, *Diccionario de la lengua nahuatl o Mexicana* (Mexico: Siglo XXI, 1984), p. 781.
81. Inga Clendinnen, *Aztecs: An Interpretation* (Cambridge: Cambridge University Press, 1991), p. 145; Christian Duverger: *L'Esprit du jeu chez les Aztèques* (Paris: Mouton, 1978).
82. Erving Goffman, *Interaction Ritual: Essays on Face-to-Face Behavior* (New York: Pantheon Books, 1982).
83. Díaz del Castillo, *Historia verdadera de la conquista de la Nueva España*, vol. 1, pp. 301–2.
84. Cortés, *Letters from Mexico*, pp. 108–9.
85. Ibid., p. 44.
86. Ibid., pp. 48, 85–6.
87. Ibid., p. 113.
88. Ibid., p. 66.
89. Ibid., pp. 85–6.
90. Ibid., p. 101.

Chapter 7

1. Quoted in T'ien-tse Chang, 'Malacca and the Failure of the First Portuguese Embassy to Peking', *Journal of Southeast Asian History*, 3, 2 (1962), p. 57.

2. Raffaella D'Intino, *Enformação das cousas da China. Textos do século XVI* (Lisbon: Imprensa nacional, Casa da Moeda, 1989), p. 7.
3. Paul Pelliot, 'Le Hoja et le Sayyid Husain de l'histoire des Ming', *T'oung Pao*, 2nd series, vol. 38, 2–5 (1948), p. 101.
4. Ibid., pp. 182–3.
5. Moctezuma's speech (to Cortés, according to Cortés) contains some improbable elements (the surrender of power) and others the conquistadors could not have known at that date (the foreign origin of the Mexicas). Moctezuma's avowal of his humanity could be interpreted as a roundabout, elegant and courteous way of making it known to the intruders that he did not take them for gods: Hernan Cortés, *Cartas y documentos*, ed. Mario Hernández Sánchez-Barba (Mexico: Porrúa, 1963); Hernán Cortés, *Letters from Mexico*, trans. and ed. Anthony Pagden (New York: Grossman Publishers, 1971), p. 86.
6. Francis Brooks, 'Motecuzoma Xoyocotl, Hernan Cortés and Bernal Díaz del Castillo: The Construction of an Arrest', *The Hispanic American Historical Review*, 75 (1995), pp. 164–5.
7. This is what emerges from the version of the Florentine Codex, in Bernardino de Sahagún, *Historia general de las cosas de Nueva España* (Mexico: Porrúa, 1977), vol. 4, p. 85 and passim.
8. Already on the offensive against the Tlaxcaltecs, the Spanish had organized lightning raids to sow terror in the villages, lighting fires, massacring women and children and capturing slaves.
9. Cortés, *Letters from Mexico*, p. 128.
10. Ibid., p. 135.
11. But it would eventually be successful, whereas the other attempts made at the same time on the Mexican coast north of Vera Cruz failed lamentably: see Pierre Chaunu, *Conquête et exploitation des Nouveaux Mondes (XVIe siècle)* (Paris: PUF, 1969), p. 142.
12. Pelliot, 'Le Hoja et le Sayyid Husain de l'histoire des Ming', p. 148, n. 136, p. 189.
13. Ibid., p. 99, nn. 26, 27.
14. D'Intino, *Enformação das cousas da China*, p. 17.
15. In fact, the Portuguese shipbuilding techniques, which consumed huge quantities of wood, did not find favour and only two small boats were built in Canton.
16. João Paulo Oliveira e Costa, 'A coroa portuguesa e a China (1508–1531): do sonho manuelino ao realismo joanino', in António Vasconcelos de Saldanha and Jorge Manuel dos Santos Alves (eds), *Estudos de história do relacionamento luso-chinês, séculos XVI–XIX* (Macau: Instituto Português do Oriente, 1996), p. 46.
17. Pelliot, 'Le Hoja et le Sayyid Husain de l'histoire des Ming', pp. 103–4.
18. The *Yue-chan ts'ong-t'an*.
19. Wang Hong became Minister of the Interior.
20. Pelliot, 'Le Hoja et le Sayyid Husain de l'histoire des Ming', p. 106, n. 41.
21. D'Intino, *Enformação das cousas da China*, p. XXVIII.

22. Ibid., p. 15.
23. Pelliot, 'Le Hoja et le Sayyid Husain de l'histoire des Ming', p. 104, n. 37.
24. Ibid., p. 15.
25. D'Intino, *Enformação das cousas da China*, pp. 13–16.
26. Ibid., pp. 16, 17, 36.
27. Chang, 'Malacca and the Failure of the first Portuguese Embassy to Peking', p. 63.
28. D'Intino, *Enformação das cousas da China*, p. 14.
29. Ibid., p. 37.
30. Oliveira e Costa, 'A coroa portuguesa e a China (1508–1531)', p. 51, quoting Fernão Lopes de Castanheda, *História dos descobrimentos e da conquista da India pelos Portugueses* [1552–61] (Porto: Lello & Irmão, 1979), vol. 2, pp. 377–8.
31. Cortés, *Letters from Mexico*, p. 142.
32. Ibid., pp. 166–7.
33. Ibid., p. 166.
34. Ibid., pp. 164–5; Sahagún, *Historia general de las cosas de Nueva España*, p. 58.
35. Bernal Díaz del Castillo, *Historia verdadera de la conquista de la Nueva España*, ed. Joaquín Ramirez Cabañas (Mexico: Porrúa, 1968), vol. 1, p. 53.
36. Ibid., vol. 1, p. 96.
37. Chaunu, *Conquête et exploitation des Nouveaux Mondes*, pp. 136, 138.
38. For Afonso de Albuquerque, see T.F. Earle and John Villiers (eds), *Afonso de Albuquerque: O Cesar do Oriente* (Lisbon: Fronteira do Caos, 2006).

Chapter 8

1. Paul Pelliot, 'Le Hoja et le Sayyid Husain de l'histoire des Ming', *T'oung Pao*, 2nd series, vol. 38, 2–5 (1948), p. 93, n. 14.
2. Ibid., p. 163, n. 180.
3. Luís Felipe Thomaz, 'Frangues', in *Dicionário de história dos descobrimentos portugueses*, ed. Luís de Albuquerque (Lisbon: Círculo de Leitores, 1994), vol. 1, p. 435.
4. Pelliot, 'Le Hoja et le Sayyid Husain de l'histoire des Ming', p. 164.
5. Ibid., pp. 86–92.
6. *Houang Ming che-fa lou*. Pelliot quotes other sources: *Chou-yu tcheou-seu lou*, in 24 chapters, preface (dated 1574) by Yen T'song kien, the official responsible for Imperial audiences (n. 67, p. 119); the biography of Leang Tch'ouo, *Nan-hai hien tche* (1573–1619).
7. Jin Guo Ping and Wu Zhiliang, 'Uma embaixada com dois embaixadores. Novos dados orientais sobre Tomé Pires e Hoja Yasan', *Administração*, 60, 16 (2003-2), pp. 706–7.

8. The *Shilu* gives *Pou-li-tou-kia*; see Raffaella D'Intino, *Enformação das cousas da China. Textos do século XVI* (Lisbon: Imprensa nacional, Casa da Moeda, 1989), p. 8, n. 7.

9. Bernal Díaz del Castillo, *Historia verdadera de la conquista de la Nueva España*, ed. Joaquín Ramirez Cabañas (Mexico: Porrúa, 1968), vol. 1, p. 48.

10. Toribio de Benavente, called Motolinía, *Memoriales o libro de las cosas de la Nueva España y de los naturales de ella*, ed. Edmundo O'Gorman (Mexico: UNAM, 1971), p. 171.

11. James Lockhart, *The Nahuas after the Conquest* (Stanford, CA: Stanford University Press, 1992), pp. 270–1, 276. An inhabitant of Castile was called *caxtiltecatl* (p. 277). The final *n* of *Castilan* was the Indian mark of the locative ('of Castile') rather than the transposition of the ending *no* of the Spanish *Castellano*.

12. James Lockhart, 'Sightings: Initial Nahua Reactions to Spanish Culture', in Stuart Schwartz (ed.), *Implicit Understandings: Observing, Reporting and Reflecting on the Encounter between Europeans and other Peoples in the Early Modern Era* (Cambridge: Cambridge University Press, 1994), p. 238.

13. Bartolomé de Las Casas, *Historia de las Indias* (Mexico: FCE, 1986), vol. 2, pp. 274–5.

14. This was the case with Gonzalo Guerrero; see Díaz del Castillo, *Historia verdadera de la conquista de la Nueva España*, vol. 1, p. 166.

15. Cortés, *Letters from America*, pp. 85–6.

16. Ibid., pp. 36, 53.

17. Anthony Pagden, *The Fall of Natural Man: The American Indian and the Origins of Comparative Ethnology* (Cambridge: Cambridge University Press, 1982), p. 17.

18. Pelliot, 'Le Hoja et le Sayyid Husain de l'histoire des Ming', p. 161. See T'ien-tse Chang, 'Malacca and the Failure of the First Portuguese Embassy to Peking', *Journal of Southeast Asian History*, 3, 2 (1962), pp. 57–8.

19. D'Intino, *Enformação das cousas da China*, p. 16.

20. Notably the memoirs of Qiu Dalong and He Ao: see D'Intino, *Enformação das cousas da China*, p. 9, n. 6; Pelliot, 'Le Hoja et le Sayyid Husain de l'histoire des Ming', p. 126.

21. D'Intino, *Enformação das cousas da China*, pp. 9, 10, 15.

22. http://sites.estvideo.net/malinal/tl/nahuatlTLACATL.html.

23. Lockhart, *The Nahuas after the Conquest*, pp. 536–7.

24. Díaz del Castillo, *Historia verdadera de la conquista de la Nueva España*, vol. 1, pp. 154–5.

25. The Mexica sovereign probably pondered the origin of his visitors at a very early stage, if only to work out how to get rid of them. It is much less sure that he had already, by the time of his encounter with Cortés, envisaged and accepted interpretations which led him to make an unconditional surrender. The 'goodwill' of Moctezuma is made all the stranger by the fact that his Tlaxcaltec neighbours, on their first contact, had

immediately fought against the intruders, using every sort of manoeuvre and cunning stratagem.

26. Motolinía, *Memoriales*, p. 171.
27. Hernán Cortés, *Letters from Mexico*, trans. and ed. Anthony Pagden (New Haven, CT/London: Yale University Press, 1986), pp. 145, 147, 165.
28. Martín Fernández de Figueroa, *Conquista de las Indias de Persia e Arabia que fizo la armada del rey don Manuel de Portugal*, ed. Luis Gil (Valladolid: University of Valladolid, 1999), p. 126.
29. Cortés, *Letters from Mexico*, p. 144.
30. Ibid., pp. 73, 158–9.
31. D'Intino, *Enformação das cousas da China*, p. 36.
32. Compiled from 1566 onwards for the Emperor Jiajing, hence retrospective.
33. Pelliot, 'Le Hoja et le Sayyid Husain de l'histoire des Ming', p. 91, n. 10.
34. Bernardino de Sahagún, *Historia general de las cosas de Nueva España* (Mexico: Porrúa, 1977), vol. 4, passim; John Bierhorst, *A Nahuatl–English Dictionary and Concordance to the Cantares mexicanos with an Analytical Transcription and Grammatical Notes* (Stanford, CA: Stanford University Press, 1985), p. 62.
35. Chang, 'Malacca and the Failure of the First Portuguese Embassy to Peking', p. 53.
36. Bierhorst, *Nahuatl–English Dictionary*, p. 64.
37. Pelliot, 'Le Hoja et le Sayyid Husain de l'histoire des Ming', p. 109.
38. D'Intino, *Enformação das cousas da China*, p. 20.
39. In the 1580s, when the Chinese knew the Portuguese rather better, it was the Spanish envoys who revived these ancient fears.
40. D'Intino, *Enformação das cousas da China*, p. 9 and n. 17.
41. Some Portuguese were supposed to have stolen some young Chinese children or bought kidnapped children to sell them as slaves: see João de Barros, *IIIa Década da Asia*, part 2, book 6, pp. 16–18. Foreign visitors from countries paying tribute were accustomed to procure children in Canton.
42. Ibid., p. 14.
43. Frank Lestringant, *Le Cannibale: Grandeur and décadence* (Paris: Perrin, 1994).
44. Michel de Montaigne, *The Complete Essays*, trans. M.A. Screech (Harmondsworth: Penguin, 1991), pp. 235–6.
45. For the Chinese sources, see D'Intino, *Enformação das cousas da China*, p. 9, n. 17; *Yueshan congtan*, trans. in Pelliot, 'Le Hoja et le Sayyid Husain de l'histoire des Ming', p. 93; *Guangdong tongahi*, p. 93; *T'ianxia jungo shu*, cap. 119, p. 43; *Mingshi*, book XXVIII, p. 842.
46. This fantasy is not without echoes of those science fiction films featuring the invasion of extra-terrestrial creatures who abduct and eat human beings; see, for example, *Intruders*, Dan Curtis, 1992.

Chapter 9

1. Paul Pelliot, 'Le Hoja et le Sayyid Husain de l'histoire des Ming', *T'oung Pao*, 2nd series, vol. 38, 2–5 (1948), pp. 202–3.
2. *Daxue wen*, trans. Chan Wing-tsit, *Source Book*, pp. 659–66, in Anne Cheng, *Histoire de la pensée chinoise* (Paris: Seuil, 1997), p. 557, n. 14.
3. Ibid., p. 532.
4. *Oeuvres*, 24, 12–13, in Pelliot, 'Le Hoja et le Sayyid Husain de l'histoire des Ming', p. 202.
5. 'Cantar LXVI', in John Bierhorst (ed.), *Cantares mexicanos: Songs of the Aztecs* (Stanford, CA: Stanford University Press, 1985), pp. 320–1.
6. Raffaella D'Intino, *Enformação das cousas da China. Textos do século XVI* (Lisbon: Imprensa nacional, Casa da Moeda, 1989), p. 19.
7. T'ien-tse Chang, 'Malacca and the Failure of the First Portuguese Embassy to Peking', *Journal of Southeast Asian History*, 3, 2 (1962), pp. 57–8.
8. Ibid.
9. *Chou-yu tcheou-tseu lou*, 9, 9b, in Pelliot, 'Le Hoja et le Sayyid Husain de l'histoire des Ming', p. 107, n. 42.
10. That is, China.
11. Bernardino de Sahagún, *Historia general de las cosas de Nueva España* (Mexico: Porrúa, 1977), book XII (trans. in James Lockhart, *We People Here: Nahuatl Accounts of the Conquest of Mexico* (Los Angeles, CA: University of California Press, 1993), pp. 48ff.).
12. Bierhorst, *Cantares mexicanos*, p. 58.
13. Ibid., pp. 322–3, 'Cantar LXVI', fols 55–55v.
14. Ibid., fol. 54v.
15. Ibid., fols 55–55v. Compare the havoc wreaked by the Portuguese cannon in South-East Asia: see Anthony Reid, 'Southeast Asia Categorizations of Europeans', in Stuart Schwartz (ed.), *Implicit Understandings: Observing, Reporting and Reflecting on the Encounter between Europeans and other Peoples in the Early Modern Era* (Cambridge: Cambridge University Press, 1994), p. 278.
16. Sahagún, *Historia general de las cosas de Nueva España*, vol. 4, pp. 60, 141.
17. Ibid., p. 62.
18. Ibid., p. 139 (Lockhart, *We People Here*, pp. 189–90).
19. Diego Durán, *Historia de las Indias de Nueva España e islas de la Tierra firme* (Mexico: Porrúa, 1967), vol. 2, p. 567.
20. Sahagún, *Historia general de las cosas de Nueva España*, vol. 4, p. 141 (Lockhart, *We People Here*, pp. 195–7).
21. Ibid., vol. 1, p. 180 (book 2, chapters 27, 42).
22. Alfredo López Austin, *Cuerpo humano e ideología* (Mexico: UNAM, 1980), vol. 1, pp. 66–7.
23. Sahagún, *Historia general de las cosas de Nueva España*, vol. 4, p. 155 (Lockhart, *We People Here*, p. 230).

24. Ibid., pp. 158–9 (Lockhart, *We People Here*, p. 240).
25. Lockhart, *Nahuas after the Conquest*, pp. 272–3.
26. Ibid., p. 267.
27. Character 395 in *Dictionnaire français de la langue chinoise* (Institut Ricci: Kuangchi Press, 1976), p. 72.
28. Taken from *Farangi*, a name given by the oriental interpreters. In Portuguese it was written *Franges* (Vieira, in D'Intino, *Enformação das cousas da China*) or *Frangues* (Barros [1777], *IIIᵃ Década,* part II, VI, p. 7). In Turkish, Babur used the word *farangi* in the sense of 'cannon' (Pelliot, 'Le Hoja et le Sayyid Husain de l'histoire des Ming', n. 39). And *piringi* means 'cannon' in Telegu.
29. Pelliot, 'Le Hoja et le Sayyid Husain de l'histoire des Ming', p. 101, n. 31.
30. Lockhart, *Nahuas after the Conquest*, p. 269.

Chapter 10

1. Stuart Schwartz (ed.), *Implicit Understandings: Observing, Reporting and Reflecting on the Encounter between Europeans and other Peoples in the Early Modern Era* (Cambridge: Cambridge University Press, 1994); on the absence of linguistic barriers, the role of Arabic and Malay as lingua francas in South-East Asia and the – still rarely acknowledged – role of indigenous women in the relationships formed by the visitors, see Anthony Reid, 'Southeast Asia Categorizations of Europeans', in Schwartz, *Implicit Understandings*, pp. 272–4.
2. João de Barros [1777], *IIIᵃ Década da Asia*, part 1, book 2, chapter 8, p. 217.
3. Ibid., p. 215.
4. Hernán Cortés, *Letters from Mexico*, trans. and ed. Anthony Pagden (New Haven, CT/London: Yale University Press, 1986), p. 71.
5. Stéphane Péquignot, 'Les diplomaties occidentales et le mouvement du monde', in Patrick Boucheron (ed.), *Histoire du monde au XVᵉ siècle* (Paris: Fayard, 2009), p. 722.
6. Ruy González de Clavijo, *Embajada a Tamorlán*, ed. Francisco López Estrada (Madrid: Castalia, 2004).
7. Jin Guo Ping and Wu Zhiliang, 'Uma embaixada com dois embaixadores. Novos dados orientais sobre Tomé Pires e Hoja Yasan', *Administração*, 60, 16 (2003-2), pp. 697.
8. Cortés, *Letters from Mexico*, pp. 100, 85.
9. Bernardino de Sahagún, *Historia general de las cosas de Nueva España* (Mexico: Porrúa, 1977), book XII, chapter 5, pp. 30–1 (trans. in James Lockhart, *We People Here: Nahuatl Accounts of the Conquest of Mexico* (Los Angeles, CA: University of California Press, 1993), pp. 71–2).
10. The expression is from Gilles Veinstein (Boucheron, *Histoire du monde au XVᵉ siècle*, p. 720).

264 *Notes to pp. 136–149*

11. Bernal Díaz del Castillo, *Historia verdadera de la conquista de la Nueva España*, ed. Joaquín Ramirez Cabañas (Mexico: Porrúa, 1968), vol. 1, pp. 60, 62, 71, 73.
12. Jin Guo Ping and Wu Zhiliang, 'Uma embaixada com dois embaixadores', p. 700, n. 78.
13. Raffaella D'Intino, *Enformação das cousas da China. Textos do século XVI* (Lisbon: Imprensa nacional, Casa da Moeda, 1989), pp. 8, 7.
14. Ibid., pp. 20, 8.
15. Lockhart, *We People Here.*
16. Barros [1777], *IIIª Década da Asia*, part 1, book 2, chapter 8, p. 211.
17. Ibid., p. 212.
18. David M. Robinson, 'The Ming Court and the Legacy of the Yuan Mongols', in David M. Robinson (ed.), *Culture, Courtiers and Competition: The Ming Court (1368–1644)* (Cambridge, MA: Harvard University Press, 2008), p. 401.
19. Ibid., according to Yu Ruji, *Libu zhigao*, 1620.
20. Guo Ping and Wu Zhiliang, 'Uma embaixada com dois embaixadores', p. 709, quoting the *True Chronicles of the Li Dynasty (Lichao Shilu).*
21. Richard White, *The Middle Ground: Indians, Empires, and Republics in the Great Lakes Region, 1650–1850* (Cambridge: Cambridge University Press, 1991).

Chapter 11

1. Raffaella D'Intino, *Enformação das cousas da China. Textos do século XVI* (Lisbon: Imprensa nacional, Casa da Moeda, 1989), pp. 48, 23, 21.
2. Ibid., p. 49.
3. Ibid., p. 25.
4. Ibid., pp. 27, 28, 49.
5. Michael E. Smith, *Aztec City-State Capitals* (Gainesville, FL: University of Florida, 2008).
6. Jianfei Zhu, *Chinese Spatial Strategies: Imperial Beijing 1420–1911* (London: RoutledgeCurzon, 2004), p. 103.
7. Ibid., p. 4; Eduardo Matos Moctezuma et al., 'Tenochtitlan y Tlatelolco', in *Siete ciudades antiguas de Mesoamérica. Sociedad y medio ambiente* (Mexico: Instituto nacional de Antropología e Historia, 2011), pp. 360–435.
8. Gilles Béguin et al., *L'ABCdaire de la Cité interdite* (Paris: Flammarion, 2007).
9. Bartolomé de Las Casas, *Apologética historia sumaria*, ed. Edmundo O'Gorman (Mexico: UNAM, 1967), vol. 1, p. 237.
10. Las Casas also claimed that Mexico had a million inhabitants: ibid., p. 265.
11. Ibid., pp. 304–5.

12. Bernal Díaz del Castillo, *Historia verdadera de la conquista de la Nueva España*, ed. Joaquín Ramirez Cabañas (Mexico: Porrúa, 1968), vol. 1, p. 45.

13. William Lithgow, *Rare Adventures and Painful Peregrinations* (London: 1632).

14. Hernán Cortés, *Letters from Mexico*, ed. Anthony Pagden (New Haven, CT/London: Yale University Press, 1986), p. 68.

15. Díaz del Castillo, *Historia verdadera de la conquista de la Nueva España*, vol. 1, pp. 47–8.

16. Cortés, *Letters from Mexico*.

17. '*Villa y fortaleza de Ceyxnacan*': ibid., p. 55; the Cempoala region had no fewer than fifty *villas y fortalezas*: ibid., p. 50.

18. Ibid., pp. 56, 57.

19. *Aldea*: from the Arabic *al-day'a*, translated into Castilian as *villa*; *alquería*: from the Arabic *al-qarîa, poblado* and, in Spanish usage, 'hamlet', even 'isolated house'.

20. Cortés, *Letters from Mexico*, p. 96.

21. Ibid., p. 57.

22. Ibid., pp. 92, 67.

23. Ibid., pp. 103–4.

24. Pires had apparently sent the governor of India, before 1524, a book, now lost, on the wealth of China: see Armando Cortesão (ed.), *The Suma oriental of Tomé Pires and the Book of Francisco Rodrigues* (London: Hakluyt Society, 1944), p. LXIII.

25. D'Intino, *Enformação das cousas da China*, p. 48.

26. Ibid., p. 44.

27. Ibid., pp. 43, 49.

28. Ibid., pp. 21–2.

29. He was drawing on the evidence of the expedition of Ferñao Peres and '*per um debuxo do natural delle que nos de là trouxeram*': see João de Barros [1777], *IIIᵃ Década da Asia*, part 1, book 2, chapter 7, p. 203.

30. D'Intino, *Enformação das cousas da China*, p. 24.

31. Barros, *IIIᵃ Década*, part 1, book 2, chapter 7, p. 188.

32. Ibid., p. 191.

33. D'Intino, *Enformação das cousas da China*, p. 27.

34. Ibid., pp. 24, 27, 43.

35. Ibid., p. 36.

36. For the rampart discovered at the entry to the province of Tlaxcala, see Cortés, *Letters from Mexico*, p. 57.

37. It appeared in the Catalan Atlas (c. 1380) under the name of *Chanbalec*, as did *Zincolan* (Canton, Guangzhou). On the world map of the Venetian fra Mauro (1459), the town of Chanbalec is shown at the centre of the noble empire of Cathay, with the appearance of a Muslim city, with its cupolas and tall minarets. In the second half of the sixteenth century, Abraham Ortelius still distinguished *Cambalu*, metropolis of Cathay, from *Pangin*, the Chinese town. At the beginning of the seventeenth

century European cartographers (Hondius, 1610) were still stubbornly distinguishing Peking and the capital of the Mongols.

38. Joan-Pau Rubiés, *Travel and Ethnology in the Renaissance: South India through European Eyes, 1250–1625* (Cambridge: Cambridge University Press, 2000), p. 293.

Chapter 12

1. Machiavelli, *The Prince* (Harmondsworth: Penguin Books, 1961), pp. 36, 133.
2. Ibid., p. 37.
3. Hernán Cortés, *Letters from Mexico*, ed. Anthony Pagden (New Haven, CT/London: Yale University Press, 1986), p. 156.
4. Ibid., p. 158.
5. Raffaella D'Intino, *Enformação das cousas da China. Textos do século XVI* (Lisbon: Imprensa nacional, Casa da Moeda, 1989), pp. 49, 31.
6. Machiavelli, *The Prince*, p. 119.
7. Quentin Skinner, *The Foundations of Modern Political Thought* (Cambridge: Cambridge University Press, 1978).
8. Marcelo Santiago Berriel, 'Cristão e sudíto. Representação social franciscana e poder régio em Portugal, 1383–1450', doctoral thesis, Fluminense Federal University, Niteroi, 2007, pp. 204, 175, 188, 189.
9. D'Intino, *Enformação das cousas da China*, pp. 25, 31, 27.
10. Cortés, *Letters from Mexico*, pp. 148–9.
11. Pedro Cardim, *Cortes e cultura política no Portugal do Antigo Regime* (Lisbon: Edições Cosmos, 1998).
12. D'Intino, *Enformação das cousas da China*, p. 37.
13. Skinner, *Foundations of Modern Political Thought*.
14. D'Intino, *Enformação das cousas da China*, p. 49.
15. Cortés, *Letters from Mexico*, pp. 98, 106.
16. D'Intino, *Enformação das cousas da China*, p. 36.
17. Cortés, *Letters from Mexico*, pp. 147–9.
18. D'Intino, *Enformação das cousas da China*, p. 42.
19. Ibid., pp. 50, 43.
20. Cortés, *Letters from Mexico*, p. 158.
21. Peter Sloterdijk, *Essai d'intoxication volontaire, Suivi de L'heure du crime et le temps de l'oeuvre d'art* (Paris: Pluriel, 2001).
22. Cortés, *Letters from Mexico*, pp. 156, 157.
23. D'Intino, *Enformação das cousas da China*, pp. 53, 48.
24. Ibid., pp. 39–40.
25. Ibid., pp. 49, 35, 10, notes 21, 42.
26. Ibid., p. 37.
27. Cortés, *Letters from Mexico*, p. 155.
28. D'Intino, *Enformação das cousas da China*, p. 45.

29. João Paulo Oliveira e Costa, 'A coroa portuguesa e a China (1508–1531) do sonho manuelino ao realismo joanino', in António Vasconcelos de Saldanha and Jorge Manuel dos Santos Alves (eds), *Estudos de história do relacionamento luso-chinês, séculos XVI–XIX* (Macau: Instituto Português do Oriente, 1996), p. 46.
30. D'Intino, *Enformação das cousas da China*, pp. 46, 43, 38, 44, 52.
31. Ibid., p. 42.
32. Ibid., pp. 45, 42.
33. Ibid., pp. 51, 49, 50, 29.
34. Ibid., p. 51.
35. Ibid., pp. 46, 52.
36. Ibid., p. 36.
37. Ibid., p. 43.
38. Cortés, *Letters from Mexico*, pp. 95, 96.
39. Isabel dos Guimarães Sá, 'Os rapazes do Congo: discursos em torno de uma experiência colonial (1480–1580)', in Leila Mezan Algranti and Ana Paula Megiani (eds), *O império por escrito. Formas de transmissão da cultura letrada no mundo ibérico, séculos XVI–XIX* (São Paulo: Alameda, 2009), p. 317.
40. Ibid., p. 322.

Chapter 13

1. Serge Gruzinski, *What Time is it There? America and Islam at the Dawn of Modern Times*, trans. Jean Birrell (Cambridge: Polity, 2010).
2. Cantar LXVIII, fol. 58, vol. 13, in John Bierhorst (ed.), *Cantares mexicanos: Songs of the Aztecs* (Stanford, CA: Stanford University Press, 1985), p. 337.
3. *Houang Ming che-fa lou*. Pelliot quotes other sources: *Chou-yu tcheou-seu lou*, in 24 chapters, preface (dated 1574) by Yen T'song kien, the official responsible for Imperial audiences (n. 67, p. 119); the biography of Leang Tch'ouo, *Nan-hai hien tche* (1573–1619).
4. Arthur Waldron, *La grande muraglia. Dalla storia al mito* (Turin: Einaudi, 1993), pp. 110, 111, 125, 134.
5. Ibid., pp. 139, 124, 141.
6. Ibid., pp. 119, 121, 208–9, 211.
7. Ibid., p. 142.
8. Ibid., pp. 104, 132, 210, 113, 105.
9. Ibid., p. 201. Owen Lattimore, 'Origins of the Great Wall of China: A Frontier Concept in Theory and Practice', in *Studies in Frontier History: Collected Papers, 1928–1958* (London: Oxford University Press, 1962), pp. 97–118.
10. Waldron, *La grande muraglia*, pp. 115, 205, 206.
11. Ibid., pp. 134, 207. The same difficulty in making political choices is apparent in the case of Vietnam, which would recur after the campaign of 1537–40.

12. Timothy Brook, *The Troubled Empire: China in the Yuan and Ming Dynasties* (Cambridge, MA: Belknap Press of Harvard University Press, 2010), p. 223.
13. Jacques Gernet, *Le Monde chinois* (Paris: Armand Colin, 1972), p. 369.
14. See the work of Claude Lévi-Strauss, passim, and Eduardo Viveiros de Castro, *Métaphysiques cannibales* (Paris: PUF, 2009).
15. Claude Lévi-Strauss, *Histoire de lynx* (Paris: Plon, 1991), p. 16.

Chapter 14

1. Dennis Owen Flynn and Arturo Giraldez, 'Cycles of Silver: Global Economic Unity through the Mid-Eighteenth Century', *Journal of World History*, 13, 2 (2002), pp. 391–427.
2. João Paulo O. Costa, 'Do sohno manuelino ao pragmatismo joanino. Novos documentos sobre as relações luso-chinesas na terceira década do século XVI', *Studia*, 50 (1991), pp. 121–56.
3. Jorge Manuel dos Santos Alves, *Um porto entre dois impérios. Estudos sobre Macau e as relações luso-chinesas* (Macau: Instituto Português do Oriente, 1999), p. 58.
4. Ibid., p. 59.
5. For the importance of this global trade, see Timothy Brook, *The Troubled Empire: China in the Yuan and Ming Dynasties* (Cambridge, MA: Belknap Press of Harvard University Press, 2010), pp. 213–37.
6. Fernão Mendes Pinto, *Peregrinação* (Lisbon: Imprensa nacional, Casa da Moeda, 1984), p. 199.
7. Geoffrey Phillip Wade, 'The Ming-shi-lu (Veritable Records of the Ming Dynasty) as a Source for Southeast Asian History, 14th to 17th centuries', doctoral thesis, University of Hong Kong, 1994, in Alves, *Um porto entre dois impérios*, p. 25, n. 23.
8. Ibid., pp. 70, n. 52, 71, n. 53; Roland L. Higgins, 'Piracy and Coastal Defence in the Ming Period. Government Response to Coastal Disturbances, 1523–1549', doctoral thesis, University of Minnesota, 1981, pp. 161–88; Jin Guo Ping and Zhang Zhengchun, 'Liampó reexaminado à luz de fontes chinesas', in Saldanha and dos Santos Alves, *Estudos de história do relacionamento luso-chinês*, pp. 85–137.
9. Ibid., p. 102.
10. Mendes Pinto, *Peregrinação*, p. 185.
11. Ibid.
12. Alves, *Um porto entre dois impérios*, p. 19, n. 3: 'Sejarak Malayu or Malay Annals', ed. C.C. Brown, *Journal of the Malayan Branch of the Royal Asiatic Society*, 25, 2/3 (1963), chapter XXL.
13. Higgins, 'Piracy and Coastal Defence in the Ming Period', p. 195.
14. Mendes Pinto, *Peregrinação*, p. 186.
15. Pierre-Yves Manguin, *Les Portugais sur les côtes du Viêt-nam et du Campa. Etude sur les routes maritimes et les relations commerciales*

d'après les sources portugaises (XVIᵉ, XVIIᵉ et XVIIIᵉ siècles) (Paris: EFEO, 1972).

16. Li Hsien-chang, 'A Research on the Private Traders along the Chekiang Coast during the Ghiaching (16th Century) Period and on the History of Captain Wang Chih: A Private Trader's Life under the Embargo Age', *Shigaku*, 34, 2 (1961), pp. 161–203 (in Japanese); Stephen T. Chang, 'The Changing Patterns of Portuguese Outposts along the Coast of China in the XVIth Century: A Socio-Ecological Perspective', in Alves, *Portugal e a China*, pp. 22–23.

17. Jin Guo Ping and Zhang Zhengchun, 'Liampó reexaminado à luz de fontes chinesas', in António Vasconcelos de Saldanha and Jorge Manuel de Santos Alves (eds), *Estudos de história do relacionamento luso-chinês, séculos XVI–XIX* (Macau: Instituto português do Oriente, 1996), pp. 104, 101, 105.

18. Alves, *Um porto entre dois impérios*, pp. 51–102.

19. Ibid., p. 42.

20. Serge Gruzinski, *La Pensée métisse* (Paris: Fayard, 1999), pp. 59–84 (trans. Deke Dusinberre as *The Mestizo Mind: The Intellectual Dynamics of Colonisation and Globalisation* (London/New York: Routledge, 2002)).

21. See Gruzinski, *The Mestizo Mind*; idem, *Les Quatre Parties du monde. Histoire d'une mondialisation* (Paris: La Martinière, 2004).

Chapter 15

1. Xavier de Castro et al., *Le Voyage de Magellan (1519–1522). La relation d'Antonio de Pigafetta & autres témoignages* (Paris: Chandeigne, 2007), vol. 2, p. 908; Peter Martyr d'Anghiera, *Décadas del Nuevo Mundo*, ed. Edmondo O'Gorman (Mexico: José Porrúa e Hijos, 1964–5), vol. II, p. 517.

2. Information which Pigafetta includes in his chapter 47: see Castro, *Le Voyage de Magellan*, vol. 1, pp. 251–7.

3. Statement of Albo in 'Les dépositions d'Elcano, Albo et Bustamente au retour de la *Victoria*', ibid., vol. 2, p. 625.

4. Ibid., vol. 1, pp. 223, 229, 254–7, 469.

5. Ibid., pp. 256, 257, 411.

6. Jean-Michel Sallmann, *Charles Quint. L'empire éphémère* (Paris: Payot, 2000), p. 123.

7. José María Ortuño Sánchez-Pedreño, 'Estudio histórico-jurídico de la expedición de García Jofre de Loaisa a las islas Molucas. La venta de los derechos sobre dichas islas al rey de Portugal por Carlos I de España', *Anales de derecho*, Murcia, 21 (2003), pp. 217–37; idem, 'Las pretensiones de Hernan Cortés en el mar del Sur. Documentos y exploraciones', ibid., 22 (2004), p. 325, n. 17.

8. António Galvão, *Tratado dos descobrimentos* (Porto: Livraria Civilização, 1987), p. 133.

9. Juan Gil, *Mitos e utopias del descubrimiento 2: El Pacífico* (Madrid: Alianza Editorial, 1989), p. 26; AGI, Patronato, 37, 9.
10. Gil, *El Pacífico*, p. 134.
11. Ortuño Sánchez-Pedreño, 'Estudio histórico-jurídico de la expedición de García Jofre de Loaisa a las islas Molucas', pp. 339, 317–53; Castro, *Le Voyage de Magellan*, vol. 1, pp. 23–4.
12. Galvão, *Tratado dos descobrimentos*, p. 125.
13. Ortuño Sánchez-Pedreño, 'Estudio histórico-jurídico de la expedición de García Jofre de Loaisa a las islas Molucas', pp. 327, 329, 331.
14. Ibid., p. 332; Cortés, *Cartas y documentos*, p. 474.
15. Galvão, *Tratado dos descobrimentos*, p. 138.
16. Ibid., p. 139.
17. The eighteen men who had been rescued from Saavedra's ship returned to Tidore. It was there that they were captured by the Portuguese, who took them to Malacca: see Ortuño Sánchez-Pedreño, 'Estudio histórico-jurídico de la expedición de García Jofre de Loaisa a las islas Molucas', p. 334; Francisco López de Gómara, *La conquista de México* (Madrid: Historia 16, 1986), p. 401.
18. Ibid., pp. 329, 330.
19. *De Moluccis* (Cologne, 1523); there were three Latin editions in 1523 and thirteen in Latin and Italian during the course of the sixteenth century: Sallmann, *Charles Quint*, p. 207.
20. Ibid., pp. 216, 225.
21. Hernán Cortés, *Cartas y documentos*, pp. 494–5, 497–8.
22. Ibid., p. 495.
23. Ibid., pp. 494–5.
24. Francisco del Paso y Troncoso, *Epistolario de la Nueva España* (Mexico: José Porrúa e Hijos, 1939), vol. 2, pp. 133, 113, 140.
25. Bernal Díaz del Castillo, *Historia verdadera de la conquista de la Nueva España*, ed. Joaquín Ramirez Cabañas (Mexico: Porrúa, 1968), vol. 2, p. 305.
26. Ibid., p. 308.
27. Galvão, *Tratado dos descobrimentos*, p. 147.
28. López de Gómara, *La conquista de México*, pp. 414–15.
29. Carlos Prieto, *El oceano pacífico: navegantes españoles del siglo XVI* (Madrid: Alianza Editorial, 1975), p. 83.
30. Peter Gerhard, *Síntesis e índico de los mandamientos virreinales, 1548–1553* (Mexico: UNAM, 1992), pp. 19–20.
31. Juan Suárez de Peralta, *Tratado del descubrimiento de las Indias* (Mexico: Secretaría de Educación Pública, 1949), p. 109.

Chapter 16

1. Carlos Prieto, *El oceano pacífico: navegantes españoles del siglo XVI* (Madrid: Alianza Editorial, 1975), pp. 89–92.

2. Fernán González de Eslava, *Coloquios espirituales y sacramentales* (Mexico: El Colegio de México, 1998), pp. 61–3.
3. Ibid., pp. 154, 298 (*Coloquio sexto*), 318, 322 (*Coloquio séptimo*).
4. AGI Filipinas 6; Pablo Pastells and Pedro Torres y Lanzas, *Catálogo de documentos relativos a las islas Filipinas* (Barcelona: Viuda de L. Tasso, 1925–1936), I, CCVCIV; Manuel Ollé, *La empresa de China. De la armada invincible al Galeón de Manila* (Barcelona: Acantilado, 2002), p. 40.
5. John M. Headley, 'Spain's Asian Presence, 1656–1590: Structures and Aspirations', *The Hispanic American Historical Review*, 75, 5 (1995), p. 633.
6. Lourdes Díaz-Trechuelo, 'Filipinas y el tratado de Tordesillas', in *Actas del primer coloquio luso-español de Historia de Ultramar* (Valladolid: University of Valladolid, 1973) pp. 229–40; Juan Gil, *Mitos e utopias del descubrimiento 2: El Pacífico* (Madrid: Alliance Editorial, 1989), p. 65.
7. Ricardo Padrón, 'A Sea of Denial: The Early Modern Spanish Invention of the Pacific Rim', *The Hispanic Review*, 77, 1 (Winter 2009), pp. 1–27.
8. Juan López de Velasco, *Geografía y descripcíon universal de las Indias* (Madrid: Ediciones Atlas, 1971), p. 289.
9. Geoffrey Parker, *The Grand Strategy of Philip II* (New Haven, CT/ London: Yale University Press, 1998), p. 62, Plate 12.
10. López de Velasco, *Geografía*, p. 295.
11. Ibid., p. 300.
12. Ibid., p. 301.
13. 'Será para lo que se puede ofrecer': ibid., p. 302.
14. *Discurso de la navegacíon que los Portugueses hazen a los reinos y provincias de Oriente y de la noticia que se tiene de las grandezas del reino de la China*; Parker, *Grand Strategy of Philip II*, p. 186.
15. Lothar Knauth, *Confrontación Transpacífica. El Japón y el Nuevo Mundo Hispánico, 1542–1639* (Mexico: UNAM, 1972), p. 42.
16. *Carta del padre Pedro de Morales*, ed. Beatriz Mariscal Hay (Mexico: El Colegio de México, 2002), p. 54.
17. *Cinco cartas de Pedro Moya de Contreras* (Madrid: Porrúa Turanzas, 1962), p. 32: extract from Cristóbal Gutiérrez de Luna, *Vida y heróicas virtudes de Pedro Moya de Contreras*, 1619.
18. Paul Claudel, *The Satin Slipper*, trans. Fr. John O'Connor (London: Sheed & Ward, 1932; repr. 1945), First Day, scene 6, p. 43.
19. Francisco del Paso y Troncoso, *Epistolario de la Nueva España* (Mexico: José Porrúa e Hijos, 1939), vol. 12, p. 124.
20. Knauth, *Confrontación Transpacífica*, p. 44.
21. 'Relación de Juan Pacheco Maldonado', in ibid., p. 46.
22. *La Cina è vicina*, directed by Marco Bellocchio, 1967.
23. Fernando Iwasaki Cauti, *Extremo Oriente y el Perú en el siglo XVI* (Lima: Pontíficia Universidad Católica del Perú, 2005).
24. Pierre Chaunu, 'Le galion de Manille. Grandeur et décadence d'une route de la soie', *Annales. Economies, Sociétiés, Civilisations*, 4 (1951),

pp. 447–62; Pierre Chaunu, *Les Philippines et le Pacifique des Ibériques (XVIᵉ, XVIIᵉ, XVIIIᵉ siècles)* (Paris: SEVPEN, 1960); Federico Sánchez Aguilar, *El lago español: Hispanoasia* (Madrid: Fuenlabrada, 2003).

Chapter 17

1. Letter from Andrés de Mirandaola to Philip II, Cebu, 8 June 1569 (AGI, Audiencia de Filipinas, 29). A factor was an official responsible for the national and economic interests of the Crown.
2. AGI, Filipinas, 79, 1, 1, in Manuel Ollé, *La empresa de China. De la armada invincible al Galeón de Manila* (Barcelona, Acantilado, 2002), pp. 41–2.
3. It is not unhelpful to reread the action of Las Casas from this perspective.
4. Ollé, *La empresa de China*, p. 52.
5. AGI, Audiencia de Filipinas, 6, 28: letter from Francisco de Sande, 7 June 1576.
6. Ibid.; letter from the town of Manila, 2 June 1576: AGI, Audiencia de Filipinas, 84.
7. AGI, Patronato, 24, 47.
8. *Diálogos militares* Mexico: Pedro Ocharte, 1983, in Joaquín Garcia Icazbalceta, *Bibliografía Mexicana del siglo XVI* (Mexico: FCE, 1981), pp. 316, 393–5; *Instrucíon nautica* (Mexico: Pedro Ocharte, 1587).
9. Bernardino de Escalante, *Discurso de la navegación que los Portugueses hacen a los reinos y provincias del Oriente y de la noticia que se tiene de las grandezas del reino de la China* (Seville, 1577), pp. 96, 98.
10. *Real cédula* of 29 April 1577, in AGI, Audiencia de Filipinas, 339, I, 80.
11. Carmen Y. Hsu, 'Writing on Behalf of a Christian Empire: Gifts, Dissimulation and Politics in the Letters of Philip II of Spain to Wanli of China', *The Hispanic Review*, 78, 3 (Summer 2010), pp. 323–44.
12. For the worlds of the Catholic Monarchy, see Serge Gruzinski, *Les Quatre Parties du monde. Histoire d'une mondialisation* (Paris: La Martinière, 2004; Points Seuil, 2006).
13. Giuseppe Marcocci, *L'invenzione di un impero. Politica e cultura nel monde portoghese (1450–1600)* (Rome: Carocci Editore, 2011), p. 135.
14. 'Relación de Alonso Sánchez (Manila, April–June 1583)', in AGI, Audiencia de Filipinas, 79, 2, 15; Ollé, *La empresa de China*, pp. 89–120. For the establishment of the Portuguese Jesuits in Macau, see Rui Manuel Loureiro, 'Origens do projecto jesuita de conquista espiritual da China' in Jorge Manuel dos Santos, *Portugal e a China. Conferências no IIIº curso livre de história das relações entre Portugal e a China (séculos XVI–XIX)* (Lisbon: Fundação Oriente, 2000), pp. 131–66.

15. Ibid., p. 114.
16. 'Ynformación sobre los impedimentos a la predicación en China ... por el Obispo Domingo de Salazar para el papa Gregorio XIII y el rey Felipe II', Manila, 19 April 1583, AGI Patronato, 25, 8; see also AGI Audiencia Filipinas, 74, 22.
17. Audiencia Filipinas, 79, 2, 15, 'Relación breve de la jornada que el P. Alonso Sánchez hizo ...'; Letter of Bishop Domingo de Salazar to Philip II, Manila, 8 June 1583.
18. For the clichés associated with the Chinese language, see Anne Cheng (ed.), *La Pensée en Chine aujourd'hui* (Paris: Gallimard, 2007).
19. Juan Bautista Román, *Relación* (1584), Archivo de la Real Academia de la Historia, Colección Juan Bautista Muñoz, 9–4797, vol. 18, fols 249–258; Ollé, *La empresa de China*, p. 157.
20. Ibid., pp. 158–9.
21. In fact it was not until later that Hideyoshi, who had reunified the country, had to attack Korea and China: this was the 'Seven Years War' (1592–8).
22. Francisco de Vitoria, *Relectio de Indis* (1539) and *Relectio de Jure Belli* (Salamanca, 19 June 1539).
23. Anthony Pagden, *The Fall of Natural Man: The American Indian and the Origins of Comparative Ethnology* (Cambridge: Cambridge University Press, 1982); Antony Anghie, *Imperialism, Sovereignty and the Making of International Law* (Cambridge: Cambridge University Press, 2005).
24. In his *Apología* of 1550; see Pagden, *Fall of Natural Man*, p. 119.
25. Vasco de Quiroga, *De debellandis Indis*, ed. René de Acuña (Mexico: UNAM, 1988) p. 57.
26. Bartolomé de Las Casas, *Obras completas* (Madrid: Alianza Editorial, 1992), vol. 1, pp. 157–8.
27. Lino Gómez Canedo, *Evangelización y conquista. Experienca francis-cana en Hispoamérica* (Mexico: Porrúa, 1988), pp. 77–9, 81, n. 35.
28. Ibid., pp. 80, 83, n. 41.
29. Ibid., pp. 81–2.
30. Ollé, *La empresa de China*, p. 146.
31. José de Acosta, *Parecer sobre la guerra de la China et Respuesta a los fundamentos que justifican la guerra contra China*, Escritos menores, in *Obras del Padre José de Acosta* (Madrid: Atlas, BAE, 1954), pp. 337–40: Francisco del Paso y Troncoso, *Epistolario de la Nueva España* (Mexico: José Porrúa e Hijos, 1939), vol. 12, pp. 132–3.
32. Ibid., pp. 223–4; Pedro Chirino, *Historia de la provincia de Philippinas de la Compañía de Jesus*, I, XXI, 1630 ms.
33. Which is not to say that all dreams of conquest died; the Moluccas, Siam and Cambodia seemed other possible targets: see Manuel Ollé, *La invencíon de China. Percepcíones y estrategias filipinas respecto a China durante el siglo XVI* (Wiesbaden: Otto Harrassowitz, 2001), pp. 86–7.

Conclusion

1. 'The discovery of the immense Chinese world was the major fact of the mid sixteenth century. The strange simultaneity of the construction of one network of penetration from Macau and another from Manila, and the chronology that are so striking … have never to my knowledge been fully brought out. In fact this history has always been described in the context of the artificial and inadequate divisions of the European states': Pierre Chaunu, *Conquête et exploitation des Nouveaux Mondes (XVIᵉ siècle)* (Paris: PUF, 1969), pp. 209–10.
2. François Hartog, *Régimes d'historicité. Présentisme et expériences du temps* (Paris: Seuil, 2002).
3. Serge Gruzinski, *What Time is it There? America and Islam at the Dawn of Modern Times*, trans. Jean Birrell (Cambridge: Polity, 2010).
4. Giuseppe Marcocci, *L'invenzione di un impero. Politica e cultura nel monde portoghese (1450–1600)* (Rome: Carocci Editore, 2011); Giuseppe Marcocci, *A consciência de um império. Portugal e o seu mundo (secs XV–XVII)* (Coimbra: University of Coimbra, 2012).
5. Gruzinski, *What Time is it There?*
6. Paul Claudel, *The Satin Slipper*, trans. Fr. John O'Connor (London: Sheed & Ward, 1932; repr. 1945), p. 26.
7. Ibid.

Bibliography

Abbreviations

AGI: Archivo General de Indias (Seville)
CSIC: Centro Superior de Investigaciones Científicas (Madrid)
FCE: Fondo de Cultura Económica (Mexico)
UNAM: Universidad Nacional Autónoma de México

Acosta, José de, *Parecer sobre la guerra de la China et Respuesta a los fundamentos que justifican la guerra contra China*, Escritos menores, in *Obras del Padre José de Acosta* (Madrid: Atlas, BAE, 1954), pp. 337–40.

Adelhofer, Otto (ed.), *Codex Vindobonensis Mexicanus*, 1 (Graz: Akademische Druck- u. Verlagsanstalt, 1963).

Alves, Jorge Manuel dos Santos, *Um porto entre dois impérios. Estudos sobre Macau e as relações luso-chinesas* (Macau: Instituto Português do Oriente, 1999).

Alves, Jorge Manuel dos Santos, *Portugal e a China. Conferências no III° curso livre de história das relações entre Portugal e a China (séculos XVI–XIX)* (Lisbon: Fundação Oriente, 2000).

Andaya, Leonard Y., *The World of Maluku. Eastern Indonesia in the Early Modern Period* (Honolulu, HI: University of Hawaii Press, 1993).

Anghie, Antony, *Imperialism, Sovereignty and the Making of International Law* (Cambridge: Cambridge University Press, 2005).

Anghiera, Peter Martyr d', *Décadas del Nuevo Mundo*, ed. Edmondo O'Gorman, 2 vols (Mexico: José Porrúa e Hijos, 1964–5).

Argensola, Bartolomé Leonardo de, *Conquista de las islas Malucas* (Madrid: Editorial Miraguano, 1992).

Barbosa, Duarte, *O livro de Duarte Barbosa*, ed. Maria Augusta da Veiga e Sousa (Lisbon: Ministério da Ciência e da Tecnologia, 1996).

Barros, João de, *Décadas da Asia*, vol. 3, part 2, books 6, 7 (Lisbon: Regia Officina typografica, 1778).

Bataillon, Marcel, 'Les premiers Mexicains envoyés en Espagne par Cortés', *Journal de la Société des américanistes*, new ser., 48 (1959), pp. 135–40.

Berriel, Marcelo Santiago, 'Cristão e sudíto. Representação social franciscana e poder régio em Portugal, 1383–1450', doctoral thesis, Fluminense Federal University, Niteroi, 2007.

Bethencourt, Francisco, and Kirti Chauduri, *História da expansão portuguesa*, vol. 2 (Círculo de Leitores, 1998).

Bierhorst, John, *A Nahuatl–English Dictionary and Concordance to the Cantares mexicanos with an Analytical Transcription and Grammatical Notes* (Stanford, CA: Stanford University Press, 1985).

Bierhorst, John (ed.), *Cantares mexicanos. Songs of the Aztecs* (Stanford, CA: Stanford University Press, 1985).

Bisaha, Nancy, *Creating East and West: Renaissance Humanists and the Ottoman Turks* (Philadelphia, PA: University of Pennsylvania Press, 2006).

Boucheron, Patrick (ed.), *Histoire du monde au XVe siècle* (Paris: Fayard, 2009).

Bourdon, Léon, 'Un projet d'invasion de la Chine par Canton à la fin du XVIe siècle', in *Actas do III° Colóquio Internacional de Estudos Luso-Brasileiros* (Lisbon: 1960), vol. 1, pp. 97–121.

Boxer, Charles Ralph, *Fidalgos in the Far East* (The Hague: Martinus Nijhoff, 1948).

Boxer, Charles Ralph, *South China in the Sixteenth Century* (London: The Hakluyt Society, 1953).

Boxer, Charles Ralph, *The Great Ship from Amacon: Annals of Macau and Old Japan Trade, 1555–1640* (Lisbon: Centro de Estudos Ultramarinos, 1963).

Boxer, Charles Ralph, 'Portuguese and Spanish Projects for the Conquest of Southeast Asia, 1580–1600', *Journal of Asian History*, 3, 2 (1969), pp. 118–36.

Brandi, Karl, *Charles Quint et son temps* (Paris: Payot, 1951), trans. C.V. Wedgewood as *The Emperor Charles V. The Growth and Destiny of a Man and of a World* (London: Jonathan Cape, 1939).

Brook, Timothy, 'Rethinking Syncretism: The Unity of the Three Teachings and their Joint Worship in Late Imperial China', *Journal of Chinese Religions*, 21 (1993), pp. 13–44.

Brook, Timothy, *The Confusions of Pleasure: Commerce and Culture in Ming China* (Berkeley, CA: University of California Press, 1998).

Brook, Timothy, *Vermeer's Hat: The Seventeenth Century and the Dawn of the Global World* (London: Bloomsbury Press, 2008), pp. 1–25.

Brook, Timothy, *The Troubled Empire: China in the Yuan and Ming Dynasties* (Cambridge, MA: Belknap Press of Harvard University Press, 2010).

Brooks, Francis, 'Motecuzoma Xoyocotl, Hernán Cortés and Bernal Díaz del Castillo: The Construction of an Arrest', *The Hispanic American Historical Review*, 75, 2 (1995), pp. 149–83.

Burkhart, Louise M., *The Slippery Earth: Nahua–Christian Moral Dialogue in Sixteenth-Century Mexico* (Tucson, AZ: University of Arizona Press, 1989).

Cardim, Pedro, *Cortes e cultura política no Portugal do Antigo Regime* (Lisbon: Edições Cosmos, 1998).

Castanheda, Fernão Lopes de, *História dos descobrimentos e da conquista da India pelos Portugueses* [1552–61] (Porto: Lello & Irmão, 1979).

Castro, Eduardo Viveiros de, *Métaphysiques cannibales* (Paris: PUF, 2009).

Castro, Xavier de, et al., *Le Voyage de Magellan (1519–1522). La relation d'Antonio de Pigafetta & autres témoignages*, 2 vols (Paris: Chandeigne, 2007).

Chang, Stephen T., 'The Changing Patterns of Portuguese Outposts along the Coast of China in the 16th Century: A Socio-Ecological Perspective', in Alves, *Portugal e a China*, pp. 15–34.

Chang, T'ien-tse, 'Malacca and the Failure of the First Portuguese Embassy to Peking', *Journal of Southeast Asian History*, 3, 2 (1962), pp. 45–64.

Chang, T'ien-tse, *Sino-Portuguese Trade from 1514–1644: A Synthesis of Portuguese and Chinese Sources* (Leiden: E.J. Brill, 1934; New York: repr. AMS Press, 1973).

Chaunu, Pierre, 'Le galion de Manille. Grandeur et décadence d'une route de la soie', *Annales. Economies, Sociétiés, Civilisations*, 4 (1951), pp. 447–62.

Chaunu, Pierre, *Les Philippines et le Pacifique des Ibériques (XVIe, XVIIe, XVIIIe siècles)* (Paris: SEVPEN, 1960).

Chaunu, Pierre, *Conquête et exploitation des Nouveaux Mondes (XVIe siècle)* (Paris: PUF, 1969).

Chaunu, Pierre, and Michèle Escamilla, *Charles Quint* (Paris: Fayard, 2000).

Cheng, Anne, *Histoire de la pensée chinoise* (Paris: Seuil, 1997).

Clark, Hugh R., 'Frontier Discourse and China's Maritime Frontier: China's Frontiers and the Encounter with the Sea through Early Imperial History', *Journal of World History*, 20, 1 (March 2009), pp. 1–33.

Clavijo, Ruy González de, *Embajada a Tamorlán*, ed. Francisco López Estrada (Madrid: Castalia, 2004).

Clendinnen, Inga, *Aztecs: An Interpretation* (Cambridge: Cambridge University Press, 1991).

Colón, Cristobal, *Textos y documentos completos*, ed. Consuelo Varela (Madrid: Alianza Editorial, 1982).

Cortés, Hernán, *Cartas y documentos*, ed. Mario Hernández Sánchez-Barba (Mexico: Porrúa, 1963).

Cortés, Hernán, *Letters from Mexico*, trans. and ed. Anthony Pagden (New York: Grossman Publishers, 1971) (New Haven, CT/London: Yale University Press, 1986).

Cortesão, Armando (ed.), *The Suma oriental of Tomé Pires and the Book of Francisco Rodrigues*, 2 vols (London: The Hakluyt Society, 1944; New Delhi/Madras: Asia Educational Services, 1990).

Costa, João Paulo O., 'Do sohno manuelino ao pragmatismo joanino. Novos documentos sobre as relações luso-chinesas na terceira década do século XVI', *Studia*, 50 (1991), pp. 121–56.

Cruz, Gaspar da, *Tratado das coisas da China*, ed. Luis Manuel Oureiro (Lisbon: Edições Cotovia, 1997).

Díaz del Castillo, Bernal, *Historia verdadera de la conquista de la Nueva España*, ed. Joaquín Ramirez Cabañas (Mexico: Porrúa, 1968).

Díaz-Trechuelo, Lourdes, 'El consejo de Indias y Filipinas', in *El consejo de Indias en el siglo XVI* (Valladolid: University of Valladolid, 1970), pp. 125–38.

Díaz-Trechuelo, Lourdes, 'Filipinas y el tratado de Tordesillas', in *Actas del primer coloquio luso-español de Historia de Ultramar* (Valladolid: University of Valladolid, 1973), pp. 229–40.

D'Intino, Raffaella, *Enformação das cousas da China. Textos do século XVI* (Lisbon: Imprensa nacional, Casa da Moeda, 1989).

Durán, Diego, *Historia de las Indias de Nueva España e islas de la Tierra firme*, 2 vols (Mexico: Porrúa, 1967).

Duverger, Christian, *L'Esprit du jeu chez les Aztèques* (Paris: Mouton, 1978).

Duverger, Christian, *L'Origine des Aztèques* (Paris: Points Seuil, 2003).

Earle, T.F., and John Villiers (eds), *Afonso de Albuquerque. O Cesar do Oriente* (Lisbon: Fronteira do Caos, 2006).

Escalante, Bernardino de, *Discurso de la navegación que los Portugueses hacen a los reinos y provincias del Oriente* (Seville, 1577).

Fernandes, Valentim, *Códice Valentim Fernandes*, ed. José Pereira da Costa (Lisbon: Academia Portuguesa da História, 1997).

Figueroa, Martín Fernández de, *Conquista de las Indias de Persia e Arabia que fizo la armada del rey don Manuel de Portugal*, ed. Luis Gil (Valladolid: University of Valladolid, 1999).

Flynn, Dennis Owen, and Arturo Giraldez, 'China and the Spanish Empire', *Revista de História Económica*, 2 (1996), pp. 309–39.

Flynn, Dennis Owen, and Arturo Giraldez, 'Cycles of Silver: Global Economic Unity through the Mid-Eighteenth Century', *Journal of World History*, 13, 2 (2002), pp. 391–427.

Fok, Kai Cheong, 'The Macau Formula. A Study of Chinese Management of Westerners from the Mid-Sixteenth Century to the Opium War Period', doctoral thesis, Honolulu, University of Hawaii, 1978.

Fok, Kai Cheong, 'The Macau Forum at Work', in Saldanha and dos Santos Alves, *Estudos de história do relacionamento luso-chinês*.

Furst, Jill Leslie (ed.), *Codex Vindobonensis Mexicanus. 1: A Commentary* (New York: University of New York at Albany, 1978).

Galvão, António, *Tratado dos descobrimentos* (Porto: Livraria Civilização, 1987).

García Abasolo, Antonio, 'La expansión mexicana hacia el Pacífico: la primera colonización de Filipinas', *Historia Mexicana*, El Colegio de México, vol. 22, 125 (1982), pp. 55–88.

García Icazbalceta, Joaquín, *Bibliografia Mexicana del siglo XVI* (Mexico: FCE, 1981).

Garcia, José Manuel, *A viagem de Fernão de Magalhães e o Portugueses* (Queluz de Baixo: Editorial Presença, 2007).

Gerbi, Antonello, *La natura delle Indie nove. Da Cristoforo Colombo a Gonzalo Fernández de Oviedo* (Milan: Riccardo Ricciardi, 1975).

Gerhard, Peter, *A Guide to the Historical Geography of New Spain* (Cambridge: Cambridge University Press, 1972).

Gerhard, Peter, *Síntesis e índice de los mandamientos virreinales, 1548–1553* (Mexico: UNAM, 1992).

Gernet, Jacques, *Le Monde chinois* (Paris: Armand Colin, 1972).

Gil, Juan, *Mitos e utopias del descubrimiento, 2: El Pacífico* (Madrid: Alianza Editorial, 1989).

Gillespie, Susan D., *The Aztec Kings. The Construction of Rulership in Mexica History* (Tucson, AZ: University of Arizona Press, 1989).

Goffman, Erving, *Interaction Ritual: Essays on Face-to-Face Behavior* (New York: Pantheon Books, 1982).

González de Mendoza, Juan, *Historia de las cosas más notables, ritos y costumbres del Gran Reyno de la China* [1585] (Madrid: Editorial Miraguano, 1990).

Graulich, Michel, *Moctezuma* (Paris: Fayard, 1994).

Gruzinski, Serge, *La Pensée métisse* (Paris: Fayard, 1999), trans. Deke Dusinberre as *The Mestizo Mind: The Intellectual Dynamics of Colonisation and Globalisation* (London/New York: Routledge, 2002).

Gruzinski, Serge, *Les Quatre Parties du monde. Histoire d'une mondialisation* (Paris: La Martinière, 2004; Points Seuil, 2006).

Gruzinski, Serge, *Quelle heure est-il là-bas?* (Paris: Seuil, 2008), trans. Jean Birrell as *What Time is it There? America and Islam at the Dawn of Modern Times* (Oxford: Polity, 2010).

Guo Ping, Jin, and Zhang Zhengchun, 'Liampó reexaminado a luz de fontes chinesas', in Saldanha and Santos Alves, *Estudos de história do relacionamento luso-chinês*, pp. 85–137.

Guo Ping, Jin, and Wu Zhiliang, 'O impactos da conquista de Malaca em relação à China quinhentista: uma abordagem sobra a periodização da história moderna da China', *Administração. Revista de Administração Pública de Macau*, 13, 49 (2000–3), pp. 939–46.

Guo Ping, Jin, and Wu Zhiliang, 'Uma embaixada com dois embaixadores. Novos dados orientais sobre Tomé Pires e Hoja Yasan', *Administração. Revista de Administração Pública de Macau*, 60, 16 (2003–2), pp. 685–716.

Gutiérrez, Lucio, 'The Affair of China at the End of the Sixteenth Century: Armed Conquest or Peaceful Evangelization', *Philippiniana sacra*, 20, 59 (1985), pp. 329–406.

Haar, Barend J. ter, *Telling Stories: Witchcraft and Scapegoating in Chinese History* (Leiden: Brill, 2006).

Hall, Kenneth R., *Maritime Trade and State Development in Early Southeast Asia* (Honolulu, HI: University of Hawaii Press, 1985).

Hartog, François, *Régimes d'historicité. Présentisme et expériences du temps* (Paris: Seuil, 2002).

Hassig, Ross, *Comercio, tributo y transportes. La economía política del valle de México en el siglo XVI* (Mexico: Alianza Editorial Mexicana, 1990).

Headley, John M., 'Spain's Asian Presence, 1565–1590: Structures and Aspirations', *The Hispanic American Historical Review*, 75, 4 (1995), pp. 623–46.

Higgins, Roland L., 'Piracy and Coastal Defence in the Ming Period. Government Response to Coastal Disturbances, 1523–1549', doctoral thesis, University of Minnesota, 1981.

Huang, Ray, *1587. A Year of no Significance* (New Haven, CT/London: Yale University Press, 1981).

Iwasaki Cauti, Fernando, *Extremo Oriente y el Perú en el siglo XVI* (Lima: Pontíficia Universidad Católica del Perú, 2005).

Karttunen, Frances, *An Analytical Dictionary of Nahuatl* (Austin, TX: University of Texas Press, 1983).

Keen, Benjamin, *The Aztec Image in Western Thought* (New Brunswick, NJ: Rutgers University Press, 1971).

Knauth, Lothar, *Confrontación Transpacífica. El Japón y el Nuevo Mundo Hispánico. 1542–1639* (Mexico: UNAM, 1972).

Lach, Donald F., *Asia in the Making of Europe,* vols 1 and 2 (Chicago, IL: University of Chicago Press, 1965–94).

Larner, John, *Marco Polo and the Discovery of the World* (New Haven, CT: Yale University Press, 1999).

Las Casas, Bartolomé de, *Apologética historia sumaria*, ed. Edmundo O'Gorman, 2 vols (Mexico: UNAM, 1967).

Las Casas, Bartolomé de, *Historia de las Indias*, 3 vols (Mexico: FCE, 1986).

Las Casas, Bartolomé de, *Obras completas*, 14 vols (Madrid: Alianza Editorial, 1992).

Lattimore, Owen, *The Inner Asian Frontiers of China* (Boston, MA: Beacon Press, 1940, repr. 1962).

Lattimore, Owen, 'Origins of the Great Wall of China: A Frontier Concept in Theory and Practice', in *Studies in Frontier History: Collected Papers, 1928–1958* (London: Oxford University Press, 1962), pp. 97–118.

León-Portilla, Miguel, *Toltecayotl. Aspectos de la cultura náhuatl* (Mexico: FCE, 1980).

León-Portilla, Miguel, *Vision de los vencidos: crónicas indígenas* (Madrid: Historia 16, 1985).

León-Portilla, Miguel, *Le Livre astrologique des marchands, Codex Fejérvary-Mayer* (Paris: La Différence, 1992).

Lestringant, Frank, *Le Cannibale. Grandeur and décadence* (Paris: Perrin, 1994).

Lévi-Strauss, Claude, *Histoire de Lynx* (Paris: Plon, 1991).

Levinson, Nancy Smiler, *Magellan and the First Voyage around the World* (New York: Clarion Books, 2001).

Lockhart, James, *The Nahuas after the Conquest* (Stanford, CA: Stanford University Press, 1992).

Lockhart, James, *We People Here: Nahuatl Accounts of the Conquest of Mexico* (Los Angeles, CA: University of California Press, 1993).

López Austin, Alfredo, *Cuerpo humano e ideología* (Mexico: UNAM, 1980).
López Austin, Alfredo, and Leonardo López Luján, *El pasado indígena* (Mexico: FCE, 1996).
López de Gómara, Francisco, *La conquista de México* (Madrid: Historia 16, 1986).
López de Velasco, Juan, *Geografía y descripción universal de las Indias* (Madrid: Ediciones Atlas, 1971).
Loureiro, Rui Manuel, 'A China na cultura portuguesa do século XVI. Noticias, imagens, vivências', doctoral thesis, 2 vols, Lisbon, Faculty of Letters of Lisbon, 1995.
Loureiro, Rui Manuel (ed.), *O manuscrito de Lisboa da 'Suma oriental' de Tomé Pires* (Macao: Instituto Português do Oriente, 1996).
Loureiro, Rui Manuel, 'Origens do projecto jesuita de conquista espiritual da China', in Alves, *Portugal e a China*, pp. 131–66.
Loureiro, Rui Manuel, *Fidalgos, missionários e mandarins. Portugal e a China no século XVI* (Lisbon: Fundação Oriente, 2000).
Loureiro, Rui Manuel, *Nas partes da China* (Lisbon: Centro Ciéntifico e Cultural de Macau, 2009).
Machiavelli, Niccolò, *The Prince* [1553] (Harmondsworth: Penguin Books, 1961).
Maffei, Laura, Franco Minonzio, and Carla Sodini, *Sperimentalismo e dimensione europea della cultura di Paolo Giovio* (Como: Società Storica Comense, 2007).
Manguin, Pierre-Yves, *Les Portugais sur les côtes du Viêt-nam et du Campa. Etude sur les routes maritimes et les relations commerciales d'après les sources portugaises (XVIᵉ, XVIIᵉ et XVIIIᵉ siècles)* (Paris: EFEO, 1972).
Manzano y Manzano, Juan, *Los Pinzones y el descubrimiento de América* (Madrid: Cultura Hispánica, 1988).
Marcocci, Giuseppe, *L'invenzione di un impero. Politica e cultura nel monde portoghese (1450–1600)* (Rome: Carocci Editore, 2011).
Martínez José Luis, *Hernán Cortés* (Mexico: FCE, 2003).
Matos Moctezuma, Eduardo, et al., 'Tenochtitlan y Tlatelolco', in *Siete ciudades antiguas de Mesoamérica. Sociedad y medio ambiente* (Mexico: Instituto Nacional de Antropología e Historia, 2011).
Mendes Pinto, Fernão, *Peregrinação* [1614] (Lisbon: Imprensa nacional, Casa da Moeda, 1984).
Michelacci, Laura, *Giovio in Parnasso: tra collezione di forme e storia universale* (Bologna: Il Mulino, 2004).
Montaigne, Michel de, *The Complete Essays*, trans. M.A. Screech (Harmondsworth: Penguin, 1991).
Morales, Pedro de, *Carta del padre Pedro de Morales*, ed. Beatriz Mariscal Hay (Mexico: El Colegio de México, 2002).
Motolinía, Toribio de Benavente, called, *Memoriales o libro de las cosas de la Nueva España y naturales de ella*, ed. Edmundo O'Gorman (Mexico: UNAM, 1971).
Moya de Contreras, Pedro, *Cinco cartas de Pedro Moya de Contreras* (Madrid: Porrúa Turanzas, 1962).

Murray, Harold, *A History of Chess* (Oxford: Clarendon Press, 1962).

Navarette, Martin Fernández de, *Coleccíon de documentos y manuscritos compilados por F. de N.* (Madrid: Museo naval, 1946).

Needham, Joseph, *Science and Civilization in China*, vol. 5: *Chemistry and Chemical Technology*, part 1, *Paper and Printing*, by Tsien Tsuen-hsuin (Cambridge: Cambridge University Press, 1985).

Niccoli, Ottavia, *Profeti e popolo nell'Italia del Rinascimento* (Bari: Laterza, 2007), trans. Lydia G. Cochrane as *Prophecy and People in Renaissaince Italy* (Princeton, NJ: Princeton University Press, 1990).

Nogueira Roque de Oliveira, Francisco Manuel de Paula, 'A construção do conhecimento europeu sobre a China', doctoral thesis, Autonomous University of Barcelona, 2003.

Oliveira e Costa, João Paulo, 'A coroa portuguesa e a China (1508–1531): do sonho manuelino ao realismo joanino', in Saldanha and Alves, *Estudos de história do relacionamento luso-chinês*, pp. 11–84.

Ollé Rodrígues, Manuel, 'Estrategias filipinas respecto a China. Alonso Sánchez y Domingo de Salazar en la empresa de China (1581–1593)', doctoral thesis, Barcelona: University Pompeu Fabra, 1998.

Ollé Rodrígues, Manuel, *La invencíon de China. Percepciones y estrategias filipinas respecto a China durante el siglo XVI* (Wiesbaden: Otto Harrassowitz, 2001).

Ollé Rodrígues, Manuel, *La empresa de China. De la armada invincible al Galeón de Manila* (Barcelona: Acantilado, 2002).

Ollé Rodrígues, Manuel, 'A inserção das Filipinas na Asia Oriental (1565–1593)', *Review of Culture*, 7 (2003), pp. 7–22.

Ortuño Sánchez-Pedreño, José María, 'Estudio histórico-jurídico de la expedición de García Jofre de Loaisa a las islas Molucas. La venta de los derechos sobre dichas islas al rey de Portugal por Carlos I de España', *Anales de derecho*, 21 (2003), pp. 217–37.

Ortuño Sánchez-Pedreño, José María, 'Las pretensiones de Hernán Cortés en el mar del Sur. Documentos y exploraciones', *Anales de derecho*, 22 (2004), pp. 317–56.

Pagden, Anthony, *The Fall of Natural Man. The American Indian and the Origins of Comparative Ethnology* (Cambridge: Cambridge University Press, 1982).

Parker, Geoffrey, *The Grand Strategy of Philip II* (New Haven, CT/London: Yale University Press, 1998).

Paso Y Troncoso, Francisco del, *Epistolario de la Nueva España*, vol. 2 (Mexico: José Porrúa & Hijos, 1939).

Pastells, Pablo, and Pedro Torres y Lanzas et al., *Catálogo de los documentos relativos a las islas Filipinas*, preceded by a *Historia general de Filipinas* (Barcelona: Viuda de L. Tasso, 1925–1936).

Pelliot, Paul, 'Le Hoja et le Sayyid Husain de l'histoire des Ming', *T'oung Pao*, 2nd series, vol. 38, 2–5 (1948), pp. 81–292.

Prieto, Carlos, *El oceano pacífico: navegantes españoles del siglo XVI* (Madrid: Alianza Editorial, 1975).

Quiroga, Vasco de, *De debellandis Indis*, ed. René de Acuña (Mexico: UNAM, 1988).

Reid, Antony, 'Southeast Asia Categorizations of Europeans', in Schwartz, *Implicit Understandings*, pp. 238–94.

Robinson, David M., 'The Ming Court and the Legacy of Yuan Mongols', in David M. Robinson (ed.), *Culture, Courtiers and Competition: The Ming Court (1368–1644)* (Cambridge, MA: Harvard University Press, 2008), pp. 365–421.

Rubiés, Joan-Pau, *Travel and Ethnology in the Renaissance: South India through European Eyes, 1250–1625* (Cambridge: Cambridge University Press, 2000).

Sá, Isabel dos Guimarães, 'Os rapazes do Congo: discursos em torno de uma experiência colonial (1480–1580)', in Leila Mezan Algranti and Ana Paula Megiani (eds), *O império por escrito. Formas de transmissão da cultura letrada no mundo ibérico, séculos XVI–XIX* (São Paulo: Alameda, 2009), pp. 313–32.

Sahagún, Bernardino de, *Historia general de las cosas de Nueva España* (Mexico: Porrúa, 1977), vol. 4; English trans. in Lockhart, *We People Here*.

Salazar, Domingo de, *Sinodo de Manila de 1582*, ed. José Luís Porras Camuñez et al. (Madrid: CSIC, 1988).

Saldanha, António Vasconcelos de, and Jorge Manuel dos Santos Alves (eds), *Estudos de história do relacionamento luso-chinês, séculos XVI–XIX* (Macau: Instituto português do Oriente, 1996).

Sallmann, Jean-Michel, *Charles Quint. L'empire éphémère* (Paris: Payot, 2000).

Sallmann, Jean-Michel, *Le Grand Désenclavement du monde, 1200–1600* (Paris: Payot, 2011).

Sánchez Aguilar, Federico, *El lago español: Hispanoasia* (Madrid: Fuenlabrada, 2003).

Schwartz, Stuart (ed.), *Implicit Understandings: Observing, Reporting and Reflecting on the Encounter between Europeans and other Peoples in the Early Modern Era* (Cambridge: Cambridge University Press, 1994).

Skinner, Quentin, *The Foundations of Modern Political Thought* (Cambridge: Cambridge University Press, 1978).

Sloterdijk, Peter, *Essai d'intoxication volontaire, Suivi de L'heure du crime et le temps de l'oeuvre d'art* (Paris: Pluriel, 2001).

Smith, Michael E., *Aztec City-State Capitals* (Gainesville, FL: University of Florida, 2008).

So, Billy K.L., *Prosperity, Region, and Institutions in Maritime China: The South Fukien Pattern, 946–1368* (Cambridge, MA: Harvard University Press, 2001).

Spallanzani, Marco, *Giovanni da Empoli: mercante navigatore fiorentino* (Florence: Spes, 1984).

Spate, O.H.K., *The Spanish Lake* (Minneapolis, MN: University of Minnesota Press, 1979).

Suárez de Peralta, Juan, *Tratado del descubrimiento de las Indias* (Mexico: Secretaría de Educación Pública, 1949).

Subrahmanyam, Sanjay, *The Portuguese Empire in Asia, 1500–1700: a Political and Economic History* (London/New York: Longman, 1993).

Tafuri, Manfredo, *Venice and the Renaissance* (Cambridge, MA: MIT Press, 1989).

Tapia, Andrés de, *Relación sobre la conquista de México* (Mexico: UNAM, 1939).

Thomaz, Luís Filipe F.R., *De Ceuta a Timor* (Algés: DIFEL, 1994).

Townsend, Camilla, 'Burying the White Gods: New Perspectives on the Conquest of Mexico', *American Historical Review*, 108, 3 (2003), pp. 659–87.

Valladares, Rafael, *Castilla y Portugal en Asia (1580–1680)* (Louvain: Leuwen University Press, 2001).

Vogeley, Nancy, 'China and the American Indies: A Sixteenth-Century History', *Colonial Latin American Review*, 6, 2 (1997), pp. 165–84.

Voretzsch, Ernst Arthur, 'Documentos acerca da primeira embaixada portuguesa à China', *Boletim da Sociedade Luso–Japonesa*, 1 (1926), pp. 30–69.

Wachtel, Nathan, *La Vision des vaincus. Les Indiens du Pérou devant la conquête espagnole* (Paris: Gallimard, 1971), trans. Ben and Siân Reynolds as *The Vision of the Vanquished: the Spanish Conquest of Peru through Indian Eyes, 1530–1570* (Hassocks: Harvester Press, 1977).

Wade, Geoffrey Philip, 'The Ming-shi-lu (Veritable Records of the Ming Dynasty) as a Source for Southeast Asian History, 14th to 17th centuries', doctoral thesis, University of Hong Kong, 1994.

Waldron, Arthur, *La grande muraglia. Dalla storia al mito* (Turin: Einaudi, 1993).

Wauchope, Robert (ed.), *Guide to Ethnohistorical Sources: Handbook of Middle American Indians*, vol. 14, part 3 (Austin, TX: University of Texas Press, 1975), pp. 235–6.

White, Richard, *The Middle Ground: Indians, Empires, and Republics in the Great Lakes Region, 1650–1850* (Cambridge: Cambridge University Press, 1991).

Zhu, Jianfei, *Chinese Spatial Strategies: Imperial Beijing 1420–1911* (London: RoutledgeCurzon, 2004).

Zimmermann, T.C. Price, *Paolo Giovio: The Historian and the Crisis of Sixteenth-Century Italy* (Princeton, NJ: Princeton University Press, 1995).

Index

CPSIA information can be obtained at www.ICGtesting.com
Printed in the USA
BVOW06*1151101115

425959BV00008B/17/P